*Darling Queen — Dear old Bones*

Miss Elizabeth Saxton Winter on the completion of her duties as governess in 1896, a position that she took up in 1886. Photograph: De Lavieter & Co.

# Darling Queen

~

# Dear old Bones

Queen Wilhelmina's Correspondence
with her English Governess
Miss Elizabeth Saxton Winter, 1886–1935

*Edited by Emerentia van Heuven-van Nes*

Amsterdam University Press

The publication of this book is made possible by grants from:
- Geschiedkundige Vereniging Oranje-Nassau
- Jan Menze van Diepen Stichting
- Koninklijke Vereniging van Leden der Nederlandse Ridderorden
- Private Foundation
- Stichting Elise Mathilde Fonds
- Stichting Fonds A.H. Martens van Sevenhoven
- Stichting Historische Verzamelingen van het Huis Oranje-Nassau

Originally published as: *Dear old Bones. Brieven van Koningin Wilhelmina aan haar Engelse gouvernante Miss Elizabeth Saxton Winter, 1886–1935.* Bezorgd door Emerentia van Heuven-van Nes. Uitgeverij THOTH, Bussum 2012 © 2012 Emerentia van Heuven-van Nes en Uitgeverij THOTH With special thanks to THOTH Publishers for the re-use of the colour images.

Translation: Vivien Collingwood

Cover illustration: Queen Wilhelmina, February 1896. Photograph: H.R.F. Kameke, The Hague
Cover design: Suzan Beijer
Lay-out: Sander Pinkse Boekproductie

Amsterdam University Press English-language titles are distributed in the US and Canada by the University of Chicago Press.

ISBN    978 94 6298 438 7
e-ISBN  978 90 4853 504 0
DOI     10.5117/9789462984387
NUR     698

© Emerentia van Heuven-van Nes / Amsterdam University Press B.V., Amsterdam 2017

# Table of contents

# Foreword to English edition

Queen Wilhelmina of the Netherlands is best known for her role during World War II. When Germany invaded the Netherlands on 10 May 1940, Wilhelmina issued a proclamation to the nation of 'flaming protest'. A few days later however, and very much against her will, she had to leave her beloved country for England with her family and members of the Cabinet. Through her radio broadcasts from London during World War II, she became the symbol of Dutch resistance to the Nazi occupation. She won respect and admiration, proving that a woman was as capable as a man in leading her people through difficult times.

Less well known is that the young Wilhelmina as a princess was already familiar with England, thanks to her governess Miss Winter, who taught her the English language from a very young age. In 1895, Wilhelmina visited Queen Victoria, who noted that the young Queen '*speaks good English and knows how to behave with charming manners*'.

Miss Winter also had great influence in shaping Wilhelmina's developing personality. Known as a bold woman herself, she embodied the positive British spirit. Miss Winter saw it as her mission to make the Princess 'a bold and noble woman'. Miss Winter most certainly succeeded in this, as we learn from none other than Winston Churchill himself. He described Wilhelmina as 'the only real man' among the governments-in-exile in London.

Wilhelmina holds the record for the longest-reigning Dutch monarch, 50 years. Especially for members of Royal families, it is always difficult to get a real insight into what truly drives them. That is what makes this book so unique. Wilhelmina and Miss Winter maintained a very personal and frank correspondence for nearly 50 years. This gives us readers a unique insight in the life of an extraordinary woman — who described herself in her memoirs as 'lonely, but not alone'.

Simon J.H. Smits
Ambassador of the Kingdom of the Netherlands in the United Kingdom

# Foreword

When Marion Crawford — the governess to Princess Elizabeth and Princess Margaret, the daughters of the British King George VI and his wife Elizabeth Bowes-Lyon — published her recollections of life at court in a book entitled *The Little Princesses* in 1950, the royal family immediately severed all contact with her.[1] The precious relationship that she had always enjoyed with the royal family had been damaged by her actions. How could she have taken it into her head to expose the internal affairs of the court? The damage proved to be irreparable. This could also have been the fate of Miss Elizabeth Saxton Winter, the governess to Queen Wilhelmina of the Netherlands between 1886 and 1896 and one of the two principal figures in this book.

After her honourable dismissal in 1896 having completed her duties as a governess, at the beginning of the twentieth century Miss Winter asked Wilhelmina's permission, as far as the queen understood it, to write about her time in the Netherlands.[2] The queen agreed to her request by telegram. In the summer of 1904, however, it proved that Miss Winter was in fact writing about her time at the Dutch court and her relationship with Wilhelmina herself. The latter was 'not amused' and wrote to her mother Emma, who paid Miss Winter's pension, asking her to keep an eye on the ex-governess. 'I shall make you responsible for what she writes.' Things ultimately turned out better than expected when Miss Winter's recollections were published in the American women's magazine *The Ladies' Home Journal* between November 1908 and January 1909. A Dutch translation by Henriette S.S. Kuyper was subsequently published, with the title *Toen onze Koningin nog Prinsesje was [When our queen was just a little princess].*[3] Miss Winter escaped Marion Crawford's fate and the contact was not broken, although it would become less frequent.

In 1989, the then director of the Paleis Het Loo National Museum in Apeldoorn, Dr Adriaan W. Vliegenthart, asked me whether I wanted to manage an upcoming exhibition on the regency of Queen Emma. In 1990, it would be one hundred years since she had become regent on behalf of her daughter, Wilhelmina, who was then still a minor. Wilhelmina had become queen at the age of ten on 23 November 1890 after the death of her father, King Willem III, but she was still too young to be able to govern. The regency had been an important period and would form an interesting subject for an exhibition.

1 For literature citations in the notes, only the author's surname (written in bold in the bibliography) has been cited, followed by page references. See Crawford. On 8 May 2004, I was informed by Prof. C.A. Tamse that there is an English expression 'to do a crawfie', meaning to commit an indiscretion. Marr, pp. 81–85.

2 Fasseur 1998, pp. 275–276.

3 Winter.

Emma's role had been an extremely difficult one. Not only was she the first queen to rule in the Netherlands, but she was also a foreigner, aged just 32, whose primary interlocutors were old men and who had to carve out a role for herself in the Netherlands. In addition, her only child had to be brought up to reign as queen in just eight years. Moreover, there was a need to breathe new life into the bond between the royal family and the Dutch people, which had been neglected by King Willem III, by appearing in public – something that had already been done on the king's seventieth birthday in 1887 – and to ascertain that 'we are still here'. This statement became the title of the exhibition.[4]

I was responsible for the themes 'Emma's youth and marriage' and 'The education of Queen Wilhelmina'. Whilst undertaking research in the Royal Archives in The Hague, I came across the correspondence between Wilhelmina and her English governess, Miss Elizabeth Saxton Winter (1855–1936), who had served the family between 1886 and 1896.[5] To my great astonishment, these unique letters had never been used.[6] Was this because there had been no occasion to do so? Or was it because they were mostly 'merely' a child's letters and, later on, letters from a young girl/young woman? Were they not sufficiently interesting? Apparently not, thought Mr R. de Beaufort, an employee of the Dutch embassy in London, who was the first to investigate the letters in 1967 when there was a possibility they might be sold. 'The whole collection is not of great value. I cannot imagine that anyone would show a great interest in them.'

In 1965, Henriette L[aman] T[rip] de Beaufort wrote her book *Wilhelmina 1880–1962, een levensverhaal [Wilhelmina, 1880–1962: A life]*, a biography commissioned by the then Dutch Ministry of Education, Arts and Sciences. She had no knowledge of the letters. The letters from Miss Saxton Winter to Wilhelmina had been destroyed by the latter during her lifetime, and Mrs de Beaufort thus made no mention of a correspondence between the two. However, the biographer did frequently cite the abovementioned memoir by Miss Winter. In 1972, ten years after Wilhelmina's death, Fred J. Lammers wrote *Wilhelmina, Moeder des Vaderlands [Wilhelmina, Mother of the Nation]*. By then, Wilhelmina's letters had been deposited in the Royal Archives, but he did not refer to them. He did refer, however, to the interesting notes on the private lessons that

4 The following seven themes were covered in the exhibition: I Introduction with historical background to and the situation of the House of Orange around 1890 and the beginning of the regency; II Emma's youth and marriage; III The education of Queen Wilhelmina; IV Governing the country; V Visiting the country; VI The queen-regent and the history of the House of Orange; and VII The end of the regency.

5 Royal Archives, G27. Items originating from Miss Saxton Winter, acquired from Miss H.I. Spanton in 1967. The letters were categorized into 26 non-chronological items, a categorization that was maintained after they were acquired.

6 It is striking that Boekholt, in his chapter in the 1990 book edited by C.A. Tamse, *Koningin Emma Opstellen over haar regentschap en voogdij [Queen Emma: Essays on her Regency and Guardianship]*, entitled 'Emma en de opvoeding van Wilhelmina [Emma and Wilhelmina's upbringing]', did not use Wilhelmina's letters to Miss Winter. However, he did use the notes made by the tutor Gediking, whom he repeatedly called 'Gedeking' (see following note).

Wilhelmina received from her tutor Fredrik Gediking, at which Miss Winter was always present.[7] The next person to write a biography of Wilhelmina, which he spent many years researching, was Prof. A.F. Manning. He would pass away in 1991 before the work was completed, although he did publish a chapter about the queen in a book entitled *Nassau en Oranje*.[8] Cees Fasseur took over Manning's work and published a biography of Wilhelmina in two volumes in 1998 and 2001, respectively.[9] Naturally, he also cited the now-familiar letters from Wilhelmina to Miss Winter. He did believe that they were of value, arguing that they shed 'interesting new light' on her youth, especially the years surrounding the investiture.[10]

In the meantime, in 1995, in addition to the letters from Emma and Juliana, eighteen letters from Wilhelmina were published for the first time, edited by L.B. Romeyn.[11] This concerned seven letters written between 1898 and 1908 to her second cousin Princess Marie of the Netherlands,[12] who married Wilhelm, the Prince of Wied, in 1871, and eleven letters written between 1910 and 1934 to her favourite lady-in-waiting, Marie Snoeck,[13] who had married Mr Frans Beelaerts van Blokland in 1905 and gone to live in Peking, where her husband was the Dutch ambassador. Van Osta provided an introduction and the notes.

For my part, I used Wilhelmina's unique letters to her governess not only for the exhibition about Emma, but also for other publications and exhibitions at Paleis Het Loo.[14] I also drew others' attention to this rich source material, full of interesting details relating to their specific subjects, whether these might be fashion, souvenirs, horses, or Wilhelmina's own paintings.[15] Gredy Huisman, who published her book *Tussen salon en souterrain. Gouvernantes in Nederland*

7  Fredrik Gediking (1852-1902), head teacher at the grammar school on Schelpkade in Scheveningen, recorded in fifty notebooks the preparation for and outcomes of the 1,215 lessons that he gave to Queen Wilhelmina between 3 January 1887 and 20 April 1897. At the time, the notebooks were in the possession of his granddaughter, Mrs A.P. Loosjes of Harderwijk. On the occasion of the exhibition 'Wij zijn er nog [We are still here]', she gave them to the Paleis Het Loo National Museum in Apeldoorn in 1990, inv.no. RL3098 (Lammers, p.13, Van Heuven 1989, p. 28).
8  Manning.
9  Fasseur 1998 and 2001.
10  Fasseur 1998, p. 152.
11  Osta, pp. 47-85.
12  Marie of the Netherlands (1841-1910) was the daughter of Prince Frederik (1797-1881), the brother of King Willem II (1792-1849), and Princess Louise of Prussia (1808-1870). On 18 July 1871 she married Wilhelm, the Prince of Wied (1845-1907).
13  Marie Snoeck's full name was Adriana Maria Snoeck (1873-1948). She entered royal service on 10 July 1900 as the successor to Idzardina Juliana Frederika 'Pixy' de Constant Rebecque (1877-1958). Emma and Wilhelmina were very fond of Marie. On 30 May 1905, she married Mr Frans Beelaerts van Blokland (1872-1956), whose positions included envoy extraordinary and minister plenipotentiary in Peking, Minister of Foreign Affairs and vice-president of the Council of State. Pixy de Constant Rebecque, see letter 51, note 71.
14  Heuven 1990, 1992, 2003, 2004, 2008, Spliethoff 2006.
15  Meij, Rooseboom, Spliethoff 2006, Conijn.

*[Between the drawing room and below stairs: Governesses in the Netherlands]* in 2000, did not tackle the subject of governesses at the Dutch court: 'their duties were of a very special nature', she wrote, without further explanation.[16]

No complete edition of Wilhelmina's letters had yet been produced, however, despite my having expressed this intention to the then director of the Royal Archives in the 1990s. Although I had transferred Wilhelmina's letters in English to my computer, I had not had sufficient time to work on them. I only managed to do so after my retirement in 2009.

At that time, Her Majesty Queen Beatrix granted me permission to publish the letters in full, something for which I am very grateful. Owing to circumstances at the time, the letters were first published in Dutch translation.[17] Now, in 2017, they are being published in their original English form, along with additional letters, including sixteen letters from Miss Winter that have since been discovered. It would have been impossible to write this book without the assistance of the Royal Archives in The Hague. Once again, the director of the Royal Archives, Ph.C.B. Maarschalkerweerd, and all of the staff of this private royal archive proved to be of inestimable value. I would like to extend a special word of thanks to the archivists Mrs Ch.J.M. Eymael and Mrs H.J. de Muij-Fleurke for their critical reading of the manuscript, and to Mr L.J.A. Pennings for his tireless provision of relevant details and for always responding so quickly to my numerous emails asking all manner of questions. I would also like to express my special gratitude for the fact that I was once again permitted to use illustrations from the archive, which is administered by Mrs M.S. Jansen, on a 'pro deo' basis. I am extremely grateful to the former director of the Royal Archives, B. Woelderink, with whom I had discussed the publication of the letters back in the 1990s, for his critical reading and comments on the introductory chapters. I am also grateful to the director of the Paleis Het Loo National Museum, M. van Maarseveen, and my former colleagues Marieke E. Spliethoff, George Sanders, Paul Rem, Anne Dirk Renting, Niels Coppes, Angelique van den Eerenbeemd, Liesbeth Schothorst and Mariska Dumas for their expertise and for their answers to my questions. I am grateful to the director for permitting me to publish the photographs for this publication from the museum's collection on a 'pro deo' basis, as well as to all the individuals, with special thanks to Archduke Markus Habsburg-Lothringen, Bad Ischl (Austria) and Gregor Antoličič, Limbus (Slovenia), and to the institutions that provided photographs. Their names are listed in the photo credits. A special word of gratitude for Kees van den Hoek, director of THOTH Publishers, Bussum, the Netherlands, who published the Dutch edition of this book with the title *Dear old Bones — Brieven van Koningin Wilhelmina aan haar Engelse gouvernante Miss Elizabeth Saxton Winter, 1886–1935*, in 2012, and gave us the use of all the colour plates for free. Credit is also due to

16 Huisman, p. 90.
17 Emerentia van Heuven-van Nes, *Dear old Bones. Brieven van koningin Wilhelmina aan haar Engelse gouvernante Miss Elizabeth Saxton Winter 1886–1935*, Bussum 2012.

my husband, Jan Willem, as yet more of our free time was devoted to preparing this English edition.

It would not have been possible to publish this book without the support of a number of funds and foundations, and I am extremely grateful to them. Their names are listed on page 4.

These days, when so many books are published and it is thus more difficult than ever to find a publisher for such a specialized subject, I was extremely glad that Jan-Peter Wissink, the director of Amsterdam University Press, also recognized the importance of this unique personal source material and appreciated the value of publishing it in its original language. I have always enjoyed a pleasant, constructive working relationship with Inge van der Bijl, the commissioning editor, and all her colleagues.

I am particularly pleased that interested parties from beyond the Netherlands will now be able to become acquainted with these unique personal letters, which also cover relations with the royal houses of Europe, including those of Great Britain, Habsburg, Italy, Mecklenburg-Schwerin, Romania, Saxe-Coburg, Saxe-Weimar, Spain, Waldeck-Pyrmont and Wied. The photographs in this book depict many royal figures. How an ostensibly 'age-old' photograph could suddenly become very real and relevant was brought home to me during a visit to Metfried, the Prince of Wied, in September 2016. When he saw the photograph of the Wied family (shown on p. 190) gathered around a radiant and proud figure, the youngest son and heir, Prince Hermann, wearing a splendid white dress, his little head covered with a feathered cap, sitting on the lap of his great-grandmother, the widowed Marie of Wied, Princess of Nassau, he said: 'That is my father.' It was an unexpected and surprising remark, which suddenly made the photograph in this book feel very topical.

My hope is that reading the heart-felt and spontaneous letters of Queen Wilhelmina will offer a deeper insight into her psyche than all of the biographies that have been written about her.

# Biographical sketch of Queen Wilhelmina, 1880–1962

As it is useful to know something about the lives of the two principal figures in this book, in what follows I offer a brief biographical sketch of both women. Detailed biographies have been written of both Queen Wilhelmina and her mother Emma in recent years.[18]

Wilhelmina Helena Pauline Maria, Princess of Orange-Nassau, was born on 31 August 1880 at Noordeinde Palace in 's-Gravenhage. She was the only daughter from the second marriage of King Willem III (1817-1890) to Queen Emma (1858-1934), Princess of Waldeck-Pyrmont. Of the three sons from the king's first marriage to Sophie (1818-1877), Princess of Württemberg — Willem (1840-1879), Maurits (1843-1850) and Alexander (1851-1884) — only the youngest was still alive. When the latter died on 21 June 1884, Wilhelmina became heir to the throne, and with King Willem III's death on 23 November 1890, Wilhelmina became queen. Queen Emma would then govern as regent until Wilhelmina reached adulthood in 1898.

Wilhelmina's early years were carefree. Queen Emma was largely responsible for her education. Wilhelmina was initially brought up bilingual, speaking Dutch and French. Emma had replaced French with Dutch as the language of the court, and thus she spoke Dutch to her only child as well. As a small child, Wilhelmina learned French from Julie Liotard, a nanny from Alsace. She was taught English in playful fashion by an Englishwoman, Miss Elizabeth Saxton Winter, when the latter was made her governess in January 1886. Queen Emma had a high opinion of English education: 'The English [approach] is, I believe, the best [...] It is friendly, but firm.' Wilhelmina had to grow up to be a strong, powerful, noble and intrepid woman. In great isolation, and in a world full of adults and with a tightly scheduled daily programme, Wilhelmina was brought up in 'gründlich', 'pünktlich' and 'tüchtig' (thorough, punctual and efficient) fashion.

Between January 1887 and July 1890, Wilhelmina received private primary-school tuition from a schoolmaster from The Hague, Fredrik Gediking. In addition to the classes he taught, she also received secondary-school tuition from a number of tutors and professors. Her confirmation on 24 October 1896 marked the end of her schooling, and was followed by a period in which Wilhelmina was prepared for her role as queen. In the meantime, visits were held to all of the provinces in order to familiarize Wilhelmina with the Netherlands, and to strengthen the bond between the Dutch people and the House of Orange.

---

18 On Wilhelmina, see: Beaufort 1965, Lammers 1972, Tamse 1981, Fasseur 1998, 2001, 2003; on Emma, see: Verburg 1989, Tamse 1990, Heuven 1989, 2008.

When travelling abroad, she visited the most important European countries and cities and met their ruling monarchs. In addition, there were many visits to the mountains for her health.

Wilhelmina's investiture was held in the Nieuwe Kerk in Amsterdam on 6 September 1898. Her marriage to Hendrik (1876–1934), Duke of Mecklenburg-Schwerin, took place on 7 February 1901 in The Hague. After three miscarriages, one of which — on 5 May 1902 — was the result of typhus, her daughter Juliana was born on 30 April 1909. This was followed by yet more miscarriages, which did little to aid her marriage to Prince Hendrik. Moreover, Wilhelmina had a strict understanding of her duties and Prince Hendrik, who loved outdoor life and companionship, was excluded from all governmental matters.

Wilhelmina was convinced that she was queen by grace of God and that there was a special bond between the Netherlands and the House of Orange. She took the fortunes of her people very much to heart. Regarding her duties with a high seriousness, she was independent, strong-willed and just, but she could also be detached and severe. Later she would say: 'I am like a pasha'. Despite this, she also had a good sense of humour.

Her upbringing, but also the fact that she, aside from Emma, was the first woman to ascend the throne, meant that she presented herself assertively. She was able to stand her ground in a man's world. She had an impatient and impulsive character, and often saw things in black and white terms. Although she was intelligent and had a good understanding of state matters, she by no means gave her ministers an easy time. In contrast to King Willem III, but just

The twelve-year-old Queen Wilhelmina accompanied by, on the left, her English governess Miss Saxton Winter, and on the right, Lady Henriette van de Poll, 'superintendent' of Wilhelmina's education from 1891, surrounded by a number of dolls, including, in the middle at the back, the 'French governess' that Wilhelmina was given as a Christmas present in 1889. This was the last time that Wilhelmina was photographed with her doll collection. As she had to devote herself to preparing for her future role, the dolls were stored in a specially made display case. Photograph: H.R.F. Kameke, The Hague, April 1893.

like Queen Emma during the regency, she drew admiration from politicians in The Hague for her considerable expertise.

There was a strong bond between Wilhelmina and the army during her lifetime, expressed in particular during the First and Second World Wars. In 1918, a revolution led by the socialist leader P.J. Troelstra was averted. Between 1940 and 1945, when she was in England — whence she had fled on 13 May 1940 — she became a great pillar of strength and symbol of resistance to Germany. As a result, she became known as the 'Mother of the Nation', a variant on the title of 'Father of the Nation' that had been given to William of Orange (1533–1584) who led the resistance against Philip II, ruler of the Netherlands, but also king of Spain, and Wilhelmina's great inspiration.

Wilhelmina's influence on the government in exile in London was not inconsiderable. Once back in the Netherlands, the queen had hopes for national renewal, spiritual unity and a new constitution. When her wishes were disappointed, and suffering from deteriorating health, she abdicated on 4 September 1948, having reigned for fifty years. Princess Juliana twice acted as regent: first, between 14 October and 1 December 1947; and second, and from 12 May 1948, the day on which Wilhelmina announced her abdication, until 30 August. This was followed by Juliana's investiture on 6 September 1948.

After the abdication, she went back to calling herself 'Princess Wilhelmina' and retreated to Paleis Het Loo, her 'dear home in Gelderland'. It was there that she wrote her biography, which was published in 1959, as well as a few pamphlets on spirituality. Although she had been accepted into the Dutch Reformed Church, she had very much followed her own spiritual path; she had a mystical streak and did not wish to bind herself to a single church. She died on 28 November 1962 in Paleis Het Loo, and lay in state in the chapel there. Placed on her coffin was the *Watersnoodbijbel,* a bible that had been given to her father after the flooding in Gelderland in 1861.[19] On 8 December, the queen, just like her husband before her, was 'buried' in white and entombed in the vault of the House of Orange in the Nieuwe Kerk in Delft.

19 Heuven 1993, pp. 86–95.

# Biographical sketch of Elizabeth Saxton Winter, 1855–1936

Elizabeth Saxton Winter was born on 6 September 1855 in Portland, Dorset, the daughter of a successful butcher, Richard Winter, and Bernice White.[20] The two had married in July 1845 in Melcombe Regis near Weymouth in Dorset, and had two sons, Robert and Richard, and three daughters, Elizabeth, Nancy and Bernice. Elizabeth's father probably died in 1863, when the youngest was two years old. It is unclear what then happened to the family, but mother and siblings were separated. The two youngest girls were sent to different orphanages, whilst Elizabeth was educated at the Royal Asylum of St Anne's Society in London, a charity school for poor children that had been founded in 1829. The children who attended the school were probably selected for their ability, and it is possible that her brother Richard was also admitted. They were given a thorough training in being of service to others. Richard later became a priest in the Anglican Church. Elizabeth's mother left Dorset to become the director of the London Road Hospital in Saffron Walden in Essex. It is likely that Elizabeth finished school when she turned sixteen and, like her two sisters, went to live with her mother in Saffron Walden. Nancy worked at the hospital as a masseuse, and would later take over her mother's role as director. In 1902 she moved to a newly built house on 39 South Road in Saffron Walden. She also ran a private nursing home in Mount Pleasant Road. During the First World War, Nancy was the director of the Red Cross Hospital at Walden Place, and was later awarded the Royal Red Cross for her service. Bernice became a milliner. Elizabeth found employment as a governess to the family of a lawyer, Augustus Henry Maule of Blithe Court in Newnham, Gloucestershire. She had the care of his three children: Lilian, Hugh and Monica. She would remain in contact with the family for the rest of her life, and Hugh would be the executor of her will when she died in 1936.

Although 'Saxton' was officially Miss Winter's Christian name, in addition to her second name 'Elizabeth', she added it to her surname, possibly to present herself as more distinguished than she was. She would always sign her letters 'E. Saxton Winter'. In the Dutch State Directory she was always referred to as 'Miss Saxton Winter', and the same was true of official papers, such as those relating to her appointment. The letter of 20 March 1929, whereby her pension

20  Zeepvat 2006, pp. 57–60. She would discover that Miss Winter was not an officer's daughter, but the daughter of a butcher. *Weekly News*, 25 September 1986. In his memoirs, aide-de-camp Count J.H.F. Dumonceau described Miss Winter as the daughter of a high-ranking officer, which is what he had been told (Cleverens 1991, p. 40). Fasseur also described Miss Winter as the daughter of an officer (Fasseur 1998, p. 86).

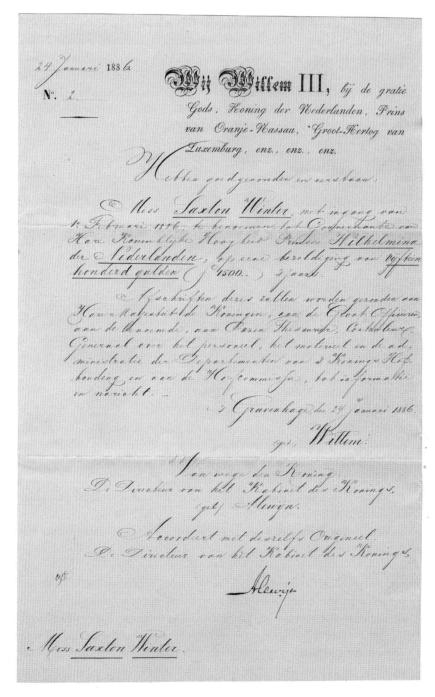

The appointment of Miss Elizabeth Saxton Winter as Governess of Her Royal Highness Princess Wilhelmina of the Netherlands as of 1 February 1886 by King Willem III, signed on 24 January 1886.

was increased by £100, was addressed to Miss E. Saxton Winter.[21]

It is likely that Miss Winter entered Queen Emma's service as the governess to Princess Wilhelmina after having been governess to the Maule family. Although it was customary in the Netherlands for well-to-do families to have a French or Swiss governess, in Queen Emma's view, nothing was better than an English education. Her parents had also employed an English governess for their children. In an interview in 1929, on the occasion of her having spent fifty years in the Netherlands, Queen Emma said:

> Choose whichever system you like, but be sure to be consistent. A child should also learn 'discipline' this way. One should dare to say: this is how it should be done [...] discipline is essential. Not discipline instilled by fear, of course; which can be the German way. Not humiliating discipline. The English [approach] is, I believe, the best [...]. If one approaches a child in the right way [...] one wins them over. [...] One has to be friendly, but firm.[22]

As is still often the case with families, the royal family probably found Miss Saxton Winter through their own contacts. One such contact may have been Julie Douglas, one of Emma's English governesses, who had married the Reverend Peter Ackland on her return from Waldeck.[23] In her memoirs, *Toen Onze Koningin nog prinsesje was [When our queen was just a little princess]*, Miss Winter began her book as follows: 'It was in the early autumn of 1885 when I was introduced by a mutual friend to a lady, who had been commissioned by Her Majesty Queen Emma of the Netherlands to find an English governess for the young crown princess, Wilhelmina, at that time a child of just five years.' Miss Winter had hoped to acquire an occupation that would enable her to 'be one of those men or women who, through their work, find a meaningful place in the world. But never, even in my wildest dreams, had I ever dared to hope that I might educate a royal child.'

On 24 January 1886, King Willem III signed the appointment of Miss Saxton Winter, then thirty years old, as governess of H.R.H. Princess Wilhelmina, as of 1 February of that year, on a salary of 1,500 guilders per annum.[24] Her travel expenses to and from England were also reimbursed.[25] The two spoke French at their first meeting. According to Miss Winter, Wilhelmina 'soon learned enough English words to be able to make herself understood, and after a few months she was speaking English with ease.' Wilhelmina would write her first

21 Royal Archives, G27–23.

22 Itallie, 9 January 1929. Heuven 1989, p. 26.

23 Royal Archives, A47-IVc-10. In a short letter from the eleven-year-old Emma to Miss Douglas on 9 August 1869, with the news of the death of her oldest sister Sophie, she addressed her as 'Miss E. Douglas' (Heuven 1989, pp. 13, 86, cat. no. 29).

24 Royal Archives, G27–23.

25 Royal Archives, A47a-III. The petty cash books of Queen Emma frequently feature sums for travel, gifts at Christmas and suchlike.

Photograph of Queen Wilhelmina and Queen Victoria: a meeting between Europe's youngest and oldest queens in May 1895. Photomontage Chits & fils.

English letters using phonetic spelling. The governess herself spent much of her time on a similar study of the Dutch language.[26] She also attended all of her pupil's lessons. The fact that she spoke Dutch can be inferred from Emma's words in a letter of December 1928, in which the latter sent her a Dutch book with the remark: '[...] As you were with me & worked with in the most serious & responsable years of my life I think you will be interested in some parts of it & quite able to understand as you do not seem to forget your dutch.'[27] Nonetheless, Miss Winter continued to write in English and she also used English between May 1887 and October 1896 when keeping her account books, in which she made a note of minor expenses relating to Wilhelmina.[28]

It was not until 23 January 1891, thus after the death of King Willem III, that Miss Winters was appointed 'English governess to Her Majesty the Queen'. This time, the appointment was signed by 'Her Majesty the Queen-Widow, Regent Emma.' Miss Winter thereafter gave her pupil lessons in the English language and literature, and she also taught her to play tennis.

The fact that Miss Winter succeeded in teaching Wilhelmina to speak English well is revealed by a remark made by Queen Victoria herself, no less. On 3 May 1895, after Queen Wilhelmina and her mother had visited Windsor Castle during

26  Winter, pp. 8–9.
27  Letter 292.
28  Royal Archives, A47a-III-14, 15 and 16. The governess received the money for this from Mrs Kreusler, Queen Emma's lectrice.

an educational trip to London, at which Miss Winter was also present, Queen Victoria wrote:

Windsor Castle, 3rd May. – Shortly before two, went downstairs to receive the Queen Regent of the Netherlands and her daughter, the young Queen Wilhelmina [...] The young Queen, who will be fifteen in August, has her hair still hanging down. She is very slight and graceful, has fine features, and seems to be very intelligent and a charming child. She speaks English extremely well, and has very pretty manners.[29]

With the exception of her holidays, Miss Winter was always in Wilhelmina's retinue; in private and in public in the Netherlands, but also during many trips abroad. She accompanied the royal pair when they went to take the waters in Germany, for example, such as during their trip to Bad Arolsen in May 1886, immediately after her appointment; and she was part of the retinue during the visits to the Dutch provinces between 1891 and 1895, for the state visit to the emperor and empress of Germany, for the celebrations of the golden wedding of the Grand Duke and Grand Duchess of Saxe-Weimar in Weimar in 1892, and for the educational trip to England in 1895; and she attended dinners, such as those to celebrate the birthdays of Queen Emma on 2 August and of Princess/Queen Wilhelmina on 31 August, and other official dinners. She also accompanied Wilhelmina to plays or concerts, or on visits to exhibitions.

At the end of October 1896, Wilhelmina's education was complete. Final ceremonial meetings were held, such as that on Friday 23 October in the study of Palace Noordeinde, when Wilhelmina was accepted into the Church by the court chaplain, G.J. van der Flier. The next day, Wilhelmina was confirmed as a member of the Dutch Reformed Church. Miss Winter was also present when, on 30 October, Wilhelmina placed a commemorative stone in the building of the Royal Archives, which was being constructed close to Palace Noordeinde, and she accompanied her to a last exhibition in Pulchri Studio. But this marked the irrevocable end. 'On the 1st of November, Miss Winter and Lady van de Poll are leaving; it will be a dreadful day [...]', Wilhelmina wrote to Lady de Kock on 5 September 1896.[30] On 2 November 1896 Miss Winter was dismissed in the most honourable fashion. As of 1 January 1897, she was to receive a pension of 150 pounds a year, a sum that was increased in 1929 to 250 pounds, to celebrate Emma having been in the Netherlands for fifty years.

Miss Winter fell into a black hole: from one moment to the next, she had gone from being employed to having no work at all. All those years, she had devoted

---

29 This visit formed part of an educational trip to London between 26 April and 10 May 1895, which included visits to the British Museum and the Natural History Museum. The visit to the British queen took place on 3 May 1895. Buckle, p. 499, Beaufort, p. 32, Heuven 1989, pp. 34-35, Fasseur 1998, pp. 146-149.
30 Royal Archives, G28. Items from Lady Marie Louise de Kock (1848-1932), the attendant of Princess Wilhelmina.

herself, day in, day out, with the sole exception of her holidays, to completing her difficult and lonely task and to helping to educate a far from easy child, without any thought for herself. Queen Emma was well aware of this fact and tried to find new employers for her. She eventually found a position with Marie, Princess of Wied and Princess of the Netherlands, who was married to Wilhelm, Prince of Wied. Miss Winter would teach English to their daughters, Louise and Elisabeth. Wilhelm was Emma's cousin, as his mother, Marie,[31] was a half-sister of Emma's mother. The governess stayed there, to everybody's satisfaction, from July 1897 until the following summer of 1898, and received a monthly salary of 100 Reichmarks.

When Wilhelm's sister Elisabeth and her husband, King Carol I of Romania,[32] were looking for a governess for Crown Prince Carol, for whose education they felt responsible, Wilhelm and Marie thus felt no hesitation in recommending Miss Winter. Carol was the eldest child of their cousin, Crown Prince Ferdinand of Romania, who had married Marie, Princess of Edinburgh.[33] Miss Winter's appointment followed in the winter of 1898. It would be a disaster, known as the 'Miss Winter affair'.[34] Carol's mother Marie was absolutely unable to get on with the governess, whom Marie cruelly nicknamed 'Hornet'. Marie — who had many love affairs, resulting in several children — accused the governess of spreading public gossip about her and of keeping her children from her. In the end, the king felt compelled to appoint a new governess and Miss Winter had to leave on 21 April 1900. When the little Carol learned of this, he was utterly distressed; he rolled on the floor screaming, declaring that he wanted to go with her.[35] With

31 Marie, Princess of Nassau (1825-1902), was the eighth child from the first marriage of Wilhelm of Nassau (1792-1839) to Louise of Saksen-Hildburghausen (1794-1825), whilst Emma's mother Helene (1831-1888) was from the second marriage to Pauline of Württemberg (1810-1856).

32 Carol (1839-1914) of Hohenzollern-Sigmaringen was first Prince (1866-1881) and then King Carol I (until 1914) of Romania. In 1869 he married Elisabeth of Wied 'Carmen Silva' (1843-1916). They had just one daughter, Marie, who died aged four in 1874. Carol's brother Leopold of Hohenzollern-Sigmaringen and his eldest son Wilhelm relinquished their right to succeed Carol I. Leopold's second son Ferdinand (1865-1927) became the heir to the throne in November 1888. See letters 227, 237, 238, 242, 245.

33 Marie 'Missy' (1875-1938), from 1893 the wife of Crown Prince Ferdinand of Romania, was the eldest daughter of Alfred (1844-1900), Duke of Saxe-Coburg and Gotha (1893-1900) and Maria Alexandrovna, Grand Duchess of Russia (1853-1920), the only daughter of Tsar Alexander II. Alfred was the second son of Queen Victoria of Great Britain and Albert of Saxe-Coburg. Because the eldest son of Marie and Ferdinand, Carol II (1893-1953), was the heir apparent, Queen Elisabeth and King Carol I felt responsible for the education of their nephew. Fasseur erroneously wrote in his book Wilhelmina, de jonge koningin [Wilhelmina, the young queen], p. 151, that Marie saw Miss Winter as her 'mother-in-law's spy'. He probably meant a spy of Queen Elisabeth of Romania, Ferdinand's aunt. Carol II would reign as king for ten years, from 1930 to 1940.

34 The 'Miss Winter affair', so called by Marie's mother, Grand Duchess Marie Alexandrovna (Fasseur, p. 151, Zeepvat 2006, pp. 168-173. Mandache, pp. 394-395, 397-399, 402, 404-405, 408, 411-416, 418, 433, 437, 439.

35 Zeepvat 2006, p. 172.2.

the installation of the new governess, Miss Anne Ffoliott, peace returned to the Romanian court.

On her return to England, Miss Winter became the director of a finishing school for girls in London. In 1901 she attended the marriage of Queen Wilhelmina. In September 1908, the former governess spent a few days at Soestdijk and Het Loo, where she was photographed with Queen Wilhelmina and two ladies-in-waiting. She was not present at the baptism of Princess Juliana in 1909.[36] The London school was closed following the outbreak of the First World War, whereupon Miss Winter went to live with her sister Nancy on South Road in Saffron Walden. In May 1922 she visited The Hague again. Princess Juliana would visit her in England in 1933 and in 1934. In September 1935, just in time – a few months, in fact, before the death of Miss Winter – Queen Wilhelmina was able to embrace her a final time in Saffron Walden. This must have brought much joy to them both. A few months later, a week after her sister Nancy, Miss Elizabeth Saxton Winter passed away on 29 January 1936, having lain unconscious for a week, according to a newspaper report.[37]

## Others' opinions of Miss Saxton Winter

Various opinions were expressed regarding the person of Miss Winter. First and foremost, we should consider that of Wilhelmina. She wrote in her auto-biography that Miss Winter had come not only as an English teacher, but also, and above all, as a governess.[38] Wilhelmina:

Miss Winter had a strong, open, sincere personality: 'to train your character, to make you into a bold and noble woman, unflinching and strong'. This also had to be expressed in 'bold' handwriting. She did not give way to anyone, nor did she seek to avoid anybody. She was a 'bold woman'. She was in possession of all the virtues that characterize the English people and that are

36 Royal Archives, E18a-D-14. Miss Winter's name does not appear in the file 'Birth and Baptism of Princess Juliana'.
37 In a detailed article published on 29 January 1936, a newspaper, possibly the *Algemeen Handelsblad*, reported: 'De Chaperonne van H.M. de Koningin overleden [death of the chaperone of Her Majesty the Queen]'. Other newspapers, such as *Het Vaderland* and *Nieuwsblad van het Noorden*, published an article on 30 January 1936 entitled 'Elisabeth [sic] Saxton-Winter †', whilst other newspapers, such as the *Limburger Koerier, Nieuwe Tilburgse Courant* and the *Leeuwarder Nieuwsblad*, included a brief report on this. There is a striking passage in Henriette de Beaufort's book (p. 155) on Queen Wilhelmina, although its source is unclear. She wrote that the queen, having just arrived in London in May 1940, sent Mr Van 't Sant to find out where her old governess, the elderly Miss Saxton Winter, was living. She was concerned that the latter would no longer be receiving her pension, which had been sent from the Netherlands. The Queen wanted to make immediate arrangements to ensure that Miss Winter would be provided for – but she had died four years previously!
38 Wilhelmina, pp. 50-60.

cultivated in every person there. These are the virtues that form the backbone of the British nation. I often heard remarks from Miss Winter that underlined this.

Miss Winter was Wilhelmina's only company when she and her mother were confined to Het Loo by her father's illness. Wilhelmina: 'Fortunately, she had a cheerful nature and was able to play with me very kindly, with endless ingenuity.' This ranged from rowing, doing 'spatter work' (*Spritzwerk*) of dried flowers on wood, velvet or leather and roasting potatoes, to building with bricks, as Miss Winter's memoirs recall. When Wilhelmina was old enough, Miss Winter taught her to play tennis and secondary-level English language and literature.[39] Initially, Wilhelmina submitted to her authority. Wilhelmina: 'When I began my education, she always attended the lessons. She took great care that my behaviour during the lessons left nothing to be desired.'[40] This was a difficult undertaking, because Wilhelmina was both capricious and stubborn. The governess had to submit constant reports to Queen Emma. Wilhelmina's tutor, the schoolmaster Gediking endorsed Miss Winter's complaint to the queen that it was almost impossible to educate a child at court: 'According to her, the task is particularly difficult because the timetable is so strict and she is constantly having to reproach the princess.'[41] On the other hand, Gediking made a plea for leniency from the queen-regent, advice that was followed when Miss Winter proposed that Wilhelmina be punished for inattentiveness.

Wilhelmina refused to allow her governess to pray with her. She was adamant on this: 'If she did not agree to my wishes, I declared the prayers invalid and said that I would pray again on my own, which I did.'[42] Although Wilhelmina, when she became more self-assured, was often at loggerheads with Miss Winter, to the extent that the governess would sometimes even threaten to leave, she held back from going too far out of respect for her mother: 'for that would only add to my mother's cares, which were already so great [...] Mother cautioned me expressly that she was unable to take on my daily education in addition to her many duties, and cautioned me to keep respecting Miss Winter's authority.'[43] One example of how difficult and impudent Wilhelmina could be was provided by Lady van de Poll in a letter to her mother dated 26 December 1891: 'She [Wilhelmina] was so cheeky to Miss W. that Miss W. left her by herself in the room. When she was first threatened with this, she had said in English: 'Oh, that makes no difference to me, this afternoon I have *de freule* [Lady van de Poll] and then I shan't be needing you at all.'[44] But she could also show that she meant

39 Royal Archives, G28–3. In a letter to her former attendant Lady de Kock, Wilhelmina wrote on 27 October 1895: 'P.S. Miss Winter is teaching me literature, that is, English literature.'
40 Wilhelmina, pp. 50–51.
41 See p. 11, note 7.
42 Wilhelmina, p. 53.
43 Wilhelmina, pp. 68–69.
44 Cleverens 1994, p. 99.

well, as can be inferred from her wish in the letter of 29 December 1894: 'I hope to that the coming jear will not make many difficulties arise between us and that we will get always more and more intimit and devoted frinds and will make us, next to the love that we have for our mothers, the <u>most</u> devoted friends on earth. You are not to poke up your nose at what I am writing, because I meen it.'

The fact that Queen Emma was very taken with Miss Winter is shown by the letters that she wrote to her, particularly the first letter after Miss Winter's dismissal on 2 December 1896, in which Emma wrote: 'Yes it was the greatest blessing for my child & both of us that we could work so well together & that there was perfect understanding between us & that in all principal things we had the same views. Therefore you were & could be <u>such</u> a <u>help</u> to me & <u>blessing</u> for my child.' The fact that Emma sometimes needed Miss Winter after the latter had left is shown by the remarkable letter of 2 January 1902, in which Emma poured out her heart to the former governess.

Someone with more influence over Wilhelmina's education was Lady van de Poll, Queen Emma's lady-in-waiting, when she was made 'superintendent' of her education in 1890, although she was an unusually modest woman and always gave credit to Miss Winter in matters of education. This made a great impression on Wilhelmina. As a result, Wilhelmina gradually began to doubt the infallibility of Miss Winter's judgement. Wilhelmina: 'My governess no longer had moral authority over me. I say "governess" here expressly, because I continued to love Miss Winter and later, when there could no longer be any squabbling, because she was no longer my governess, a close friendship developed between us.'[45]

Lady van de Poll often mentioned Miss Winter in her letters to her mother. On 20 June 1886 she wrote from Wildungen: 'I think that Miss Winter is a very good governess and has a very kind way of dealing with the child; the *Kin* [Queen] is very taken with her and rightly so, I believe.'[46]

The fact that children had difficulty with the well-meaning, disciplined, strict, but not 'warm' Miss Winter is revealed by the following two examples. On a long drive taken by Wilhelmina and her Bentheim cousins on 29 July 1893 in the surroundings of Het Loo, the children constantly changed places on the box, the dicky seat and the carriage, their antics accompanied by all kinds of tricks and silliness. According to Lady van de Poll, in a letter to her mother on 30 July 1893, one of the cousins told her 'that she should like to come out with me every day, because I grumble much less than Miss W. The other two immediately agreed. Fortunately, the confession was in German, so perhaps the Queen [Wilhelmina] did not understand it.'[47]

Wilhelmina's contemporary and playmate Sara van Steijn,[48] the daughter of the house steward of Paleis Het Loo, Van Steijn, who was often invited to come and play, along with her little sister Ina and brother Joan, recalled Miss Winter as

45 Wilhelmina, pp. 67–68.
46 Cleverens, 1994, p. 86.
47 Cleverens, 1994, p. 101.
48 See letter 32, note 44.

follows: 'Miss Saxton-Winter was a robust, strict woman with penetrating eyes. She meant well, but we were sometimes a little afraid of her.'[49]

By contrast, the aide-de-camp Count J.H.F. Dumonceau[50] described Miss Winter in his *Souvenirs* as 'the amiable and cheerful governess.' He also devoted a short paragraph to her in which he described her as the daughter of a high-ranking officer, as he had been told. Dumonceau: 'I admired her greatly for her appearance — she looked well — and for her jovial way of managing the Princess, who was ten years old!' And he praised the excellent education that she gave Wilhelmina.

When Miss Winter had completed her duties in 1896, she received two affectionate letters from Wilhelmina's aunt Sophie, Grand Duchess of Saxe-Weimar,[51] and from Emma's sister, Pauline, Princess of Bentheim-Steinfurt,[52] in which both expressed their gratitude for the way in which Miss Winter had contributed to her pupil's education. Both women also understood how difficult it would now be for Miss Winter to have to leave the Netherlands. Wilhelmina's history tutor, Professor Krämer, was likewise full of praise — also on behalf of his colleagues, professors Blok and Kan — for Miss Winter's ceaseless and painstaking care and for her show of judgement during the lessons with Wilhelmina, as they told her in a letter upon her departure.

It seems that men were better able to get along with Miss Winter than women, because the above opinion forms a contrast to that of Mrs H.A. Insinger-van

**49** Steyn, p. 14.

**50** Dumonceau 1991, pp. 27, 40. In 1890, Count Joseph Henri Felix Dumonceau (1859–1952), became aide-de-camp to the court of King Willem III. In 1904 was appointed adjutant to Queen Wilhelmina. Between 1919 and 1946 he was her master of ceremonies and grand master of the royal household. In 1900 he married Wilhelmina's lady-in-waiting Pixy de Constant Rebeque (see letter 51, note 71).

**51** Sophie of Saxe-Weimar (1824–1897) was the only sister of King Willem III and the youngest child of King Willem II and Queen Anna Paulowna. In 1842 she married the later Grand Duke Carl Alexander of Saxe-Weimar and lived in Weimar, where she was highly respected and played a significant part in cultural life there. In 1885 and 1889 she inherited the archives of the German playwrights, writers, poets and philosophers Johann Wolfgang von Goethe (1749–1832) and Friedrich von Schiller (1759–1805), respectively. On Sophie's initiative, Goethe's 143 works were published in four volumes — literature, science, diaries and letters — in the period between 1887 and 1919, forming the so-called *Sophienausgabe* or Goethe Edition. She had a new archive built to house them that was completed in 1896. She was just able to attend the opening on 28 June 1896, for she would die in March 1897. The archive building would later serve as an example for Emma when the latter commissioned the building of the Royal Archives in The Hague, as the place where all of the archives that were kept in the different palaces could be assimilated. This was achieved in 1898, the year of Wilhelmina's investiture. Queen Emma and Queen Wilhelmina were very fond of Sophie, because she was able to tell them a great deal about Dutch affairs. She was a mine of information for both women after the death of King Willem III.

**52** Princess Pauline of Waldeck-Pyrmont (1855–1925) was the elder sister of Queen Emma. In 1881 she married heir apparent Prince Alexis of Bentheim-Steinfurt (1845–1919). Between 28 September 1890 and his death on 21 January 1919, Alexis was the reigning sovereign. They lived in Burgsteinfurt, close to the Dutch border. They had five sons and three daughters.

Grand Duchess Sophie sitting surrounded by her family, on the occasion of her 65th birthday in 1889. Seated, from left to right: her daughter-in-law Pauline, Grand Duchess apparent; her daughter Princess Marie Alexandrine Reuss; Grand Duchess Sophie; her grandson Bernhard; her daughter Elisabeth of Mecklenburg-Schwerin; and her husband, Grand Duke Carl Alexander. Standing: her grandson, Prince Wilhelm Ernst; her sons-in-law Johann Albrecht, Duke of Mecklenburg-Schwerin, half-brother of Prince Hendrik, and Prince Heinrich VII Reuss, and her son Carl August, Grand Duke apparent. The latter died in 1894, after which his son Wilhelm Ernst would succeed his grandfather in 1901. Photograph: Louis Held, Weimar.

Loon,[53] Dame du Palais to Queen Emma in Amsterdam. She noted in her diary of Monday 5 September 1898 that when she and others 'including Miss Saxton Winter, Miss Joarmes,[54] Mrs Hoeffer van Heemstra,[55] and the whole series of governesses' were waiting in the throne room of the Royal Palace in Amsterdam for the queens to return from their drive, '[...] Saxton Winter was just as unpleasant as always, and displayed the most dreadful manners. What an unfortunate choice that proved to be [...].'

This opinion was shared by Marie, Crown Princess of Romania, who called

**53** Cleverens 1984, p. 51. Groenveld, p. 27. Mrs H.A. Insinger-van Loon (1825–1902) was made Dame du Palais for Amsterdam by Queen Emma as of 1 January 1879.
**54** Cleverens 1984, p. 51. Mrs Insinger mistakenly referred to Ada de Joannis (after 1863–1951), who was appointed by Emma as a French lady-companion to Wilhelmina in the summer of 1897, as Miss Joarmes (see also letter 167, note 429).
**55** Baroness Cornelia Martina van Heemstra (1847–1931) was honorary lady-in-waiting to Queen Emma. She was appointed governess on 5 April 1882 and remained in the post until 1887. In 1890, she married the later brevet Major General Frederic A. Hoefer (1850–1938). She would remain in touch with Wilhelmina for the rest of her life.

the governess 'Hornet' when she was working in Bucharest in 1899. The crown princess described the governess in her biography in most unfriendly terms: 'The woman was just everything that could not be borne, thick-set, heavy with staring, goggle-eyes, a large fleshy nose and repulsive mouth; she was common, with a commonness that only one of her own nationality could rightly appreciate.'[56] By contrast, King Carol I and Queen Elizabeth of Romania, who had appointed Miss Winter, shared a high opinion of the Englishwoman. Carol would write to the hereditary prince's father: 'One could not make a better selection.'[57]

The liberal politician Willem Hendrik de Beaufort[58] met the former governess at a dinner at Soestdijk Palace on 2 September 1908, when Miss Winter was staying with Queen Emma for a few days. At that time, De Beaufort was Minister of Foreign Affairs and was receiving the 'Duitsche depêches' (official dispatches) about the court scandal between the crown prince and the crown princess. Queen Emma wanted to read them, and they contained the most dreadful things. 'I presume they were not edifying' was Miss Winter's response. The crown prince, according to Miss Winter was 'a non-entity'; she had thought that it would come to a divorce, but the crown princess, 'a skilful but very immoral woman', was opposed. Miss Winter described the barbarity of the Romanian people with reference to an incident involving a tramp, whose ears were cut off by the gardeners after he had stolen a cucumber from the royal kitchen gardens. The statesman offered no opinion on Miss Winter, but he found her recollections of Romania so interesting that he recorded them in his diary.[59]

56 Marie, II, p. 141; Fasseur, p. 151.
57 Zeepvat, p. 169.
58 Willem Hendrik de Beaufort (1845-1918) was a lawyer and liberal statesman, and would become Minister of Foreign Affairs in the Pierson Cabinet of 1897-1901. He worked hard to achieve the First Hague Peace Conference in 1899, of which he was honorary chairman. He led the Dutch delegation to the Second Hague Peace Conference in 1907.
59 Beaufort, W.H. de, I. pp. 442-443.

# About the letters

The Royal Archives acquired the letters that had belonged to Miss Saxton Winter on 15 June 1967.[60] The correspondence proved to be a fine addition to the Royal Archive's collections, although Mr R. de Beaufort, a member of staff at the Dutch embassy in England, was of a different opinion. The letters had been kept in England by a cousin of Miss Saxton Winter, Miss Hilda Spanton. Having consulted the letters, De Beaufort told Mr E. Pelinck, who was then the director of the Royal Archives, that the collection was of no great value and that he could not imagine anyone showing great interest in them. Pelinck noted that in the nineteenth century, it had been customary for a royal figure's correspondence to be returned to the letter-writer's family after the member of the royal family had died. Unlike De Beaufort, he did consider the letters to be of some interest to the Royal Archives, because few letters from Queen Wilhelmina and none — with a few exceptions — from Miss Saxton Winter had been kept.

In the meantime, more than twenty years would pass before the letters would first be used by myself, as described above, for the exhibition on the regency of Queen Emma. Now, in 2017, exactly fifty years later, they are being published for the first time as a book, unabridged and in their original English form.

## The letters

A total of 320 letters were kept, 249 of which were written by Princess/Queen Wilhelmina. They include greetings cards to celebrate Christmas, New Year and Easter, some of which were made by Wilhelmina herself, and a series of telegrams, most of which concern Miss Winter's stays in England. In addition, there are 39 letters from Queen Emma and five from Princess Juliana (after 1927), as well as letters from the following: Pauline, Princess of Bentheim-Stein-furt (letter 130), Sophie, Grand Duchess of Saxe-Weimar (letter 131), the Dutch ambassador in London, Mr de Marees van Swinderen (letter 274), and two from Jenny Reichardt, Emma's lectrice (letters 313 and 315). Only four letters from Miss Winter herself seem to have been kept in the Royal Archives. Queen Wilhelmina burned many letters. Recently, however, another sixteen letters from the governess were found in a newly-opened file in the Royal Archives: numbers 15, 20, 22, 26, 31, 35, 48, 52, 56, 67, 73, 79, 81, 86, 90 and 93.[61] A letter from Miss

60 See foreword, note 5.
61 Royal Archives, A50-VIIa-01. These letters formed part of a package of letters that was sealed by Queen Emma with the following description in the inventory: 'Sealed package of letters with the title "Private letters (unimportant) sent to my daughter in the years 1888–1893, which she gave to me. For the eyes of the Queen, my daughter, only. I urgently request her

came in my dressing
room to put down
something she had
brought, shewing
my dressingroom to
the maid of miss o.
Ittersum and miss de
Vries believes the maid

Het Loo.
August 9
1895

Dear Bones,
Thank you so
much for your two
dear lettres. My day
at Middachten past
off well; it was very
stiff. Miss van Harden

In this letter featuring a crowned 'Het Loo' monogram, Wilhelmina wrote about what she considered to have been a very 'stiff visit' to Middachten Castle; Het Loo, 9 August 1895.

Winter also came to light unexpectedly in the archive of the Dutch faith-based broadcasting association, the Evangelische Omroep. It is a reply to a letter of thanks from Wilhelmina's history tutor, Professor Krämer,[62] when her position as governess ended in 1896 (letters 132 and 133). Finally, a letter from Miss Winter had been kept in one of Gediking's exercise books in the Paleis Het Loo National Museum, Apeldoorn (letter 111), and recently a picture postcard that Wilhelmina sent to Miss Winter was bought at auction by the author of this book (letter 278).

The first letters were written on small sheets of writing paper; children's writing paper, sometimes decorated with little bouquets or other pictures. Much of the writing paper featured a personal or general royal monogram, varying from a crowned 'W' in various forms to Wilhelmina's name in capital letters, printed next to each other in the form of a small medallion, or Wilhelmina's name in capital letters arranged in a crowned monogram. Wilhelmina also used writing paper from the various palaces: 'Het Loo', with a crown over the 'H', or 'Paleis, 's Gravenhage', featuring a crown over the 'P', or 'Soestdijk', with a crown over the 'S' (see Colour plate 1-2 and the various letters shown throughout the book).

not to destroy these after my death" (signed Emma).' Although the seal on the package was broken in 1995 by Mr B. Woelderink, then director of the Royal Archives, for the biography of Wilhelmina by Cees Fasseur, it was then forgotten again.
62 Prof. F.J.L. Krämer (1850-1928) was made a professor of history at Utrecht University in 1893. Between 1894 and 1898 he gave Wilhelmina lessons in general history, while in the winter of 1896 he also gave her lessons in art history. In March 1897, these lessons would be taken over by C. Hofstede de Groot. In 1903 Krämer was appointed director of the Royal Archives.

When a member of the family died, the letters were written on black-edged mourning paper. This was the case, for example, between December 1890 and August 1891 after the death of King Willem III and between 28 March and 20 June 1897 after Grand Duchess Sophie of Saxe-Weimar passed away. Emma continued to write on mourning paper for longer. When the queens were staying abroad, they sometimes made use of the writing paper provided by the hotel in which they were staying. The envelopes for many of the letters were kept. The envelopes were addressed by the sender herself from 6 August 1893 onwards, and many featured a red wax seal (black in times of mourning).

The correspondence began on 14 November 1886, when Miss Winter was spending her holidays at her mother's in Saffron Walden in Essex. Most of the letters were written on Sundays. The first short letters were written in English by Queen Emma herself, as though she were Wilhelmina. Emma signed them 'Wilhelmine'. Between 6 December 1888 and 3 August 1894, Wilhelmina signed the letters 'Poekie', 'Poekie Woekie', 'Poekieoekie', 'PoekiePoes', 'OeksiePoeksie' or 'Wilhelmina and old Poekie'. Wilhelmina wrote a few letters in Dutch in 1891 with the salutation 'Lieve Darling [Dear Darling]'. Between 15 April 1892 and 27 December 1895, they were addressed to 'Dear old Bones' or 'Dear Bones', then 'Darling' in various forms, and from 1900, 'My dear old friend'.

In 1888, Wilhelmina began to write her first letters herself, using phonetic spelling, and would continue to do so until 1890. These short English letters are downright entertaining and they can only be understood when read out loud. Emma wanted her daughter to have a large, clear hand, as she herself did, for 'a queen should have clear handwriting, and unfortunately too many monarchs have a scrawly, unclear hand.'[63] This particular task fell to Wilhelmina's tutor, Gediking. On 3 November 1890, Wilhelmina wrote in beautiful calligraphy with a thin upwards stroke and a thick downwards one, this time in Dutch, always writing the 'u' with a capital letter.[64] Her next letter, written on 24 December 1890, was on black-edged mourning paper. Her father had just died. One would not know this from the letter, which was written as though nothing had happened, although the old king's death did in fact affect her deeply.[65] In 1891 she also wrote a single letter in Dutch, while another, in English, was written for her by her superintendent, Miss van de Poll.[66]

63 Heuven 1989, p. 29; Lammers, p. 12.
64 For this reason, in the Dutch translation of the letters, 'U' is always written with a capital letter.
65 Wilhelmina, pp. 28–30. '... And then that deathly silence everywhere, and the thick shutters, all those heavy forms with long veils, ... and above all mother so unhappy and swathed in an alarming amount of crêpe. I was utterly unable to stand it. ... The plan had been that I should escort father to the door. For this, I had to wear a crêpe hat with a veil covering my whole face. I was so frightened by this prospect that my nerves did not hold. I had to stay in bed with a headache and stomach ache.' All of this affected Wilhelmina so much that she even stopped growing during this period.
66 On 18 October 1879, Miss F.L.H. (Henriette) van de Poll (1853–1946) was, like Baroness E.G. van Ittersum (see introduction under letter 52, note 72) appointed lady-in-waiting to

On 19 August 1895, Wilhelmina demanded much perseverance on the part of her governess. Reading with intense concentration was the only way to decipher this eight-page letter, in which her writing filled the page in two directions. The paper featured a beautiful crowned monogram in blue and gold.

Just like any young person who wants to try everything, Wilhelmina would sometimes joke around; when she was twelve, for example, she imitated her mother, who wrote the letter 'd' with a big stroke to the left (23, 25 and 29 October 1892), and she would write letters with a splendid flourish (see Colour plate 1-2), as had been done in the seventeenth century (3 November 1892). On 13 August 1893, she addressed the envelope herself in calligraphy. The eight-page letter of 19 August 1895 is particularly difficult to read, as she wrote back across the text she had already written on the first four pages.

Now and then, the letters reveal Wilhelmina's own opinion of her handwriting and spelling. On 7 November 1892, she fished for a compliment from Miss Winter: 'I hope you will admire the beauty of my writing.' From the letter, it seems that she first wrote on top of pencil lines, which she then rubbed out. As regards her English spelling, one comes across many a mistake. In 1892, in a short undated letter (letter 68), she wrote: 'I only ask mother the words I have not written befor.' And on 23 October 1892: 'I have not asked so meny tims about the spelling'; as evident from the 'meny tims'! Her later letters would also include numerous errors. On 3 August 1893, we come across 'hear – here', 'first – furst', 'writing – ritting' and 'written – ritten'; and on 6 August 1893, 'imagine

Queen Emma. By a royal decree of 23 January 1891, Lady van de Poll was charged with the supervision of Queen Wilhelmina's education. She was also known as the 'Superintendent of the education of Her Majesty the Queen'. She fulfilled this role until the confirmation of Queen Wilhelmina at the end of October 1896, whereupon she resumed her previous role until the death of Queen Emma in 1934.

— immadgine'. The fact that she really was trying her hardest is evident from the letter of 2 December 1896: 'I always try to write nicely not to shock you with my spelling and stile!' And on 21 March 1897 she wrote: 'I now don't anymore let mother read my letters so all faults come down upon me. Do say if you think my handwriting & spelling has improved.' She was overjoyed with Miss Winter's response to her letter of 28 August 1897: 'You don't know how glad I am about your saying that my spelling was improving; I think that by writing to you so often I will perhaps get to write without mistakes!'

But on 30 December 1898, she had again crossed out the 'e' in 'sure', although she did write 'sure' correctly a little further on. Wilhelmina used a wide range of adjectives, alternating 'beautiful', for example, with 'pretty', 'cosy' and 'lovely'. She followed the common English custom of abbreviating the word 'Christmas' as 'Xmas'. And just as members of the British court emphasized particular words in their private correspondence by underlining them, sometimes multiple times, and always wrote the word 'and' as '&', we also frequently encounter these practices in Wilhelmina's and Emma's letters.[67] Now and then Wilhelmina would abbreviate a word, such as 'comfy — comfortable' (27 December 1888, 28 November 1897, 8 May 1900). Some of the more unusual words and phrases that she used were: 'come down a cropper' (13 November 1898), 'jibberjabbered' (3 January 1897), 'plucky' (4 December 1898), 'heartrending' (11 December 1898), 'I wonder if you feel "tungyhangy" out (as we used to say) about the new year' (30 December 1898). She used the Dutch word 'benauwd [anxious, oppressive]' a number of times without ever translating it into English (13 December 1896, 3 January, 31 January and 4 August 1897, 20 March and 5 October 1898, 31 March and 25 April 1899).

One is particularly struck by the sometimes surprising terms that Wilhelmina used to her address her governess. This clearly reveals the intense relationship between the two, and Wilhelmina did not hold back from addressing her with a certain degree of cheekiness. The following names offer a good picture of Wilhelmina's imaginative use of terms to address her governess: 'Dear old Bones/bones' (from April 1892 until the end of December 1895); 'wretch', 'Hearty' (9 November 1896); 'deary' (a number of times); 'Noddle' (15 November 1896); 'Your poor old heady' (19 December 1897); 'You dear old thing' (2 June 1898); 'You sweet old Darling!' (1 July 1898); 'You poor old Friendy' (10 December 1900); and 'Poor old Friendy' (26 December 1900).

Wilhelmina certainly had a way with words. At dinner on her fifth birthday, Wilhelmina said to her father King Willem III, when he asked his daughter whether she had eaten the cake with her mouth: 'Did father think I'd eaten it with my nose?'[68] And she once said to Emma's lady-in-waiting, Lady van de Poll: 'Freule Hanjet play with me.'[69] The Dutch royal family were known for their

67  Zeepvat 2005.
68  Cleverens 1994, p. 85.
69  By 'Hanjet', Wilhelmina meant 'Henriette' (Lady de Poll's first name); a name that is difficult for a small child to pronounce.

habit of giving others nicknames. King Willem III called his sister Sophie, Grand Duchess of Saxe-Weimar, 'La Chattemitte', and called the girl who taught the young Wilhelmina to speak French, Julie Liotard from Alsace, 'La belle Julie'.[70] Wilhelmina called Lady van Heemstra (her first governess, between 1882 and 1887) 'Brown-eyes',[71] and a lord-in-waiting, Taets van Amerongen, 'Curlyhead'.[72] Wilhelmina would later bestow nicknames on various dignitaries in her own humorous way.

Wilhelmina also wrote expressively, as shown by the following sign-off: 'With all dearest love I remain your most affectionately devotedly, stickily melting friend. Wilhelmina' (14 August 1898). She often skipped from one subject to another when writing. The most diverse subjects followed one another in the same paragraph, without any transition. Standard themes in the letters were: an opening thanking Miss Winter for the letters she had received; an enquiry after Miss Winter's fortunes and those of her family, especially with regard to her mother's health, about which the governess was often greatly concerned; and then the weather. Every letter made reference to the weather. Indeed, this was a habit that was not unique to Wilhelmina. The letters from Wilhelmina's contemporary Marie (Missy), Crown Princess of Romania, also contain frequent remarks about the weather. In his diaries, King Carol I of Romania described the weather in the minutest detail.[73] Emperor Franz Joseph of Austria could also write at length about the weather in his letters.[74] Wilhelmina enjoyed the weather when it snowed or was icy; as she wrote on 27 December 1899, 'It is just as if you quite get an other being on the ice!' By contrast, she hated the heat, which she was quite unable to endure. Her holidays were therefore always spent in cooler climes, such as Norway or Switzerland. Having to wear royal regalia in the heat of August 1898 was unbearable; and 'the hottest day I have ever felt!' happened to fall on 15 July 1900. Not only snow, storms and downpours, but also the budding trees or beautiful autumn colours and her great love for her dear Loo Palace are described in her letters. Wilhelmina frequently underlined words, sometimes multiple times, for extra emphasis, in imitation of her mother and her governess. She also abbreviated words, something that was also done by Queen Victoria of England, as well as the latter's son Leopold, for example, who would marry Emma's sister Helena in 1882, in their private correspondence.[75]

Wilhelmina and her English governess always enjoyed a good relationship. After the latter was dismissed in 1896, Queen Wilhelmina wrote her long letters on an almost weekly basis, always on Sundays, until her investiture in 1898. In

---

70  Cleverens 1989, p. 88.

71  Baroness Cornelia Martina van Heemstra (1847–1931) was honorary lady-in-waiting to Queen Emma. She was appointed governess on 5 April 1882 and remained in this position until 1887. She would stay in touch with Wilhelmina until her death.

72  Taets van Amerongen, see letter 96, note 201.

73  Mandache, p. 7.

74  Hamann, p. 448.

75  Zeepvat 2005.

fact, Miss Winter was the only person, aside from her mother, whom she fully trusted. As someone who always took a rather distanced stance, Wilhelmina expressed herself in strikingly open fashion in her letters to her ex-governess. In them, the young queen described what she had done; what she thought; her belief in the Almighty; whom she had met; how her lessons were progressing; her great love for Paleis Het Loo; her painting hobby (Colour plate IV-7); the trips that she made; the monuments, churches and museums that she visited; and her favourite painters. It is fascinating to read how Wilhelmina slowly grew towards her role as a monarch and the investiture. She also touched on political issues, such as the Aceh War, the Dreyfus Affair and the Boer War, and her commitment to the army. 'I always have had such a military heart and I feel myself half like a soldier at his post and duty!'(6 March 1898). One is struck by the way she lectured Miss Saxton Winter, someone who had of course herself lectured Wilhelmina on how she ought to behave. In addition, the teenage queen often wrote in strikingly complicated sentences, in which she wanted to cover a whole range of things.

A few tragic letters attest to the lonely situation in which Emma and Wilhelmina found themselves in the 'glass cage' of the court. One moving example is the letter dated 28 March 1897, which Wilhelmina wrote after the death of her aunt Sophie, Grand Duchess of Saxe-Weimar. It reveals in heart-rending terms how lonely she felt. Sophie had had a good understanding of how things had traditionally been done in the Netherlands and had made regular visits to the country, giving Emma and Wilhelmina wise counsel on how to manage court affairs.[76] One such piece of advice was to avoid, above all, being on too confidential a footing with the members of the royal household; one should always maintain one's distance. The two women therefore isolated themselves, and there was hardly anyone to whom they could pour out their feelings when they needed to, certainly not after Sophie's death. Emma's letter of 2 January 1902 also attests to this. In the letter, the queen mother expressed her need to confide her concerns to the former governess about what she considered to be the odd behaviour of her youthful, newly-married daughter to her husband, Prince Hendrik.

The correspondence steadily declined after the investiture, but Miss Winter was not forgotten on her birthday and at Easter, Christmas and New Year. It is unclear why no letters were kept from the periods between 1903 and 1917 and between 1918 and 1921.

When Princess Juliana was old enough, she also wrote a number of letters expressing friendship. Juliana even visited Miss Winter herself when she went to England in 1933.[77] In 1934, on her next trip to England, she would cancel a meeting with the governess because she had to rush back to the Netherlands

---

76 A50-VIIa-6. Fasseur 1998, p. 155, note 41.
77 Princess Juliana was in London between 1 and 12 July 1933. This is where she must have met Miss Winter.

following the death of her father.[78] At the marriage of Prince George, the Duke of Kent, to Princess Marina of Greece on 29 November of that year, Juliana was one of the bridesmaids and was able to visit Miss Winter after all.

The only visit that Wilhelmina paid to her old governess was that of September 1935. On 10 November, Wilhelmina wrote her final letter to 'My dear old Friend', signing off: 'With a hug ever your dear old friend Wilhelmina.' A few months later, on 29 January 1936, Miss Winter died aged 78, shortly after the death of her sister, with whom she had shared the house in Saffron Walden.

---

78 Princess Juliana was in England between 14 June and 4 July 1934, where she was the guest of the British Royal Family and the Count and Countess of Athlone (Aunt Alice). Prince Hendrik died of a heart attack on 3 July.

# The letters
# 1886–1935

When the logo of the palace where the letter was written is printed on the writing paper, the name of the palace is always written one line above the date of the letter. When Wilhelmina wrote 'Het Loo' herself, for example, then the palace and the date have been written in a single line. Just like her mother and Miss Winter, Wilhelmina frequently underlined a word to give it extra emphasis, sometimes a number of times. When a word was underlined multiple times, the number of times is included in square brackets.

   Punctuation has occasionally been added, in the interests of readability. The errors that Wilhelmina made in her letters have been left as she wrote them. Wilhelmina sometimes wrote a word in Dutch, such as the word 'benauwd [stressful, oppressive]', for example, in an English letter. These words have been left in Dutch with the translation given in brackets. The inventory numbers provided in the notes refer to the records in the Royal Archives, unless stated otherwise.

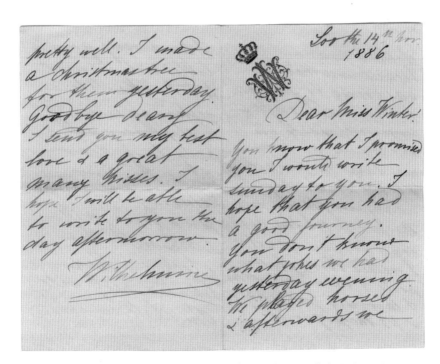

Wilhelmina's first letter to Miss Winter, written by her mother on Wilhelmina's writing paper, which featured a gold-coloured crowned monogram; Het Loo, 14 November 1886.

# 1886

On Saturday 13 November 1886, Miss Elizabeth Saxton Winter spent her holiday visiting her family in Saffron Walden in Essex, England. Wilhelmina had turned six on 31 August of the same year.

Loo the 14<sup>th</sup> Nov. 1886

1 Dear Miss Winter!

You know that I promised you I would write sunday to you. I hope that you had a good journey.

You don't know what jokes we had yesterday evening. We played horses & afterwards we dressed mother, because mother was going to put me to bed.

— This afternoon we went in the woods of Soeren, we saw many stags & a big buck.[1] Afterwards we played with the hoops on the high road to Amersfoort. I walked through the pools & the mud & than I saw my pet rabbits & fed the pigeons.[2]

I am a very good little girl. I went to bed rather late yesterday evening. I slept very well & very long dear Miss Winter.

Saturday I went for a drive with Julie[3] with Eros & Jockey.[4] They behaved very well. The children behaved pretty well.[5] I made a christmastree for them yesterday. Goodbye deary I send you my best love & a great many kisses. I hope I will be able to write to you the day aftermorrow.

Wilhelmine

1 This refers to Hoog Soeren, a village in the municipality of Apeldoorn, lying 85 m above Normal Amsterdam Water Level (NAP) and surrounded by the woodlands of the Royal Forest, 5 km from Apeldoorn. King-Stadholder Willem III (1650-1702), who built Paleis Het Loo, had a hunting lodge there in the 17th century. He and his wife Mary Stuart (1662-1695) were crowned King and Queen of Great Britain and Ireland in 1689.

2 King Willem III (1817-1890) had a playhouse in Swiss style, known as the 'little chalet', built for his daughter Wilhelmina in the park of Paleis Het Loo, in the place where an 18th-century summerhouse (the *Schellenhuisje*) had stood. There, she had a seesaw, a swing, a dovecot and a garden for growing flowers and vegetables.

3 Julie Liotard, the nanny from Alsace, was employed in 1883 thanks to the mediation of Emile Bourlier (1845-1911), a clergyman from Wallonia and, from 28 November 1878, chaplain of the court (Cleverens 1989, p.88). She remained in royal service until 1886. Later, she would often return when Miss Winter was on holiday. In a letter dated 10 November 1895 to her former attendant, Lady de Kock, Wilhelmina called her 'Julie Liotard my "francaise"' (G28-3). Julie taught Princess Wilhelmina French in playful fashion and encouraged her love of playing with dolls. This was considered important by Queen Emma, for 'the trait of protective tenderness — which should form a principal trait in the character of the adult woman — can already be gradually developed in small girls by encouraging them to treat and care for their dolls as though they were not dolls at all, but little human beings.' Wilhelmina acted out her own life with her dolls (Winter, pp. 11-14, Heuven 1990, Carvalho, pp. 51-77).

4 Eros and Jockey are two horses.

5 By 'the children', Wilhelmina is referring to her family of dolls.

2    Dear Miss Winter!

I thank you very much indeed for your dear letter. I find it a great pity that you were sea sick. I did not write so soon as I promised, as I waited for a letter from you deary. Father is very well & Mother too. I have a new child, which is called Caroline[6] & which I hope you will like.— The other day Julie let Theodora fall, she broke her head & is still with the physician. Father will give me four Shetland ponies with two carriages one for myself & one for the coachmen to exercise them. Father also ordered a pretty little harness.—

I am on the whole a very good little girl.

This afternoon I saw with the children the magic lantern; it was very amusing. Willy & all the children send you many kisses & compliments.

I send you many kisses & my best love. Goodbye for the present dear Miss Winter.

Wilhelmine

Postscript from Emma:

Everything is going on quite well just now dear Miss Winter. Julie keeps the child out of mischief & makes her happy & Mademoiselle[7] interferes very little till now. I can only hope she will go on like that. I sincerely hope you are enjoying yourself very much & that you found all your dear ones well        E

Loo the 27<sup>th</sup> of Nov 1886

3    Dear Miss Winter!

I thank you very much indeed for your dear letter. The twins are very glad, that Uncle Trousers arrived well in England.

Caroline will be very glad to see her uncle & I promise that your nieces will send you a nice little card one day.

The table for Father succeeded very well indeed. I make now a pretty dark vase.

This morning Julie mended Willy, she looks very nice now.

I would have liked to be with you & see the little monkey.

I hope that you are happy at home. I am a good little girl & Mother says that I don't give any trouble to her or Julie.

All the children are happy & don't give any trouble either to their father or mother.

Goodbye dear Miss Winter for the present. I send you my best love & many kisses

Wilhelmine

---

6 Caroline is a doll, as are Theodora and Willy in this letter. The family of dolls also included the twins Marie and Frederik ter Hansch, Uncle Trousers, Dora, Marguerite, Bertha and Suzanna (in the following letters).

7 'Mademoiselle' probably refers to one of Queen Emma's two ladies-in-waiting: Baroness E. (Elise) G. van Ittersum (1851–1936) or Lady F.L.H. (Henriette) van de Poll (1853–1946). Lady Marie Louise de Kock (1848–1932), the daughter of a naval officer, who would also look after Wilhelmina when Miss Winter was on holiday, was not at Paleis Het Loo at that time.

Princess Wilhelmina in her duc carriage, supplied by Thorn of London, accompanied by her mother, on the square in front of the Royal Stables on Hoge Wal, The Hague, April 1887. Photograph: H.R.F. Kameke, The Hague.

Loo the 4 Dec 1886

**4**  Dear Miss Winter!

I thank you very much indeed for your letter.

The ponies are darlings. I took two for a walk today. One of them tumbled in the water, his foot slipped of the bridge. First he kicked mother, his manners are none.

The first thing he was very greedy & he was inclined to run. This one is called Brownie & the name of the other I took for a walk is Baby.[8] The two others are called Puck and Blackie.[9] I love them very dearly.

We went for a day to Soestdijk, we came back here at 6 o'clock.—

Bud is a much better child now & she promises Uncle Trousers that she will remain good. I have new ducks at Soestdijk. We went to see the little & the big farm.[10] I showed Julie everything.

8  Baby, mare, 1.01 m, Shetland, chestnut, bought in London on 2 December 1886, died (put down) on 20 November 1901. Brownie, mare, 1.05 m, red roan, bought in London on 2 December 1886, transferred to the royal hunting stables. Puck, mare, 1.05 m, Shetland, blue roan, put down on 4 November 1896. Blacky is not mentioned in the studbook (*Stamboek van de Paarden*) (E11c-11b-4).

9  Of the four ponies — Baby, Brownie, Puck and Blacky — Baby and Brownie were buried in the animal cemetery in the park of Paleis Het Loo. Baby was Wilhelmina's favourite pony. The inscription on his gravestone reads: 'Here lies buried / Baby / 25 years old / the first saddle horse / of H.M. the Queen. / 2 Dec. 1886=20 Nov. 1901.' Brownie's gravestone reads: 'Here lies / BROWNIE / Pony of H.M. the Queen. / Born 1881. Died 1905.'

10  The 'little farm' in the park of Soestdijk Palace is the small farm that King Willem II had built for his daughter Sophie (1824–1897). The princess laid the first stone in 1833.

I am making a tiny christmastree for Father & for Mother, I will not allow any one to help me.

The dear twins are good. Today I gave them a big picnic.

I am trying to be very good indeed.

Mademoiselle sends you her compliments & I give You a big hug & thirty tiny kisses

Wilhelmine

Loo the 19<sup>th</sup> Dec. 1886

**5**  Dear Miss Winter!

I thank you very much for your darling letter. May I offer you these little pictures I did them quite alone?[11] There is a great deal of snow, today also, I threw Julie with snow so well, that she was nearly white.

Old father Christmas came here in my room, he had not a big waterproof like last year but a big furcloak, he threw a good lot of bonbons & I have them now still. He brought Julie a pretty dress & the next morning I found my presents & many sweets. We each found the beginning of our name. Old father Xmas brought me a pretty screan [screen]. Only think what I found the next morning in my slipper a box like a piece of money, a letter & another little box, all filled with chocolades. The next day a conjuror came & played tricks in the theater, that is in the palace.[12] He had also some 'marionettes'.—

Aunt Pauline was here for a week & Grandfather for one evening & a morning.[13] I help Mother with the Christmas trees.— My chickens give eggs now for father. The rabbits are very well. My ponies are very good, Julie can ride on one of them.

Goodbye dear Miss Winter. Many compliments from Mademoiselle.

I send you a hug.

We will see one another again very quickly & I will be very glad.

Much love from your girlie

Wilhelmine

11  Wilhelmina may be referring to a number of stencilled pictures that were kept with Miss Winter's letters.

12  The theatre was built at the time of King Louis Napoleon, on the site of the 17th-century orangery in the East Wing of Paleis Het Loo. It was redecorated by King Willem III around 1875. When renovations were carried out between 1911 and 1914, the theatre was demolished once again and moved to the West Wing. When the palace was restored between 1977 and 1984, the room was demolished for good.

13  See p. 26, note 52. There had always been a close bond between Emma, her older sister Pauline and her husband Alexis. The Prince and Princess of Bentheim-Steinfurt arrived on 11 December and left on 15 and 18 December, respectively. 'Grandfather' refers to Emma's father, Georg Viktor, Prince of Waldeck-Pyrmont (1831–1893). He arrived on 11 December and left the following day. They had a family dinner together on 11 December.

Undated Christmas card; the text is partly printed and partly written by Emma:

6 With 'many kisses from Wilhelmina' and best wishes for a Happy Christmas to 'dear Miss Winter';
On the reverse: 'Today it is de day before Xmas eve. I have a great deal of fun. There was ice yesterday & I could walk on it & slide.'

# 1887

Miss Winter was on holiday between Sunday 5 November and Saturday 3 December 1887. Her duties were taken over by Lady Marie Louise de Kock.[14]

The Loo Nov. th 8

7 Dear Miss Winter!
I thank you very much for your dear little telegram which I received sunday.
I am very glad you had a good journey. Will you excuse my not writing sooner but I thought you would know more about my behaviour after a few days. I dont think I will have to keep some chocolate for you deary because you will be here for old father Xmas but if you are not yet back, I will keep some for you. I have been till now very good deary & I have had very good lessons. I learnt today about the trees & coal mine. Yesterday we made a long walk, Julie was to show the way but made a mistake. You dont know what I invented deary, I gave little sticks to the young dogs. I played yesterday such a long time with them, first they looked very stupidly at the little sticks but afterwards they took them; all in their little house.
Theodora was very naughty yesterday, but she is good now. She was so impertinent that I had to put her to bed. I send you very many kisses & hugs.

Wilhelmine

Loo the 18<sup>th</sup> Nov. 1887

8 Dear Miss Winter
I thank you very much indeed for your two charming letters. I hope you had a lot of pleasure at the seaside.
Baby is a little pickle in front of the carriage. I drove with mother on sunday with the ponies. —
I wrote to-day beautifully with Miss de Kock the word "vreugd [joy]".
I am going to learn to-morrow the latin figures because I have finished with 12.
— Mr. Gediking says 12 is such a funny number it leads to all kinds of things.
Deary I would like to offer you a little bookmark. I enclose it. I dried & stuck the leaves myself.[15] I am again going out. I am on the whole very good indeed. I am always amusing myself very much.

---

14 Lady Marie Louise de Kock; see letter 2, note 7.
15 Princess Wilhelmina would pick many flowers and leaves in the park around Paleis Het

The children have been very good except Dora & Marguerite. Now 4 children are going away also Suzan.[16] Suzan is going to your wife. Bertha is ill & has been today very impertinent, she may not come down before sunday she is with her father. Goodbye deary. Many compliments from Miss de Kock & Julie. I send you many many kisses.[17]

Fredrik Gediking, principal tutor at the secondary school in Scheveningen, was recommended to Queen Emma by Dr L.R. Beijnen, the former headmaster of the grammar school in The Hague, who had tutored Emma in Dutch when she became engaged to King Willem III. Between 1887 and 1897, Gediking would tutor Wilhelmina in primary education (until July 1890), numeracy, natural history, physics, chemistry, economics (loans, stocks and monetary systems) and mathematics. When saying farewell on 20 April 1897, Wilhelmina thanked Gediking warmly for everything that he had done for her in the preceding years and for the patience he had shown when explaining things to her that she had not understood. By way of thanks, she gave him a signed photograph of herself with the inscription: 'In grateful memory of the years 1887-97'.

Loo the 30th Nov. 1887

9    Dear Miss Winter!
I thank you very much indeed for your charming letter. The fact of the matter is that I am going on well with my reading. My lessons are very good only the writing is not very good. I did not hold my pencil well. I have been good on the whole. Suzan is coming back when her uncle comes. Bertha has been a pickle, she shut herself up in a cupboard, wanting to pay a visit to the sunday children. One whole day she had no food except her breakfast. Mothers sachet came, and I gave it her. Did not your holidays seem to pass as a wind? Now I am making all kind of pleasant surprises for the children's hospital. I am making a cache-nez[18] for father, you will see how I do it.
    Goodbye Deary.
    Very many kisses from your loving                          Wilhelmine

Loo and dry them in the form of separate flowers or bouquets, so that they could be used to decorate all kinds of objects made of wood, velvet and leather, such as bookmarks, trays, albums, and so forth. This was known as 'spatter work' or *Spritzwerk*. Around 1889, she made her tutor Gediking a keepsake album with a leather cover, decorated with a bouquet of flowers. It is kept at Paleis Het Loo (RL4000).
16  Suzan, or Suzanna, was Wilhelmina's favourite doll and Miss Saxton Winter's godchild, with whom she would travel when she spent her holidays in England. The doll, made of porcelain, composition, wood and mohair, was made by Kestner & Co in Ohrdruf (Thuringia).
17  Wilhelmina did not sign the letter.
18  A *cache-nez* is a muffler/comforter.

# 1888

The Hague<br>
March the 31 1888[19]

**10**  Dear Miss Winter!

I thank you very much indeed for your dear telegramm. I am glad you arrived safely. I hope Suzan is a very good girl. I have been very good on the whole, especially yesterday & today.

My music-lesson went well to, mother teaches me in another way than you do Deary. Mother makes me play all the old exercises over again, what I don't like at all, & makes me read many notes, which I cant guess. I walked at Sorgvliet yesterday & brought home many flowers. I send you many many loving kisses. Your loving

Signed by Wilhelmina herself: Wilhelmina[20]

Postcript from Queen Emma:

Dear Miss Winter, We are getting on all right. The child is very good. This night she did not feel quite comfortable & I already feared a stomach attack, but this morning she is quite bright & happy & well again. As the weather is colder again, I keep her in house by ? of Tienhoven,[21] so that she should be quite well for Monday.

Please bring me from England a pot of zink ointment as my pot does not close well & two pots of good cold cream. I hope you are enjoying yourself & that you did not frighten your mother!

A small envelope with a black border from Esher, England, sent on 30 August 1888 to:

**11**  'H.R.H. The Princess Wilhelmina of the Netherlands, Het Loo, Holland'

With a crowned monogram on the reverse, contained thirteen small stencilled pictures, probably made by Wilhelmina. The envelope would have originally contained a letter from Miss Winter to her pupil.

The following card, written in calligraphy between drawn-in lines, would have been sent by Wilhelmina to her governess on the occasion of her birthday, which was on 5 September:

**12**  'With my warmest / congratulations / Wilhelmine / 1888'

---

19  The envelope is marked Saffron Walden, 'Sussex', but Saffron Walden is in the county of Essex.

20  Wilhelmina wrote her name in calligraphy.

21  'Van Tienhoven' probably refers to the court physician, Dr G.P. van Tienhoven; see letter 113, note 150.

Princess Wilhelmina standing by the chalet that she was given by her father, feeding her doves in the park of Paleis Het Loo. On the left is Miss Winter; c. 1888.
Photograph: Roeloffzen & Hübner.

Wilhelmina wrote the following letter phonetically; it is written unevenly, between drawn-in lines:

Oktober 8 1888

**13**    Dier Loeieza,

ij em bled toe hew hed wram u. Ij woed lijk toe sie end kam toe u. IJ Fijnd Loeieza koed hev e prizent wrom her ongti. IJ Odet e pir ov Fik lijnboets vor ol of jor tsjilden.

  Boed Bijj Mij dir loeieza

  Jor lawing                                 Wilhelmina

Transcription:
Dear Louisa[22]
I am glad to have heard from you. I would like to see and come to you. I find Louiza could have a present from her auntie. I ordered a pair of thick lined boots for all of your children. Goodbye my dear Louiza

  Your loving                                  Wilhelmina

22 'Louise' most probably refers to a doll. It could also refer to Louise Muller of Apeldoorn, whose name appears in the notebook listing Wilhelmina's playmates, and who was also invited to the Christmas party in 1889.

**14**   Dear Miss Winter!

You know I promised you I should tell you all about St. Kl.[23] I will begin quite from the beginning. I drove out yesterday afternoon with Julie with the ponies. I drove through the village, the boys looked so mischievous, at Mr. Bentinck's[24] house music played. I walked afterwards in the park, I decorated myself with a dead fern & gras. Afterwards I threw it in the stove.

I took tea early & St. Kl. arrived soon after.

Smelting[25] announced him. I think you would like to know how he was dressed. He had a brilliant read cloak with gold braid & under that a kind of read satin frock trimmed with white lace. His trowsers were white with yellow braids. He had a big stick with a nice handle to it. His face was very funny; his eyes seemed quite dry, I think he wore a mask, only his lips seemed natural. He told me that my writing was tidy but my reading ought to be better. He poked fun at Julie & said that there was a family called at Paris Liotôt, but that they ought to be called Liotard as one member of the family was always late & missed the trains. St.KL. told me he had seen you & Suzan in England, I gave him your message. He sent me lots of presents. First a mother monkey with a baby. All the children got two parcels; even Suzan. The boys got heats (Charlie's has the name "le terrible" Maurice's "le vainquer") & overcoats. I got a box to sculpture pretty things. First we got parcels in turns, first the children, then I & Julie, but after dinner Smelting brought in a whole basket full & threw it down on the ground. Julie had much fun. St.Kl. played her the trick of giving her a sent bottle filled with amonia; she put it to her nose & was nicely caught.

He gave her french butter, inside was dutch cheese that smelt <u>awfully</u>, she also smelt it & got it all in her nose & eyes.— There were many more things to frighten both of us.

I have had to day very good lessons, I worked well with Mlle Henriette.[26] I have been a good girl.

---

23 By 'St. Kl.' Wilhelmina is referring to 'Sinterklaas', St Nicolas, who brings presents to Dutch children each year on 5 December.

24 In 1861, Baron Volkier W.R. Bentinck tot Schoonheten (1833-1915) married Miss Pauline A. van Beresteyn (1840-1906). On 3 April 1880, he was made Master of the Royal Shoot for Gelderland by King Willem III. According to the *Erica Adres- en jaarboekje 1887 van Apeldoorn*, Bentinck lived in 'L1'; a house, demolished between 1960 and 1965, on Waldeck Pyrmont (Zwolseweg), now the site of the block of flats known as *De Loohorst*.

25 According to the register of the department of the Marshal of the Court (Stamboek Departement Hofmaarschalk), E10a, sect. 11a, Nos 8 and 9, Georg Frederik Smelting (born in 1835 in 's Gravenhage) entered the service of King Willem III as a footman on 1 October 1877. On 1 May 1885 he became chamber servant to Princess Wilhelmina, and as of 4 December 1896 was promoted to valet.

26 See p. 25. In *Eenzaam maar niet alleen,* Wilhelmina praised Lady van de Poll's modesty and calm judgement on many things, whereby she had more influence over Wilhelmina than Miss Winter. During the Christmas holidays, Lady van de Poll allowed Wilhelmina to read for fifteen minutes every morning. Once, the 'Princesje [Little Princess]', as Lady van de Poll called her in

Your loving pupil
    Signed by Wilhelmina in calligraphy written between two short lines: Poekie[27]

The following letter is the first of sixteen letters from Miss Winter that were recently found in a sealed file in the Royal Archives in The Hague:[28]

Saffron Walden Essex December 8<sup>th</sup> 1888

**15**    My darling little Poekie

I was <u>so</u> happy to have such a long letter & to read the account of St Claus that I really much send you an answer <u>at once</u>! Your beautiful description of the kind old man & all his mischievous tricks makes me wish I could have been there!

How wonderful it seems that he should know all about <u>your</u> lessons & Julie having missed her train. I imagine from the long conversation you evidently had with him, that you were not any longer afraid of him? His costume must have been most gorgeous. I cannot understand <u>when</u> he saw Susan & myself. Most likely he was hiding somewhere at the station in London the day I came home to see if we arrived safely.

I am <u>so</u> glad darling to hear you are a good child & working well. My mind is much easier for knowing it.

I am tremendously busy in preparing for the Bazaar which is to be on Thursday.

My mother liked your cigars <u>so</u> much dearie & thought it very sweet of you to have sent them. They will be on <u>my</u> stall, so I shall think of my little Poeki when I see them!

If I remain in England long enough, I mean to go & spend a few days with my brother in the North before Xmas & shall take Susan with me. I fancy the change of scenery may interest her.

Have you been cooking much since I came away?

I am very happy and enjoying the rest not think much about the dear little pupil who is trying so bravely to do her utmost to be good, on the other side of the water.

With heaps of love darling ever believe me

Your very loving                                E. Saxton Winter

Wilhelmina wrote the following letter phonetically, in calligraphy:

Loo 18-12 1888

**16**    Dir mis Winter!

I em soo gled toe hev hud vram joe.

---

the letter she wrote to her mother on 23 December 1888, said: 'Lady, isn't it a bothersome affair for you to teach me like this?' 'Whereupon I was fortunately able to reply that I found it a very pleasurable affair' (Cleverens 1994, p. 90).

**27** Here Wilhelmina uses a nickname for herself, *Poekie,* for the first time. She would continue to use it in all kinds of variations until 4 August 1894. She wrote the name in calligraphy.

**28** See The letters, p. 29, note 61.

Juli hed e wirre plizzent bufti. I besprinkeld hur a boekmaak end bod a wielberro with a littel buddi.

Poeki iz viri goed end works wil.

Julie hed satch offel toetheek thet shi hed toe goo toe the dintist et Utrecht.

Nouw I em verre bizze with Xmas. Wirre match law. Poekie.

Emma added:

We only finished the letter today the 23<sup>th</sup>. The child is well & <u>very</u> good.

The King is no better, but also not worse since you heard last.[29]

Transcription:

Dear Miss Winter,

I'm so glad to have heard from you. Juli had a very pleasant birthday. I besprinkled her a bookmark and bought a wheelbarrow with a little birdie. Poeki is very good and works well. Julie had such awfull toothache that she had to go to the dentist at Utrecht. Now I'm very busy with Xmas.

Very much love. Poekie

The Loo Dec. the 27 1888

**17** Dear Miss Winter!

I thank you very much indeed for your dear letter and the pretty little book, but still more for Susan's pictures I like them <u>so</u> much![30] Susan looks charming & like a real child.

I would like to know very much how you spent your Xmas? I know I did not write to you for a long time but writing myself it took so much time. —

I had a <u>very</u> happy Christmas Eve darling, & enjoyed the fun with the children very much.

I got such nice presents. Father gave me the rest of the pretty silver[31] I got for my birthday [Colour plate 1-1] & a carriage & a silver buckle. Mother gave me

---

**29** King Willem III was not in good health; he was suffering from a kidney condition. From the spring of 1888, the royal family would stay at Paleis Het Loo and no longer go to The Hague. Although he initially did better, in November the king collapsed again as a result of diabetes.

**30** In her book *Toen onze koningin nog prinsesje was*, Saxton Winter described visiting a photographer with the doll, Suzanna, while on holiday in Saffron Walden (see letter 8, note 16) as follows: 'I had her portrait taken and sent to her mother, so that she could see the good that the English climate was doing her. But the photographer to whom I brought her, when I expressed my wish that the doll should be photographed in various poses, regarded me with such a pitiful expression that I strongly suspect that he took me for someone who was not in her right mind, and only agreed to my request as the surest way to keep a harmless lunatic calm!'

**31** This refers to a large silver table centrepiece (*surtout de table*), originally consisting of 81 pieces, which King Willem III commissioned from Anthonie Begeer (1856–1910) of Utrecht as a Christmas gift for his eight-year-old daughter in 1888. Designed by Maurits Johannes Lens (1829-1897), it included a large vase, mirror plates in various forms, candelabras, sweet boxes and *compotiers*. Every item was decorated with the crowned monogram *PWN* [Princess Wilhelmina of the Netherlands]. The bill, dated 24 December 1888, came to 100,000 guilders (Jan Rudolf de Lorm, 'Edelsmeedkunst', in exhibition catalogue '*De Lelijke Tijd*', Rijksmuseum

Wilhelmina's favourite doll, Suzanna.
Photo: C. A. Sadman, Saffron Walden (Essex), 1888.

a pretty little sewing machine, two fur cloaks for Charlie & Maurice, a new brother for the children called William, & a pretty carriage with a charming horse & another little dear horse for the children to ride with two saddles (lady and gentleman). I got a machine to photograph, I will be able to photograph the children.[32]

I play the whole day in the grey drawing room,[33] where the Xmas tree is, it is very comfy.

I got a pretty little broach & a silver watch-chain.

Mother gave me many pretty little ornaments & many more things, charming games. —

Poekie is good until now. Julie had to had a tooth pulled out, now she is all right again. — Good bye darling. Many loving kisses from your

Signed by Wilhelmina as: Poekie

Christmas card from Wilhelmina, showing cows in water and trees, with the following text on the other side:

18   Printed: With every good wish for a happy Christmas from
Signed by Wilhelmina in calligraphy: Poekie 1888'

Emma also signed a Christmas card with the text:

19   'Emma 1888'

Amsterdam 1995, pp. 251–257). Lady van de Poll's opinion on the present was as follows: 'Het Loo, 23 December 1888 ... All the silver from Begeer has been on display in the Great Hall since Friday. The candelabras are particularly beautiful, but it is an odd gift for an eight-year-old child ...' (see Cleverens 1994, p. 90). The large piece of silver tableware in rococo style is kept at Noordeinde Palace, The Hague.

32  Archives of CODA (Cultuur Onder Dak Apeldoorn), Apeldoorn. The local chronicle, the *Kroniek van Apeldoorn*, recorded on 8 January 1889: 'For a few days now, H.R.H. has been receiving lessons in photography from Mr E.A. Kerkmeijer. The princess is showing great pleasure in these lessons.'

33  The grey drawing room was in the place where the Bentinck Room has been since the restoration of Paleis Het Loo in 1984, to the east of the vestibule. This was where Sophie, Grand Duchess of Saxe-Weimar, stayed when she was visiting Het Loo.

# 1889

Letter from Miss Winter, with the year '1889' written in pencil:

Sunday, August 18th

**20** My darling Princess.

Very many thanks for your dear letter, as you said it seemed "very funny" that it should have been written by Julie! I am <u>so</u> glad Poekie dear to hear you are good and obedient — but wish the weather would get finer- Tomorrow you will be beginning lessons again. I shall think so much about you. Accept very much love sweet little girlie & give "Swell" many pats from yours lovingly

E. Saxton Winter.

Undated, probably written in 1889 by someone other than Queen Emma. Wilhelmina has signed 'Swell' herself, but not neatly:

**21** Wauw, wauw, wauw, wauw, wauw, dear Miss Winter,

I write in the name of my mistress. I will sign my letter. I want to tell you that I think very much about you. I have been very wild and excited today. I have been sick the other day, but now I am quite well.

Much love from your a obedient wauw wauw                    Swell[34]

Letter from Miss Winter:

Saffron Walden. August 24th

**22** Darling little Princess

You cannot possibly imagine how delighted I was last evening when I unpacked the box & discovered the heather. It was <u>so</u> kind & sweet of you dearie to have thought of sending it & the quantity was so great that I know you must have had some trouble & patience to pick it! Where did you find the <u>white</u> heather? My mother rejoiced over the parcel as if it were worth untold gold!

I'm dreadfully sorry to hear of poor old "Swell" having been sick though if, as your letter leads me to suppose it was occasioned by his gobbling up his liver too quickly, I am inclined to think it may teach him a good lesson. I only hope that <u>Mother</u> was not in the room, when the affair happened, or it would have ended more seriously I fancy!

It is such pleasure to hear the work has begun well, in a very short time, if all goes well, we shall be doing the lessons together Poeks dear. I hope sincerely that the boat will get into Flushing at the proper time & thus enable me to get to

---

34 Swell, an Irish setter, was Wilhelmina's favourite dog. She appears with him a number of times in photographs and in work by the sculptor Bartholomeus J.W.M. 'Bart' van Hove (1850–1914). In 1897 the latter made a bronze statuette of them that is kept in the Paleis Het Loo National Museum, on loan from the Queen Sophia Association for the Protection of Animals, inv.no. X19770021. Swell was bred by Mr Sodenkamp of Schaerbeek, from the he-dog Mate and the bitch Rousotte (Departement Koninklijke Stallen E111-11b).

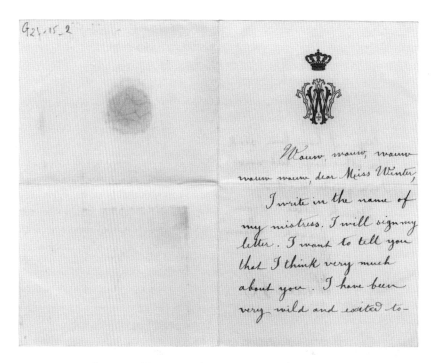

On writing paper featuring a blue crowned monogram in the form of a double 'W',
Wilhelmina wrote on behalf of her favourite dog, the Irish setter Swell, in 1889. Wilhelmina
signed the letter 'Swell'.

the Loo on Monday evening, but the sea has been terribly rough all this week, &
I see from the newspapers that the boats have been delayed in consequences.

 With very many thanks & much love.

 Believe me always yours most lovingly       E. Saxton Winter

This short letter was originally written in Dutch by Queen Emma as though it were from
the doll Marie Hansch, on behalf of her twin brother, to the doll Uncle Trousers:

**23**   Dear Uncle Trousers!

On behalf of Frederik, I should like to thank you for your lovely letter. Frederik
is making great progress in his gymnastics and in his Greek and Latin. We are on
holiday.

 Our warmest greetings to you and to Suzanna.

 Always your obedient           Marie

The following two short letters, written phonetically in English, were kept in a single
envelope with two stamps, postmarked Apeldoorn 13 Dec. 1889 and with a wax seal. The
explanations for a few words had been written above the word in question.
Wilhelmina wrote the letter to Uncle Trousers on behalf of Marie ter Hansch in quite neat
calligraphy, between double lines. On the reverse, in much more slapdash handwriting
and without lines, she wrote the part on behalf of Frederik ter Hansch. Marie and

Frederik ter Hansch were twin dolls. Uncle Trousers had joined Suzanna on a trip to England with Miss Winter.

**24**    D. 13 1889.

Mij dir ankel, ij mien toe rijt toe Joe, end cho Joe dhet ij ken rijt. Vader skeetid, bet nat in a wiire plissent menner. Bekas hie nirle! nirle! fel. Mader ren kwikle uwwee bet oonle a fjoe stips uwwee. Nou mij dir ankel ij mast see goedbij toe Joe.                                                                                    Fram Marie t. Hansc.

Transcription:

My dear uncle, I mean to write to you and show you that I can write. Father skated, but not in a very pleasant manner. Because he nearly fell. Mother ran quickly away but only a few steps away. Now my dear uncle I must say goodbye.
                                                                                            From Marie ter Hansch

On the reverse:

Mij dir ankel, ij em wire sorre dit Marie kant rijd mor distnkle, end floiendle. Bekaze ij noo dit it wil giwe joe a lat aw annissere trabel. Swelle hezze bienne ieting ijs.

   Goedbij mij dir ankel!          Joer oelwiz a-biedjent Freederik ter Hansch.

Transcription:

My dear uncle, I'm very sorry that Marie can't write more distinctly, and fluently. Because I know that it will give you a lot of unnecessary trouble. Swell has been eating ice.

   Goodbye my dear uncle          Your always obedient Frederik ten Hansch.

Wilhelmina began by writing the salutation, but Emma then continued the letter:
                                                                                    December 13 1889

**25**    Dir Bwajer

Fridderic [followed by Emma:] & Marie have been writing very indistinctly because they do not know the english language. I hope you will not be shipwrecked & arrive safely at your mothers house. I took a nice walk through the Enkhout & the nursery. It is now four o'clock & till now I have been good. I met Ina & Sara[35]

---

**35**  A50-V-16. Gezina 'Ina' (1881–1945) and Sara (1882–1950) were the daughters of Joan A. van Steijn (1855–1926). With their little brother Joan (born 1884), the little girls were the first to be listed in the notebook that contained the names of Wilhelmina's playmates. They received numerous invitations to attend on special occasions. On 27 December 1887, their father became Comptroller-General of the Royal Palace and Estate of Het Loo. His first wife, Agatha Wesseling (born 1850), died at Paleis Het Loo in 1910. Van Steijn remarried in 1914. His second wife was Mary Adelaïde van Overzee (1860–1925), who had been appointed lady-of-the-bedchamber and later lectrice to Queen Wilhelmina in December 1896 (letter 140, note 240). In 1902 Ina married the artist Baron Ernst H.K.A.F.H. von Stenglin (1862–1914. He painted the picture 'Prince Hendrik in his hunting wagon on the moor at Soeren, near Het Loo',

walking in the Enkhout with their nursery governess. I am now making a chain for the Xmas tree. Please insist upon Susan doing her work properly during the one week.

I am thinking very much of you & I believe, I believe I will feel nervous when I know that you are going to get on the boot. (Nice phrase!).

Swell is snoaring. I will try to keep my word & be a good girl. Many kisses from your loving

Poeks

Then continued by Emma:
Wilhelmina is quite happy & seems in a better mood, for the moment at least. So enjoy yourself & dont worry,          E.

The following letter from Miss Winter is undated. Although the year '1888' was written in pencil under 'Sunday', the content suggests that it should follow on from letters 23–25:

Saffron Walden
Sunday

**26**     Dearest Princess
Very, very many thanks for writing so soon. I had your dear little letter this morning. Will you please thank Marie & Frederik for their charming notes, which considering they have not as yet learnt English I thought very well written.

I found your telegram waiting for me at Flushing & it cheered me up very much. It was then snowing hard & I was like a walking "snow man" before I reached the boat. The sea was very calm & I had a good sleep. I was <u>so</u> glad not to be shipwrecked. In London there was a thick fog & I thought how delighted Julie would have been if she could only have seen it!

Suzan bore the journey <u>well</u>. She is now sitting on the couch talking gently to herself. My mother & sister gave her a warm welcome but wondered why none of her <u>sisters</u> ever came! How delightful that you were able to get some skating, Sweet little Poekie! I think of you <u>so</u> much & rejoice to hear that <u>so far</u> you have managed to be good. I hope the lessons will go on satisfactionely for the last days that the ? work may end well.

Good bye, little Darling. Always your very loving E. Saxton Winter

Letters 27–29 were written by Wilhelmina herself, mostly phonetically.

**27**     Mather heving noo wissel, kood nat mennids swell. End thi kansikkens waz thet swell ren rijt eewee.

Thi tint was poet ap ez last jir. Friderik end Marie end jis ol thi tchildren sind jou law. Mather end Julie sind joe match lav. End swell a lik. Poekie sinds lav toe soeen end bwajen.

which hangs in the stairwell at Paleis Het Loo, inv.no. PL 290. Von Stenglin fell at Dixmuiden (Belgium) during the First World War in 1914. His wife Ina died in Berlin in 1945.

In the first letters she wrote in English, Wilhelmina used phonetic spelling, such as in this letter of 15 December 1889: 'Dir swiet! ij em gooing', etc.

On a separate page, Emma has added:
W. has been very good today. She began the day by dressing quickly & has been sweet the whole day apparently without great effort.

Transcription:
Mother having no whistle, could not manage Swell. And the consequence was that Swell ran right away. The tent was put up as last year. Frederik and Marie and yes all the children send you love. Mother and Julie send you much love. And Swell a lick. Poekie sends love to Susan and Bryar.

December 14. 1889.

28    Dir swiet!
ij hev bien skeeting this monning uppan thi littel ditch behijnd mij kunsuvve-tree end this aafternoen uppan thi big leks. Juli hez bien volling bat offelle tiesd. Ienna hez bien skeeting a rees with mie, bat sara olsoo, chie vil twijs ij vil olsoo bat nat in reesing. Mister van den Bos hed a stiepeltchees with mister van Ziulen thi last hed teeken af his het.

Transcription:
Dear Sweet,
I have been skating this morning upon the little ditch behind the conservatory and this afternoon upon the big lakes.[36] Julie has been falling but awfully teased.

36 'Big lakes' refers to the two large ponds to the north-eastern side of Het Loo park. At the time of the King-Stadholder Willem iii, there were six rectangular fishponds, which were subsequently dug into two asymmetrical ponds in the 19th century. In one of them was an island where Queen Wilhelmina often used to play as a child. She could reach it by means of a little boat that could be pulled along on chains.

Ina has been skating a race with me, but Sara also, she fell twice, I fell also, but not racing. Mister van den Bosch[37] had a steeplechase[38] with mister van Ziulen,[39] the last had taken of his hat.

December 15. 1889

**29**    Dir swiet!

ij em gooing toe thi frinch surwis ave mister Bourlier, in thi tcheppel. End this afternoon, ij em gooing toe skeet wiz thi toe littel Roepelaas uppan thi big leek. if it dazent begin toe sor. Sink wans, wie ar going toe skeet vor toe hool awers. It is nouw hafpastnijn end in a kwotter av a nouw ij mast goo end dris. Thi pipel ar olriddi errijving. minni kissis fram

Poekie.


Transcription:

Dear Sweet!

I am going to the French service of mr Bourlier,[40] in the chapel. And this afternoon I'm going to skate with the little Roepelaas[41] upon the big lake.

   If it doesn't begin to thaw, think once, we are going to skate for two whole hours. It is now half past nine and in a quarter of an hour I must go and dress. The people are already arriving. Many kisses from

Poekie


Wilhelmina originally wrote this letter in Dutch between two drawn lines:

December 16.1889

**30**    Dear Miswinter

I (Poek) have had a great deal of fun. (That was yesterday) Adrienne came alone with her mother. We went racing. Ina, Sara, Adrienne and Poeks raced. Ina and Adrienne were almost always ahead, every time we raced.

   Joan wanted to skate on the stick with me.[42] The snow had been swept into neat rows and it was so much fun to skate across them. Swell almost slipped on

---

**37** 'Mr. van den Bos' probably refers to Mr W.J.P. van den Bosch (1848–1914), appointed aide-de-camp to King Willem III on 2 June 1877. In January 1890 he became his adjutant and in April 1891 he was appointed adjutant to Queen Wilhelmina. In 1908 he became her first chamberlain.

**38** The steeplechase is a high-speed race on a racecourse with various hurdles.

**39** 'Mr. van Ziulen' probably refers to Baron J.A.H. van Zuylen van Nijevelt (1854–1940), who was made chamberlain to King Willem III on 22 December 1883.

**40** Emile Bourlier (1845–1911) was a clergyman at the Walloon Church in The Hague and became court chaplain in 1878. Queen Wilhelmina and her predecessors were faithful attendees of the Walloon Church.

**41** A50-V-16. The 'Roepelaas' are the children Adrienne (born 1879) and Mimi Repelaer, the daughters of Mr and Mrs Repelaer-van Haeften, who lived in Apeldoorn but who later moved to Baarn.

**42** This refers to how the skaters would skate in a line, holding on to a long stick. See photograph on p. 89.

the ice. How is Susanna? This afternoon I will go skating again. Lots of kisses from

Poekie.

On the reverse:

Dear Uncle Trousers,[43] we have come to tell you about our skating, we skated lots. Marie and I learned lots and we fell. Lots of kisses from us

Frederik and Marie.

The following undated letter was written by Miss Winter as though she were the doll Suzan. It is only dated 1889, in pencil:

31 My darling Mother,

I am writing to wish you a very happy Xmas. Dear old Uncle Trousers has had my phtograph taken, & says I am to send it to you as a Xmas present. I hope you will like them Mother dear. I think them lovely & had no idea what a very pretty child I was until I saw them. I hope you & all my brothers & sisters are well? I must not forget Father either! Much love to all at home, your loving little girl Suzan.

With the exception of the signature, this letter was written by Emma, because Wilhelmina was ill. Wilhelmina signed the letter between two lines:

the Loo Dec the 22. 1889

32 Dear Miss Winter!

I thank you very much indeed for your dear three letters. You see I have not been writing so much any more as you ordered me not to do so. I wish you a very merry merry merry merry merry merry merry merry merry merry Christmas. I send you a card, I made myself. I hope it will please you.

I send Susan many kisses. I am glad she is good.

I worked well, now I have a cold. My Xmas tree is nearly readdy & all the presents are arranged, I did that to-day. I invited the children myself,[44] I went in a closed carriage. The weather is very bad especially today. It is pouring with rain. All the children of my Xmas tree will get lots of cakes. There is quite room enough at the chalet[45] for all the children.

I am reading a little book, which is a history book in my free time (29 p. since yesterday evening) I like it. It is called "Van vroeger en later".[46] Now goodbye my dear sweet.

43 Uncle Trousers was one of Wilhelmina's dolls. The letter is from Frederik and Marie, twin dolls.

44 The following children were invited: Ina, Sara and Joan van Steyn; Adrienne and Mimi Repelaer; Loula and Otteline Boissevain; Louise Muller; Anna Tydeman; Cornelia Wilkens; Jan Hattink; Hendrik Mollerus; and Louis Goedhart, all from Apeldoorn; and Armand Crommelin from Twello.

45 Wilhelmina's playhouse in Het Loo park (see letter 1, note 2).

46 Wilhelmina may be referring here to: Mr H. van A. *Herinneringen van vroeger en later*

Your loving little                                      Poekie

Emma had added the following report, but she did not sign it:

In a great hurry a short account of W.[47]

   Friday morning she woke very bright & worked beautifully but before luncheon
she complained of a headache giddiness (she was arranging my trees). I was
rather anxious for the moment, not knowing what was the matter with the child.
W. sleeping well digestion well & having good appetite. But after luncheon, I
had the explanation W. vomited & I saw she had a cold on her stomach. She
since than looks much better, less pale & drawn then when you left. I starve
her, the docter gave her a medicin. She has a little appetite, sleeps well & is
bright & happy & nomore so nervous & tired. I think this cold must have been
hanging about the child for a long time, I am only glad it comes out well now, I
think she is getting a cold in her head also. W. is very good, she & all her people
make things very easy for me. Friday the poor child thought she was getting the
influenza & would be ill for Xmas. I hope you will be able to read. I am awfully
occupied. I hope you will have a very merry & happy Xmas

Letter written by Emma:

HET LOO
the 29th of Dec. 1889

**33**   Dear Sweet!
I send you my best wishes for the New Year.
   I send you as well a card I chose on purpose for the verse. I thank you very
much for your dear letters and Suzan for hers. I was so pleased with the Xmas
cards you sent me for my Xmas tree & for myself.[48] My tree succeeded <u>very</u> well.
The children were very happy. The little Peters & Veenhuizen[49] showed it the

---

*leeftijd, en aan gedenkwaardige land- en tijdgenooten: ten vervolge op 'Uit de gedenkschriften van een
voornaam Nederlandsch beambte, over de tweede helft der 18e en het begin der 19e eeuw' [Recollections
at a younger and older age, and of memorable compatriots and contemporaries: the sequel to 'From the
memoirs of a prominent Dutch official, concerning the second half of the 18th and the beginning of the
19th century'],* Tiel 1884. A note in pencil on the title page of the book in the library of the Royal
Archives records that this official was A.W. Engelen. A.W. Engelen (1804–1890) also wrote
under the pseudonym Herman van Apeltern. My thanks to H. Robaard, the librarian of the
Royal Archives, for this information.

**47**  Queen Emma probably wrote this brief report on Wilhelmina's short illness around 22
December 1889. It was enclosed with the short letter from Wilhelmina of this date, which was
also written by Emma.

**48**  A50-VII-C5. Christmas card with two birds for: *Poekie! E. Saxton Winter 1889* with a small
hole in the centre, which may have been hung in the Christmas tree.

**49**  Wilhelmina, p. 20. The 'kleine [small] Peters' and 'Veenhuizen' are the children of Mr
Peters, King Willem III's head gamekeeper, and Mr Veenhuizen, the keeper of the dogs and the
deer park at Het Loo, respectively. Wilhelmina visited Mr Peters at home on the Koningslaan
and played with his children. Wilhelmina wrote to Lady de Kock on 23 December 1889: 'I am

most. Marie[50] cooked everything for the tea. There was quite enough room. The tree was so very pretty. Evertjes little boy[51] was much nicer than when we saw him this summer.

I have had such pretty presents for Xmas. Mother gave me a big Punch & Judy. Father gave me beautiful lace. I had a big doll,[52] a governess for the children. I got a beautiful guitar & many other things. I am reading an other book, also about history. I walked yesterday again. This afternoon I will make a Xmas tree for the children.

We had delightful romps on Xmaseve.

Many kisses from Poeks for you & Suzan & a lick from Swell. Your loving

Signed by Wilhelmina: Poekietje.

The following poem was printed on the card mentioned in the letter above:

**34**　A Happy New Year to you
A glad and bright New Year!
Thro' paths, by sorrow unknown,
May joy your footsteps gleer!
And making your heart its throne,
Convert it into a dear
And bright little World of its own!

| | |
|---|---|
| With greetings written by Emma: | For my dear Miss Winter from |
| Signed by Wilhelmina in calligraphy: | Poekie. |
| | 1889 |

making an Xmas tree for poor people. The three Peters children, the two [children] of Mekking, the gamekeeper, the two [children] of the dog-keeper, etc., etc.' (G28–3).

50  A47a-III-2, *Weihnachten* 1896, p. 167. 'Marie' is probably Marie Benner. Maria J.J. Benner (1853-1900) was appointed on 1 August 1888 as supervisor of the royal wardrobe, and on 1 December 1896 became 'supervisor of the office', probably an administrative role in the Marshal of the Court's office relating to the royal kitchens (see E1b-I-10, and letter 155, note 293).

51  Heuven 2004. 'Evertje' is Mrs van der Zande, who called herself Evertje Schouten and entered service in December 1880 as Princess Wilhelmina's nurse. Another solution had to be found for her own family. She replaced the first nurse, Mrs Oskam of Voorburg. Evertje not only stayed in Apeldoorn and The Hague, but she also accompanied the royal family to Arolsen, Germany, when Queen Emma went to visit her family there and the king wished to take the waters.

52  This French doll, a metre-high 'Parisienne', was ordered from Paris by Queen Emma as a Christmas present in 1889. F. Gaultier made the head and shoulders from biscuit porcelain. The body was made of leather and the light-brown wig was made of real hair. Such dolls were in fact intended for the wealthy bourgoisie, to be shown off in opulent interiors or used for displaying clothes (Winter, pp. 81–84, Nihom, pp. 18–21, Heuven 1990, Carvalho, pp. 68–69). Wilhelmina used the doll as a governess for her own dolls. To her former attendant Lady de Kock, she wrote on 29 December 1889: 'Mother also gave me a carriage. A puppet theatre, a real doll, who must be a governess ....' (G28–3).

Letter from Miss Winter:

Saffron Walden December 30<sup>th</sup> [1889]

**35**   Darling little Princess,

I am writing to wish you a <u>very</u> happy & bright New Year. Looking back upon this old one which is so quickly slipping away from us, I think we may, on the whole, be satisfied with Poekie's efforts & work. Each year you live Darling you will more clearly realize the responsibilities of life that God lays even upon little children, & you & I will both begin this New Year with a brave determination to work hard together to overcome the difficulties & temptations of daily life.

You can't understand dearie how happy and relieved I felt to hear you were getting well again & now that work is not to begin till next Monday I'm happier still!

How did all the children enjoy their Xmastree? I am going up to London for the day, so shall not wait to write any more.

God bless & keep you sweet child.

Very much love from Susan & myself.

Always yours most loving                                    E. Saxton Winter

This letter was written and signed by someone other than Wilhelmina or Emma:

HET LOO [1889]<sup>53</sup>
31 X<sup>bre</sup>

**36**   Dear Miss Winter,

My cold is nearly better. I can already go out-of-door. I spent a very merry christmas. To-day it is new year even. I am going to church at seven o'clock evening.

To-morrow is the birthday of Frédéric and Mary.

Dominee Hattinck<sup>54</sup> is going to preach this evening.

The children are going to receive very pretty presents from me and Julie.

We have rekindled the two tiniest Christmas trees of Mother.

How is Suzan?

Many Kisses from                                    Pokiege

---

53   The letter was written by someone other than Emma or Wilhelmina. On the envelope, the English town 'Saffron Walden' has been spelled 'Saffron Valden'.

54   C. Hattink (1859-1928) was a clergyman from Apeldoorn.

# 1890

37  Dear Sir,

I am commanded by the Queen to request you <u>not</u> to come for the French lesson of the Princess, as Her Royal Highness is not very well.

Her Majesty begs you to abstain from mentioning the fact, as the Princess is only suffering from a <u>slight</u> indisposition. Small details connected with the Court get sometimes terribly exaggerated & the Queen is anxious to avoid any such reports in consequence of the near approach of the King's birthday.

Believe me

Yours truly

E: Saxton Winter

Dr J.J. Salverda de Grave started teaching Wilhelmina French at the end of 1889, and would continue until the autumn of 1896. He also gave her tuition in Dutch, beginning in mid-1890. In the course of 1890, he began teaching her geography (until 1894) and general history (until 1893), and he taught her Dutch history between 1891 and 1893.

In August 1890 Miss Winter spent her holiday in England, staying with the Rev. Winter in New Brighton.

On 4 August 1890 she received a telegram from Wilhelmina that communicated the following:

38  Many thanks telegram, visited flowershow, went to Zutphen,<sup>56</sup> much love Wilhelmina

The following letter was once again written phonetically by Wilhelmina. Miss Winter was now staying at Khandalla Sandroch Park, Siscard-Cheshire (postmarked Birkenhead, 10 August 1890):

---

55  This is one of the four letters already published in the Dutch edition of *Dear Old Bones*, written by Miss Saxton Winter and kept in the Royal Archives: A50-V-4b. The year is not given, but it must have been 1890, in view of the fact that the French lessons were being taught by J.J. Salverda de Grave (1863–1947), who had taken a doctorate in French literature in 1888 and had begun teaching Wilhelmina French at the end of 1889, and King Willem III's birthday was on 19 February. Salverda de Grave would also teach Dutch, history and geography, and he would continue to teach French and Dutch until 1896.

56  Zutphen is located c. 21 km to the south-east of Apeldoorn, on the opposite side of the River IJssel.

**39** Dir dalling switte!

IJ wasse wire gled toe rissiw Joer dir litter. The dee win ij wint toe Zitfen wie wint over the IJssel, win djast the treen wasse going over the bridg.

Fotdjennetle wie hed Hallas and Pako, (the toe Hongaarsche hosses) witch ar newwer frijtend af enneething, soo it wint stil. Zutfen it silf isse wiire proettee, end it toeks ennouwer toe drijf ther. The dee befor jisterdee ij wint behijnd Hoog Buurloo, and! and! and! sor the bunt huthther. Joe noo wat ij mien? Wie gat a megnifissent wiu. Jisterdee ij wint toe the kemp af oldenbroek, wie mesoek the rood. Wie mint toe goo toe Hattem. (Joe noo wer that isse.)

(8th of Aug.)

It isse nauw wan (one) dee verthe. Jisterdee wie meedde the piknik. Mij wuk isse gooing wirre wille. Matche lav fram Poekie

Dirrist angkel!

I emme fitting wirri matchche                                     Jor obedient Suzan

Emma has added: I discover Wilhelmina has been writing with a dreadful pen!

Transcription:

Dear Darling Sweety

I was very glad to receive your dear letter. The day when we went to Zutphen, we went over the IJssel, when just the train was going over the bridge.

Fortunately we had Hellas (Hallas) and Pako (the two Hungarian horses)[57] which are never frightened of anything, so it went still. Zutphen itself is very pretty, and it took an hour to drive there. The day before yesterday I went behind Hoog Buurloo[58] and! and! and! saw the burned heather. You know what I mean? We got a magnificent view. Yesterday I went to the camp of Oldebroek[59], we mistook the road. We ment to go to Hattem[60] (You know where that is.)

(8 Aug.)

It is now one day further. Yesterday we made the picnic. My work is going very well. Much love from Poekie

Dearest uncle!!!

I am fitting very much                                     Your obedient Suzan

---

**57** Departement Koninklijke Stallen, E11i-11b-2. Halos and Pako were two geldings from Hungary, bought for 1,940 guilders apiece on 15 October 1885 from Schlesingen Fattensäl of Vienna, exclusively for the use of Her Majesty the Queen, and given as a gift on 22 July 1889 (third quarter).

**58** Hoog Buurloo is an old agricultural area in the midst of forests and moors, to the west of Apeldoorn and to the east of the Radio Kootwijk broadcasting station.

**59** At the beginning of the 1870s, an artillery camp was established at Oldebroek between Epe and Elburg, known as the 'camp at Oldebroek'. A few of the chalet-like constructions from those early years are now listed buildings.

**60** Hattem lies 33 km to the north of Apeldoorn.

And the telegram from Emma to Miss Winter, c/o the Rev. Winter in New Brighton, on 9 August 1890, informed the governess of the following:

40 Wilhelmina very well, good and happy, she wrote yesterday evening. Emma

On 14 August Miss Winter was actually back in Saffron Walden, in view of the telegram sent that day:

41 Many thanks for both dear letters, made me very happy, am going on well and happily, much love Wilhelmina

Telegram dated 18 August 1890:

42 Am getting on very well, longing for your return, much love, telegraph mother if you cannot catch one o clock train. Wilhelmina

Government telegram to Miss Winter at the Royal Palace, The Hague:

43 Many thanks for dear letters. Am very happy. Cooked and sprinkled.[61] A lick from Swell. Much love from Wilhelmina

Miss Winter felt unwell in November and stayed at Noordeinde Palace in The Hague, while Lady van de Poll looked after the young princess.[62] According to Lady de Poll (letter from Het Loo, 8 November 1890), Miss Winter was over-tired and over-strained. The doctor had said that her sickness was due solely to a disorder of the stomach nerves. At that time, it had been announced that Lady van de Poll would be charged with supervising the education of Her Royal Highness Princess Wilhelmina. As we have seen, Wilhelmina had a particularly good relationship with the modest, engaging and friendly Lady van de Poll. Miss Winter would also have noted this many a time, and she may have interpreted the lady-in-waiting's appointment as a threat to her own position, something that expressed itself in her bad state of health. When Wilhelmina heard of Van de Poll's appointment, she said: 'Do you know, lady, there is something that I find so wonderful, you must guess what it is … I am so happy that you are going to be completely with me, I am so used to you…'. And in the same letter of 8 November: 'Yesterday morning she asked: "Lady, are you pleased that Miss Winter is coming back today?" "Yes, little princess, I am pleased for Miss Winter that she is well enough to come back." "Yes, but for yourself?" "Oh, I could have carried on like this for a little longer." "Yes lady, me too; you know, one isn't grumbled at the whole time." Nevertheless, she was pleased when Miss W. returned.'

61 Spatter work or 'Spritzwerk' (see letter 8, note 15)
62 Cleverens 1994, p. 95.

Wilhelmina, now aged ten, wrote the following letter in calligraphy, originally in Dutch:

Het Loo

3.11.1890

**44** Dear Miss Winter!

Thank you very much for your dear letter. You won't be able to understand this, as I'm writing in Dutch, but perhaps you can understand it a little. Maybe you'll be able to guess? I am very pleased to hear that since yesterday, you've no longer been feeling sick. Has your brother been on lots of day-trips? Or is he planning to? I wrote part of this letter in my calligraphy class. On Sunday I decorated a sewing box [spatter work]. It was very difficult, but in the end it turned out really beautifully. Emma wrote the letter from here onwards: I have decorated all the little items, aside from the ruler. This afternoon I went for a walk with Baby and she became very excited, I was quite tired when we got home. My work is going very well. Mother finished this letter for me. Lots of kisses from me and a scratch from Swell. Lots of kisses from Poekie

## King Willem III dies and Wilhelmina becomes queen

By this time, King Willem III was no longer able to govern, and on 20 November 1890 Queen Emma took the oath as regent in The Hague. At 5:45 a.m. on 23 November, the king died at Paleis Het Loo. Thirty-nine weeks of mourning were declared: 26 of full mourning, ten of half mourning, and three of light mourning.

The register of the Marshal of the Court immediately recorded the new status of the two remaining women in the following announcement: 'Her Majesty the Queen-Regent and Her Majesty the Queen to dine at 6:30.'[63]

On 26 November, the king's body was laid in a coffin and placed in the large audience chamber above the vestibule. On Sunday 30 November, in the presence of 'Her Majesties', Professor Nicolaas Beets[64] read out a funeral oration. A day later, the two queens travelled to The Hague, followed by the king's funeral transport. The internment took place in the Nieuwe Kerk in Delft on 4 December; a date that was specially chosen by Queen Emma, so that the Dutch population would still be able to celebrate the feast of St Nicolas on 5 December.

In December 1890 Miss Saxton Winter was once more visiting her mother in Saffron Walden. She received the following telegram from The Hague on 16 December:

**45** Many thanks for dear telegram, am going on nicely, much love, hope you have safely arrived at your mothers,

Wilhelmina

---

63 Department of the Marshal of the Court, E10-IVb.
64 Nicolaas Beets (1814-1903), also known by the pseudonym 'Hildebrand', was a Dutch author, poet, clergyman and professor.

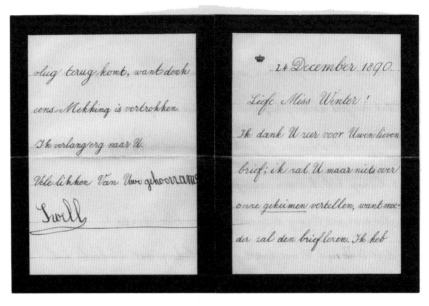

In the first letter after her father's death, written by Wilhelmina on mourning paper to Miss Winter on behalf of Swell, Wilhelmina made no mention of her father.

And on 19 December 1890, another telegram:

**46**  Many thanks for dear kind letter am quite well and getting on beautifully hope that you will have great success today

Wilhelmina

The following letters were written on black-edged mourning paper, decorated with a small black crown. Wilhelmina drew guidelines for the first letter and wrote it very nicely in Dutch:

24 December 1890

**47**  Dear Miss Winter!
Thank you very much for your dear letter; I shall not mention anything of our <u>secrets</u>, as mother shall read this letter. I had lots of fun yesterday, for I helped mother in the morning and in the morning I also wrote the Christmas cards. I did other things in the afternoon. Such a shame that the bazaar did not work out on Friday. I am sending you a card. Exci is sending you a letter.

Lots of kisses from your Poekie

Added separately:
Miss Winter!
I hope that you come back very, very soon, because just imagine, Mekking[65] has left. I am longing to see you.

Lots of licks from your obedient Swell

---

65  Cleverens 1994, p. 94. Mekking was the gamekeeper.

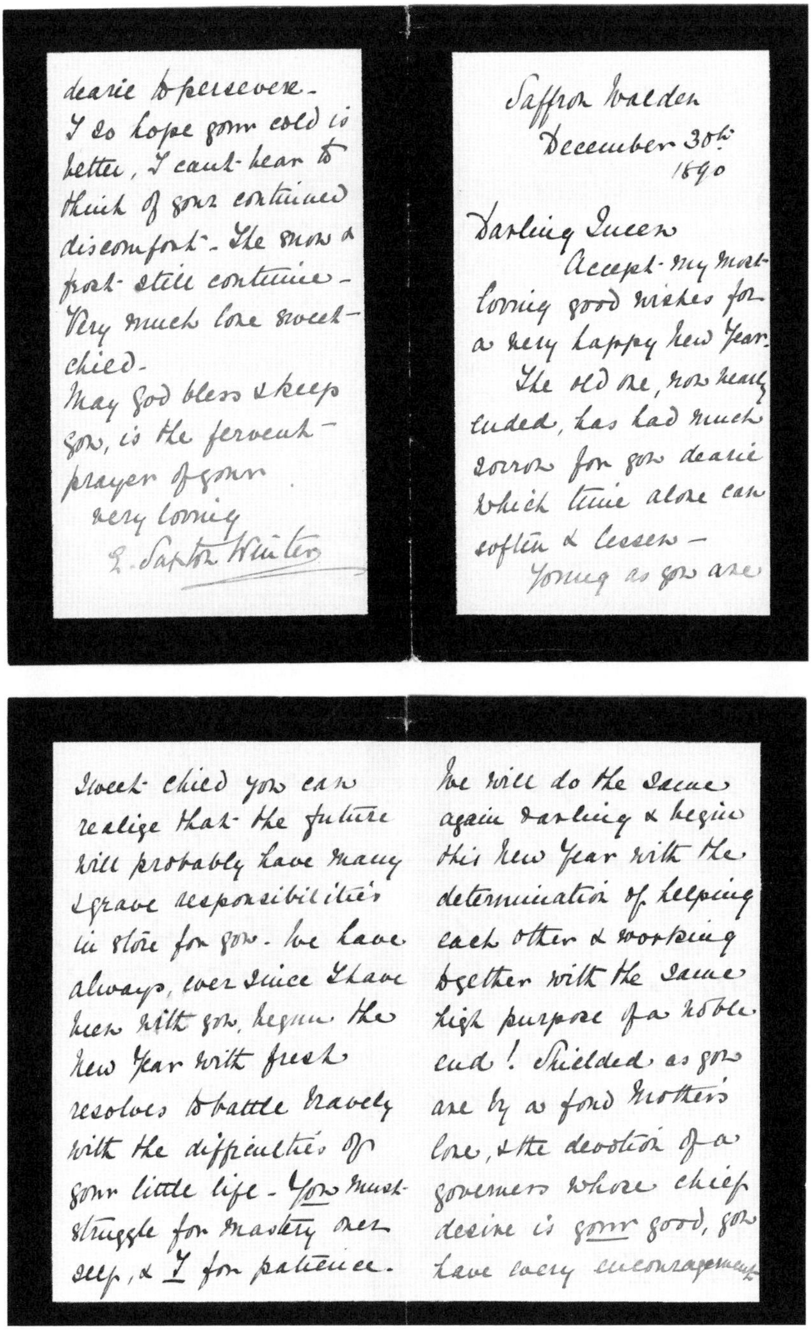

Saffron Walden
December 30th
1890

Darling Queen

Accept my most loving good wishes for a very happy New Year. The old one, now nearly ended, has had much sorrow for you dearie which time alone can soften & lessen —

Young as you are Sweet child you can realize that the future will probably have many & grave responsibilities in store for you. We have always, ever since I have been with you, begun the New Year with fresh resolves to battle bravely with the difficulties of your little life — You must struggle for mastery over self, & _I_ for patience.

We will do the same again darling & begin this New Year with the determination of helping each other & working together with the same high purpose of a noble end! Shielded, as you are by a fond Mother's love, & the devotion of a governess whose chief desire is _your_ good, you have every encouragement dearie to persevere.

I do hope your cold is better, I can't bear to think of your continued discomfort. The snow & frost still continue —

Very much love sweet-child.

May God bless & keep you, is the fervent prayer of your

very loving
E. Saxton Winter

Letter from Miss Winter in which she alludes to the great responsibilities awaiting the ten-year-old Queen Wilhelmina, 30 December 1890.

Letter from Miss Winter:

Saffron Walden December 30<sup>th</sup> 1890

**48** Darling Queen

The old one, now nearly ended, has had much sorrow for you dearie which time alone can soften & lessen —

Young as you are sweet child you can realize that the future will probably have many & grave responsibilities in store for you. We have always, ever since I have been with you, begun the New Year with fresh resolves to battle bravely with the difficulties of your little life. <u>You</u> must struggle for mastery ones self, & <u>I</u> for patience.

We will do the same again Darling & begin this New Year with the determination of helping each other & working together with the same high purpose of a noble end! Shielded as you are by a fond Mother's love, & the devotion of a governess whose chief desine is <u>your</u> good, you have every encouragement dearie to persevere.

I so hope your cold is better, I can't bear to think of your continued discomfort. The snow & frost still continue. Very much love sweet child.

May God bless & keep you, is the fervent prayer of your very loving

E. Saxton Winter.

New Year was always marked with an exchange of calendars. This was something that Queen Wilhelmina continued to do for many years, mostly making the calendars herself. To Miss Winter, she sent a twelve-page calendar bound with a ribbon. On the first page is written:

**49** 'Calender for 1891', signed: 'From Wilhelmina'

# 1891

Telegram from The Hague, arrived in Saffron Walden on 1 January 1891:

**50** I send you many many good wishes for the New Year, am well, enjoying holidays tremendously. Wilhelmina

The following letter was written by Lady van de Poll on behalf of Wilhelmina, on mourning paper, following the death of King Willem III on 23 November 1890:

The Hague Jan. 1<sup>st</sup> 1891.

**51** Dear Darling!

I thank you very much for your dear letter, and now I am going to tell you about Mother's presents. The chair was exquisite, the cushion which I began to make, when you were going away, got very pretty because Miss v.d. P. mounted it for me and now Mother has taken it into use. I made a second one for Mother's tinier pins, which got nearly prettier than the other one. The cushion that you and I made together got sweet.

I got a beautiful inkstand with chandeliers and penholder for Mother's school-room (you know what I mean by that). Guess once what I got for beautiful things! I got a beautiful screen with all sorts and kinds of views of the Loo[66], and one of them where Dash and Daisy and his Lordship[67] and Mekking were painted on. [Colour plate II-3] I got also a cart[68] and lots of little bronze things. I had much pleasure on Christmas eve with lots of little children,[69] which you don't know, the only big ones were Lita de Ranitz[70] and Pixey Constant.[71] I have had much pleasure with Julie. I am longing dreadfully for you Darling. Much love from

Poekie Woekie.

66  Archive of the Royal Household of Queen Emma A47a-III-2, p. 124; Eigen Haard, page unknown; Meddens, p. 26, image p. 95. Commissioned by Queen Emma, Willem Roelofs (1822–1897), Julius J. van de Sande Bakhuyzen (1835–1925), Johannes M. 'Jan' Vrolijk (1845–1894) and Jan Willem van Borselen (1825–1892) painted the panels for the gilded wooden four-piece folding screen in Louis XV style, with vernis Martin panels below and framed watercolours above. Jan Willem van Borselen painted the panel mentioned by Wilhelmina, staying at Het Loo in 1890 in order to do so. Mekking has been painted discretely on the right, behind a bush. Meddens did not know the exact year and wrote 'Around 1891 [...].' The folding screen (188 × 311 × 5 cm; 81.5 × 74 × 74 × 81.5) was designed and manufactured by P.L. Warnaer of 's Gravenhage. Royal Archives, inv.no. PLV/191. Until 1983, it stood in Lange Voorhout Palace, The Hague. It has been kept in the Royal Archives since 1986.

67  Dash and Daisy and His Lordship were dogs belonging to Wilhelmina. His Lordship was the Irish setter Swell (see also the letter of 6 Augustus 1893).

68  A47a-III-2, p. 124. The cart was a horse-drawn carriage known as a break.

69  These children were: under the heading '24 December 1890 Christmas tree': Corrie van Hogendorp, Pikky van de Poll, Bertha van den Bosch, Tea van Heeckeren, Aggie Grovestins, Charlotte van Spengler, Lita de Ranitz and Pixy de Constant (Archive of Queen Wilhelmina, A50-V-16, notebook beginning with '1891–1892 Girls and Boys' with at the back, parties held between 24 December 1890 and 24 December 1900, as well as the birthday party of Juliana on 23 May 1917 from 4–6).

70  Miss Lita de Ranitz (1876–1960) was the daughter of Mr S.M.S. de Ranitz (1846–1916), who since 2 September 1881 had been private secretary to King Willem III and, after his death, on 11 December 1890 became private secretary to Queen-Regent Emma. Queen Emma was particularly fond of him. De Ranitz once wrote that if Lita were troublesome again, she should be sent to Paleis Het Loo 'for a beating' (Lit, p. 14). Lita de Ranitz married the artist Willem Bastiaan Tholen in 1919. She is best known for her dolls house, which is kept in the Municipal Museum of The Hague (Lit).

71  'Pixy' refers to Baroness Idzardina Juliana Frederika de Constant Rebecque (1877–1958), the youngest daughter of the Marshal of the Court, Jan Daniël C.C.W. de Constant Rebecque. She was a playmate of Queen Wilhelmina's and one of the two regular dance partners at Wilhelmina's dance lessons at Noordeinde Palace. On 15 September 1898, together with Lady C.E.B. Sloet van Marxveld, she was made Queen Wilhelmina's lady-in-waiting. On 10 February 1900, she became engaged to the Catholic aide-de-camp Count J.H.F. Dumonceau (1859–1952), son of Count C.H.F. Dumonceau, Chief of the Military House, and eighteen years her senior. Her parents were initially opposed to the union due to the difference in religion and the lack of a fortune on both sides. Dumonceau requested official permission from the Pope to marry the protestant lady. The marriage took place on 31 July 1900. It was probably due to her poor health that Queen Wilhelmina did not make her a lady-in-waiting or honorary Dame du Palais.

Lita de Ranitz with her father Mr S.M.S. de Ranitz.
Lita's name was first to appear on the 1891-1892
list of girls and boys who could be invited to
attend festive occasions at Court (A50-5-16).
She was born on 4 March 1876. The second was
Pixy de Constant Rebecque, who was born on
21 November 1877.
Photo: De Lavieter & Co, The Hague

Letter from Miss Winter:

Saffron Walden Jan[ua]ry 9<sup>th</sup> 1891

**52** Darling Queen

I am sending only a little message to be quickly followed by my own arrival!

Will you please thank the Queen Regent for her telegram which I received this morning?

You see now dearie that I am <u>not</u> remaining, this time at least, in England for ever!

You, who are so devoted to your own Mother, will understand how sad I feel at the idea of leaving <u>mine</u>. I so wish she could have been stronger, however, we all hope that in the Spring she may revive. Much dear love sweet child until we meet.

Ever your very loving                                    E. Saxton Winter

I had just finished signing my name when your sweet loving letter arrived, so I hope darling you will excuse my adding a word of thanks, instead of re-writing the whole. I am <u>so</u> glad all your cushions for Mother succeeded so well — how pleased you must have been dearie. I leave all other chattering till Thursday & only send now a <u>very</u> dear big hug for little

"Poekie Woekie"

Between Wednesday 2 April and 6 May 1891, the royal party travelled to Arolsen and to Gersau in Switzerland, where the company stayed in the Hotel Schiller on Lake Lucerne. Emma and Wilhelmina's retinue included the Baroness van Ittersum,[72] the principal lady-in-waiting to Queen-Regent, Miss van de Poll, Miss Saxton Winter, Adjutant General

---

72 'Baroness van Ittersum' is Baroness E. (Elise) G. van Ittersum (1851–1936). She was made Queen Emma's lady-in-waiting on 18 October 1879. In 1898 she became the principal lady-in-

Dumonceau,[73] Captain Baron Sirtema de Grovestins,[74] adjutant, chamberlain Baron H.W.J.E. Taets van Amerongen[75] and senior official to the Cabinet, Mr Petrus J. Vegelin van Claerbergen.[76] On Wednesday 6 May, the company left Gersau to return to Het Loo. Probably due to her mother's illness, Miss Winter left Gersau unexpectedly to spend three weeks in England.

Telegram from Emma, sent from Gersau to Saffron Walden, arrived on 22 April 1891:

**53** Am glad to know you with your mother, wilhelmine well good, my warmest wishes for your mother

Emma

Telegram from Wilhelmina, sent from Gersau, 22 April 1891:

**54** Many thanks telegramm, am happy, to day Rigi, yesterday other side of the lake, much love

Wilhelmina

Plus a letter written in Dutch between drawn lines, undated:
Dear Darling!
I did write after all, as you can see. I will write everything down faithfully in my diary, so that I will know precisely what I have done during your three weeks of leave.[77] I hope that you arrive home safely.

Many kisses from your Poekie

waiting to Her Majesty the Queen Mother and honorary Dame du Palais to Her Majesty the Queen.

**73**  On 24 April 1891, Count C.H.F. Dumonceau (1827–1918), aide-de-camp, adjutant, private secretary and librarian to King Willem III, was made Adjutant General and Chief of the Military House of Queen Wilhelmina. He also arranged the travel abroad.

**74**  On 17 April 1891, Baron Jan E.N. Sirtema van Grovestins (1842–1919) was appointed adjutant to Queen Wilhelmina. As the oldest adjutant, he helped to bear Wilhelmina's royal robes on the day of her investiture on 6 September 1898. In 1899 he was made Grand Master of the House of Her Majesty the Queen. He was a mine of information and confidante for many courtiers (Cleverens 1994, p. 188).

**75**  The chamberlain Baron Hendrik W.J.E. Taets van Amerongen (1840–1920) was also known as 'Jetje'. See letter 96, note 123).

**76**  Between 1876 and 1878, Mr Petrus J. Vegelin van Claerbergen (1845–1918) was chamberlain and second private secretary to King Willem III. Between 1879 and 1910 he fulfilled various roles, from clerk to director of the King's/Queen's Cabinet.

**77**  A50-V-1 contains five attempts by Queen Wilhelmina to keep a diary: 1. an exercise book without a cover: 'On Saturday, 25 July 1891, I began to write this diary so that I would have a souvenir of my youth'; 2. an exercise book without a cover: 'My monthly journal, 1892'; 3. an exercise book without a cover: 'My monthly journal, 1893-2'; 4. a tiny book, bound in black leather, with a lock and gilt-edged pages: 'Friesland'; 5. an extremely small book bound in brown leather with an empty coat of arms on the front: 'My monthly journal, which I began in November 1893', which runs until December 1894 and ends with a hiatus: 'Know thyself. 26 February 1896 Wilhelmina'.

On mourning paper with drawn lines, undated, no envelope. Wilhelmina wrote the next original letter in Dutch:

Gersau 24 April 1891

**55**    Dear Darling,

Thank you for your dear letter. As you can see, I am writing despite your having forbidden me to do so, because one can say so little in telegrams, and in letters I can tell you much more — don't you think?

The weather stayed fine until yesterday. But it became unsettled yesterday, and today, or rather, this morning, it rained. We went up the Rigi[78] by [cogwheel] train and came to Rigi Kaltbad, where we dined, but I have to remark upon the English manners. There were English people sitting at the table next to ours who had the most dreadful manners. I shall tell you more about that when you return. We descended the Rigi partly on foot. Bleuette[79] hurt her foot, but now is it almost better. Yesterday I went to see a farm. It was not as neat and tidy as a Dutch farm. There was a very gentle foal, but nearly all the cows were up in the mountains. They do not make cheese and butter. They sell any milk that they do not need themselves.

Many kisses from Poekie

Included separately was a stamp from Hotel Bellevue in Rigi Kaltbad, on the back of which Wilhelmina had written: 'for You'

Letter from Miss Winter:

Saffron Walden<br>April, 28th 1891

**56**    Darling Queen,

In spite of my having, as you said in your letter, forbidden you to write, it was very pleasant to receive your dear letter & to read all your news. I was indeed glad to know that the poor little leg was all right again about her? The nightingales have already arrived home. I heard them singing so sweetty the whole of last night but they rather angered me. They seemed so cheerful & I was feeling so sad.

You will be sorry for my sake Poekie dear to knew that my Mother today is very much worse again & scarceley knows us.

I can't write any more now sweetie. I wish I will back again with you with a light heart.

I am always thinking of you & feeling sure you are trying bravely to do your best.

God bless your efforts darling. Heaps of dear love from your lovingly

E. Saxton Winter

---

78  The Rigi is a massif by Lake Lucerne. The highest peak is the Rigikulm, c. 1800 m. It is the site of the oldest cogwheel railway in Europe, built in 1871.

79  Bleuette is a doll; she is also mentioned by name in letter 74, April 1892.

Telegram from Emma, arrived in Saffron Walden on 25 April 1891:

**57**  Received second letter, [?] not expect you to come back to Gersau, we leave 4 or 5 may for the Loo, [?] very bad your mother continues same destressing state,

Emma


Telegram from Wilhelmina, arrived in Saffron Walden on 25 April 1891:

**58**  Many thanks telegram, leg all right, happy and good, much love,

Wilhelmina


Telegram from Wilhelmina: 3 May 1891:

**59**  Many thanks for all dear letters, could not write, out all day making expeditions, am all right, much love.[80]                          Wilhelmina


Telegram from Emma, arrived on 3 May 1891:

**60**  Thanks, wait letter and news sent Mrs Kreusler,[81] please write again next Saturday, will then decide about your return, do not expect you before 12th, Wilhelmina all right well and bright.                          Emma


Telegram from Het Loo from Wilhelmina, arrived in Saffron Walden on 6 May 1891:

**61**  Left Gersau yesterday before 2 oclock, arrived here this morning at nine, excellent pleasant journey, very happy to be here, much love

Wilhelmina


Telegram from Emma, arrived in Saffron Walden on 8 May 1891:

**62**  Thanks letter, would like you to decide about return after receiving second letter of mrs Kreusler, she will write to morrow,                          Emma


From 1891 onwards, Emma and Wilhelmina spent the summer at Het Loo in uneven years, alternating with summer at Soestdijk Palace. Between 5 and 30 August 1891, Miss Winter spent her holidays in England. She was back for Wilhelmina's birthday on 31 August, so that she could take part in the gala dinner that was held the following day in the Gallery of Paleis Het Loo, attended by representatives of all state institutions, as well as the Council of Guardians.


80  With a little bunch of Alpine flowers and leaves, Miss Winter wrote: 'Sent me by the Queen in 1891 from the Alps'.
81  Mrs Mathilda Kreusler (1833–1902) from Arolsen came to the Netherlands in 1879 when Emma got married. She was her lectrice, a role that lay between that of a lady-of-the-bed-chamber and a lady-in-waiting. In addition, she kept the books for the personal expenditure of Queen Emma and Princess Wilhelmina's so-called 'petty cash'. She also kept a separate registry for the pair's orders. In 1902 she fell ill and returned to Germany, where she died in Bonn in 1902, aged 62. She was succeeded by Mrs Jenny Reichardt (see letter 313, note 742).

Telegram from Wilhelmina, arrived in Saffron Walden on 7 August 1891:

**63** Many thanks news, happy you not shipwrecked, am well and happy, Suzan goes with us to Hattem,[82] much love, Wilhelmina

Two pages on black-edged mourning paper with drawn-in lines, undated, no envelope, written by Wilhelmina in Dutch:

**64** Dear Darling!

I did write after all, as you can see. I will write everything down faithfully in my diary, so that I will know precisely what I have done during your three weeks of leave.[83] I hope that you arrive home safely.

Many kisses from your Poekie

Telegram from Wilhelmina, sent from Het Loo on 20 August 1891, to Miss Winter, Wilton Lodge Grayt. Rd, Worthing, Engl.:

**65** Many thanks dear letters, am well and happy, yesterday Wieds,[84] to day Oranjenassauoord,[85] much love,

Wilhelmina

The last letter on mourning paper, written by Wilhelmina in Dutch, postmarked: Apeldoorn 21 Aug. 91

**66** Dear Darling,[86]

I went horse riding this morning. Once I was well on my way, it began to thunder quite hard. We got home safely. The weather is like November. You have terrified me by telling me that you have become quite brown. I get the shivers just thinking of it.

I have sent you some apricots — I just hope that they haven't turned into mush. Yesterday we went to Orange Nasausoord.[87] Swell sends you a lick. Lots of kisses from

Poekieoekie.

**82** On Friday 7 August, Wilhelmina wrote in the diary that she kept between Saturday 25 July and 30 August 1891, 'because I want to have a souvenir of my youth': 'Early in the afternoon we went to Hattem. The way there is pretty much all the same: farmland, meadows, woods and moorland alternate with one another. We alighted at Molecaten, near Hattem. The Heekrens gave us a warm welcome. I believe that they showed us everything that belongs to them. The tour takes 5 ½ hours. We were home late.'

**83** See p. 69, note 77.

**84** The Prince and Princess of Wied were at Het Loo with their two daughters, Louise and Elisabeth. They had a family dinner together, among other things.

**85** On 20 August there was a visit to the estate of Orange Nassausoord in Renkum. King Willem III had bought the estate in 1881 as a country estate and widow's chattel for Emma. In 1898 she would spend the National Gift of c. 300,000 guilders that she received at the end of her regency on transforming the house into the first Dutch sanatorium for patients suffering from lung disease. It would be opened by Wilhelmina in 1901.

**86** At that time, Miss Winter was staying in Wilton Lodge, Gratwicke Road, Worthing, Sussex.

**87** In the diary that she kept between 25 July and 30 August 1891, Wilhelmina wrote: 'On

Letter from Miss Winter:

Wilton Lodge
Gratwricke Road
Worthing
Aug 23<sup>d</sup> 1891

**67**   Darling Queen Poekieoekie,

It was so very sweet of you to send the apricots which were <u>not</u> either bruised or shaken on the road here, they travelled splendidly & I thank you heartily for them dearie.

Poor little Poekie, I am <u>so</u> distressed for your shivering fits and general fright over my brown face but I thought it wiser to prepare you by degrees for my changed appearance!

There was a very terrible thunder storm here on Friday probably <u>your</u> storm come over from the Netherlands, but like you Darling — though I happened to be out in it — I reached home alive!

I shall be curious to hear all about Oranje Nassausoord when we meet: only a few more days Darling & then we shall be able to chatter to any extend.

The sea this morning was <u>lovely</u>. I was floating, & lying under the water gazing up into the blue sky until I almost fancied I had become a fish, you would feel still more uncomfortable were I to return covered with scales & fins!

Many thanks to Swell for his kindly greeting in return of which I send him a loving pat.

Much dear love Darling from your ever loving          E. Saxton Winter

I forgot to thank you for the dear telegram.

Wilhelmina's sense of humour is revealed by these two drawings of her governess that she made in c. 1892, with the captions: 'Miss Winter, O how bad' and 'Miss Winter at her best.'

Thursday 20 August we took an early train to Arnhem. There, we stepped in the carriage and drove to Orange Nassausoord. When we had arrived in Orange Nassausoord, I visited my little garden, my chickens and the stable. After that, we had lunch. After dining, Jakline and Bertha [the dolls], who had accompanied us, had a rest. During that time, I looked at the toys of mine that were there. Then we drove to Wageningen, crossed the Lek [river] by ferry and drove through the Betuwe for a while. After that, we took the steamboat back to Arnhem (...).'

# 1892

From the end of March, shortly before the annual visit to Amsterdam of 22-28 April 1892, for which she joined the retinue, Miss Winter took a holiday in England.

This letter, written on writing paper decorated with a small bouquet of flowers, is probably dated 28 March 1892, judging from the postmark on the envelope:

68  Dear old darling,
Mother does not know what clothes I am to pot on to go to church. I am writing this evening. I only ask mother the words I have not written befor. Do write back to say if you caught the train? I never cried ocean's after you had left. Do not forget to tell me howlong it took to cross the Hollandschediep. I hope you have not suffocated an board the baot. Swell sends you his love. And so does your dear old

Poeksie

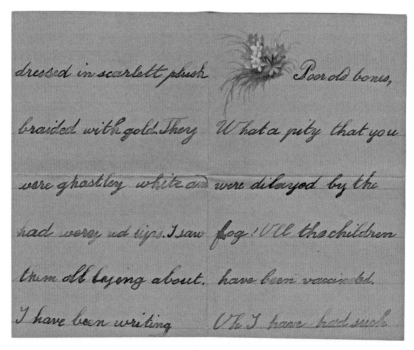

In 1892, Wilhelmina began to address her letters to 'Poor old Bones' or 'Dear old Bones', something she would continue to do until the end of 1895. In this case, on writing paper featuring a small bouquet of flowers in the corner, undated and signed 'Poekie'.

Telegram from Wilhelmina sent from The Hague, arrived in Saffron Walden on 28 March 1892:

69  Many thanks telegram, so sorry you were late, rather homesick, went church, stables romped, much love. Wilhelmina

Undated, the same writing paper as for letter 68:

70  Poor old bones,

What a pity that you were dilayed by the fog! Oll the children have been vacci-nated. Oh I have had such nightmare. I dreamt that we, mother you and I, were seeing a small battle in the Franco-German war from a distance on a mountain. The German's won and marched past us. They had a tight fitting tan uniform. Mother allowed them to camp her in the palace. The germans were wery rough. The French were dressed in scarlett plush braided with gold. They were ghastley white and had wery red lips. I saw them all lajing about.

I have been writing monday and tuesday. I have just got your letter. I thank you very much for it. The sores are quite better. I rode on tuesday. It went very well. I will send the woman at Scheveningen 14 eggs for three weeks. Mother let me go to church in my grey coat.

Many hug's from your                                                        Poeks

Telegram from Wilhelmina, sent from The Hague, arrived in Saffron Walden on 1 April 1892:

71  Many thanks for dear letter, primroses, sending you Pluvereggs,[88] well and happy, much love

Wilhelmina

Telegram from Wilhelmina, sent from The Hague, arrived in Saffron Walden on 4 April 1892:

72  Loving thanks letter, well happy, Friday children hospital, long drives, romped to day, love

Wilhelmina

Letter from Miss Winter:

April 7th 1892

73  My sweetest Queen

So very many thanks for your dear telegram. I am so glad darling that you are well & happy, & having such an enjoyable time, with this glorious weather you will much prefer being out, to sitting still at the lessons I expect?

I have been spending 2 days with my friends at Kensington, & each day we drove in the Park to watch the people riding in the Row. London just now is very full, & there were always hundreds of people riding. You may guess how I watched them all, ladies & girls, to know they were dressed, held their reins, sat

88  By 'Pluvereggs', Wilhelmina must mean plovers' eggs.

in their saddles, & managed their steeds, in order that we could talk about it all on my return!

I am so dreadfully baked with the heat, that I really think you will find me <u>much</u> thinner. I have nothing but my thick winter clothes, & my general appearance is much like that of a large beettroot!

How are all the children? Give them my dear love & impress upon them my hope of having an excellent report of their behaviour!

There have been several friends calling, so I must quickly finish my letter.

Good bye darling Poeks,

Ever with dearest love

your fondly attached

E. Saxton Winter

Undated, April 1892:

**74** Dear old bones,

I thank you very much for your dear letter. Bleuettes, Jacquelines and Bertha arms have taken,[89] but the others not. I went to the childrens hospital on Friday and rode on Saturday and Tuesday.

To day (Wednesday) some children of the schools came to sing at the palace. They sang very well. I know the second second pleasure in Store for me. Mother told me it. I hope that the day you ment to take your mother was fine. Oh I am mad about the pleasure. Many hugs so dear to stifle you

From your old Poekie

April 15<sup>th</sup> 1892

**75** Dear old Bones,

I thank you very much for your dear letters and primroses, they arrived not faded. I have been playing war, I won. I am sending you photo's of the children. I rode four times and began to ride some figur's. The weather has changed very suddenly. The children are all right. I am allright.

Much love from your Poekie

Telegram from Emma to Miss Winter Saffron Walden, 16 April 1892:

**76** Wilhelmina well and happy, departure Amsterdam fryd twentysecond, return Hague twentyeight for several days, you need only return with dayboat wednesday twentyeight,[90] please write me decision Emma

---

89 Wilhelmina may mean that the dolls' arms had been sent to the doll hospital.
90 The telegram is rather unclear, because according to the registry of the Marshal of the Court, Miss Winter was also present at the annual visit to Amsterdam between 22 and 28 April 1892. This must mean that Miss Winter returned on Wednesday 20 April, because 28 April fell on a Thursday.

*April 15th 1892*

*Dear old Bones,*

*I thank you very much*
*for your dear letters*
*and primroses they*
*arrived not faded. I*

*have been playing war, ther has changed very*
*I won. I am sending suddenly. The children*
*you photo's of the chil- are all right. I am all*
*dren. I rode four times right.*
*and began to ride Much love from your*
*some figur's. The wea- Poekie.*

This letter, dated 15 April 1892 and featuring a crowned, circular emblem of Wilhelmina's name in gold, was written by Wilhelmina in calligraphy and signed 'Poekie'.

Between 3 and 10 October 1892 (the whole trip lasted until 17 October), Emma and Wilhelmina were in Weimar to attend the Golden Wedding celebrations of Sophie and Carl Alexander, Grand Duchess and Grand Duke of Saxe-Weimar, with their usual retinue: the mistress of the robes Baroness G.E.J. van Hardenbroek van Bergambacht;[91] superintendent Miss F.L.H. van de Poll; lady-in-waiting A.J. Juckema van Burmania, Baroness Rengers;[92] the English governess Miss Saxton Winter; the Lord Chamberlain/acting Grand Master R.J. Schimmelpenninck van Nijenhuis;[93] private secretary Mr S.M.S. de Ranitz; adjutant troop captain Mr W.F.H. van de Poll;[94] and senior official to the Cabinet Mr P.H. Gevers Deynoot.[95]
Miss Winter then stayed in England between 22 October and 15 November 1892.

---

**91** In 1872, Mrs G.E.J. (Julie) van Hardenbroek of 's Heeraartsberg and Bergambacht, Countess of Limburg Stirum (1842–1921) was made Dame du Palais to Queen Sophie (1818–1877), the wife of King Willem III and, as of 15 December 1878, to Queen Emma. In 1891 she became Mistress of the Robes to Queen-Widow Regent Emma. Between 26 October 1896 and 1913, she fulfilled this role for Queen Wilhelmina.

**92** Miss Rengers is A. 'Annie' J. Juckema van Burmania, Baroness Rengers (1868–1944), who would become lady-in-waiting to Queen Emma on 25 November 1890, but served Queen Wilhelmina; after Wilhelmina's confirmation in 1896, she became her principal lady-in-waiting. She would remain in service until 1917.

**93** Rutger Jan Schimmelpenninck van Nijenhuis (1821–1893) was made Lord Chamberlain on 26 April 1881.

**94** Mr Willem F.H. van de Poll (1843–1918), who was a Catholic, unlike Lady van de Poll, was made adjutant to Queen Wilhelmina on 20 April 1891.

**95** Mr P.H. Gevers Deynoot (1848–1899), the son of the mayor of The Hague, Gevers Deynoot, was senior official to the Queen's Cabinet between 1875 and 1894 and thereafter its director.

**77** Many thanks telegram, am quite well, miss you very much but am not homesick, dreadfull rain and snowstorm, pleasant morning, much love

Wilhelmina

In the following letters, Wilhelmina attempts to imitate her mother's handwriting by writing the letter 'd' with a large flourish to the right.

23 October 1892

**78** Dear Darling,

I was so glad to her that you had passed the sae all rightly. You can not imagine how dreadful the weather is, it is doggy weather, now other word for it. I have not been out to day. This morning I have played with Peter, I bathed him and nursed him.[96] Aftre luncheon I decided about the poor piples things,[97] and then I played battledoor and chattlekock with Mother, and other odds and ends. I behaved properly in the train.[98] Swell never looked for you, (la rage) he smells very doggy.

Many hugs from ekky
Poeksie

I forgot to ask you for Juli's adress, if you have got it please send it, if not don't bother. I have not asked so meny tims about the spelling.

Letter from Miss Winter:

Saffron Walden
24 October 1892

**79** My sweet darling Queen

Very many thanks for your dear telegram of this morning. I hope little darling that the "missing" me will soon pass over. I shall try & write very often, but you are not to think of answering each letter. You can reserve all your news until we meet! The weather during the journey to Flushing was something terrible, & the passage across the channel was the roughest, I have ever had. The waves dashed over the decks in such an awful way, that from time to time it seemed as if the roof of the cabin must be smashed in. My poor old heart felt rather lonely, & I could only hope your remarks of being shipwrecked were not going to be verified! Will you please dearie tell the Queen Regent that I find a great improvement in my Mother, she can move so much more easily, & she certainly looks much stronger. You may imagine how delighted she is to have me. I hope dear

96 This must have been a dog.
97 A50-V-19–19b Between 1888 and 1896 Wilhelmina kept her own account books, in which she wrote down how she spent her monthly allowance of 10 guilders; for example, 2 guilders for 'the poor' and in August 1894 20 guilders 'for the poor' from a monthly allowance of what was by then 50 guilders (Fasseur 1998, p.94).
98 On 22 October, Wilhelmina ceremonially launched the armoured cruiser 'Queen Wilhelmina of the Netherlands' in Amsterdam.

old girlie that you will thoroughly enjoy the time with Mother, work bravely, & have a grandly good account for me on my return.

Fondest love & a dear hug

from your very devoted                                    E. Saxton Winter

25 Octobre 1892

**80**  Dear Darling,

I thank you very much for your letter. I thought by the weather the sea would by very rough.

Yesterday (Monday) I rode, the horses were very wild. Woyko[99] was exitded by the other horses. In the afternoon I drove in the chaise.[100] I was rather homesick. O darling I rode in my new riding pantaloons, Guterbock[101] has made them 1 ¾ inches smaller at the top then those of this summer...... I thought you would like to no it. In the evening we had dinner with the tails. Mister van Bylandt[102] was invited with his wife, she has not got more lovely. To day I tooke a walk. In the afternoon I walked with Mother on the Postweg.[103]

Your Poekie

Letter from Miss Winter:

St James'Mount, Liverpool<br>27th October 1892

**81**  Sweet little Queen

Very many many thanks for your dear letter, but really I shall get <u>rather</u> [?] with "ekky Poeksie" if she writes too often, for she must make the most of her spare time & not spend in letter writing! I thought the spelling <u>very</u> well dearie and the writing quite tidy. I hope that poor Peter is feeling better, that the fever has

---

**99**  E1ii-11b-2. Woyko was a dark-brown Arab gelding, bought on 12 November 1891 from the horse trader's Woltman & Co. of Berlin, and presented as a gift to Queen Wilhelmina on 26 March 1892. Woyko died in 1903.

**100**  The 'chaise' refers to the West-Frisian pony-chaise that Princess Wilhelmina received as a birthday gift in 1885. It was made by Abraham Frank and painted with scenes of country life and with pictures of Dutch provincial costumes at the front and back. It was supplied by the Groote Koninklijke Bazar, a department store in The Hague; property of the Crown Goods Association (Conijn, pp. 114–115).

**101**  A47a-III-9 Güterbock & Sons, 16 New Burlington St Regent Street, London, supplied Wilhelmina's horse-riding clothes (Conijn, p. 109). On 28 December, an invoice for 876.84 guilders (72 pounds, 8 shillings and 6 pence) was paid.

**102**  This refers to Count Charles M.E.G. van Bylandt (1818–1893), who had been envoy extraordinary and minister plenipotentiary in London since 1871. He married Adelaide Petrowna Yasikoff (1827–1903) in St Petersburg in 1852. The Van Bylandt couple arrived at Het Loo in the afternoon. In the evening, a dinner was held in the small dining room at Het Loo, in the presence of Mr J.A. van Hasselt, Mayor of Apeldoorn between 1872 and 1897, among others. The couple left again the following morning.

**103**  The Postweg in Apeldoorn, until 1919 the continuation of the Loseweg, ran along the eastern side of the park of Het Loo. On the corner was the Posthuis, home to the postmaster of Het Loo in the 17th and 18th centuries.

gone & that you dear little Mother are no longer disturbed at night? I found at a
gardeners in Walden some lovely thistles which I thought would be just the thing
for adding to your collection of dried flowers for the vault. They must not be put
in water, if you arrange them in a vase in a warm room they will dry gradually &
retain their form. I hope they will reach you all right. I came here this morning &
return to Walden on Saturday morning. The weather is terrible, such rain & wind.
I have no idea where Julie is at present, she was leaving her last position early in
September & though she promised to send me her new address, she has not yet
done so.

I am not going to send any message to Swell, for it is much too bad of him not
to have noticed my absence!

I did the Queen Regents' commissions in London yesterday, & blew the people
up most thoroughly!

I tried to find what you wanted but have not quite succeeded & mean to try
again on Saturday.

Much dear love sweet darling. I hope you escaped a cold after the wetting of
last Saturday?

Kind messages to the children.

Ever your devoted                                                    E. Saxton Winter

29 Octobre 1892

**82**   Dear Darling,
I thank you very much for the lovely thistles and for your dear lettre. How
beautiful they are. Peter is nearly well. To day Thea van Heeckeren[104] came to
play with me. We saw Beppo[105] excercised and Carrots[106] and afterwards oll 5
poneys loose. To morrow it will be Arnulf's birthday.[107] He is going to have some
presents. Thursday Mrs Hoefer[108] hase been her. I rode thursday and to day.
Yesterday I walked home from the Doelen Eik bij de zeven weegen.[109]

Your dear old loving                                                Oekie, Poekie

---

104  Antoinette A.M. 'Thea' van Heeckeren (1882–1967) was the daughter of Baron J.A. van
Heeckeren van Molecaten (1820–1885), Master of the Royal Shoot to King Willem III and
steward of Het Loo, and his second wife, Baroness M.A. van Heeckeren van Molecaten,
Baroness van der Goes of Dirxland (1844- 1926), who was Dame du Palais to Queen Emma.
105  E11c-11b-4. Beppo, a black stallion from Hungary, was bought on 16 June 1892 at Nicholas'
in Berlin for 1560.62 guilders, and was sold in October 1897 for 250 guilders to the horse trader
Mulder.
106  E11c-11b-2. 'Carrots' was an Arab gelding, a golden chestnut. Like Woyko, he was bought
from the horse trader's Woltmann & Co. of Berlin on 12 November 1891. Presented as a gift to
Her Majesty the Queen on 6 December 1891.
107  Arnulf is probably a doll.
108  Baroness Cornelia M. Hoefer van Heemstra (see p. 27, note 55).
109  The Doelen Eik, 'the oak tree at the seven roads', lies to the right, when coming from Paleis
Het Loo, shortly before the end of the Koningslaan, where this road meets the Amersfoortseweg
in the Hoog Soeren woods. On the Topographical Map of the Netherlands, p. 33A 'Hoog Soeren',
the tree is described as the 'Doeleboom [target tree]'.

Letter from Emma, written in pencil on black-edged paper:

The Loo Nov 1 1892

**83**  Dear Miss Winter,

I send you to-day inclosed the promised two thousand florins,[110] I hope that will be sufficient for the expenses for this moment. In December I can give you the other two thousand.

Yours affectionately,

Emma

In the following letter, Wilhelmina attempts to write with many flourishes, imitating the style of centuries gone by (Colour plate 1-2):

3 Novembre 1892

**84**  Dear Darling,

I thank you very much for your dear letre and for your good advice to write with flourishes.

Evertje has been her with some of her children.[111] I have not been able to ride till now, this week. First it has been to cot and then to wet. I have been working well. The homesciknis! larsted 4 ouwers!

Your old Poekie

Added by Emma in pencil:

You will be very glad to hear that Wilhelmina is very well, happy and good. Only yesterday morning (still after luncheon) she was depressed & felt lonely & her homesickness, as she calls it, made her feel uncomfortable also physically.

In the afternoon she quite recovered & is all right since than. She really is very sweet and good, so I can make things pleasant and easy for her. — Guterbock[112] really made the band of her riding pantaloons 1 ¾ inches narrower than the band of the thin ones. Please scold him for it. It is too stupid. I have had new bands put on by the maids, because I could not do without the thing for a week, the time required to send it to London.

I am very glad you found your mother stronger than she was in the spring & trust you will be able to enjoy your holiday very much. Yours affectionately,

E.

Het Loo, Nov. the 7th 1892

**85**  Dear Darling,

I thank you very much for your dear letter. I hope you will admire the beauty of my writing. I am getting on very well with the poor people things. For a second time I have sent them work.

Much love from your

Poeksie

---

110  Until 1971, the florin was an English coin worth two shillings.
111  See letter 33, note 51.
112  See letter 80, note 101.

This letter, written in calligraphy and signed 'Poeksie' by Wilhelmina, featured a crown and 'Het Loo' printed in gold; 7 November 1892.

Letter from Miss Winter:

Saffron Walden
November 10<sup>th</sup> 1892

86 Most darling Queen,

Your sweet and <u>beautifully</u> written letter reached me yesterday & from the <u>exquisite</u> [?] & careful formation of all the letters, I am inclined to think it was written during an English lesson & probably finished as "schoonschrijven", am I right? I can see dearie that you took a great deal of trouble over the whole letter & thank you very much.

You must indeed be getting on well with the poor people's things if you have already twice sent them work. I shall have to hurry up too with the shawls, hoods etc.

I think I have a little touch of Influenza again for my left eye is swoollen in the same ridiculous way as last winter in the Hague & my body aches all over, however I am taking large doses of quinine & hope by tomorrow to be all right again.

How are you sweet girlie?

You never say!

The days now seem to fly by in the most extraordinary manner.

Heaps & heaps of love darling

Ever your very devoted
E. Saxton Winter

Telegram from Wilhelmina sent from Het Loo, arrived in Saffron Walden on 14 November 1892:

87 Could not write, many thanks for letter, romped yesterday, am happy and well, much love, looking forward to meeting, Wilhelmina

# 1893

Between 3 and 30 August 1893, Miss Saxton Winter stayed in England. Emma and Wilhelmina spent the summer at Het Loo. The following letters were written neatly by Wilhelmina. She also addressed the envelopes herself.

3 August 1893.

88    Dear old Bones,

I hope to here that you have arrived safe and sound at home.

As soon as you had left Swell was let into my room. Furst he ran through to Mothers room were I was. After he had greeted Mother and me he ran to my room to look for you. He seemed very astoneshed not to find you there. So he thought he would bark and djump about a little, and afterwerds ly down a little. I helped Mother to clear up her presents.

I could not help shedding a tear but I was soon bright again. Do not wory about the mony you had forgotten to give to the page, Mother gave it. I hope you will admire my ritting. I have ritten without lines. The envelope to.

With a hundred and fifty kisseses your own, reel, loving

Wilhelmina and old Poekie

On 4 August, Miss Winter received a telegram from Wilhelmina:

89    Many thanks for dear telegram, am getting on quite rightly, have quite settled down, much love

Wilhelmina

A letter from Miss Winter:

Saffron Walden<br>August 6. 1893

90    My very darling Queen,

A thousand thanks for your telegram of yesterday and loving letter this morning. If this is the way you are going to attend to my orders about not writing many letters, I cant say that I think you very obedient upon that point! You dear girl! I'm so glad to know that after the "tear was shed" you quickly "settled down". There is no reason in the world why you should not. It is very good, for both of us to be separated now and then, and when re-united it draws one love into yet closer bonds. I felt very lonely and depressed until I reached Flushing. The wind was extremely high but as the weather was quite fine I determined to remain a while on deck and have the cob-webs blown away!

I walked bravely up and down for an hour and a half, at the end of which time feeling ravenously hungry and rather happier in my mind. I went down & had some supper & then to bed!

The passage was rather rough but that I never mind. It was fearfully wet in London the whole morning and about 2 o'clock a most acopl. thunderstorm.

I reached home about 4 o'clock, and was so glad to get here. My Mother looks wonderfully well & is so bright. She asks me to offer you her most respectful & grateful thanks for the lovely grapes. They travelled beautifully, scarcely any of the bloom brushed off, and as soon as they were unpacked my Mother began to feast upon them!

Please thank the Queen-Regent for giving the money to the page, I was so stupid to have forgotten it after all. I attended to Her Majesty's commissions, but will write about them separately.

Pat dear old Swell for me & try to grunt for him as I do! I am wondering what you will be doing this afternoon?

The garden is looking so pretty & gay & the dear little house is flooded with sunshine.

I shall lose the post unless I leave off at once dear. Ever with dearest love darling.

Your very devoted                                             old "Bones"


I must just add my congratulations upon the really tidy appearance of the letter & envelope, it is a great improvement darling. Good bye.
Not signed

August 6 1893

91    Dear old Bones

I went out on Friday-morning with Mother in the cart with Carrots. It went very well. Carrots was very lasy. Mother walked all the time next to the cart. Downt you find it quite an undertaking with out the cochman?

Satterday-morning I rode, it pored so hard that I could not ride ase long ase I had wanted. I have quite forgotten to tell you that Mother and I drove after diner Friday evening. We had such a schower that the straatweg van Amersfoort [the road to Amersfoort] wich had been very dusty the hole day was positifly floded in three minits. We seemed to be in thick mist.

Satterday my uncle of Sax-Weimar[113] came at one acloc and went away again at five acloc. I offered him Swell's photograph and he asked me to signe mine and his lordships name on it. As you may well immadgine I hated this task.

In the evening we dined with the sweete. We had a German officer to dine. The poor man had broken his skul and had come to a cure at scheveningen, he did not look ill. Now downt you find it clevre of him to have made his skul heel up again.

To day I went to the service in the chaple. After church I gave Miss van de Poll[114] a driving lesson well understood a dirving lesson, it went very well and was very amusing. Miss van de Poll drove Carrots and May.[115] In the afternoon

113  On Saturday 5 August there was a visit from Carl Alexander, Grand Duke of Saxe-Weimar, the husband of Grand Duchess Sophie, Princess of the Netherlands and the sister of King Willem III.
114  See p. 25 and letter 14, note 26.
115  E11c-11b-4. Pony May, mare, 1.02 m, Shetland, blue-grey, born on 20 May 1887 to the pony

I had Carrots infront of the little cart with Mother. He seemed to have gott more ambition.

I have been finnishing the lettre on Monday. This morning I just gott your darling letter. I thank you very much for it. I am so glad that you found your Mother so well.

I have nothing more to tell you, dear old bones, so I send you boxses and boxses of hugs and love and kisseses and remane olways your loving and devoted and affectionned dear old

Poekie and Wilhelmina

The following letter was written and addressed very neatly by Wilhelmina:

the 11<sup>th</sup> [sent on 13 Aug. 1893]

**92**   Dear old Bones

I thank you for your dear letter. The groing panes in my leggs have quite gonn. It is quite troo about the scul.

Munday at one aklok the queen and king of Sax[116] came. The queen is a short little woman and has a very big stomac. She has a rimpled face and is dredfully imbarrased, speshely in making sercle after diner.

The king was quite polite but, oh dear, he positifly did not no ennething about making sercle. He stood and tolked all the time with one gentleman. They sore my cotadge and chaise and went away again the same evening.

Eberwyn[117] rote a lettre to Mother and asced her to greet you.

The wether is very hotte.

The feast of the children pased very gayly.[118] We began at four aclok to see a clown who poot three little munkies thro there trikes. It was very proty.

Then we sore a clown who made mwsic. all sorts of curius instements, like an ocarina and a lot of half filled bottles and bells that he poot on his head and leggs and arms.

After that we sore a lot of clever tricks dun by a cungerar.

---

Puck in The Hague, died at Het Loo on 1 August 1901.

**116** Albert of Saxony (1828–1902) had become King of Saxony in 1873. In 1853 he had married Caroline Vasa (1833–1907), daughter of Gustavus, Prince of Sweden (1799–1877). The visit took place on Monday 7 August.

**117** Eberwijn, Prince of Bentheim-Steinfurt (1882–1949), was the eldest son of Emma's sister Pauline and Alexis, Prince of Bentheim-Steinfurt.

**118** A50-V-16. On 8 August 1893 between 4 and 6 p.m. a children's party was held in the theatre of Paleis Het Loo, with a performance by Professor Chambly and Clowns, followed by play. There were 27 children: Ina, Sara and Joan van Steyn (Apeldoorn), Lita de Ranitz (The Hague), Annie de With, Madeleine Lucassen, Adriana Wilkens, Louise Muller, Anna Tydeman, Hendrik Mollerus (Apeldoorn), Jenny and René van der Borch (Vorden), Jacoba and Henri van der Borch (Verwolde, Laren), Cornelie and Egbert van Nagell (Schaffelaar Barneveld), Jaqueline van Nagell (Laren), Maud and Henriette van Kattendyke (Arnhem), Armand Crommelin and Theodoor van der Feltz (Twello), Cornelie van Heemstra (Hattem) and Eleonore Walter (Apeldoorn). Jeannette Mollerus, Jan Hattink, Otteline Boissevain and Maurits de With (Apeldoorn) were unable to attend.

Then we sore three clowns wich were dressed like {((diables))} and wich twisted themselfes in such a clever way that one could not see what and where were there feets and there head.

After that came a clown who drew very kwikly the pickchurs of all sorts of poeple.

And to finnish up the hole afaire the cungerar did still a few tricks.

I am getting to feel much less tiered.

With heeps and heeps of love and kissises, dear old bones I am and will allways remane your

loving and devoted old                                   Poeksie and Wilhelmina

A letter from Miss Winter:

Saffron Walden
August. 23. 1893

93   Most darling Queen

It was very sweet & dear of you to send me another letter, and I was deeply touched by my old friend Swell greeting me in such an affectionate manner & highly appreciate the beauty of his signature! I can well imagine how much you will have enjoyed the visit of the baby prince!

Hearing that you "stuck to your seat on Sunday last in the village church" I am quite at a loss to know how to address my letter, are you still sitting in the church court-bench or are you home & the bench with you? Pray inform me the present state of the case when next you write.

I rejoice to say that the weather here has changed & become <u>much</u> cooler.

Last week I had a most delightful time in Cambridge, we have a friend who is now under graduate there, & he showed us all the beauties of the place & took us on the river for hours. I have been making an effort to do a little cooking, but was laughed at in such an unmerciful way that I am scarcely inclined to begin again!

I hope Swell will excuse my not sending him an answer, but I am trying to make the most of the last days.

Hoping you keep well darling,

Ever with dearest love

Your most devoted                                          "old Bones"

Telegram from Wilhelmina sent from Het Loo, arrived in Saffron Walden on 26 August 1893:

94   Many thanks letter, shall not write again, races[119] very nice, driving much myself, very happy to meet soon, much love,

Wilhelmine

---

119  On Thursday 24 August 1893, Emma and Wilhelmina went to the races in Arnhem.

Miss Winter left for Saffron Walden on Thursday 21 December in order to spend Christmas with her family. She returned to The Hague on 9 January 1894.

Telegram from Wilhelmina sent from The Hague, arrived in Saffron Walden op 22 December 1893:

95    So glad you arrived safe and sound, am sure I had better night and dinner than you, all right, flourishing, very busy, much love

Wilhelmina

Christmas 1893

96    Dear old Bones,

I thank you very much for your dear letter and carde. How pretty it is! I can quite well read your riting and find your tale of your railwayfriend [underlined three times] very amusing but told (à la Winter) [underlined four times]. Mother told me that you knew about my new horses. I do [underlined eight times] finde them such [underlined five times] dears.

I got a lot of pretty things like works, lampshades and from Aunty Sophie[120] a casse with stones, I am so glad with that last.

There were invited a lot of people but it takes such a time to rite alle there names. We romped very merryly. We played blindemansbuf. Every body was cort besides Mʳˢ Schimmelpenninck[121] and Mother and the dear old general[122] and Mʳ van Amerongen.[123]

Mʳ van Amerongen (Curlyhead) had to be blindfolded al so, was not that a joke ?????????????

We are just home from church. With heaps of love I am your loving

OekieOeksiePoesie
Poekie and Wilhelmina

120  Sophie, Grand Duchess of Saxe-Weimar, Princess of the Netherlands, and the sister of King Willem III. The box of stones collected in the Grand Duchy of Saxe-Weimar was one of a hundred boxes transferred to the management of the Museum of Natural History (now Naturalis) in Leiden in the 1960s. This natural-historical collection contains fossils, stones and minerals, especially from the Netherlands, Europe and the former colonies. As a young girl, Wilhelmina was extremely interested in geology. Whilst out walking, she hoped to discover 'fossils or strata still unknown to the scientific world' (Saxton Winter, pp. 95-96). Based on her own searches, her pocket money and gifts, she managed to build up a good collection. J. Karl L. Martin, born in Germany, a professor at Leiden University (1877-1922) and the first director of the National Museum of Geology and Mineralogy, tutored her on this subject (Brus, pp. 50-51).
121  This is dowager Baroness Cornelia M. Schimmelpenninck van der Oije-Steengracht (1831-1906), the wife of the Lord Chamberlain and Grand Master Baron Willem A.J. Schimmelpenninck van der Oije (1834-1886).
122  The 'dear old general' is Count C.H.F. Dumonceau; see introduction after letter 52.
123  The nickname 'Curlyhead' suggests that this refers to the chamberlain Baron Hendrik W.J.E. Taets van Amerongen, nicknamed 'Jetje' (1840-1920), and not to Baron G.L.M. Taets van Amerongen van Natewisch (1837-1901), a balding man who became Marshal of the Court of Her Majesty Queen Wilhelmina on 24 April 1891; see introduction after letter 52, p. 69, note 73.

Telegram from Wilhelmina, The Hague, 24 December 1893:

97 Many thanks letter card, have had delightful evening, everything great success, much love,

Wilhelmina

[Undated letter[124]]

98 Dear old Bones,

Thank you very much for your dear letter. The chair for Mother came still in time. My <u>itchings</u> [underlined eight times] have all gone. My new horses had no names and so Ise[125] have named them Dot, meening darling, Duty and the one that I do not use, Dear.[126] Do you not finde they are pretty names. Yow <u>must</u> get to love them very dearly, wont you? You old Dear! I drove them already twice, they go very well and ar very soft in the mouth. I have just got your dear letter, thank you very much for it, what a pickel you are growing into, it is realy dredful. The days are not a bit long without lessons. I felt rather lownly and homesick during the dansinglesson[127] and loked rather in a bad temper. It will be better to prepare you that Dot, Duty and Dear are no bigger then Woyko and so you must not think of elephants.

With piles of loving hugs I am you sweet old

Poekie and Wilhelmina

[Undated letter[128]]

99 Dear old Bones,

I thank you very much for your loving and dear letter. I hope to that this year will bring many a cumfy causy day with us together. I hope that also for you and your family the year will be a happy one. I mean to try if this year we can gett through life without gowling and grumping endlesly, but you can not expect me to never be nauty, can you ????????????

How can you even dream that I would finde your (((((((((((( sermon)))))))))))) to long, I found it so nice to think that you had taken such trubbel for me.

With heaps of love I am your loving

Poekie and Wilhelmina

124 Miss Winter dated the letter '29 December 1893'.
125 The identity of Ise is unclear.
126 E11C-11b-2. Dot, mare, 1.50 m, East Prussian, black, bought on 17 December 1893 from Woltmann's of Berlijn for 750 guilders, sent to Dobbin-Linstow (Germany) on 21 August 1901; Duty, mare, 1.50 m, East Prussian, black, bought on 17 December 1893 from Woltmann's of Berlin, put down on 5 February 1898 (see Wilhelmina's letter of 6 February 1898); Dear, mare, 1.47 m, East Prussian, black, bought on 17 December 1893 from Woltmann's of Berlin for 750 guilders, had foal named Dartel in 1894, transferred to Soestdijk on 20 November 1900.
127 Queen Wilhelmina had a dance lesson every Thursday; the first half-hour alone, the second in the company of Pixy de Constant (see letter 51, note 71) and Anna Bentinck (see letter 123, note 171), so that she could dance the quadrille and the minuet (Cleverens 1994, p. 103).
128 Miss Winter dated the letter herself '31 December 1893'.

The twelve-year-old Queen Wilhelmina with the Court and Miss Winter to her right, skating holding onto a pole, on part of the canal near Huis Ten Bosch in The Hague that had been cleared especially for her. The text on the board reads: 'Reserved for H.M. the Queen', January 1893. Photograph: H. Fuchs, The Hague.

# 1894

Telegram from Emma, The Hague, 1 January [18]94:

**100** Many thanks letters, I send you my very best wishes for the new year, Wilhelmina all right and happy, shows only signs of a coming cold, hope you are enjoying yourself, Emma

'ized="center">'s Gravenhage [postmarked: 4 Jan. 94]

**101** Dear old Bones !!!!!

Rejoys for me ......... I can skate; but I must first thank you for your dear lettre. How noghty your ladyship is to think that I only immadginid about the dancing. The lessons are going quite well. M^r Stortenbeker[129] did scearsly blow at all.

We have also had a little snow, but not very much. You were quite right to think that M^r Gladstone[130] [underlined three times] would finde a very loving friend here [underlined three times]. But now about the could, it is fearful 7 degrees R.[131] I am mad with pleasure.

With very much loving kisses I your loving          Poekie and Wilhelmina

---

129 Mr I. Stortenbeker, who was appointed court pianist on 18 March 1880, taught Wilhelmina piano between 1888 and the beginning of 1896.
130 William Ewart Gladstone (1809–1898), British Liberal statesman, was prime minister four times: 1868–1874, 1880–1885, February-July 1886 and 1892–1894.
131 R = réaumur. Seven degrees R is roughly equivalent to 9 degrees Celsius.

Between 31 May and 19 July 1894, the two queens stayed in Vulpera, near Tarasp in the Engadin region of Switzerland. Miss Winter was in the retinue. Shortly afterwards, she travelled to England to spend her holidays there, from c. 24 July until 29 August 1894.

Telegram from Soestdijk, 24 July 1894:

102 Many thanks telegram, glad to know you arrived safely, killing heat, am all right and send most loving kisses,

Wilhelmina

Soestdijk July 25 [written in tiny letters,<br>with a magnifying glass drawn underneath] 1894

103 Dear Bones,
It has been so very hot yesterday and the weather had made me se lasy that, I could not write before this. I hope you will have not quite arived in a "gillet" in London; did you sit the whole night on deck? I am all of an ick and a slimy — stick, but not to impatient. Geeske[132] gave us your message and I was very sorry that you had not quite quieted down because you will have helped yourself uncomfortibly much with your fists iff [underlined six times] there had comme down a man on your lap as before. Yor "Guterbock-frind"[133] left yesterday after having tried, after your order, the habit on, and having made a few alterassions he thought it was rite. I am driving much my self and do not feel to home-sick. It has been thondering and lightening very much but it makes if possible the weather still hotter. I petted Swell in the morning in sted of you and he grunted just as he dose with you. Yesterday-evening I went out with "Mess" van Ittersum[134] and four of the gentlemen after diner in the yellow brake.[135] I have put a loup so that you cane reede my writing,
With ever so many kisses and heapes of love I remain your loving

Poekie and Wilhelmina

Soestdijk 29th of July 1894

104 Dear old Bones,
I thank you very much for your dear letter, was it a big farm that was on fire? So you were not seasick, I suppose. I have been driving very often with four horses in the yellow brake with the gentlemen after dinner. The

132 'Geeske' is Geeske Peters, the daughter of Mr Peters, King Willem III's head gamekeeper, who lived on Koningslaan in Het Loo park. Queen Wilhelmina wrote in *Eenzaam maar niet alleen*: 'We often visited them at home; there I found children of my age, who played with me.'
133 See letter 80, note 101.
134 By 'Miss', Wilhelmina is referring to Baroness (Elise) G. van Ittersum (see introduction under letter 52, note 72).
135 From here onwards, the letter has been written in tiny letters, and over the last sentences an arm has been drawn holding a 'loupe' (small magnifying glass).

races[136] were lovely; I enjoyed them very much; the same officer wun as at Arnhem, I was very glad. Mister Metelerkamp[137] nearly wun, but fortunatly he did not. We gave a lovely cub and a souvenir. Mother gave me praise for my good behaveyor. I rode friday, and had a two small saddle, my riding-stays pressed me and gave me a sore place, we do not know what we are to do. It is very hot and I am driving my self for long turns with Bavo and Beppo, they do not make me so tired as Dot and Duty.[138]

With heaps of love I am you most loving          Poekie and Wilhelmina

[Postscript with the header:] Private
Thank you very much for all your toubel for the frame in London; I find it is quite wright that you had it made the most fationable lether.

Wilhelmina

Telegram from Wilhelmina, sent from Soestdijk, arrived in Saffron Walden at the beginning of August 1894:

**105**    Many thanks dear letter, frame great success, arrangements going on, all right, am very busy, will write after Thursday,[139] much dear love

Wilhelmina.

Telegram from Wilhelmina, sent from Soestdijk, arrived in Saffron Walden on 2 August 1894:

**106**    Many thanks dear letter, birthday arrangements splendid, mother very pleased, think much of you, sorry you cannot admire, much love

Wilhelmina

Telegram from Emma, sent from Soestdijk, arrived in Saffron Walden on ? August 1894:

**107**    Many thanks for your good wishes and all trouble you took with Wilhelmina to make day happy for me, Wilhelmina quite well since Tuesday afternoon.

Emma

Wilhelmina's illness on Tuesday morning is also discussed in the following letter!

The address on the following two letters suggests that around 4-8 August, Miss Winter was staying at 9 East Parade, Rhyl, North Wales. On the back of the first envelope, Wilhelmina wrote: I was ill on Tuesday morning.

---

136  On 28 July, Emma and Wilhelmina attended the races at the Cruysbergen estate in Bussum.
137  This may refer to Adriaan J.P. Metelerkamp (1856–1920), who was a colonel in the cavalry.
138  No details on Bavo were found in the Royal Archives. For Beppo, see letter 82, note 105; for Dot and Duty, see letter 98, note 126.
139  Emma's birthday was on Thursday 2 August.

**108**     Dear old Bones,

I thank you very much for your dear letters, what a nasty name for a little dog your sister has immagined! How dos the walking without the knee cap go? I must realy give you grammar lessons if you write "sukkel" with "kle" in sted of with "kel".

I am enjoying very much my holy days and I have had such success with Mothers bithday it was very difficult to arange the golden frame, étagère, and esel the two first we aranged on esels and the service we put partly on the table and partly on the ground; the whole looked very pretty and Mother found the service lovely, the frame came tuseday evening, I saw it wednesday, I found it very nice, but it was too big and so we had to send for a passe-partout which came still in time, I wrote Viracks[140] name on the photograph. I was busy the hwole of wedesday afte noon. I drank Mothers heth and very many people admired it, but I must tell you all about it when you are back.

I have been too busy to play tennis and I rode only once and am very curious to kno if the photographer took good photographs.

You must tell me all about Guess[141] when you come back, will you?

Mother did not have a party of children and is meaning to give it me when she finds clowns and other people to amuse uss, she has not found them hither to.

[From here onwards, she writes back between the previous lines] I am beginning to write the other way, as you see, it is good to learn every thing.

With heaps of love, dear sweet old bones, I remain Your loving

Poekie and Wilhelmina

Miss Saxton Winter was in Wales for her holidays, judging from the address that Queen Emma wrote on the envelope: Miss Saxton Winter, 9 East Parade, Rhyl, North Wales, England:

Soestdijk August 8 1894
Very private

**109**     Dear old Bones,

I thank you very much for your dear lettre, it was not very, very bad about the frame, only I was rather anksious iff the passe-partout would comme in time; you would better reserve your tears for your swollen knee, because I suppose that you will want them very badly, or no, you will still more want <u>me</u> [underlined twice] to help you over your impatience and C°, you poor old thing, I am so sorry for you, it must not be plesant, specialy because the one ailment is so closly connected with the other. But it is rather hard lines to tease you over such a thing, but now quite jenjuen I am very sorry that you can not go without your knee-cap. Please do not ceep this lettre.

---

140  The identity of 'Viracks' is unknown.
141  'Guess' is a dog; see also letters 109 and 115.

Did you find that Dolly[142] looked for her doing well? I can very well immagine your not very soft carresses and would not very much have liked being "Guess", is he or she very disobedient? I am very glad your enjoying the sea, how long is your sister going to stay? I so glad that you admire my style, behaps you could still improve it during my coppy-book-writing. The Albanys/ies[143] are comming to morrow and the childrens party[144] is going to be given on tuseday.

With heaps of love and kisses (and hoping your knee will be better at the same time as patience & C⁰) I am your loving                                        Wilhelmina

Telegram from Wilhelmina, Soestdijk, to Miss Saxton Winter, Saffron Walden, 16 August 1894:

110    Many thanks [?] am all right, very busy, lessons and Albany's, representation[145] great success, yesterday visit Uncle Charles,[146] much love, very happy, meeting soon, Wilhelmina

Undated [Sunday 19 August 1894][147]

111    Dear Bones,

I have gone to chuch and can not welcome you on your arrival. I have been out with the Albanys yesterday after noon, I had no time for picking flowers, I thought about it, I hope you will not take that amiss, I have already gobbled down my braekfast in 10 minutes, I <u>realy</u> [underlined twice] had no time for enything else.

With a loving welcome I remain your loving

Wilhelmina

---

142  This may refer to Dolly Maule, a member of the Maule family, to whom Miss Winter had been governess; see the biography of Miss Winter, p. 19.

143  'The Albanys' refers to Helene and her two children, Alice and Charles Edward, who came to stay at Soestdijk Palace between 9 and 18 August 1894. Helena (1861–1922), the Duchess of Albany and Emma's younger sister, married Queen Victoria's youngest son Leopold (1853–1884) in St George's Chapel, Windsor, on 27 April 1882. Leopold suffered from haemophilia and died on 28 March 1884 in Cannes, at the youthful age of almost 31. Their only daughter, Alice (1883–1981), was named after Leopold's favourite sister, Alice (1843–1878), who died of diphtheria aged 35 on 14 December 1878. Their only son, Charles Edward 'Charlie' (1884–1954), was born on 19 July, a few months after Leopold's death. See Charlotte Zeepvat, *Queen Victoria's Youngest Son*. Charles Edward was the Duke of Albany and, from 30 July until 13 November 1918, the last Duke of Saxe-Coburg and Gotha.

144  This refers to a children's party with 54 guests, where there was a performance by the 'Fritz van Haarlem' company in the Orangery at Soestdijk on 14 August 1894. Frits van Haarlem, director of Circus Carré (now the Royal Theatre Carré), had a travelling company that included comedians, jugglers, acrobats and animal tamers, which gave annual performances between 1893 and 1915 with an alternating range of artists.

145  See previous note.

146  On 15 August 1894, there was a visit from Carl August, Hereditary Grand Duke of Saxe-Weimar (1844–1894), and his sister Elisabeth 'Elsi', the Duchess of Mecklenburg (1854–1908). Carl August would die on 24 November 1894.

147  The letter was kept in an envelope labelled 'Letters from the Queen 1894'.

Miss Winter was back just in time to accompany the two queens on their provincial visit to Zeeland between 21 and 25 August 1894.

Notebook XLVIII, one of the fifty notebooks containing the 1,215 lessons given by Wilhelmina's tutor Fredrik Gediking, proved to contain the following letter to Gediking from Miss Winter:[148]

The Loo

October 1. 1894

112   Dear M^r Gediking

I enclose the list & hours of your lessons to H.M. the Queen according to the new time table. The Queen-Regent has arranged (as you will observe) for the first lesson to last an hour; but as the Queen always throws herself entirely into the subject in hand, the Queen Regent wishes you to arrange the lesson in such a manner that the house work should always be examined during the morning lesson & not in the afternoon. By this means the hour will not be so very fatiguing to Her Majesty.

With kind regards

Yours sincerely

E. Saxton Winter

Dinsdag [Tuesday]   4–4³⁰

Vrijdag [Friday]      4³⁰–5³⁰

New time table to begin
at the Hague on
December 4^th 1894

Between 15 December 1894 and 6 January 1895, Miss Winter was again on holiday in England.

December 16 1894

113   Dear old Bones,

I have been having a very happy morning and afternoon, mother is realy [under-lined twice] better, she is lying down and has not yet gone out. the weather has been very rainy. I was very happy to hear that you had not been shipwrekked, was the sea very raugh? I hope you appreciate that I am writing so large.

I do not know what to tell you more, I have slept till nine oclock this morning.

With a hug and heaps of love I am your sweet, loving

Wilhelmina.

Followed by a page on which Emma had written in pencil:

You need realy not worry about me dear Miss Winter, I am much better, even without fever this afternoon, so I am sure to be quite myself tomorrow. I move

---

148  Paleis Het Loo National Museum, Apeldoorn, RL3098, notebook XLVIII.

about without any effort today & am only on my couch to prevent fever coming back. W. is very well & bright.

E

19 December 1894

**114** Dear old Bones

Thank you so much for your dear letter, you are such a brick to have writen from Ealing, I had never hoped that you would have been such a darling. I am glad I was not the station master at Rozendaal to have to tell you to "overstappen". I am very glad that you went to see the Connaught[149] people,

I suppose you were also very interested in them.

Mother is realy much better, she feels still a little week, she went out under the hood this afternoon, "Tientje"[150] would not alow her yet to go in an open caridge. To day I have been helping at the chrismas trees, the one I am doing is getting very nice. Your notes for the lessons of the professors helpt very well, I could answer them quite well.

... [text missing here]

I have finished mothers card besides the writing, I have asked M$^r$ de Ranitz's[151] advice about the colouring of the ... [text missing here].

I have finisched my handwork to night. I showed Miss van de Poll the presents, she found them lovely.

I dreamt of you the other night.

With heapes of love I am your loving, loving                    Wilhelmina

December 22 1894

**115** Dear old Bones,

Thank you so much for your dear letter. How gastly about "Guess"; are you going to by another little dog? Did you not pich into them dreadfully for not announcing you his death, where is he or she buried?

Mother is quite well and so am I. I have heather to been "giving no truble"

I was very good in receiving the audience from Breda, the picture that they gave is realy very nice, it represents the "Botermarkt"[152] with all the costumes of the paisants. I received another audience this afternoon, it was to receve a present of the German Emperor.[153] It consisted, not in soldiers, like we had feared, but in

---

149  It is unclear who is meant by the 'Connaught people'. The seventh child of Queen Victoria was Arthur, Duke of Connaught (1850-1942). He was married to Louise of Prussia (1860-1917).
150  'Tientje' is Dr G.P. van Tienhoven (1836-1901), who was made personal physician to Queen Wilhelmina on 28 August 1891.
151  Mr S.M.S. de Ranitz (1846-1916) was a fairly good amateur watercolourist (see letter 51, note 70).
152  The painting 'De Botermarkt [The Butter Market]', 131 x 150.5 cm, was painted by the Dutch artist Heinrich M. Krabbé (1886-1931); collection of the Stichting Officiële Geschenken (Official Gifts Foundation), Royal Archives, The Hague, inv. no. sc/1507.
153  Emperor Wilhelm II of Germany (1859-1941) was proud of the fact that he was a descendant of William of Orange (1533-1584) via Louise Henriette (1627-1667), William's

a lovely painting of William the silent,[154] represented as a young man. [Colour plate III-4] The emperor sent an aîde de camp and a very nice letter that I must answer, I promis you that I'l write my best.

The picture of the "vaandeluitreiking"[155] is pretty nice [Colour plate III-5], Mother and I do not resemble very well, M^r Schimmelpenninck[156] is made with two [underlined three times] drumacs.

I do not know what I am to say to your anymore, except that I wish you a very happy, pieceful, merry, blessed Christmas and that I have painted you quite alone the card I am sending you.

With heaps of love and lots of kisses I am ever and always your loving

Wilhelmina

25 December 1894

116    Dear old Bones,

You can not immagine what pleasure you gave me by making me that pretty little picture; I wish I had you here to be able to give you a tremendous [underlined twice] hug for it. I thank you heaps and heaps of times for it, and also for your pretty card and dear letter. How could you only think that I could say that your dear painting was only fit for the stove, I am quite indignent.

Mother was very pleased with her presents. She liked very much the silver trays and specialy my card, every thing was a great succes [underlined three times].

I got a very pretty couch and tabel and a beautiful ivory brush and handglass, enleyed with gold and nine [underlined nine times] handworks and heaps of the other things. We had a delightful evening, we played blindmansbuff, even M^r

granddaughter. In 1646 the latter had married Frederik Willem, Elector of Brandenburg (1620–1688). Their descendants became kings of Prussia and later emperors of Germany. Emperor Wilhelm's titles included Prince of Orange (See 'Epiloog: Keizer Wilhelm II en de Oranjes [Epilogue: Emperor Wilhelm II and the House of Orange]', *Onder den Oranje boom*, pp. 445–456).

154  The painting is a copy of the portrait of William the Silent (William of Orange) painted by Anthonis Mor (1519–1575) in Kassel. The portrait — with the subject turned to the right, looking at the viewer, in richly decorated armour with a general's baton in his right hand and his helmet to the left on the table — has a little shield on its frame with the inscription: 'Ihrer Majestät der Königin der Niederlanden von Seiner Majestät dem deutschen Kaiser Wilhelm II / Weihnachten 1894.' It hangs in the painting gallery of the Paleis Het Loo National Museum, on loan from the Royal Collections, The Hague, inv.no. SC/0366 (previously PL234).

155  The painting entitled *Vaandeluitreiking [Presentation of the flag]*, 170 x 300 cm, was commissioned by Queen-Regent Emma and painted by Jan Hoynck van Papendrecht (1858–1933); Royal Collections, The Hague, inv. no. SC/0871. It shows Queen Wilhelmina on 21 September 1893 during a large demonstration on the Malieveld in The Hague, standing in a carriage accompanied by her mother and presenting new flags to twelve regiments whose flags and standards were worn-out. This marked the beginning of the strong bond between Wilhelmina and the army.

156  On 17 April 1891, Count R.J. Schimmelpenninck (1855–1935) was appointed aide-de-camp to Queen Wilhelmina. He was made her adjutant on 4 December 1899.

van Hardenbroek[157] was blindfolded, you can immagine what a carricature he looked! Ever body was very nice, people which I would never have thought that they would have allowed them selves to be blindfolded, were. Supposing M<sup>r</sup> Kattendyke[158] and M<sup>r</sup> van Randwijck.[159] I had mad fun and did not at all feel myself a grand lady.

[in the margin at the top:] 'rather private'

I have been to church to day, the whole place was tronged, I hope you will have had a nice service. How is your mother, sister and patients?

[at the top of the third page, in the margin:] (this need not be cept private)

We had here the whole of satterday a fearlful storm. The shore of Scheveningen is like desert, all the ships were tosed up against the road, the road quite broken up and I can really say, not <u>one</u> ship without a large hole in it, some have nearly quite disappeared in the sand. I walked all the way along the beach to see the catastrofy, with Miss van de Poll and the aide-de-camp on duty, the shore was thronged with people which came to see it.

One would not beleave it was possible if one has not seen it, all ships are lying one on the top of the other, it looks a dry marmelade, luckily there was only <u>one</u> man that was killed.

With heaps of love and lots of kisses.

I am your loving                                                            Wilhelmina


P.S The letter to the German <u>Imperor got very nice.</u>
P.S I got a lovely broche and braslet in emeralds.


Dec 29 The Hague 1894

**117**  Darling old Bones,

I hope you will not say that I am doing things against my <u>prinsibles</u> when I wish you a very happy and in all ways blessed <u>New Jear</u>; I hope so much, darling, that your mother may be spared to you for stil many jears and that your <u>dear</u> little home may prosper for a long time and will cure many people. I hope to that the coming jear will not make many difficulties arise between us and that we will get always more and more intimit and devoted frinds and will make us, next to the love that we have for our mothers, the <u>most</u> devoted frinds on earth. You are not to poke up your nose at what I am writing, because I meen it.

Thank you soo much for your dear long and interesting letter. The cushion was extreamly prettily mounted and I sent a mesage to Winkoop to say that I was very satisfied.

---

157  Baron K.J.G. van Hardenbroek (1830–1908), Lord of 's Heeraartsberg and Bergambacht, was chamberlain to Queen Sophie (1818–1877) until her death. On 12 October 1893, he became Lord Chamberlain to Queen Wilhelmina.

158  On 24 April 1891, Knight J.W.F. Huyssen van Kattendijke (1844–1903) was appointed chamberlain to Queen Wilhelmina.

159  On the same date, Count F.S.K.J. van Randwijck (1838–1913) was made Master of Ceremonies to Queen Wilhelmina.

It is not trew that you were glad not to have had a finger in the py in making the letter to the German Emperor, at leest I do not believe soo and I kwon you do not mean it.

We have been having dredful weather, hale and a second storm.

Take care that you do not come back with a upset drummac and a nose as big as a barrel. Your poor mother, she will be also ill if she eats so much cake. You seem to entirely forget you are "always a sight not to be easily forgotten" and that everybody who has seen you once will never forget you.

My holidays are over the second. I have had to day a headake but it passed very quicly. I have been riding once. Mother is going to give the second a "Bal Gala", this has not happened sins mothers mariage balls.

With heaps of love and good wishes I hope to become in 1895 your more and more loving

Wilhelmina

A New Year's card, possibly for 1894-1895, featured a short printed poem:

118 A happy New Year to you.
Though times may after years depart,
May old friends grow more dear,
And deeper pleasures fill your heart
As year succeeds to year
Clifton Bingham

Wilhelmina

# 1895

Januari 1895

119 Dear old Bones,

Thank you so much for your dear letter with good wishes and the pretty calender. I find you have chosen such a pretty [text missing] one. I hope very much for you, but specially for me, that your good wishes will reallised because then I will get a perfection. Mother found the calender very nice and it was a great succes. The reception[160] went very well, I got very much paise from Mother and I thought about my stockings, skirt and cheeks, but as I was as red as a poppy I did not rekire much rubbing. I will not be quite able to feel comfortable if you are 4 houres late, you must forgive me that. I hope so much that your mother will be quite well before you go!

Did she remain up, or awake, till twelve o'clock on munday?

160 On 1 January 1895, a reception was held for all state institutions at Noordeinde Palace, The Hague.

98

I went to church on munday, we had a lovely service, M[161] van der Flier[161] preeched, the church was thronged.

I am looking forward to my lessons. We have not yet been able to scate, it has scarcely been freesing. I rode yesterday out of doors, I began at Zorgvliet[162] and went through the woods of Scheveningen and on the publiek rodes. I rode with Mr Bentinck[163] and the aide-de-camp and Miss van Ittersum.[164]

With heapes of love I am your very loving

Wilhelmina

The following three short letters from Wilhelmina were dated by Miss Saxton Winter 7, 8 and 9 March 1895. The governess had a throat infection and had to stay in bed.

Wilhelmina wrote letter 120 in pencil:

[Thursday 7th March 1895]

120    Dear old Darling,

Thank you so much for your dear letters and good night hug. It feels so empty and horrid to know you in the house and can't come down. I wish I could give you ten hugs in sted of one. I find you are bearing it so bravely, you seemed so plucky this morning. You must only paint very much, that will pass the time. The preparation for prof. Blok went off alright. I did not learn much new in the German lesson. I hope you will [underlined twice] be able to come down to morrow. My ride was very pleasant. The diner went off all right. You must go to bed early, it is your duty. Good night, you darling, I hope you will be quite well. With hugs and love your loving

Wilhelmina

[Friday 8 March 1895]

121    Dear darling old Bones,

How norty your horrid throght is not yet to have got better. I am missing you very much. I have been out with miss de Kock[165] this morning and this after noon I was out with the de Struve girls,[166] I enjoied myself very much, they

---

161  Dr J.G. van der Flier (1841–1909) studied theology at Utrecht University and became a clergyman in The Hague in 1878. He became court pastor on 1 May 1894, succeeding C.E. van Koetsveld (1807–1893). He gave Wilhelmina religious instruction. At the end of October 1896, Wilhelmina was admitted into and confirmed as a member of the Dutch Reformed Church.

162  Zorgvliet was bought in 1837 by King Willem II and later belonged to Grand Duchess Sophie. It is a neighbourhood and estate to the north-west of the centre of The Hague, including the Catshuis (the official residence of the prime minister) and the Peace Palace (since 1913).

163  In April 1891, Baron Constant A. Bentinck (1848–1925) was made Principal Equerry. As of 1 April 1903, he became Crown Equerry to Queen Wilhelmina.

164  Miss van Ittersum; see introduction after letter 52, note 72.

165  See letter 2, note 7.

166  The girls are Marousse (born 1878) and Olga (born 1879), the daughters of Knight de Struve, who had represented Russia as envoy extraordinary and minister plenipotentiary

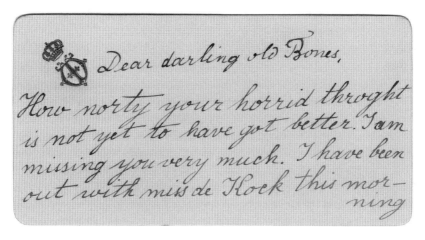

'Dear darling Old Bones' was how Wilhelmina addressed her governess in these letters, as the latter was confined to her bed with a sore throat. Miss Winter added dates to the letters (she would receive another two). Each was decorated with a fine crowned monogram.

were very nice. I hird you have been painting, I hope your sea has got on. My dressingroom has been cleaned to day, I have had to do my dressing in the service room, it was not very comfortable. You must go to bed again early and sleep well. I read English for you so that I will be able to read the part, that I have read, to you very fluently. I had a very stif arithmetique lesson, I had to calculate the whole [text missing] but I am not tired. The m [text missing] in Zorg-vliet was dreadfull [text missing] ly then when you walked in it.

 With heeps of love and good night wishes I am your loving and devoted

Wilhelmina

[Saturday 9 March 1895]

122 Darling old Bones,
How norty of your throght not to be better!. Have you had a fit when docter Evert told you to remain upstairs? I hope you will come down to morrow. Irma[167] rode with me, it was very nice. She had such a darling littel horse. I went out with mother this afternoon, it is very muddy and not so cold out. I hear you have

since 11 January 1893 (A50-V-16 and Registry of the Marshal of the Court, 11 January 1893). De Struve would be Wilhelmina's dance partner at the ball of 2 January 1897 (see letter 150, note 267).

167 This refers to Baroness Irmgard Thecla (Irma) van Hardenbroek (1871–1958), daughter of the Lord Chamberlain Baron K.J.G. Hardenbroek van 's Heeraartsberg and Bergambacht and the Mistress of the Robes Gertrude Elise Julie, Countess of Limburg Stirum (see p. 77, note 91). In 1896, Irma would marry Hans Willem, Baron of Pallandt and Lord of Waardenburg and Neerijnen (1866–1929). Wilhelmina painted a baby bath and water jug for her on the occasion of the birth of her first child, Julie Eliza, in 1898 (see Wilhelmina's letters of January and February 1898).

been painting very much. Have you finished the thing of Rochussen,[168] or not yet? I am going to church to morrow.

Marie[169] has been in a <u>very</u> bad temper to day. She got up with her leftest leg this morning, I wonder if you had had yesterday a row with her. I hear you have had bad news from home, I hope so much that your mother is better to day.

With heaps of love and good night wishes I remain your with a hug loving

Wilhelmina.

Miss Winter visited England in August 1895.

[Het Loo]
August 9, 1895

**123** Dear Bones,

Thank you so much for your two dear lettres. My day at Middachten past off well;[170] it was very stiff. Miss van Hardenbroek came with us. I drove back with the carriage. I cooked yesterday with Miss van Hardenbroek and Anna Bentinck,[171] it was very pleasant, but it did not succeede all together well.

I am very sorry to have to tell you that my maid has not been behaving well: Miss de Vries[172] caught her when she came in my dressingroom to put down something she had brought, shewing mij dressingroom to the maid of miss v. Ittersum and miss de Vries believes the maid of miss v. Hardenbroek, at least quite a stranger, the day we were at Middachten. Mother skolded her very much but hopes you will do it stil once in coming back.

---

168 Charles Rochussen (1814–1894), a painter from Rotterdam and friend of King Willem III; he did many paintings at Paleis Het Loo and was also invited to all kinds of meetings there. His portrait was included in the art gallery built by King Willem III (see Halbertsma, pp. 118–130).

169 As of 1 August 1888, Maria J.J. Benner (1853–1900) was employed as supervisor of the royal wardrobe and in 1896 became supervisor of the office (see letter 33, note 50).

170 At 2:30 p.m. on 7 August 1895, Wilhelmina and Emma, accompanied by their retinue (lady-in-waiting Baroness van Ittersum, Mistress of the Robes Baroness van Hardenbroek, adjutant Baron van Tuyll van Serooskerken, chamberlain Count W.P. van Bylandt), took a special train to Middachten, and returned at 8 p.m. by carriage at Het Loo. 'Middachten' is Middachten Castle in De Steeg, first mentioned in the records in 1190; it was built at a bend in the River IJssel. Under Godard van Reede, the ruined fortress was rebuilt in 1697. Always passed down the male or female line, it is now in the hands of the Ortenburg family. The castle has essentially remained the same since then. When Wilhelmina visited, the resident and then hostess was Caroline Mechtild, Countess of Aldenburg Bentinck and Countess of Waldeck-Pyrmont (1826–1899).

171 A50-V-16, notebook containing the names of Wilhelmina's playmates. Anna Bentinck (1880–1951) was the daughter of the Crown Equerry Baron C.A. Bentinck (1848–1925) and Baroness A.E. Bentinck-Countess of Limburg Stirum (1847–1923). Anna would never marry. Her brothers were Rudolf (1877–1943), who would also later also become Crown Equerry, Otto (1879–1930), and Volker (1886–1928).

172 A47a-III. Miss de Vries is Hanna de Vries, lady of the bedchamber. In Queen Emma's petty cash books, she is always given a rank below that of Miss van Overzee.

On 7 August 1895, Queen Wilhelmina, Queen Regent Emma and their retinue paid a visit to Middachten Castle. Photograph: Brainich & Leusink, Arnhem.

Don't wory, but bottle up your fury till you are back. I am very bright and well, so is mother. I have had mij two first lessons at driving four-in-hand, I find it delightfull and I have not yet run into something. You must show me Dolly Maule's[173] picture when you are here again, I am very curious to see it.

With heapes of love.

I remain your loving

Wilhelmina

In order to attend the entry of Emma's brother Fritz, who had married Bathildis of Schaumburg-Lippe on 9 August 1895, Emma and Wilhelmina stayed in Arolsen between 13 and 16 August 1895.

Arolsen August 14 1895

**124** Dear old Bones,

Thank you so much for your dear letter, as you will have heared from my telegram the wedding has taken place.[174] It to day the day of the entry. Everybody is in a great exitement. The whole town of Arolsen is decorated, there are "des arcs de triomphe" (I do not know the english word) being put up.[175]

---

173 Zeepvat 2006, p. 59. Dolly Maule may have been a member of the Maule family, for whom Miss Winter had been governess (see the biography of Miss Winter, p. 19).

174 The marriage of Friedrich 'Fritz' (1865–1946), Queen Emma's only brother, to Bathildis, Princess of Schaumburg-Lippe (1873–1962), took place on 9 August 1895 in Náchod in the north of the Czech Republic. Bathildis was born in the Kingdom of Bohemia (which existed until 1918 and is now the Czech Republic).

175 Triumphal arch.

This evening there is going to be illumination, but I suppose it will be a swimming affaire, it is poring so tremendously. I am very glad to hear you can drive during your holyday, but I pitty you if you have to drive a horse with such a hard mouth. When are Ethel & Hilda[176] going away, or are they remaining on till you come back?

I have no messages for you in London. I shall only address my letter to Saffron Walden as I do not know where to send it otherwise. I can very well imagine that your mother admires your painting because you know with all the tesing I do admire your painting very much. I have not very much been riding not tennising, but very much driving.

I hope very that pakking has gone all right and that I have not forgotten any thing. My maid has been behaving better, but she still likes to have a high tone.

I think you will have your hands full with her if you want to keep her in her propre place.................

I travaled with Mother quite alone, I got the lunch ready. In coming back we will travel with my uncle and aunt Bentheim,[177] the three Albanys,[178] we dop all of them at Burgsteinfurt;[179] dont you think it will be a merry journey?

With heapes of love I am your loving

Wilhelmina

Het Loo, Augustus 19 1895

**125** Dear old Bones,

Thank you so much for your dear letter and telegram, I got your letter at my return from Arolsen. How dreadful for you have been out in that thunderstorm; it must have been very bad for you to have been frightened! I can still give you one more detail about the packing: that & that I did not forget anything, but that my maid took one mackingtosh to many so you see that was not a very bad misdeed of her esspecialy as we had very horride weather; I was very 'benauwd' that everything would go wright. I missed very much somebody who looked after the things like you do always. The day of the entry of my uncle the weather was very bad. The boys Bentheim have left this morning; they were very gay but missed you very much. Luckily I got on better with them than last year, but I think they also have got easier; they went to Amsterdam and I took them to Millingen; unluckily there were few horses.

---

176 Ethel and Hilda were probably the children of Miss Winter's brother. Ethel is also mentioned in the letters of 7, 14 and 21 March 1897 and 11 May 1898.

177 Alexis and Pauline of Bentheim-Steinfurt, Emma's older sister.

178 See letter 109, note 143.

179 The Bentheims lived in Burgsteinfurt Castle, the oldest *Wasserschloss* in Westphalia; it is first mentioned in the records in 1129. Nowadays the complex consists of three buildings: the Oberburg, the Unterburg and the Schlossmühle. In 1421, the family called themselves the Counts of Bentheim and Steinfurt when they inherited the County of Bentheim. The castle has been destroyed, rebuilt and restored over the centuries. Since 2009, the castle has been back in the hands of private occupants.

The marriage of Emma's brother Friedrich 'Fritz' to Bathildis of Schaumburg-Lippe. At the front, from left to right: Queen Wilhelmina, Princess Louise of Holstein-Glücksburg (Emma's father's second wife), Prince Charles Edward and Princess Alice (the two children of Emma's sister Helena), Queen Emma. At the back: Emma's nephew Prince Otto of Schaumburg-Lippe, Grand Duke Adolf of Luxembourg (Emma's mother's half-brother), Emma's sister Pauline, Princess of Bentheim-Steinfurth, Alexis, Prince of Bentheim-Steinfurth, the bridal couple Princess Bathildis of Schaumburg-Lippe and Prince Friedrich of Waldeck-Pyrmont, and Emma's sisters the princesses Elisabeth and Helena, Duchess of Albany, August 1895. Photograph: Th. Molsberger, Arolsen.

Yesterday I began with them the day at ten o'clock and ended it at a little before half past nine, do you think I occupied myself enough with then? I began by letting them eat grapes (not a very wise thing), then I went to the punt and played with the little boats, we lost some of the sails, Swell was sent after them and after a great deal of trouble we made him get it; them we got stil a few grapes, because we were so hungry, and then lunched; after that I had to look pleasent for the boys to photograf me, this was done six times, then we drove; then we flew kites, which would not fly, then we took tea, then we got the ponys and chassed then in the ridingschool and tried to ride on them bare backed, (this was only [from here onwards, she has written back across the lines of pages 1-4] done and atchived by the boys), after that we went stil to the chalet and then we dined, afterwards I played "Phidex" and cards with them and gave two of them black moustaches, because we played old maid. Yesterday I was twice your complection; once in the morning and once in the afternoon. I am very glad to be freeed from the professors.

The Albanys are coming but I do not know quite when. I forgot to tell you that mother and I fell down in the train, there were awful shock, we thought once we were being tipped over, nobody was hurt.

▲ Hereditary Prince Leopold Friedrich of Anhalt and his wife Princess Sophie of Baden, whom he married in 1889, visited Het Loo on 20 August 1895. In 1904, Leopold took the name Friedrich II to become the reigning duke. Their marriage was a childless one. Photograph: A. Hartmann, court photographer, Dessau.

◄ Queen Wilhelmina and her favourite aunt Elisabeth ('Lily'), Emma's youngest sister, around 1895. Lily was seven years older than Wilhelmina. She often came to stay or accompanied the two queens on holidays abroad. Photograph: H.W. Wollrabe, The Hague.

I served lunch for all seven people. I was very prowd. Tomorrow I am going to have the visite of herrediterry prince of Anhalt and his wife.[180] I had no time to write to you before but I hope have not forgotten to tell you anything.

With heapes of love I remain you devotedly affectionate and loving

Wilhelmina

Around 20 December, Miss Winter returned to England. In her letter to her mother of 12 December 1895, Lady van de Poll mentioned that the Queen-Regent had said that the Queen had recently been very difficult and unmanageable. She had not noticed this herself, and she only hoped that the fourteen days on which Miss Winter was on leave would also go well.[181]

December the 22 1895

**126** Dearest Bones,

I must first wish you a happy Christmas and a comfortable time at home befor I can tell you about Saturday and to day. I hope you will <u>realy</u> have a nice and blessed Christmas. Yesterday I prepared the presents; they look very pretty, it

180 'By the hereditary prince and hereditary princess, she can only be referring to my Great-Great-Uncle Leopold Friedrich of Anhalt (born 1856 — married Sophie of Baden in 1889 — became duke in 1904 — died in 1918, without any children)', wrote Eduard, Prince of Anhalt, in an email to the author on 4 May 2011.
181 Cleverens 1994, p. 105.

Photograph of Queen Wilhelmina taken on 14 February 1896 by H.R.F. Kameke, The Hague.

only always remains a collection of plates and it was very difficult to make it look artistic.

My pincushin I finished also, I have made it quite alone, even the bows!!!! They got quite nice. Auntie Lyly arived all right. We are <u>very</u> [underlined twice] good friends. To day I painted the whole morning. I think my card has got nice, I went on changing and changing it untill I could no more find any thing to change. How did you find your Mother and Sister and patient? I do not know any thing more to tell you of. So I end. With heapes of love I remain your very devôted

Wilhelmina

[Palais La Haye]
27 December 1895

**127** Dearest Bones.

Thank you so very much for your <u>lovely</u>, <u>lovely</u> card and dear letter. How very nicely you have made it. I find it looks so artistic, how prettily you did the flowers specialy the bud and the background; I am going to hade it framed.

What a misfortune you had in London. I hope you liked rushing all over the town in the way you did!! We have had a delightful Xmas, specialy the eve. Mother was very pleased with her presents. I got a workbox, which Mother worked me, a writingtabel, a cabord, a bronze, notepaper and last (not least) a beautiful fan; I am going to use it this evening. I am still very busy, I am peinting very much. [In the margin:] 'P.S. I receved lot still of other presents. Excuse my writing, I have just dansed'. I have had to day my dansinglesson, the quadrils.[182] I dansed with the gentlemen, it was: 'benaud"..........

I am reserving a lot of things to speek to you about till you come back, when we can have quiet talk. With heapes of love I remain your devoted

Wilhelmina

# 1896

Wilhelmina painted her own Easter greetings – Easter fell on 5 April in 1896 – in water-colour for Miss Winter: a broken tympan resting on two pillars, with two palm trees against a pillar, with the text in pencil and red watercolour:

**128** Easter Joy to you Wilhelmina 1896

For the final time while in Queen Emma's service, Miss Winter spent her holidays in England while Queen Wilhelmina and Queen Emma stayed in Switzerland, between 27 April and 16 May. The royal party travelled by train from Amsterdam to Honnef,

---

182 A quadrille is an 18th-century French *contredanse* in which squares of four pairs are formed, performing various figures.

where they often met with Emma's family, and from there, to Faulenseebad near Spiez in Berner-Oberland. In addition to the retinue, Irma van Hardenbroek accompanied them as a guest. On 16 May, Miss Winter also joined them for her final period in service.

Wilhelmina's letter, sent on 30 April from Spiez in Switzerland to Saffron Walden, and forwarded to Atlair, Sutherland Road, Ealing:

Faulenseebad. April the 28<sup>th</sup> 1896

129  Dearest Sweet,

Thank you so much for your dear telegram. As you will have heared from the news of my good arrival here, I had a very good yourney. Lunch went of very well, I served it; the afternoon was hot, but quiet till Honnef.[183] There I got out of the train and took a little drive, which refreshed me very much. There were comparatively speeking many Duch people about. After a good half hours journey we came to the secont haltingplace: Neu Wied.[184] There I walked for a good time till it was time to get in again. Both times mother had a quiet time, as there were only the aunties at the station. At Coblence the dinner was brought in, the serving of which was done by the page and went off very well. Afterwards we went to bed, but I did not sleep very soundly.

We arrived at the station of Spiez[185] at about 8 oclock. The country is lovely. The hotel is situated a little height above the lake, which I see the whole day from my sittingroom-windows. The rooms are very small and low, but mine are fairly large. Miss van Hardenbroek[186] does every thing with me, we are very gay together. I forgot to tell you that in the evening in the train there was a lovely light on the Rhine by the fulmoon shining on it.

I have already unpacked every thing. This afternoon we made an excursion to Thun,[187] a place we passed this morning shortly before arriving at Spiez. We went on board the boat and came back by carriage. On the borders of the lake I saw a lot of old castles bild most in Roman or middleage Gothic stile; they look so pretty among the fruittrees which are partly in blossom, and against the steep

---

183  Bad Honnef is situated in the German federal state of North Rhine-Westphalia. On the journeys to Switzerland, Emma would often use Honnef as a location at which to meet her mother's sisters: her aunt Sophie (1836–1913), who was married to King Oscar II of Sweden, or her aunt Marie (1825–1902), the dowager Princess of Wied.

184  Neuwied, in Rijnland-Paltz, c. 10 km to the north-west of Koblenz, founded in 1653, was one of the first cities to offer sanctuary to German refugees fleeing religious persecution. The construction of the present-day Residenzschloss, home to the princes of Wied, began in 1709. Emma and Wilhelmina would also stop there during their trips to meet family members.

185  Spiez nestles among hills and vineyards and is dominated by a fort; it lies in the Swiss Canton of Bern, by Lake Thun.

186  This is Irmgard Thecla 'Irma' van Hardenbroek (1871–1958); see letter 122, note 167.

187  The name 'Thun' is derived from the Celtic word 'Dunum', meaning 'walled city'. The city, which is crossed by the River Aare, lies on the western banks of Lake Thun. The city became a real centre of trade when the dukes of Zähringen took the place from the counts of Thun in 1175.

and in some places quite barren borders. Thun itself posesses such a misterious, this one is only not in a very good condition. This castle[188] is situated on a hight and we got up to it through archways and in a way quite resembling that of the middleages. I of corse went up the tower and discovered halfway up this dingy old place a museum containing Swis fayance, handsome antiq cubbords, old prints, armour, old Roman utentensils and sculpture, misterious looking boxes which must be coffins and old flags. Up in the top of the tower the boy which was leading us round told us that there were prisonners kept up there, which amused us very much as it seemed <u>so</u> very romantic. Thun is a very old town, very dirty and smelly and has not got any pretty shops.

We saw today the Junkfrau,[189] the Mönch and many other renouned mountains. The weather has been very fine today and the air is deliteful. I am inclosing a diogram of the lake so that you can follow on the otherside of the paper the excursions I will be describing. Hoping that every thing may go well at your home I am your very devoted and loving

Wilhelmina

Faulenseebad May 5 1896

130 Dearest Darling,

Thank you so much for your dear letter. How dreadful for you that your finger has become gauty, I hope it will soon pass off; I can imagine how trying it must be for you. I could very well read your letter, you do not seem to have a great idea of my cappicities on that point! Did you find your mother very changed? Are you taking care of her yourself keeping her company? Can s[text missing] any nourrishment? I hope so that the time after the danger is over may also pass off well.

How did you find your sister at home and your maried sister and Dolly?[190] Were you able to have a quiet talk with Bob?[191] I was very glad you could write such good news of Mrs Kreusler.[192]

We have had from Thursday till Sunday awful weather: incessant rain. But yesterday and today the weather has become fine and is a shade warmer although I still drive about in my winter cloths. The sunrays are still scarce. I therefore could not make many expeditions. I do not very much enjoy the sitting at home; I try to occupy myself with painting and drawing; I tried to paint an old woman in the fields; the people excell in posessing enormous mouths faces

---

188 Thun Castle was built around 1190 by Bertold v, Duke of Zähringen. The castle tower is still completely intact. In 1218 the castle was taken by the counts of Kyburg and in 1348 by Bern.

189 The Jungfrau and the Mönch, 4158 m and 4109 m respectively, lie in the Bernese Highlands. The Eiger, 3970 m high, is the third mountain that is usually mentioned in the same breath as the Jungfrau and the Mönch.

190 Dolly Maule; see the biography of Miss Winter, p. 19.

191 Miss Winter's brother Robert?

192 Mrs Kreusler; see telegram 60, note 81.

Group photograph taken during the three-week trip to Faulenseebad in Berner-Oberland, Switzerland, on 13 May 1896. From left to right: adjutant P. Zegers Veeckens; Irma, daughter of the lord chamberlain Van Hardenbroek; director of the Queen's Cabinet P.J. Vegelin van Claerbergen; Queen Emma; chamberlain W.P. van Bylandt; Queen Wilhelmina; superintendent Henriette van de Poll; Chief of the Military House C.H.F. Dumonceau; lady-in-waiting Anny Juckema van Burmania Rengers. Photograph: Mögle, Thun.

covered with rinkels and frekkels. Here in the hotel there is a sweet St. Bernard which some-times follows the carriage and goes out with every body; I painted his head. I also painted one of the girls here; she is dressed in the costume of Bern, I am affraid I did not flatter her very much !!!!!!

We made another expedition to Thun and we went to Interlaken;[193] both places sworm with shops of woudcarving and clocks. At Thun we saw a factory of earthenware which is caracteristic to Switserland. It looks like my "emaille" painting. I thought about bying some of it for mother for Soestdijk, but I am affraid it will not go with the other china I have already given mother — I am not going to by it. The paysants themselves make it also in there own houses. Interlaken seems only to consist of hotels; the place looks very dreary as there are no people arrived and a great many hotels are shut. I went shopping there and bought many pretty things. I ordered for mothers colonades at Soestdijk a simpel wouden tabel with four chairs; I hope they will be ready by the time we leave, they had to be made. There is a shop where I got a lovely little tile which is painted so finely that one could imagine it to be a miniature; I have not be able to find out if this is Swiss manufacture.

---

**193** Interlaken ('between the lakes') lies between Lake Thun and Lake Brienz in the Bernese Highlands, at the foot of the three famous summits: Eiger, Mönch and Jungfrau.

We profited yesterday of the dry weather to make an excursion to Lauter-brunnen; a place we reached by railway from Interlaken. We went up a vally to the <u>west</u> of Interlaken. It was beautiful; we saw everywhere around us waterfalls; they are not large but fall from immense hights nearly from every rock one sees one. The rocks are very steep; just like towering walls. In arriving at Lauter-brunnen[194] (the name of the place means: "everywhere or nothing but sources") we went to the Staubbach; this is a very renouned cascade which falls from such a hight that it comes down like dust; it does not tuch the rock from the top of the mountain till it reaches the bottom of the vally. On the opposite side of the vally there is still something much more extrordinary namely: the "Trümmel-bach". There a little stream has worked its way down the rock by hollowing out a tunnel it descendes in the shape of corkscrew. Only in some places the light can penatrate in this tunnel. We went up a very steep path and saw it in three different landings. At different highs the tunnel has been overbrigded; it was from there that we had the view upon the hollowed out rock and the water coming sirringing out of the narrow round hole. The higher bridge we were on, the greater deapth we looked into; it was something like the "Tamina Schlucht" at Ragatz.[195] Now I must stop writing, Darling other wise I will not be rested for my lesson in "Maleisch". With heaps of love and an excuse for writing to you on such paper, but on can get so much more in this sheet than in the more elegant ones, I remain your very devoted

Wilhelmina

## At the age of sixteen, Queen Wilhelmina is deemed to have reached adulthood

On Friday 23 October 1896, in the study of Noordeinde Palace, Wilhelmina was accepted into the church by the court chaplain J.G. van der Flier, who had given the queen religious instruction since May 1894, in the presence of Lady van de Poll, Miss Winter and the church elders Baron T.P. Mackay and L.J. Wijsman. On Saturday 24 October, this was followed by her confirmation as a member of the Dutch Reformed Church.

This event also took place at the palace, in the presence of her governesses, tutors and the court. The following morning, mother and daughter took Holy Communion

194 Lauterbrunnen lies between giant rock faces and summits. The name, meaning 'many springs', refers to the region's 72 waterfalls. It is one of the largest nature reserves in Switzer-land.

195 Between 31 May and 19 July 1894, the queens stayed in Vulpera, Switzerland, in hotel-pension Waldhaus near Tarasp in the Engadin region. Miss Winter was also in the retinue. Ragatz, in the canton of St Gallen, known for its natural springs and a famous health resort, was the first stop. The party stayed there for a day before travelling on to Vulpera via Davos. Emma took the waters at the spa (Wilhelmina in a letter to Lady de Kock, dated 1 July 1894, G28-3).

The theologian Dr J.G. van der Flier succeeded C.E. van Koetsveld (1807-1893) as court pastor on 1 May 1894. Queen Emma had herself given Wilhelmina religious instruction from the age of four, just as her mother had done for her. Only in 1894 would Wilhelmina receive religious instruction from the court pastor. At the end of October 1896, Wilhelmina was accepted into and confirmed as a member of the Dutch Reformed Church.

at the Kloosterkerk, and in the evening they attended a service of thanksgiving at the Groote Kerk. The last activities at which Miss Winter was present were the presentation of a Bible by a delegation of the oldest pastor, oldest elder and oldest deacon on 26 October, and Wilhelmina's placing of a commemorative stone in the building of the Royal Archives, then under construction, on 30 October. The final, irrevocable activity was a visit by both queens to an exhibition in Pulchri Studio[196] on 31 October.

Wilhelmina was now deemed have reached adulthood, bringing an end to the duties of Miss Saxton Winter and Lady van de Poll.[197] Shortly beforehand, Miss Winter had had a nasty fall on the stairs when making made a farewell visit in The Hague.[198] Her right arm was rather bruised, her left knee – which had been playing up – was injured again, and she had a black eye and a few bumps on her head, as well as other bruises. And on top of that, she faced the sadness of her impending departure!

An item in one of Queen Emma's petty cash books, 260 guilders for a ring, dated 13 October 1896, suggests that Queen Emma gave Miss Winter a ring as a farewell gift.[199] That not only Queen Emma expressed her gratitude to Miss Saxton Winter, but also the family members and several professors expressed their appreciation, is shown by the following three letters: one from Pauline, Princess of Bentheim-Steinfurt, the sister of Queen Emma; one from Sophie, Grand Duchess of Saxe-Weimar and the sister of King Willem III; and finally, one from Professor Krämer, who also expressed his appreciation to Miss Winter on behalf of two other professors.

---

196  The artists' society and studio known as 'Pulchri Studio' ('for the study of beauty') was founded in The Hague in 1847. In 1901 the society moved to the Lange Voorhout. On 22 November 1932, Queen Wilhelmina was invited to join the society as a working member, an invitation she accepted with great pleasure (Spliethoff 2006, pp. 22–23).

197  See letter 2, note 87. Op 5 September 1896, Wilhelmina wrote to Lady de Kock that she would be accepted into the Church on 23 October and confirmed on 24 October, and that Miss Winter and Lady de Poll would take their leave on 1 November. 'It will be a terrible day. On the second, Lady Rengers will enter my service.'

198  Cleverens 1994, p. 106.

199  A47a-VII-9. The sum of 200 guilders for her journey to England was recorded in the petty cash book.

Princess Pauline wrote:

Burgsteinfurt Oct. the 27<sup>th</sup> 1896

**131**   Dear Miss Winter!

I can not let you leave the Netherlands without saying you a kind word of farewell. I know how great a help you were to my Sister in the education of the Queen and with what love and ardor you devoted yourself to this task. With much thankfullness you can look back on what with God's help you were able to attain.

The best reward for all your trouble and work is to see how beautifully the character of the Queen has developed. I heartily feel for you how hard it must be and how sorry you must be to leave her now.

May I ask you to accept my photograph as a sign of my good wishes for your welfare.

Believe me always

Yours

Most sincerely                                            Pauline Prss of Bentheim

added by Miss Winter: 'born Princess of Waldeck-Pyrmont'

Grand Duchess Sophie wrote:

Heinrichau[200] the 30 of October 1896

**132**   My dear Miss Winter,

Although I am sure you know me not different is it my wish to express to you my sincerest sympathy during the last days of your stay in the Netherlands.

With intense interest have I followed the Queen's development and the progress of your responsible task during many difficult years. Let me tell you my deap sense of gratitude for all you did in the true interest of my Niece. She had in your person the example of real and persuaded energy and the recollection of that example will be important to the queen, the more she will know life and its difficulties. My heart and my thought are with you. I feel naturally what these last days are to you, but also how trying it will be to experience so great a change on your return to England.

Happily you find there other duties and the possibility to devote yourself to your mother.

With heartfelt sympathy and the sincerest wishes do I remain dear Miss Winter

Sophie

---

**200**  Heinrichau is a former abbey in Silesia, which came into the possession of the House of Orange in 1812. Owing to a series of inheritances and divisions, it came into the possession of Grand Duchess Sophie, the sister of Willem III, in 1863. After her death in 1897, it was inherited by Wilhelm-Ernst, the last ruling Grand Duke of Saxe-Weimar (1876–1923). The estate fell to the Polish state in 1945. Nowadays, it is used as a seminary for priests (see Brena, pp. 7–33).

Prof. F. J. L. Krämer, who was appointed professor of history at Utrecht University in 1893, tutored Wilhelmina in general history between 1894 and 1898. He also gave her lessons in art history in the winter of 1896. In March 1897, these lessons were taken over by Dr C. Hofstede de Groot. In 1903, Krämer was made the director of the Royal Archives.

When appointing a tutor in Dutch history, Emma consulted Dr Beijnen, who recommended Prof. R. J. Fruin. The latter was of the opinion that Prof. Krämer could also teach this subject well and that it would be inadvisable for the queen to have too many tutors. The regent expressly wished to engage an additional tutor, however, 'because the circle in which she and her daughter moved was a closed circle, where ideas that had been accepted elsewhere permeated with difficulty, and where the opinions that they held were rarely challenged.' Fruin's successor, Prof. P. J. Blok of Leiden University, therefore tutored Wilhelmina in Dutch history from the end of 1894 until the end of 1897. Emma specified that the lessons should cover the period until the constitutional revision of 1887. Moreover, Blok was required to provide impartial instruction with respect to both politics and religion (Heuven 1989, pp. 32-33).

Prof. C. M. Kan, professor of geography at the municipal University of Amsterdam, taught Wilhelmina between September 1894 and the end of 1897, with an interlude in 1897. According to Wilhelmina, the lessons were 'certainly fascinating lectures', which paid special attention to the Netherlands and the Dutch colonies in the East and West (Wilhelmina, pp. 74-75).

Prof. F. J. L. Krämer          Prof. P. J. Blok          Prof. C. M. Kan

Professor Krämer wrote:[201]

Utrecht/Leiden/Amsterdam
October 31 1896.

133    Dear Miss Winter

For nearly three years you have assisted to our lectures on History and Geography to Her Majesty the Queen, and during the whole of that time each of us was equally pleased with the particular heed you always took of those lectures. Of course it was for Her Majesty's sake you did so, but still we want to thank you most heartily and sincerely for your constant and scrupulous care in

201  I am grateful to Arjan Mitzer, who works for the Dutch evangelical broadcasting association in Hilversum (Evangelische Omroep, EO), who drew my attention to this letter from Professor Krämer (see p. 30, note 62) and the response from Miss Winter; see letter 134. The letters and other archive material from the professor's estate are kept in the archives of the EO in Hilversum.

selecting, noting down and discussing, in so judicious a manner, the very same matters and considerations we might have desired to be dwelt upon as the most important and useful to Her Majesty. If our instruction may prove to have given some profit to Her Majesty, as we hope it will, we are sure you have a great deal contributed to it.

Believe us, Miss Winter, Yours truly

| | |
|---|---|
| To | J.L. Krämer, Prof<sup>r</sup> in the Univ<sup>ty</sup> of Utrecht |
| Miss E. Saxton Winter, | P.J. Blok, Prof<sup>r</sup> in the Univ<sup>ty</sup> of Leiden |
| Governess to | C.M. Kan, Prof<sup>r</sup> in the Univ<sup>ty</sup> of Amsterdam |
| Her Majesty the Queen | |

The response from Miss Winter:

The Hague
November 1. 1896

**134** Dear Professor Krämer

I am most deeply touched by the kindness & good wishes expressed in the letter I received from your hands yesterday, & would beg you to accept yourself & offer to your colleages Professor Blok and Professor Kan my very sincere and appreciative thanks.

It is needless to say that the task I undertook nearly eleven years ago, was entered upon with grave misgivings of my own unworthiness for such a heavy responsibility and honour.

Working as I have done, hand in hand with the Queen-Regent, I have learnt to love & reverence Her Majesty while my whole being is filled with devotion for our sweet Queen. I have always felt most keenly the seriousness of the <u>moral</u> training for which I was more particularly responsible, but have tried to blend with it an undivided interest & participation in the <u>educational</u> development of Her Majesty. And to know that the small part I have played in that matter, has met with your united approval, is a satisfaction indeed!

I should like to say that apart from following the lectures as a matter of "duty", I have positively <u>revelled</u> in the further enlightenment I have myself received, & always listened humbly as one who has yet so much to learn! It is a matter of keen regret that I cannot follow the lectures to their close, but for the fuller development of the Queen, the right moment for our separation has arrived. I believe her to be possessed of those qualities which will get make her a blessing and joy to her people, & I cannot feel otherwise than drawn in deepest sympathy to those, who have worked in their various ways, towards the achievement of such a result.

Believe me with sincere regards
Yours very truly

E. Saxton Winter

# The departure of Miss E. Saxton Winter

Op Monday 2 November 1896, Lady van de Poll, lady-in-waiting, and Miss Saxton Winter, 'former English Governess', as it was recorded in the Journal of the Marshal of the Court, were escorted by Her Majesties to the vestibule below and took their leave at 4:15 p.m. and 5:20 p.m., respectively.[202]

This marked an end to the two ladies' positions as superintendent and governess. Whilst Lady van de Poll became a lady-in-waiting again, Miss Winter faced an uncertain future. It did not turn out to be easy for her, as will become clear from the following correspondence.

After Wilhelmina's confirmation, Queen Emma and Queen Wilhelmina travelled to France and Italy. They stayed in Pugny-les-Corbières near Aix les Bains between 3 and 20 November, in Milan between 20 and 26 November, in Venice between 26 November and 1 December, and in Pallanza between 1 and 9 December. They were accompanied by the ladies-in-waiting Baroness van Ittersum and Baroness Rengers, the Adjutant General, the Chief of the Military House Count Dumonceau, chamberlain Mr R.W.J. van Pabst van Bingerden, Adjutant Lieutenant Colonel Mr W.F.H. van de Poll, and senior official to the Cabinet, Mr P.J. Vegelin van Claerbergen. The company left for the royal capital on 10 December.

Every week after her dismissal, Wilhelmina would write Miss Winter a long letter in which she described what she and her mother had done and said, whom they had met and what they had seen. But her letters also clearly reveal her awareness of the miserable situation in which Miss Winter found herself after her dismissal.

Pugny les Corbières
November 4 1896

**135** Dearest Darling,

Thank you still very much for your dear telegrams. I have just arrived here. But let me tell you all I did in a logical manner. The day, you started I first went to my room to crie and be alone. In the evening I helped poor mother pack the juwelery and we had miss van Ittersum down to tell us how things went at the station. Poor Darling, so M^rs van de Poll and M^rs van Suchtelen[203] were there to see you off. Luckily you traveled alone in the compartement. How did you find Lady Kilmourey?[204]

---

202 Department of the Marshal of the Court ivb, no. 9, Journal of 23 October 1895.
203 'Mrs van Suchtelen' is Baroness Hortense C.W. Taets van Amerongen (1865-1950), the wife of Mr Cornelis L. van Suchtelen van de Haare (1860-1943), whom she married in 1885. On 17 April 1891 her husband was made an aide-de-camp, and one day before Wilhelmina's wedding in 1901, he was made adjutant in regular service, and as such, in the service of Prince Hendrik.
204 It is unclear to whom 'Lady Kilmourey' refers. She is mentioned again in the letter dated 9 November 1896.

Tuesday I did my packing and drove out with miss Rengers;[205] I rode later in the morning; first Woyko and then Dear.

I can't tell you how I miss you at every moment; it is getting worse and worse. It was so dreadfully sad to see the empty place at the breakfest table and not to see your sweet old face opposite me. And then in coming into my room not to find you sitting there with the newspaper; for you know sweet, notwithstanding that I sometimes liked to be alone, it was such a comfort to me that you came in by yourself — and now?

Everywhere where your darling face shou in olden times, there is a large vacant space. Now that I am writing this to you, I wish I could hug you up to pieces; alas, now I can only do it in thoughts! You dearest Darling! I dream very much about you, and then the waking gives me such a sad feeling of melancholiness. When I am still sleepy in the morning early I make plans about the day I always think what I will do with you. Then I imagine that you are no more here and then, excuse my naughtiness, I realise the time of being impatient belongs to the past and I have to be grown up; dear, I wish I could be still allowed to be a mischief; the "deftigheid [gentility]" weight awfully heavily upon me and I feel all my responsabilities.

But I see I have been wandering from my subject.

In the afternoon we started at half past four. In Arnhem we had soop and for the rest a cold dinner; Dʳ van de Stadt[206] was on the platform and saw me. We slept both well. After Basel the views were beautiful. It was quite another country than Tyrol. You will remember from Prof. Kan's lessons that the mountains between Basel and Genève are the Jura-Alps. He told us also that the "bergketens [mountain ranges]" were situated like "coulisses achter elkander [series of layers]". The mountains are composed of much less massive stones; some rock resemble the Flimser Stein. In general the sides of the mountains are more fruitful, vines are very much grown here. I could sometimes imagine myself on the boarders of the Rhine with their hills sloping gently down to the river and with brows which are rounded off. Then again I seemed to be amidst the higher Alps with steep rocks, only overgrown with pinetrees. From Basel we went on the line which goes along the lakes of Biel, Neuchâtel, Genève and Bourget. These lakes were lovely. The railway follows partly the course of the Rhône, there the valley is very broad and boggy. We were received in great style at Aix;[207] you can imagine how tiresome I found it. The road up to Pugny les Corbières is very

---

**205** 'Miss Rengers' is A. 'Annie' J. Juckema van Burmania, Baroness Rengers (1868–1944), who became lady-in-waiting to Queen Emma on 25 November 1890, but served Queen Wilhelmina. After Wilhelmina's confirmation in 1896, she became her principal lady-in-waiting. She would remain in royal service until 1917.

**206** Dr H. van de Stadt (1842–1915), who taught at the high school in Arnhem, taught Wilhelmina physics between October 1894 and February 1896. She had previously been taught this subject by her tutor Gediking.

**207** Aix-les-Bains lies on Lake Bourget in the *department* of Savoie (Chambéry). It is known for its healing spring water.

pretty; my rooms have a sweet view upon the lake and the mountains opposite. Please excuse my spelling and my writing; I have nor my dictionary nor my pen. I wish I could let you feel how I love you, you sweetest darling! How is your poor arm?

With heaps of love and a large hug, I remain, Deary, your very affectionately devoted

Wilhelmina

Pugny les Corbières<br>November 9 1896

**136**    Dearest Darling,

Thank you very much for your two sweet letters. Your poor old hearty; I hope so much that it will soon get better. I so well understand that you feel lownly amidst strange people. But you <u>must</u> not think that being separated from each other, means not confiding the one in the other! If all other friends desert you, never fear, for you may always be sure of me and of my friendship. Never, never will I be able to give you back what you gave me; I will always remain indetted to you for all your devotion and love.

How sorry Lady Kilmorey will be that you are going away from her so soon! I can understand you do not like to stay there very long. It will interest you to here that things are going very well with the new surroundings; I am slowly getting accustomed to miss Rengers. We take in the mornings beautiful walks together. The other day we climbed over an avalanche; I specially enjoy the freedom of being able to take all roads I like and of not having to come home so punctually.

Queen Wilhelmina drawing, during her stay at the Grand Hotel Pugny-Corbières, near Aix-les-Bains, from *L'Illustration*, 21 November 1896.

The country about her is lovely. The houses are built of grau stone; they are quaint, dirty, artistic. I wish you were here to paint. With a few strokes with your large oilcolor-brush you could make the sweetest pictures. The tints of the leaves are so pretty. The foliage is no more so thick and the colors are so deep that they fill you with poetic-feeling. I draw every day an hour after breakfast, generally from a little before nine till ten; then I take my walk; then I have luncheon at 11.45 and at 1 o'clock I go out for a drive and walk till a little past four. Then I take tea and at half past six we dine.

I go to bed early and get up early.

Yesterday I went tot church at Aix, we had a nice sermon. In the summer the place must be crowded with Brittish subjects.

I drew lately a donkey, a mule and a horse. The cattle is bautiful here. One uses lovely oxen to plough the fields. I can notice that we are in a more southernly country. They grow vines and "Mais". I mean to sew diligently at mother's work. Yesterday I made my first attempts at mothers biography;[208] it was but the intro-duction; it seems very difficult.

I forgot to tell you that I made a lovely expedition on the Mont Revard,[209] a mountain behind the hotel. We ascended it in the "tandradbaan [cogwheel railway]". We had a very extended view; we even saw the "Mont Blanc".

How are you getting on with the Cramers?[210] How is your mother? Mother sends you her dearest love and thanks you for your letter.

With heaps of very dear love, I remain always your most affectionately devoted

Wilhelmina

I am sending you some of my sketches, only rough coppies.

Pugny les Corbières,
November 15 1896

137    Sweetest Darling,

I have got so much a lot to tell you that I do not know where to begin. First I will telll you what Mother wishes you to know. She wants you to say how your poor dear old noddle and your arm is. Do the dear upper stories pain still? As we are out nearly the whole day, mother has not been able to find time to write to you; she is very sorry, but she is still meaning to do it.

And now, Darling, where do you think we went yesterday? We went to the "Grande Chartreuse"[211] you know what that is? Not only the cloister was very interesting but also the road going up to it.

---

208  Wilhelmina's biography of her mother was not found in the Royal Archives.
209  Mount Revard is 1538 m high.
210  The Cramers also appear in Wilhelmina's letter of 23 November, but then as the 'Cremers'.
211  'Grande Chartreuse' is the head monastery of the Carthusian Order, which was founded by the German Saint Bruno of Cologne in 1084. It is located in the municipality of Saint-Pierre-de-Chartreuse, to the north of French Grenoble. One source of income is the liqueur produced there, *Chartreuse.*

(November 16) I have just got your dear letter; thank you very much for it. I found all you tell about your self and your drives and the country round Thorn and Roermond very interesting. I would very much like to have a small paintbox if you would get it for me. We are leaving here the 20th; our address at Milan will be: "Hôtel de la Ville". We leave for Venice the 26th and stop a few hours on the road at Verona. "Hôtel Royal Danieli" is the place we are stopping at at Venice. The 1st of December we arrive at Pallanza "Hôtel Eden".

And now to return to the Grande Chartreuse; I saw the whole building; there were fine chapels and churches and beautiful corridors. The Prior General showed us round and brought us in a cell of a Dutch Father; we spoke to him. Can you imagine some body leaving his country and people to bury himself in such a place? The order of the Chartreuse is very severe.

Queen Wilhelmina and Queen Emma were granted special permission by Pope Leo XIII to visit the monastery of La Grande Chartreuse of the Carthusian Order in St Pierre-de-Chartreuse, north of Grenoble, on 14 November 1896.

The Fathers and Brothers live in complete solitude and are only alowed to speak with the permission of the Prior. In church all their services are sung; their devotions are not only preformed in the day but also at night: they always get up at midnight to assist at a service which lasts till two o'clock. I will send you a book I got, describing their life, at your address at Saffron Walden. I think it will interest you as one seldom hears anything about that monastery; I am not in a hurry to get it back. It may interest you to know that no ladies are admitted and that we got permission from the Pope.

Your Queen was there too a few years ago. We drove down over the Sappey[212] and Grenoble. The views we got from time to time were beautiful. During the descent to Grenoble I was terrified for we had very firy horses which dashed down hill and our coachman had the greatest difficulty to prevent the animals from bolting into the carrriage before them. At Grenoble we were received by the "maire", a thing I objected to very much, but I am growing accustomed to it, for we have to put up with it frequently.

We have been making many expeditions lately; the most interesting were those to two grottos and to the Abby of "Haute Combe".[213] We crossed lake to get there. The abby is situated on a rock overhanging the water. It contains the graves and monuments of many Ducs of Savoie. The church was built in the Gothic style; it is overloded with statues and other ornaments. Both at the Chartreuse and at Haute Combe, we were made to drink the home made wine; at Haute Combe it was very acid and at the Chartreuse it was liqueur.

Dont you pitty me that I had to drink that nasty stuff? The weather is settling down for the bad. It has been snowing on the mountains, a thing that gave me yesterday gripes. We have had an awful storm during Sunday night, I thought the house was going to be blown down. To day we drove down to Aix; I bought some crockery for my studio. We saw the bathing house. It didnt look very inviting, every thing looked so dirty. I thought of you in seeing the baths, about the size of a large room, and filled with water of a temperature of $\pm 45°$ coming up to the chin, where all the females of the establishment get in together; the men's arrangements were the same. Then we saw turkish baths of the most different sorts, pipes filled with hot vapour to stick or your arm or your legs in, still more awful were the "douches"; you stick the part of your body in treatment through a whole, then you draw the pipe of a "douche" towards you with a string so that the water comes full force on the bad place; then you are massaged. I went to se

---

**212**  Le Sappey-en-Chartreuse is a municipality in the French *arrondissement* of Grenoble.
**213**  The abbey of Hautecombe, lying on Lake Bourget, was founded in 1125 by Amadeus III of Savoy. It was occupied by the Cistercians from 1135. During the French Revolution, the abbey was abolished and the building was used as a faience (ceramic ware) factory. In 1824 the abbey was purchased by King Charles Felix of Sardinia, who had the church rebuilt in neo-Gothic style. The Cistercians returned to live there. Between 1922 and 1992, the abbey was occupied by the Benedictines. Members of the House of Savoy were buried in the abbey church for centuries. Umberto II of Italy (1904–1983), who was the last king of Italy between 9 May and 12 June 1946, and his wife, Marie José of Belgium (1906–2001), are buried there.

the "sources"; you have to go through an underground way. It is a hot "source"; the hot sulphur vapour which you inhale upon nearing the "source", is suffocating; the water it self is not very appetising; a dirty looking crust of sulphur drifts on its surface. Close to the "source", there is the old reservoir; this one has been made by nature and you would nearly think you stood in a gothic vault, so much the rock has been scooped out both on the walls and the top. Afterwards I saw a museum, specially remarkable for the old weapons of the stoneperiode and for the walls of the building itself which had formerly belonged to a Roman temple.

"Marie" is very good she was quite "op" of all the packing she had had to do; she was rather seady in arriving here, but now she is better. I wish I could still have your wise advice, you sweet Darling; now I can't ask you if I have done this or that rightly. I hope you will realy be able to get some sleep and that your stay at the Maules[214] will do you good; otherwise your mother will be so sad to get you home upset!

Mother and I have been disagreeing on a point in history; do tell me if it was the same wife of James II that was the mother of queen Mary and the prince of Wales, born in 1688![215]

As I dont know your address at the Maules I will send my letter to Walden.

Now I <u>must</u> finish; with dearest love and hugs, I remain, Sweety, your affectionately devoted

Wilhelmina

[Hôtel de la Ville Milan]<br>November 23 1896

**138** Sweetes Darling,

I was very happy to hear you have arrived safe and sound in England; thank you very much for your dear letter. Don't trouble about the distance you are away from me — we can love each other just as deary if we are separated by water or by land — if our hearts only remain just as close to one and other! –

I will as usual tell you what I did and what you will find interesting. We were received in great stile at Aix on starting. The journey lasted nine hours and was beautiful; we passed through the tunnel of Mont Senis.[216] Every thing was covered with snow. The white peaks of the mountains stood out splendidly against the deap blue sky. In coming down into the valley the view upon the Alps was lovely: the sun was going down and its last rays lighted up the mountains

---

214 This concerns the Maule family; see the biography of Miss Winter, p. 17.

215 The first wife of King James II of England was Ann Hyde, the mother of Mary II, who married the Dutch prince Willem III in 1677; his second wife was the Italian Catholic Mary of Modena, who gave birth to a son in 1688. For a number of prominent Englishmen, this was one reason to ask Mary II to take her father's place on the British throne. She and her husband, William III, were crowned queen and king of Great Britain on 21 April 1689.

216 The tunnel under Mount Cenis (2081 m), which opened in 1871, formed a key link between France and Italy.

which were coloured deep red. Shortly afterwards the sinking sun lighted up the ranges of peaks gowing southward from the Alps to the Mediterranian. The sky was of a firy red. You will understand what a contrast it was coming from that fine scenery into a dense fog which only could find its equivalant in the London mist. In arriving at Milan (do tell me how you write that name in English?) the coachman could scarcely see to drive and I could not have said if I was in a town or in the country. The weather has been more or less foggy till yesterday.

Saturday morning we went to have a little look at the cathedral. It is or rather it is being build in a pure gothic stile. The marble is so finely carved, that you would think it were lacework. All the windows are ornamented with statues; their number amounts to thousands. Along the roof by the arches the points go up into little towers and also in those there are little statues.

November 24) The inside is very imposing; upon entering you are quite awed by the immense proportions of the arches which stand before you in all their imposing simplicity. For the church is not overloaded with ornaments: there are few chapels, images, monuments or tombstones which would render less important the three ailes and the original shape of the building. As is generally the case, the cathedral possesses a lot of fine gold and silver. Next to the cripta there is buried St. Carolo.[217] His outside shrine is made of refin copper; the miner case consists of kristal du rock and gold; his body is overloaded with gems.

After having visited the Dom, we went to the "Brera", a museum of pictures; I can't say that I found this very interesting, but I <u>had</u> to see the works of art of the old Italian masters. In the afternoon we went shopping. The shops are very fine and immense. The marble shops are by far the most renowned; I bought some marbles for mother besides many other things. Later in the day we paid a visit to the Queen of Italy[218] at Monza, a little town a quarter of an hour in the railway from Milan.

The Queen is a beautiful, charming woman, very clever and intellectual and evidently most practical. The King I can't judge about so well; he seems to be very much liked by his people and was very polite and kind. Of course I enjoyed my visit thouroughly. In the evening I went to the opera. You can imagine how mad I was. I heard "La Force du Destin" in Italian.[219]

Unluckily the Scala, the renowned theatre is still closed, so it was not the best acting I saw but still it must have been quite as good as what I will see at home. In the second act there was a scene, acted by a woman dressed up as a man (you know it came into the plot of the story). This creature had made herself

---

**217** 'St Carolo' refers to Carlo Borromeo (1538–1584), archbishop of Milan between 1564 and 1584. He was the leading figure during the Counter-Reformation and responsible for important reforms in the Catholic Church. He was canonized in 1610.

**218** The king and queen of Italy were Umberto I (1844–1900) and Margherita of Savoye (1851–1926), whom the former married in 1868. They had one child, Victor Emanuel III (1869–1947). The 'pizza margarita' is named after Margaret.

**219** The opera *La Forza del Destino* (The force of destiny) by the Italian composer Giuseppe Verdi (1813–1901) was premiered in St Petersburg in 1862.

Queen Margherita of Italy (1851-1926), the wife of King Umberto I (1844-1900).

look such a fright! She had stuck on her head a black feather hat, an old fashioned manscaot covered her, a pair of wide blackvelvet trousers and half high boots accomplished this costume; she looked for all the world like a black frog; and this had to preduce a tragical effect!!

Sunday we had the return visit of the Queen and King. Later I went to the German church. In the afternoon we went up the Dom; I climbed as high as one could go; the view was beautiful. We saw the "Sacristie" and the treasures and St. Carolo Baromée's tomb and body. The shrine had to be opened with a lot op pomp and state. We went to see also the burial place as being very remarkable. I must say it made a very gay impression. You went in through a building of an Eastern stile. The place itself seemed to be a public amusement ground. The people and little children after having crossed themselves upon entering seemed to forget that they were upon sacred ground and walked about as if it were a public garden. The graves were most elaborate; there were some fine and innumerable hidious erections. Mondaymorning I went shopping alone. After lunch we went to the Dom for the last time. Then we saw the church called: "Santa Maria de Grazie";[220] it is built in Roman stile and dates from an ancient period. In a building next to it we saw the renowned "fresco" Leonardo da Vinchi:[221] the Holy Communion. I <u>realy did</u> admire this; it is such a shame that it is so spoilt. The whole painting is very impressive! In all the picture-galleries there are artists copying the originals. That afternoon we still visited the church of St. Abrosius.[222] This was built in a more remote period than de Santa Maria de la Grazie. It is 3 centuries older. In the "cripta" the sepulchre of St. Abrosius and of some bishops of Milan are shown. The altar in the church is decorated

220 Together with a Dominican convent, the *Santa Maria delle Grazie* church was founded by Francesco Sforza, the Duke of Milan, in 1492. Owing to Leonardo da Vinci's *The Last Supper*, it is included in the UNESCO List of World Cultural Heritage Sites.

221 Between 1495 and 1498, Leonardo da Vinci (1452–1519), the celebrated Italian genius, artist and scientist of the Renaissance, painted *The Last Supper*, 460 x 880 cm, in the dining hall of the Dominican convent of Santa Maria delle Grazie in Milan. The painting was commissioned by Duke Ludovico Sforza.

222 Saint Ambrose (339–397) hailed from a Roman family that had converted to Christianity and lived in Trier. A church father and Bishop of Milan, he wrote many works on the Church.

with "bas-reliefs" of massive gold with precious stones on all four sides. It values 3000000 frs. To day we went in the morning to a library: I was shown some interesting manuscripts; some were of the letters of St. Paul[223] and of the gothic bibletranslation. But the most interesting of all were the drawings of Rafael[224] and Leonardo. I saw lots of sketches which they had made. Some were very expressive heads drawn with a few strokes; I was quite inspired! We saw still a church of less importance. This afternoon we visited the "Chartreuse de Pivée".[225] This is an old cloister which is now deserted. The church is built in the Renaissance stile. Every little detail is finely worked but the whole is overloaded specially outside. The altars are ornamented with "bas reliefs" in marble and precious stones. The floor round the altar is inlaid with marbles of the finest qualities. In the "sacristie" there was also a bas-relief in ivory. The long corridors looked desolate. They were decorated with fresco's and up along and over the arches the ornament were of "terra cotta". I climbed up on the tower.

I find the people behave in a disrespectful way in church; I have seen them saying up there prayers in walking about the church and admiring what there was to be seen. The streets and houses are dirty and badly kept.

I have just received your dear letter. All you say about the Maules and Cremers interests me very much. Your poor dear Mother, I hope her rhumatism will be better. How is the dear hearty? My dromack is since long quite better. I will write to you later once a long letter about how things are going with Mother ect. Now I scarcely find time to write about all I do. With heaps of thanks for your dearest letter which warms up my old heart and makes it bound within me from you at hearing something from you and all the devotion you have for me; I remain with hugs your most of all devoted

Wilhelmina

Grand Hôtel Eden, Pallanza
December 2 1896

139    Dearest Darling,
Thank you very very much for your dear letter, I am very touched by your loving way of taking care of the things I asked you to get for me, you sweet

223 After initially persecuting the early Christians, the apostle Paul (c. AD 3-64 or 67) underwent a conversion and played an important role in the development and dissemination of Christianity in the Mediterranean countries. He died in Rome.
224 Raphael (Raffaello Sanzio) (1483-1520) was a celebrated artist from the time of the High Renaissance. He came from Urbino and worked in Florence and Rome. Initially, he expressed his great talent in particular in his drawings. His work radiates a calm, harmonious beauty. Along with the all-round Italian geniuses Michelangelo Buonarotti (1475-1564) and Leonardo da Vinci, he was one of the most important artists of the High Renaissance.
225 The Certosa di Pavia is a monastery lying 8 km to the north of Pavia, built on the orders of Gian Galeazzo Visconti in the 15th century and the most important Italian monument from the Late Gothic period. The monastery became a national monument in 1866 and Benedictine monks lived there until 1880. The building has been home to Cistercian monks since 1960.

Darling; how kind of you to have thought of every thing! I can quite imagine how imposing the eveningsong must have been, and I am very glad people behave better in church in England than in this country for it is most deplorable. You poor Darling! how desperate you must feel about your unpacking, I will be very astonished if you can get all your belongings into your house! Your poor dear leg! how dreadful that it still pains, are you having it massaged? How about the arm? You have quite made me blush with all the praise you gave me! I always try to write nicely not to shock you with my spelling and stile!

I think that the last of my doings I told you about was the Chartreuse of Pavia. Wednesday morning I went to Monza to see the Dom.[226] In this church there is kept the iron crown of Lumbardy.[227] It is a golden coronet with precious jewels; a nail of the Holy Cros has been stretched to the shape of the crown and attached in it so as to form a ring inwardly. Of course this is a precious relic! We drove about the park and saw the town. The afternoon was first devoted to seeing a palladzo (a patrician house) in which there was a fine collection of furniture and things of art. Then we saw a picture gallery of modern Italian art (hidious) (worse than what we see at Pulchri[228] sometimes). The next morning we started for Verona. We stayed there about two hours and saw lots of things; first a church San Seno,[229] it is an old basilica in pure roman stile; then we went to the arena; this I found very interesting; we poked our noses every where and looked at it from all sides. It seems built for eternity.

Then we saw the marketplace, this was very quaint amidst the old houses and the three monuments in the middel, surrounded with black Italians, the women in large shawls and the men in furlined coats sitting in or standing before their tents or else walking in front of the tables on which they had their goods under a large white sort of artistsparasol. We had a look into a court or square with pretty houses. You could nearly think yourself in a city of the middleages for the large houses look so old and desolate; nobody puts out a hand to restore them and they stand there from generation to generation falling slowly to pieces. The castle is also in a lamentable condition, it is now the barracks. Near the square we saw the graves of the Scaligers[230] (a pratrician family). They are

---

226 The Cathedral of Monza was built in the sixth century on the orders of Queen Theodolinda. The frescoes in the church, the outside of which is coloured green and white, are dedicated to her.

227 The Byzantine 'iron crown', the crown of Emperor Constantine the Great (c. 280–337), is named after the iron of the nail. With a diameter of 15 cm, it is made of gold plate and decorated with precious stones and enamel in white, green and blue. It was seen as the 'crown of Italy' and was worn, among others, by Charlemagne (742 or 748–814), Charles V (1500–1559) and Napoleon (1769–1821).

228 Pulchri; see introduction above letter 131, note 196.

229 The Romanesque basilica of San Zeno was built in 967. After an earthquake in 1117, it was restored and enlarged. Saint Zeno died in 380 and his body is buried in the crypt of the church.

230 The Scaliger family ruled Verona between the 13th and the late 14th centuries. The five

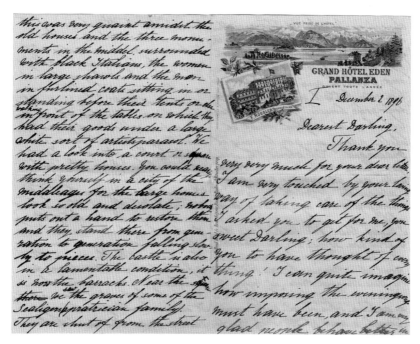

At the end of the trip, they stayed at the Grand Hotel Eden in Pallanza between 1 and 9 December, where Wilhelmina used the hotel's writing paper. This letter, dated 2 December 1896, ran to thirteen pages.

shut of from the street by a fine iron gate. Two of the tombs were placed on a little hight and surrounded by the finest gothic archways.[231] (the graves of our dear Romeo and Juliet are also in Verona). We went still to one church of I don't know what saint; it was not so very fine. A museum of things of art was the last we saw. I was very interested in the fine collection of phosiles there were there.

In arriving at Venise we were rowed in "gondoles" to the hotel. [here is a drawing of a gondola] The men row with great hability and standing; the formost rower staying lower than the backmost so as to alow him to see what is coming. We of course had the gondoles without hood. It we lovely; we first came down the large canal but afterwards we traversed the narrow waterways. On both side there are palladzo's of gothic and renaissance stile; it is awful how delaborated and desolate they look. Venise is realy a "ville morte". The view from the hotel upon the large canal was very fine. The hotel as well the people, houses, canals and streets are very dirty and are not fumigated with sweet smells.

gravestones were erected at the Church of Santa Maria Antica and are particularly beautiful examples of Gothic art.
231 'Romeo and Juliet' is an early tragedy play written by William Shakespeare, probably around 1594/95, about the doomed love between Juliet Capulet and Romeo Montague, two young people from feuding families. Shakespeare sets the marriage of the two lovers in the crypt of San Zeno in Verona.

Fridaymorning was devoted to seeing the church San Marco[232] situated on the square of the same name; the only place for walking in whole town. The church is built in Bysantian stile and is not impressive by its stile nor by its proportions. The round arches are covered with mosaic as well as the floor. I have never seen an as fine "maître autel" in my life. It consists of a basrelief in massive gold and large, precious stones and "email."

The next thing we saw was the "Palais des Doges." The walls in this palace are ornamented with pictures of the great masters and so are the ceilings. It is an enormous building; the Senate, the counsil of ten and the counsil of three and lawcourt, this last consisting of the Doge and members of the Senate, have each their room of assembly.

The afternoon was spent in rowing through the town and seeing a church of some saint or other (all churches are nearly dedicated to the Virgin and to distinguish them one gives them a second name: sup. Santa Maria Formosa, or Santa Maria di Frati.) There were fine pictures and the monuments of a Doge of Canova[233] and Titian.[234] [here is a drawing of a 'Doge's cap'] Afterwards we saw other pictures and admired the shops. Saturday was morning given up to the gallery of old pictures which anoyed me very much; there were only few that I admired: the most renowned is the ascension of the Virgin by Titian. There was a collection of drawings and sketches of the great masters in pencil and watercolour in one shade. This was quite to my taste; the paper on which they worked had such beautiful soft tints: reds or browns; I wonder how they coloured it! Later in the morning we saw a palladzo. The elegant floor consists of a large antiroom with four or six doors. Ceilings and walls are decorated often with the works of the great masters; the stile is, renaissance, Louis XIV, XV or XVI.

The chairs and woodwork are painted white; the luxury is immense. At one end two doors leed into the private appartments at the other end the doors give accession to a suite of receptionrooms in the same stile as the antiroom. I did not go upstairs, but downstairs there is a dirty looking vestibule and the main entrance is at the canal, the backdoor comes out upon the street. The afternoon was devoted to shopping and the visit to two churches. We only went into the one to see a picture of St. Barbara by Paul Veronese.[235] I admired very much

---

232  The Basilica of San Marco, which lies next to the Doge's Palace, dates from 1030 and was built in Byzantine/Gothic style to house the remains of Saint Mark.

233  Antonio Canova (1757-1822) was a neoclassical sculptor from Rome. Among other things, between 1806 and 1807 he created a marble tombstone for Prince Willem George Frederik (1774-1799), the brother of the later King Willem I, who died in Padua of wounds that he had sustained earlier. On the orders of Queen Emma, the monument, which had been housed in the Church of the Erimitani in Padua, was transferred, together with the coffin, to Delft on 3 July 1896, where the tombstone was placed in the wall of the choir aisle of the Nieuwe Kerk (see Heuven 2004-1, pp. 117-119).

234  Titian, whose real name was Tiziano Vecelli of Vecellio (c. 1487-1576), was one of the most important painters of the High Renaissance in Venice.

235  Paolo Veronese (1528-1588) was an important artist of the Renaissance. Just like Titian, he worked in Venice.

this altarpiece. In the evening I went to the opera and heard the same piece as at Milan. It was very pretty going there in gondoles at night with the stars shining and the dark water overwhich our black boat (for all gondoles are black) glided slowly and softly. The opera itself gave me the next day a headache and flees! Sunday I went to church and saw later a church renowned for its marbel basreliefs! During the time we were looking about some of the edifices, there was a service going on, a thing which keenly interested me. I find the chanting of the priests so annoying, they make a noise indistinguishable from the tunes of pigs under a gate. In the afternoon we rowed over the one of the islands to an Armenian cloister, which is very known for the studies which one has made there.

December 3) I went shopping Monday morning on my own account. Glaswork, lace and filigranwork are specially good. I went to a large laceshop where they made it also. Two Dutch ladies were associated to the business. It was very interesting to see how they made the lace; it must be very figating. I climbed still up a tower to have a general view upon Venise. In the afternoon I went to the "Pont des soupires" where formerly the prisonners were thrown into the canal. I saw the dongeons and the place of execution; the prison of your dear Byron[236] was shown to me; it was a black, damp, dark hole with a stone to ly upon at night; in the daytime one was attached to a post; it appears that he wrote "Child Harold" there. We rowed still over to an island to see the glasfactories. There are only few men working in each factory; 20 or 25, all of the same family. Each experienced workman has his own oven inwhich he melted glas of one colour is kept.

We are going to celebrate St. Nikolas grandly; you poor old Dear how sad it will feel not for you to feast it! I am sending you a roll of photograpfs of Milan and Venise; don't throw away the inner roll without a close inspection for there is a surprise inside. My biography is waiting till I have a more quiet time to write. I am arriving at the Hague on Thursday the 10th. I can't say very much about Pallanza; I believe it would be pretty in another season but now it looks barren and quite desolate. I must now finish for my preparations for the 5th are taking a long time.

With dearest love and hugs I am and will always remain your most affectionately devoted

Wilhelmina

On the same day that Queen Wilhelmina wrote to her governess, the latter also received a letter from Queen Emma with the same date.

236 George Gordon Byron, 'Lord Byron' (1788-1824), was an English writer and poet. He wrote his masterpiece, *Childe Harold's Pilgrimage*, in 1812.

Pallanza Dec. the 2$^\text{d}$ 1896

**140**  Dear Miss Winter,

I have to thank you for two dear letters, but more particularly for your first one written from Groenenberg. I was so glad & relieved to hear from you. I need not tell you that my thoughts were with you constantly, that I really <u>suffered</u> to see you & know you <u>so</u> unhappy and wretched, & not be able to help you & comfort you. On the contrary it was myself who inflicted all that pain & sorrow on you. And yet I could not do otherwise!

I am very much touched by everything you say to me dear Miss Winter about your thankfulness for what I have been able to do for you or be for you in all these years, & about your pleasure of having worked with me. Yes it was the greatest blessing for my child & both of us that we could work so well together & that there was perfect understanding between us & that in all principal things we had the same views. Therefore you were & could be <u>such</u> a <u>help</u> to me & <u>blessing</u> for my child. Because I best know <u>what</u> your life was in my service, I also can understand best what you are going through now! I can only pray God that He may help you to bear the sorrow in the wright way & give you strength to bear it.

As I told you I can never thank you enough for everything you did for my girl, you gave your whole soul & heart to your work & always gave the very best you had to my child. Before giving you some news of us I want to explain my telegramm of this morning. Miss Mackworth wrote to me (I got the letter yesterday) that she was going to write to you to ask what <u>kind</u> of work you wished for, this is the answer to my letter I wrote after consulting you about it. I was afraid you would be inclined to reject her help as you naturaly do not wish for work immediately. As a true friend I wanted to give you the advice not to do so. Tell her that you want a rest, but let her look out for work for you. I think she could be useful to you, especially if you feel inclined to make a home for Indian children. And if you do not yet quite know what you would like on the long run, let her look out for something temporarily for instance taking young girls travelling.— I believe nothing would give you so much comfort as even the idea of some work waiting for you & once at work then the necessity of putting your sad thoughts on one side & the feeling of being useful. You would also quickly be interested & put your heart in your work. I hope you feel that only real interest prompts me to give you this advice. I am convinced Miss Mackworth can be useful to you, in a certain way more than your own people.

I am glad you liked the flowers so much & that you enjoy having the Dagblad. Wilhelmina keeps you well "au courant" of what we have been doing. We arrived here on tuesday evening after very nice stay's in the town's, which I hope will prove useful to Wilh. We shall be at home thursday the 10$^\text{th}$ in the morning. — I really had rest at Corbières & enjoyed it. The air was delightful. I was out much & only did the work I had to do. I went to bed early. I really had not time to write to you sooner. In the towns I was out the whole day & had to rush to get through the work I really had to do. — Wilh. has been <u>very</u> well all the time. Sightseeing fatigued her a little at last & she only just escaped a migraine at Venice. But she escaped it happily. On the whole she sleeps very well & feeds well & takes good excercise. At Corbière she walked 3 or 3 ½ hours, sometimes more. – She looks very well indeed. She is very sweet just now, you would be very happy if you could see & watch her. She is not at all to profit anxious of her liberty or greater independance, on the contrary she just now lets herself be led & advised very easily, more easily than for a long time. The responsability weighs upon her, & as she is most anxious to do right & afraid of doing stupid or wrong things, she asks more frequently for advice, she does not feel sure yet of herself. I think it is very happy it should be like that in the beginning, it makes her more careful. She naturaly must get more assurance but it is better if it comes gradually after having aquired a little more experience, than that she should start with that assurance she sometimes had. She gets on very nicely with M^lle Rengers.

Expecially at Corbières & here they are much together in the morning, in the towns they never had any tête á tête. I try to let Wilh. free where I can & in matters of smaller importance, she than listens so much more willingly when it is necessary for me to interfere. But it seems very strange still to me to leave her more to herself, to let her decide & take care herself of her little matters. It is a great effort not to do & arrange everything for her. She happily occupies herself in a very sensible way & accustoms herself very well to being alone in her room. This has been more easy for her travelling, because our sittingrooms have always been side by side. I think it is a great thing for her that she can be alone in a room for a couple of hours. It is good for her nerves & temper & impatience. At Corbières & here we breakfast at 8 then Wilh. did one or the other little thing in her room, her [?] or finished a letter than M^lle Rengers came to her whilst she drew & played [here an asterisk has been added and Emma wrote vertically in the margin: 'dont comment about this to Wilh. She wants to tell herself'] – or read or talked to her till 10 ¼. Then they generally walked together till 11 ¾. Then we had luncheon. At 12 ¼ we all went out together till 4.³⁰ or 5. Then Wilh. was alone in her room till dinner 6 ¾. After dinner we were together. In the towns we breakfasted at 8 ½ went out at 9 ¼ till nearly 12. After luncheon again at 1 ¼ till 4 ½. In coming home Wilh. spent the time alone till dinner. Happily she did no "Maleisch". I think we will both only quite realise that you have quite left us at the Hague, how it often seems as if you had only gone for a holiday. Wilh. will miss you still more at the Hague, where she cannot get hold of me so much & easily & where everything reminds her of you. I am thankful she is so well, she will be better able to bear it. She must begin work soon if she is well occupied she will feel less lonely. But it will be a dreadful time for her, & than all the new people! Please burn this last sheet. I must come to an end, my work is waiting. I hope you are trying to get quite well again. If you do not get any sleep soon you really ought to have medical advice.

Goodbye dear Miss Winter.

With much love I remain

Your affectionate                                                        Emma

141    Dearest Sweety,

Thank you very much for your darling letter of yesterday. It was so sweet of
you to have thought of working or sending me something; I quite understand
you could not this year. It felt so empty, so strange not having you here and
not being able to tease you like formerly. I could not resist the temptation of
writing to you already today, although I had meant only to do so in arriving
at the Hague as then I would have more interesting things to write about. I
enjoyed my evening immensely; everybody was very gay, of course we were all
together. Just fancy how lovely mother is giving me a new saddlehorse. I got its
photograph. She is called Zarif and is a thorough bred Arab.[237] But mother told
me you new about it. I am longing to see it and wish I were back at the Hague.
I will ride it immediately. I got a lot of nice things: from mother a cardcase, a
silverbox for matches, a marble statuette, a lovely box of Boissier[238] and other
jokes.

The ladies and gentlemen sent me also most mysterious parcels. The first
thing I got was an alive little dog from miss van Ittersum which she had hired
for the occasion; I drew it this morning.

I sent mother a few parcels which I did up myself and the poems belonging
to them were composed and written by me. I gave mother a statuette she had
admired at Milan, two thermometers, a lampmat, a penwiper and two vases.
The other day I went to the marblequay where they get the stone for building
the dom of Milan; it was very interesting to see how they take the marble out
of the rock; it has such pretty shades; pink, mauve, gray and white. Yesterday
I woke up and found the ground covered with snow; it was so funny to see the
palmtrees in the garden under the snow. The weather seems to be setting for
the bad for today, we have had an incessant rain; I have not yet seen the sun
shining here! A dim bluegray vapour covers the mountains and makes the
landscape look dreary and melancholy.

I forgot to tell you just now that I sent a lot of things to the ladies and
gentlemen, some of which they have not yet discovered from whom they got
their parcels. The journey home is 24 hours, quite a long time! We arrive a
little past ten at the Hague. The serious life will immediately be beginning for
the day I arrive miss van Stirum[239] also comes and I will have to receive her; I

237  The Royal Archives contain a page, written in calligraphy, entitled *Saddle horse Zarif II*;
Arabian breed, dark-brown mare, 1.55 m, born in 1890, father Zarif and mother Jussuf, both
from the Babolna stud farm (E11c-11b-2).
238  Maison Boissier was a confectioner and chocolate-maker, established in 1827 on the
Boulevard des Capucines in Paris.
239  Countess A.W.A. van Limburg Stirum (1877–1961) was appointed lady-in-waiting to
Queen Wilhelmina on 26 October 1896. She would only remain in the position until after the
investiture in September 1898, because she married Baron Carel A.A.W. van Lynden (1865–
1923) on 24 November 1898.

wonder who will be more agitated she or I? Fryday evening Marie leaves me and miss van Overzee[240] arrives. Poor old Marie is quite brokenhearted about it, I am trying to be specially nice to her these last days. It has been such a comfort having her still during this journey for I did not want to run after her and could rely upon her in all ways & I could alow myself liberties with her & be up to mischief whereas had I had Geeske,[241] I would have had to behave quite sedately. It will interest you to know that mij hair has not yet been dressed but mother is rolling the frunthair up at night to make it curl, for it has grown so long that it would otherwise hang in my eyes. Poor miss van Overzee! how I pitty her that she will have to dress it!

I am coming back with the intention to have the patience of Job for I think it will be <u>most</u> [underlined three times] necessary! With new arrangements, new servants, a new maid, miss van Overzee & new ladies it will be very necessary to be provided with a heap of the virtue one calls "patience". This remains always still a quality which I don't posses! Oh, if I only had that, I would be quite another creature! I am sorry to say I can still be very impatient. It comes quite without my knowing or wishing it for I always try to not get irritable and in principal I never wish to be so, already a progress upon formerly, because I used to try and get tiresome. I had thought that in being grown up the impatience would have vanished, but this is not the case. Now I hope upon coming home that the patience of Job <u>will</u> really come to me.

I have considered travelling as a time of rest & I have heaped up all my sweetness for my people not giving to strangers more than what was absolutely necessary. I mean to make a great effort to display all the best I have in me at the Hague, not only to outsiders and where it is in my power also to really the people, but also to my surroundings & of course in the very most of first of places to my dearest little mother whom I mean to facilitate the task of looking after me and my people.

I hope you will be satisfied with my intentions! If only I carry them out; intentions are all very good, but if they are not carried out, they are worthless. Let us hope the best.

And now Darling, that I have written to you what is & has been going on in my own private life, I think it will be your turn to tell me what is going on inside you and your little home. Don't think I will find it annoying for I am just

---

240 According to the registers of the Marshal of the Court, Mary Adelaide van Overzee (1860–1925) entered royal service on 11 December 1896 as lady-of-the-bedchamber to Queen Wilhelmina (E10-IVb-19). According to Fasseur 1998, p. 186, she was appointed as lectrice (but this was not until 1898!), a position lying between that of a lady-in-waiting and a chamber-maid. She became the second wife of Van Steijn, Comptroller General of the Het Loo Royal Palace and Estate; see letter 25, note 35.

241 Over time, Geeske, the daughter of Mr Peters, head gamekeeper to King Willem III, regularly sent photos of Queen Wilhelmina and her family to Miss Winter, after the latter had ceased to be governess to the queen. Queen Wilhelmina's affection for Geeske is revealed a few letters later on, starting with letter 240 (18 June 1899) and letter 248 (15 July 1900).

as interested in what you are doing on the otherside of the Channel as I was in the happy times when we could still talk & be together. I have a just as great yearning to know what is going through your dear mind as you showed a few weeks ago to know what I was thinking about.

I won't write before getting home any more and before having seen both my new horse and people; I will then be able to tell you about them. How is the dear old knee keeping?

With heaps of hugs & love, Darling, I will always remain your most affectionnately devoted

Wilhelmina

Palace, 's Gravenhage
December 13 1896

**142**    Dearest Darling,

Thank you very much for your dear, sweet, long letter & parcel. I am so pleased with the brushes; they are just what I wanted & the dear little box & pan of blue paint! How sweet Darling of you to have thought of that too. Please send the account of all three things. You poor Darling, I wish I <u>could</u> cure the dear hearty! It seems so strange to be back here and not to see your darling old face about here; but what I <u>do</u> notice every day a fresh again, that is all your loving care; every day I find new proofs of all the thought you devoted to my things and the way you had imagined every thing to make things easy for me to find upon returning here, you have thought of every little detail. And now Darling, I am amidst all my new little world which I have to help mother to keep going! But I won't begin with the end, but with the beginning.

The last few days at Pallanza the weather was splendid. The day before leaving we made a trip on the water and went to "Isola Bella", an island onwhich a Palazzo is situated, very known for its floors, which are inlaid, its immense rooms, its beautiful furniture, its collection of glas and china and its fine garden and terraces. It belongs to the family Boromée.[242] The gardens were lovely; they produce quite tropical plants, like tea, kamfer, magnolia's, ect. We visited still another island where the vegetation was still more elaborate.

You may imagine how happy I was to start the next day for home, my own sweet home with all my people. I never yet had slept <u>so</u> well in the train. Upon arriving here I had first my bath and then I received Miss van Stirum; the interview went of quite well. She has a very nice manner about her and I hope to soon get accustumed to her, for that is the great thing. That day I felt very agitated. Friday I got up with a headache which however past off soon enough. But it prevented me from riding Zarif, a thing that disappointed me very much for after she had been shown to me I wanted to get soon on her back. I find

---

242  The Borromeo family had owned a group of islands in Lake Maggiore, the Borromean Islands, since the 12th century. Isola Bella and Isola Madre were transformed into pleasure gardens in the 17th century.

her a perfect darling; she steps so very prettily and is so soft, she is really the sweetest animal I ever saw. Friday I had my first sewing lesson. It went off perfectly although both miss Wichers[243] and I were rather "benauwd [anxious]". That evening I said goodbey to Marie; it was very dreadful. I gave her my picture singed a tray & silver teapot, sugarbasin & milkjug, mother made her a present of a black silk gown. Marie has been very very good till the last, for she has behaved perfectly in clearing up and unpacking every thing just as tidily as always; I can't really praise her enough. But the very worst of all things was the interview with miss van Overzee. Now I have got through that, the worst is over. As much as I can judge, she is very handy, most soft and scrupulously tidy and she has a pleasing manner. She has been dressing my hair & I am ageably surprised at finding myself look quite respectable. I seem much taller with the long skirts and I believe if you were to see my headdress you would scarcely recognise my hair, so much I seem now to have, now that it is curled with tongs. Today I went to church. I am trying to be kind to everybody and patient. A thing I don't find so difficult with the new people when they do things I don't care for, but in trying on the new gowns which I am already so sick of for the times. I have seen them are innumerable! Yesterday I gave Miss van Overzee all the money I had in my keeping. I am pretty well occupied. But you must not think Darling, that I have no time to write to you, because I always have a spare moment for a darling old friend; it is to me like talking to you! My first lesson with Professor Krämer[244] in the history of art went off perfectly. Old Smeltings & Hamburg[245] look so funny in their new livery; specially Hamburg looks very sedate and as pleased as punch.

I will send you by the first occasion I get some lace I bought at Venise and which I had thought you could use or down the front of your gown or as a collar on your body. How is your mother keeping. I forgot to say that the cour is going to be held this week, I find it a great joke and will try to look amiable. Now I must <u>really</u> cease, with heaps of hugs and love I remain your most affection- nately of all devoted

Wilhelmina

Palace, 's Gravenhage
December 20 1896,

**143**  Dearest of Darlings,

You don't know how happy your last sweet long letter made me! Thank you a thousand times for everything you tell me about yourself and your own feelings.

243 In the winter of 1896-1897, Miss A. Wichers taught Wilhelmina how to sew linen.
244 Prof. Krämer (see p. 30 note 62).
245 Smelting (see letter 14, note 25). Pieter Hamburg (born January 1839) entered service on 1 January 1870 as a messenger. He became a footman in 1872, was made footman to Queen Sophie on 1 June 1877, and on 1 January 1879 he was appointed chamber servant to Queen Emma. Register of the Marshal of the Court of the Royal Palace/to Her Majesty the Queen, E10a, sect. 11a, Nos 8 and 9.

Poor sweet old Darling! I can so well understand how difficult life must now be for you; I wish, I wish I could make you happy, but with that horrid sea between us, I can impossibly just come over for an hour to comfort you. It is such a pity you had to begin upon coming home to make your mother understand that your sister was to have a change; it was certainly not an agreable beginning; nor for you, nor for your poor dear mother! But if you really get your sister away, I am sure you will have a great satisfaction in having <u>done</u> your <u>duty</u>, for I know you well enough to be able to say on the other side of the sea that <u>that</u> is the thing you aim at in life and you were the happiest when you had done it. I feel so much for you Darling, in the difficult times you are going through, how horrid it must feel & be to have to hold your tongue when you see something you don't find right in the household; I suppose that your mother and sister have lived so long alone that they hate changes and new ideas! Poor Darling, when you run upstairs to forcome difficulties, I suppose you cry it out; could I only come and comfort you! It must be horrid if they don't understand you, I am sure you have to bottle up your grief & that is a thing your nature can't bear. I hope very much you will soon find something to do for then you need not fret so much about your grief, you will have something else to think about. I am also having a difficult time: I find it a great effort to thing of every thing & I am constantly worried that I will forget things, I suppose this is a natural state of affaires which will by & by pass over! My impatience is moderate, I am trying to make life easy for mother, for she has very much to do at present. I am making an effort to remain patient with my people. I don't believe I would attain any thing by being impatient with them. I believe you were quite right in saying one of the last days we were together that I would change very much; I feel I am changing; I have much more experience of life & by being forced to do many things which formerly did not ly upon my way to do, I am less shy to receive and to talk to people. Receiving miss van Stirum and some of the gentlemen alone has done me a great deel of good, for I am much less embarrassed. I dare say things to my people which formerly I would have been too shy to utter and which I must necessarily say. I know also better to "shut up" were it is necessary! I am sure you will find this a very happy thing! I have just got your dear letter; you poor old Darling how dreadful for you that this should have accured just now when you are already having such a trying time! I only hope you will be prudent not to get anything afresh in your finger; but you are certainly in a good keeping, your sister is sure to look after you; if you are only obedient! I think it must be one of the worst things which could happen to you, for you are compelled to sit still and if you had plans about painting it must be dreadful; Oh, I wish I could make you feel how I pity you, you poor, sweet, old Darling! And then not being able to help yourself; you must only not write for it <u>must</u> be bad for the dear old thumb. I will telegraph by & by to get news. The gloves for miss van Ittersum are beautiful, I am so pleased with them; thank you heaps of times that you ordered them. The lampshades have come, but I have not unpacked them yet. Don't trouble to send the bill while your finger

F. (Frits) J. Jansen (1856-1928) tutored Queen Wilhelmina in drawing and painting.

is bad, for Ronger[246] can quite well wait for the money. My "cour" went off all right. I was quite satisfied with my appearance, I wore my emeralds and in the hearts of some of my flowers were sown a few of my new brillants. The whole thing lasted two hours; I looked kindly at the people; there were nearly sevenhundred. I received mothers "dames du palais" alone in my room; it went very well. We have had 2 diners which I found very amusing. In the evenings I have received the wives of the diplomats & of the ministers in my drawing-room; Misses van Hardenbroek[247] was present at both audiences. I look quite otherwise with my hair dressed; it makes me look very important!

I have now riden Zarif; she is such a darling & goes splendidly, I don't think I ever saw such a sweet horse in all my life! Now I am very busy for Xmas; I have much more to do than ever I had during schoolroom life, there are so many little things which somehow take a lot of time to attend to. Both my ladies are taking drawing lessons with me, my first lesson in oils was very amusing. Mr. Jansen[248] said I did'n do it badly for the first time.

Miss van Stirum has begun to read to me "the last of the Barons" by Lytton.[249] I make you responsible that it is a good book & that their do not come disageable parts to read.

I envy you with the earthquake you must have had in England! It must have been very interesting to feel yourself go up and down like on a ship! When your thumb is well again, you must write & tell me all about it. I suppose that will have made your mother so seady. I hope so much she will be getting better now that the earthquake is out of the air! I must really finish now, Darling; hoping that the dear thumb will soon be better, I remain with heaps & heaps of love, your most affectionnately & most devoted

Wilhelmina

246  The identity of Ronger is unclear.
247  Mrs van Hardenbroek: see introduction after telegram 76, note 91.
248  F. (Frits) J. Jansen (1856–1928), assistant director of the Royal Academy of Art The Hague, tutored Queen Wilhelmina in drawing and watercolour painting between the autumn of 1890 and the beginning of 1896, and between 1897 and the beginning of 1898. He also gave her instruction in pastel and oil-painting techniques.
249  *The Last of the Barons* is a historical novel published in 1843 by the English writer Edward Bulwer-Lytton (1803–1873). The plot is about the power struggle between the English king Edward IV (1442–1483) and his powerful minister, the Earl of Warwick (1428–1471).

Letter from Emma to Miss Winter:

The Hague 22<sup>d</sup> of Dec 1896

**144**  Dear Miss Winter!

Although I am in one perpetual rush I cannot let Christmas come without sending you a few words to assure you that my thoughts are with you & my very best wishes. I understand & feel that these days must be very trying for you, the happiness merriness & cheerfulness all round you must make you feel doutly sad. I hope you will have such services as can give you comfort & help you & give you the feeling of peace. I am <u>so</u> sorry that you have injured your finger. What an extra trial for you!

I have sent you a little Xmas present. I hope you will like the basket & use it for breakfast & afternoon tea when you have visitors. The little box was to be sent to you from London on the 21 or 22 I think, but you are not to unpack it quite till Christmaseve. We are getting on very well; we are both <u>very</u> occupied just now. I must say goodbye dear miss Winter. God help you.

Yours very affectionate                                     Emma

PALAIS LA HAYE<br/>December 23 1896

**145**  My most dearest Darling,

Although I am sending you a card, I must just write you a few words to wish you a very happy Xmas. You will have sad recollections about Xmas eves spent with us & so much thought & preparations for the 24<sup>th</sup>, Darling. I so much wanted to

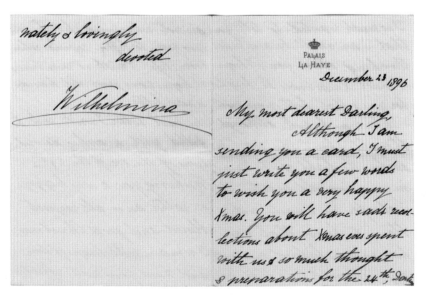

With this letter featuring the crowned monogram of 'PALAIS LA HAYE' (Noordeinde Palace), Wilhelmina wished Miss Winter a happy Christmas; the first Christmas that she was no longer in the service of Queen Emma, December 23 1896.

tell you that I am & will be very much thinking about you; I hope so much Xmas may be bright for you & that both your mother & sister may be well although thoughts about the past may darken the light of the Xmastree in your poor old hearty. It is also for me nasty wide blanc to know that you have no more helped me with my preparations & that you are not returning shortly after New Year to begin regular schoolroom life; I wish it were true! I hope your poor old handy is now better!

The next letter I write will be filled with graphic describtions of the eve of the 24th.

Wishing you a very happy, or rather an in all respects blessed and good Christmas, I remain with heaps of love and kisses, your most affectionately & lovingly devoted

Wilhelmina

December 27 1896

146 My very dearest Darling,

Thank you heaps of times for your sweet card and dear letter. You don't know how pretty I find the card, I find it very artistic & so softy washed in! The bouquet is so nicely composed & the colours are chosen so softly. You can't imagine what pleasure you gave me! We passed a happy evening: I got as usual heaps of pretty things: a table & cupboard for the Loo, a tablecloth, a floorlamp, a bronze I admired very much at Milan, a diadem with emeralds,[250] a silver matchbox & candlestick, a jeweltray & some statuettes, a fan from my aunt Sophy[251] & from aunt Helen[252] a powderbox. Mother gave me just the same marble statuette as I gave her & we gave eachother the same sort of cloth; the only difference was that I had destined mine for mothers bed & she hers for a table in my sitting room. My work got ready in time & looks very nice. I have had it mounted with a quilted dark green satin & finished off with a fringe & scallops of the same cloth as the work. I gave mother two glas chandeliers for Soestdijk which unluckily arrived too late, a ornamented lookingglas for hanging up, a vase with a pedestal[253] also for Soestdijk, two vases for the toilettable, a

250 A47a-III-2: Petty cash books of Queen Emma: *Weihnachten*, p. 161: 'Diamond and emerald diadem, Schürmann'. At the end of the 19th century, court jeweller Schürmann was established on Rossmarkt 11 in Frankfurt, under the name 'Fabrik & Handlung in Gold und Silberwaaren'. He supplied the courts of the Netherlands and Luxembourg (Brus, p. 147). This diadem is still worn. It was originally smaller, but for her silver wedding celebrations in 1926, Queen Emma gave Wilhelmina stones from a so-called 'devant de corsage', part of the Waldeck family jewels, to extend the diadem at the sides. The pear-shaped emeralds have nowadays been replaced with pear-shaped pearls, according to M. Loonstra, former curator of the Royal Archives.
251 Grand Duchess Sophie of Saxe-Weimar, Princess of the Netherlands; see p. 26, note 51.
252 Aunt Helena, Emma's younger sister; see letter 109, note 143.
253 This could be the white porcelain vase with a brown-patterned base that was found in the attics of Soestdijk Palace after the death of Princess Juliana. The vase is now at Het Loo. As suggested by M. Loonstra, former curator of the Royal Archives.

glas & gold toiletservice for Soestdijk and then the lampshades which succeeded very well thanks to you. The one was pink, the other strawcolour. We had quite little children this year, they were very merry & enjoyed themselves famously; we romped as always & I found myself not too old to take part in the blindmansbuf. It was a great pity that miss Rengers could n' be there too; she has not been well lately and the cough she always had, has been getting worse travelling so that your dear doctor Coert sent her to bed last Wednesday; she has been in her room eversince. I find it a great pity for I get on with her the best & I talk more openly with her than with my quite new surroundings. But talking about sick people, I have quite forgotten to ask you how the poor old knee & finger is, never the less your news about your cycling interested me very much, how do the brused & poisoned parts of you feel? I was quite touched about the trouble you took, Darling, to look up the parts of "the last of the barons" which I had better not let miss van Stirum read alout; you are a sweet to had given it up in books & chapters. You need never for an instant be affraid that I will get so perfect that you won't be able to recognise me, for there always remain many little failings which make me recognisable. I still find it difficult to accustome myself to being with young people, I always still prefer & feel more at home with older people. I fall back with pleasure upon mothers people, supposing miss van Ittersum. We went to the "Groote Kerk"[254] on Xmasday & to day to the "Klooster Kerk".[255] Xmasday M^r v.d. Flier preached & to day I heard a new clergyman called M^r Kramer who has a great power of speach & preaches very pretty sermons. Could you go to church with your bad knee?

   I think I will be very busy next week; all the new year & "ball gala" preparations take lots of time. With heaps of love, sweetest Darling, I remain your most affectionnately devoted

Wilhelmina

P.S. I have made a beginning for the calender but I don't know if I will have time to finish it.

PALAIS LA HAYE
December 30 1896

147   My very dearest Darling,
   I wish you a <u>very</u> <u>very</u> happy & blessed New Year & I hope that 1897 will really bring great happiness into your life. Our bond of friendship is such that at a trying moment like the ending & beginning of a year we know exactly of eachother what our feelings are — few words are necessary to explain them.

254  The Grote- of St. Jacobskerk in The Hague, used for Catholic worship until 1566, was built in its current form, typical of The Hague, in the 15th and 16th centuries. The marriages and baptisms of the House of Orange were and still are held in the church, including the marriages of Queen Wilhelmina (1901), Princess Juliana (1937) and Princess Margriet (1967) and the baptism of Princess Amalia (2004).
255  The Kloosterkerk on the corner of Parkstraat/Lange Voorhout was originally the church of the Dominican monastery. It dates from 1400, with later additions from around 1500.

You know how I wish that there would come happiness into your dear life & how I should bless the moment inwhich it might be given to me to contribute to your happiness for I think it is the worst trial to <u>know</u> that some body you love is going through a difficult time & not be able to do any thing than hope for them that it may pass. I wish, I wish you would be happy, I wish their might come some great happiness in your life which would make you bear more easily ifnot quite forget all the great grief which you have had in this year. Would that '97 might be the year in which that happiness might come to you! But let us hope; when one is beginning a new year it is so good & only right to hope; for '97 has not yet given us grievous disappointments! Poor old Darling the year we are ending has been most sad & trying for us both: a nasty parting to which we had to look up to, but now it is all over, the whole time of our comfortable life together belongs alass to the past, but the recollection of those years is a most happy one & I hope it will be always made happier also in this year by our meeting again. How much we have to tell & although that both I & circomstances will be changed, our love will never change — your pupil will have grown to be your friend, I will be still more able to understand & appreciate you, now that I have learned what it is to without my old "Darling"! Thank you so much for your dear letter; how dreadful that the poor old thumb is not getting better, does your sister attend to it properly? I hope so much that your mother will be well! How is your knee? I will adress this letter to Walden for I suppose you will be home again by the 31. I am sending you two cards, one I painted myself; as I was rather afraid you may not know what it represents, I have written it underneath! Excuse for my long sermon at the beginning of my letter, but at the end of the year I always feel rather sermony!

With dearest love, I always remain your most affectionately devoted

Wilhelmina

The Hague Dec the 30th 1896

**148** Dear Miss Winter!

I cannot let this year go to end & the new one begin without sending you a few words even if they must again be written in a hurry.

My thoughts are with you very much. You must feel so sad just now, looking back on the year that has brought you such trouble & pain & not having anything to look forward to just now. I hope your faith in Gods love and "getrouwheid [fidelity]" will help you to begin the new year with courage. I send you my <u>very</u> best wishes for the new year, I hope sincerely you will get over the acute pain of the separation from my child & that there is happiness in store for you still. — I thank you very much for your letter, I am so glad that you were pleased with my present & that my letter gave you pleasure, I am very distressed to hear that your thumb is not right yet. I am still very occupied. Wilhelmina also. Today we had audiences 5 ministers (diplomates) a "beediging [swearing-in]". Wilh. dancing lesson trying on & trying hairdress for the 2d. These things are very trying for her.

She is for <u>her</u> very patient. She has a cold just now, but she is quite well with it & looks well. She was very happy on Xmas eve I must close the letter.

With many many most sincere good wishes I remain dear Miss Winter
Your affectionate

Emma

Letter from Miss Saxton Winter to Queen Wilhelmina:[256]

York House, Kensington.W.
December 31. 96

**149**    My most darling Queen

Your dear letter as usual gave me keen pleasure, but before commenting upon that, I wish to tell you how full of thought I am for you, on this New Year's Eve. Oh! my sweet one, if love & good wishes can crown the New Year with happiness for you — be assured that it will be like a glorious sun light! Shadows must necessarily come where bright light is — but you are so full of good intentions & brave efforts, that the end <u>must</u> be a grand & satisfactory result! God bless you sweet darling & crown your efforts with success & surround your life with the love of truly devoted people. I hope that the <u>most</u> difficult time is already over for you and that before the year gets very old, you will be comfortably settled down into all the new arrangements & surroundings.

You will see I am in London, but it is uncertain when I return home — I wised to go today — but my kind friends have made me in any event promise to remain till the end of the week — I scarcely think I shall stay longer — I am <u>very</u> glad dearie the card pleased you, but you are <u>too</u> flattering in all the generous praise you gave it. I was personally most dissatisfied, though realizing <u>some</u> of the washing was rather well done — but my thumb was such a hindrance all the time!

You have indeed had a lot of lovely presents dearie! & what a delightful time you must have had with all the small children!

My knee is much less stiff, thank you sweetie but the joint seems to have got into a way of easely rolling about — for 2 days ago in stepping into the carriage it quite gave way again & the horrid sensation makes one feel as sick as a dog! By the bye, have you ever had your <u>new</u> dog, for you have never mentioned it? The thumb is <u>at last</u> beginning to get a little better — I am still rather helpless in fastening things etc & I cant do any sewing — but the maids here are all so kind & anxious to give me any help they can. I have been seeing <u>such</u> a lot of pictures, and enjoyed some of them immensely — A collection of Tissot[257] a French artist, is making a great sensation here just now — All scenes painted by

256 A50-VIIc-S-02 Archive of Queen Wilhelmina, Letters from Miss Saxton Winter.
257 James (Jacques-Joseph) Tissot (1836–1902) was an Anglo-French artist who trained in Paris and established himself in London, where his painting and etchings proved popular. In the later years of his life, he made three trips to Palestine and painted many scenes from the Bible. Between 1896 and 1897, three books of his sketches of scenes from the New Testament were published. These drawings were exhibited in England, France and the United States.

him in the Holy land, where he travelled for 10 years — mostly illustrating scenes or incidents in the life of Christ — They are all watercolours — on a very small scale but the wonderful working up of groups and scenery are astonishing — his stone work, pillars, & floors make me think very much of Bosboom's[258] work, & he often has those same shades of warm brown — I have also been 2 or 3 times to the theatre & that you know is always a <u>great</u> treat to me — London just now is very full and every street & gallery, to say nothing of the shops, seem crowded! The weather today has been more like spring — I am sending you, according to the old custom — a calendar for your room if you can manage to find a place to hang it! I often wonder what changes have been made to the "studio" and if any more "artistic" draperies & so on, have been placed on the wall?-

Do you remember you dear, how excited you were to arrange it all on that particular Sunday? or was it Saterday? I shall be thinking <u>all</u> the time of you darling on Saterday evening. I hope you may find the people's hearts to you more than ever, by a loving, tender graciousness — that you may also extract <u>some</u> pleasure out of the evening. I am wondering if you will <u>dance</u> & if so, if Madame Dupres[259] has been to coach you up a little bit beforehand?-

My thumb warns me that I must end — ever sweet darling — your very most lovingly devoted

E. Saxton Winter

# 1897

Forty-nine long letters date from 1897, fourteen of which were written on black-edged mourning paper due to the death of Sophie, Grand Duchess of Saxe-Weimar and Princess of the Netherlands.

PALAIS LA HAYE<br>January 3 1897

**150**   Most darling Deary,

Thank you so much for your pretty calendar & sweet letter & loving wishes. How very pretty the words & the pictures on the calender are — I'm so pleased with it. How dreadful, Darling that your knee still gives way! I have not yet got my dog, Mr. de With has it still in his keeping. All you tell me about what you are doing in London interests me very much; how delightful for you to have gone to the theatre. You ask about my studio — I will tell you what I am doing there. I brought home with me a lot of plates to hang up along the wall; some earth-

---

**258**  Johannes Bosboom (1817–1891), a precursor of the Hague School, was renowned for his paintings and watercolours of church interiors.

**259**  For two winters, Madame L. Duprez-Sacré gave Wilhelmina and a few other girls (Pixy de Constant, see letter 51, note 71 and Anna Bentinck, see letter 123, note 171) dance lessons, after Mademoiselle Delphine Mees had rehearsed the court dances in 1892–93.

enware, some also in metal; my simple oaken easel is drown in the middle of that part of the room, both little stools stand before it, one bearing my paintbox, the other covred with an artistic cushion of leather to sit upon; my stick & rag ofcourse ly upon my easel. My model stands on the table with a bit of plush behind it. Materials I did not by any more, but pots & pans, some of which are quite artistic. I also bought basrelief-heads of the great Italian masters, like Raffael,[260] Leonardo da Vinci, Michelangelo, Titian[261] & Dante. My studio is just beginning to look like it ought to.

I have had three lessons in oilpainting, ofcourse I find it very interesting, yesterday I began to paint an old kettel I got at Aix in oils without M$^r$ Jansen[262], I find it most amusing.

As usual I dreaded my reception of the 1$^{st}$ very much; I got afterwards a lot of praise that I had done it well, so I had the satisfaction one was pleased with me. You guessed rightly — I had M$^{sse}$ Dupree[263] over to dance the rounddances with me. The 2$^d$ a grand repetition was held for the quadrilles under the upper command of M$^r$ van Stirum.[264] The ball began at eight o'clock & ended at 11 o'clock. I found it before hand very "benauwd [oppressive]". Just before the ball Mother & I received M$^{rss}$ Howard.[265]

Upon entering the first drawingroom I thought my knees would give way in under me, so embarrassed was I, but soon it passed all over & I did 'n even notice all the people round me. It is a dreadful moment coming in those two drawing rooms crowded with people which you have nearly all to talk to; the circle went very well. The people seemed to nearly stare their eyes out of their heads, so they wanted to absorbe in my little person. After having jibberjab-bered to the gests in the two red rooms, we marched upon music all along people up the whole large ball room & sate down in state to see the first dance, which was 'n very animated. Miss van Stirum opened the ball with M$^r$ van Stirum. The view on the room was quite fairy like, the gowns of the ladies & the gold of the gentlemen made a very good effect together. The first dance over, the ladies were presented to me sup. Piksy de Constant.[266] It was delightful to meet my old playfellow out in society. Then a few officers were introduced & later some civile gentlemen. Then came one of the great moments for me — the quadrille. My cavalier, M$^r$ de Struve[267] (the Russian ambassador) came &

260 Raphael (see letter 138, note 224), Leonardo da Vinci (see letter 138, note 221) and Michel-angelo (see letter 138, note 224).

261 Titian (see letter 139, note 234) and Dante Alighieri (1265–1321), one of the world's greatest poets and author of the *Divina Commedia* [Divine Comedy].

262 F.'Frits' J. Jansen (see letter 143, note 248). The location of this painting is not known.

263 L. Duprez (See letter 149, note 337).

264 This is probably chamberlain Count E.L. van Limburg Stirum, who was appointed acting chamberlain on 9 December 1893.

265 Mrs Howard was the wife of Mr H. Howard, who had been envoy extraordinary and minister plenipotentiary for Great Britain and Ireland since 27 October 1896.

266 Pixy de Constant Rebeque (see letter 51, note 71).

267 Mr de Struve (see letter 121, note 166).

fetched me from my chair & brought me to my place in the quadrille. It went very well; M^r van Stirum stood on the opposite of the room to make me signs if I forgot a figure. Between the two cadrils I went alone, M^rss van Hardenbroek & the gentlemen following me, where I pleased having now a then people called to talk to & talking to everybody I knew & happened to meet on my walks through the rooms. I stood, talked & did 'n eat the whole three hours & was not tired after it.

I had a substancial meal in my own room afterward.

My cavalier for the 2^d cadrille was my general Dumonceau.[268] I delighted to have him & so was he. This dance went perfectly & was <u>most</u> amusing. I had heaps of praise.[269] Ofcourse from Mother & both she & I heard from many sides that the people found I behaved very nicely. I really <u>did n'</u> feel ambarrassed; I felt myself that I was smiling all the time & the people were satisfied with very little: my saying only good evening or bowing to them was quite enough to make their face light up & grin all over.

I felt so free & independent & soon forgot all the people around me when speeking to some of them. I wore as dress my Paris gown with marguerites & all my new brillants some in a zigsag row in front of my bodace, some on my sleaves & round the back whilst I wore my finest stones upon my head as diadem.[270] Miss van Overzee had done my headdress <u>very</u> well.

The weather here has also been very mild but just yesterday it has begun to freeze.

Just fancy, I had such a fright upon the first: Mother had take a little cold, nothing very much, & her whole voice had gone; she could not talk scarcely, what an awful thing for the ball. The doctor luckily gave her back her voice, but she still feels shaky.

With dearest love, Darling, I remain your most affectionnately devoted

Wilhelmina

PALAIS LA HAYE
January 10 1897

**151**  Dearest of Darlings,

Thank you so much for your two sweet letters. But before I begin to write about those, I must thank you in mother's name for the letter you wrote her; she is very very sorry that you had such a trouble with your luggage, M^rs Kreusler[271] will send you the money. And now, Darling I must thank you again & again for your sweet confiding way of writing to me; you don't know how happy you made me by telling me about all your feelings, I feel very flattered that you talk

---

268  Generaal Dumonceau (see intro after letter 52, note 73).
269  Cleverens 1994, p. 107. Lady van de Poll wrote: '(...) that, too, she did in the most enchanting and gracious fashion.'
270  Cleverens 1994, p. 107. Lady van de Poll wrote to her mother on 4 January 1897: '(...) a diamond diadem and diamonds, or rather brilliants, sewn on the bodice, with the neck bare.'
271  Mrs Mathilde Kreusler (see telegram 60, note 81).

openly to me, you a person old enough to be my mother; I wish I were a worthier confident! You povrest of Darlings, it must be horrid to feel such a "wretch" as you call yourself. I suppose such times come in every body's life someday & I know I have also gone through them, just remember last Xmas!! But I hope & I am also sure they will pass off, they can't last long! I can understand what an effort it must cost you to bottle up all your feelings & I all the same don't quite see what you can do otherwise.

It must be dreadful to not confide in anybody! But you must be full of hope: it is only right we should hope at the beginning of the year. I must also say there moments in which I despair & I then feel the weight of my responsabilities too heavy for me & then I go & have it out alone & forget all around me & feel that it is a comfort that I need not depend upon myself but that there is a Power which can support me if I only alow myself to be supported. Only don't think that I am not getting on well, for if what I have just said gave you that impression, it is quite wrong one; for everybody is trying their best & making things very easy; I would be a wretch if I were not satisfied. I have only said this to comfort you & to show you that I also, although I have a much easier life than you, find sometimes difficulty to keep straight. Don't either think I am growing goody-goody, but you see I am getting older & ought not to be affraid of showing my feelings & your letter made me feel so sad for your sake. I feel very incapable of fulfilling my task for I must stand as firm as a rock if I wish to work upon others for the good & there are so many little ways open to me to do good if I only look out for them. I heared this morning a lovely sermon upon what a christian ought to be & I felt how very much too little I did for my fellow people, but I must really stop this subject otherwise you will think I have changed into a professional preacher!!!

How is your mother, has she really one of her bad attacks? I am glad hear your knee & thumb are getting better — it must be a troublesome time till your nail grows over!

I hear you are going to Liverpool, when are you starting? Mother is now nearly better from her cold, I believe she must have had a little influenza.

Last Wednesday I went to the theatre & saw "Gijsbrecht van Aemstel"[272] acted, you know that is the renowned piece of Vondel. It was acted very well for the verses which otherwise are very annoying, did n't seem uninteresting or long & I got quite enthusiastic about the beautiful language & the patriotism Vondel

---

272 The tragedy *De Gijsbrecht van Aemstel* was written in 1637 by Joost van den Vondel (1587–1679). The play was premiered on 3 January 1638, on the occasion of the opening of the first stone-built theatre on the Keizersgracht (canal) in Amsterdam. The play is set on Christmas Night in c. 1300, and concerns the siege of Amsterdam by the surrounding villages, due to Gijsbrecht's suspected involvement in the murder of Floris V (1254–1296) in 1296. There are parallels between the play and Virgil's Aeneas: Amsterdam is Troy, a direct link to the classics. The play also recalls the Eighty Years' War with Spain. The plundering of the Catholic churches is reminiscent of the iconoclastic fury of the 16th century. The siege of Amsterdam resembles the siege of Leiden by the Spanish. (Programme from 'Het toneel speelt', *Gijsbrecht van Amstel van Joost van den Vondel*, January 2012.)

makes his hero show. I am now painting as much as I can & find it delightful. The professors have taken upon themselves to take holidays for both prof. Krämer & prof. Blok[273] have been ill, but now they have begun regular work. I have lately received many audiences; yesterday I had Piksy de Constant, Anna Bentinck & Mrss van Pallandt (Irma van Hardenbroek),[274] all between 4 & 6½ o'clock. I have not yet been able to skate, although it has been freezing lately. Yesterday it was so slippery that one could scarcely walk. The roads were covered with ice. Thank you very much for sending me the accounts, I will have them payed.

  With dearest love & hugs, I always will remain your most truly & affectionnately devoted

Wilhelmina

PALAIS LA HAYE<br>January 17 1897

**152**   Dearest of Darlings,

I am only addressing my letter to Liverpool as I hear from mother that you are staying there with your brother. I hope, Darling, that you will like your stay there & be able to go often to picture-galleries & to the theatre, for I am sure that will freshen you up a little, a thing that is very good for you after all you have been going through at present with your knee & your thumb. I have also heard that you poor mother has again had one of her bad attacks, how is she now? Has she allowed you to do little things for her, or would n't she have any body than your sister help her, if so, I am afraid you will have a sad time of it, poor old Darling!

  Is the old thumb & knee quite well now?

  I have had a very exciting week, for I have been twice at a concert & have been at the ball of the Cassino.[275] The first concert was Tuesday; I heard a quartet[276] from Amsterdam which sang without accompaniment; it was beautiful, I think I never heard any thing so lovely; they sang so well together & they had chosen

---

273  The Leiden-based Professor P.J. Blok (1855-1929) taught Dutch history from the end of 1894 until the end of 1897.

274  All three were old friends of Queen Wilhelmina. Pixy, see letter 51, note 71; Anna, see letter 123, note 171; Irma, see letter 122, note 167.

275  By 'Cassino', Wilhelmina means the Casino in the Oude Doelen, where the Casino ball was held on 15 January 1897.

276  On 12 January 1897 Wilhelmina and her mother attended a concert in the Gebouw van Kunsten & Wetenschappen (GK&W) concert hall given by the Amsterdams Vocaal Kwartet, composed of the soprano Aaltje Noordewier-Reddingius (1868-1949), the alto Catharina (Cato) Loman (1866-1951), the tenor Johannes J. Rogmans (1852-1911) and the bass Johan M. Messchaert (1857-1922), who founded the quartet in 1896. Partly thanks to their performance, there was greater appreciation of Dutch singing and the Netherlands became a player in the international music world. The quartet did not last for very long. Aside from Cato Loman, the other three sang during the investiture of Queen Wilhelmina in the elite choir led by Willem Mengelberg (1871-1951).

half religious & half wordly music. One of the ladies you heard once for a repetition in the palace, you remember we agreed she resembled a little miss de Vries!! The second concert was Wednesday & was one of Diligentia. One of your compatriots mrs. Davies[277] sang. He had a very fine voice but made such grimaces in singing & before beginning he made eyes at the audience, a thing I did not approve of. Friday was the day of the Cassino. I went for about an hour & wore my chiffon gown with pink roses from Paris & my rubies; in my hair I had had stuck a few roses with some of my brillants sewn in.[278] I danced one quadrille with mrs. van Amerongen with the beard.[279]

They have such pretty rooms at the old "Doelen"! I tried to be very polite to the people & put on my sweetest smile — I hope I succeed! Yesterday it froze so hard that I thought I would nearly be able to skate. I have lately taken the bad habit of taking easily headaches, I don't think you would find them very bad, but for me are horrid. The last three days however I have no more had them.

By the by, how is your poor dear old noddle? I shewed the card you painted for me to mrs. Jansen[280] who found you had done it very very well, he specially admired your light primroses.

I shall have an exciting day to morrow for having finished Asia, prof. Kan will have a large repetition before beginning with our archipelligo. As he has n't had time to go over all the states in detail with me, he has done it only with the most important. China, Japan, British India & Siberia were gone through very carefully. Ofcourse British India interested me very much. I also have to morrow the dinner of the diplomats, a thing I am looking forward to very much.

Now I think, Darling, I have told you every thing interesting which has happened & which I know is going to happen. I must therefore end!

With my most dearest love & hugs I shall always remain your most devoted & affectionnately loving

Wilhelmina

277  Wilhelmina writes 'Mrs' here instead of 'Mr' Davies, who sang at Diligentia (a learned society) on 13 January 1897.
278  Cleverens 1994, p. 108. On 26 January 1897, Lady van de Poll wrote to her mother: '... the Queen looked most enchanting and wore a very elegant ballgown: white satin underskirts, over which she wore a white gauze dress embroidered with a parsemé of small pink rosebuds. The bottom of the skirt was trimmed with a scallop-shaped festoon of tiny little pink roses, with the same little roses on the bodice and in her hair. Her Majesty danced only the quadrille, in which I also had the honour of taking part.'
279  This is acting chamberlain Baron H.W.M.J.E. Taets van Amerongen. Wilhelmina put 'Mrs' in front of his name instead of 'Mr'.
280  Mr Jansen, see letter 143, note 248. Wilhelmina mistakenly wrote 'Mrs' here instead of 'Mr' Jansen.

**153**     My very dearest Darling,

Thank you so very much for your dear long letter. You poor old Darling, how
I pity you with your fall! You are an unlucky old sweety to come down again —
I hope it was not so bad as at the Loo although you must have come down hard
to have knocked your front teeth half out of your mouth! Poor old Dear & just
now with the ice!

I have skated since last Friday & the ice is getting much better, in the beginning
it was so soft & it cracked very frequently! I am now beginning to get on better
but the first day I felt a misery & could not go alone. You are really dreadful —
there I believe you are going to kill yourself with that bicycle of yours — what
ever good can it do you to go flying about on that machine — if you go on like
that I will get quite angry with you — I am sure it can't be good for your knee —
do listen to me & leave that exercise! Mother and I approve much more of your
idea of going out in future with a stick — for then you can't come to grief.

How amusing for you Darling to have three boys stopping with you at your
brothers!

I suppose you are always playing with them — I am not astonished that they
are frightened at your big eyes!!!!!! How is your mother keeping?

My dinner went off quite well & I as usual tried my best to be polite. Miss
Rengers has since last Tuesday taken up her usual duty, she may only not fatigue
herself to much & is forbidden to drive out in a bitter Eastwind. Of course I am
delighted she is now duing her duty again. During her illness mothers ladies
have frequently been out with me. You will perhaps have read in the paper that
Mother has named me two "dames du Palais" the countess of Knobelsdorff[281] &
M[rs] van Loon Egidius[282] — the latter living in Amsterdam. I think I have not yet
told you what a dreadful thing has happened to old M[rs] van Nagel — just fancy
she was paying a visit at Haarlem to somebody & had a fit! The doctors think she
will remain speechless for the rest of her life. She is completely paralysed on one
side! Just think how dreadful not to be able to talk for the whole of your life — it
would not do for you or for me — I don't think I could live without speaking.

Auntie Lily is coming next Friday — I am madly delighted, it will be such a
joke to see her dancing. Tomorrow there is going to be the dinner given to the
military men.[283] Last monday[284] I wore my blue Paris gown with white stripes &
my pearl-broches & three strings of pearls round my neck. My pearls have been
restrung so as to be able to wear three strings at a time with a larger fastening.

281  On 22 January 1897, Baroness A.J.H. van Knobelsdorff-Baroness van Pallandt (1838–1912),
was made Dame du Palais to Queen Wilhelmina.
282  On 22 January 1897, Mrs Thora N. van Loon-Egidius (1865–1945) was also made Dame du
Palais to Queen Wilhelmina.
283  This took place on Monday 25 January in the Gallery of Noordeinde Palace.
284  On Monday 18 January 1897 there was also a dinner in the Gallery, at which Queen
Wilhelmina wore one of the three dresses that she had ordered from Niceaud in Paris.

Friday I went to the theatre & heard "Inkwartiering [billeting]"[285] a very amusing piece — I thought I would have been quite ill from laughter. You know that "inkwartieren [billeting]" means when there are manoeuvres the men & officers have to be lodged in different houses generally in those of the rich people of the neighbourhood, that is called "inkwartieren [billeting]." Every thing is made funny & all the same the whole thing remains so very proper & refined. I am reading through with miss van Stirum "the last of the barons" & am going to leave only out the chapter you indicated.

Hoping all your poor old bones are getting better, I remain with love & hugs, your most affectionnately devoted

Wilhelmina

PALAIS LA HAYE
January 31 1897

**154** Dearest of Darlings,

You don't know how often I have been asking myself how you are keeping & if your poor old knee & other bruised parts are getting better. How is your mother — is she still so bad? I wonder if you have been able after all to skate?

I have no more skated since last Sunday, but just to day it has been freezing so I hope the ice will soon be strong. I am only afraid that it will not be very good for the lot of snow we have been having during this week, coming on the thawing ice & now freezing upon it, won't have improved it!!!

I have been sledging three times, a thing I found very amusing. [Colour plate IV-6] Just fancy dreadful auntie Lily has not yet come for she is in bed with a cold at Arolsen, don't you find that <u>too</u> [underlined four times] bad? She might have really done this a little earlier! My military dinner ofcourse went off all right, I wore the same gown I wore for the cour -- you know the white one of Haefely[286] with my brillants. I went to a Diligentia concert last Wednesday & heard a very renowned pianist & a lady who had not a sympathetic voice in singing.[287] They played such classical music that I could n't at all understand it — the tragical consequence was that I almost fell asleep!! Friday I went to the

285 The comedy 'Inkwartiering [billeting]' was written by Gustav von Moser (1825-1903) and Franz von Schönthan (1849-1913). Although all the catalogues state that it was premiered in 1890, it had been staged before it was published in print.

286 According to Ietse Meij, this should be spelled 'Haesely', although 'Haefeli' is written on the invoice of January 1897, and Wilhelmina also writes 'Haefeli' clearly in her letter (see Meij, pp. 72-73, with the invoice, image 60). A total of 1,406 guilders was paid for clothing supplied in September, October and November 1896, including a gown of watered silk for 325 guilders and a 'toilette blanche' for 250 guilders in November.

287 Wilhelmina and Emma attended the fifth concert at the Diligentia society on Wednesday 27 January 1897. Having entered the hall after the performance of the Symphony in E-flat major by W.A. Mozart, they listened to the soloists Miss Blanc of Paris (voice) and Mr Busoni of Berlin (piano). *Algemeen Handelsblad*, 28 January 1897. Ferrucio Busoni (1866-1924), born in Italy and the son of celebrated pianist, was a child prodigy and already a virtuoso on the piano by the age of seven. Also a composer and a conductor, he later lived in Berlin.

theatre & saw "Om de kroon [For the crown]", a tragedy translated from the French which is written by Coppé.[288] We saw the four first acts & I did not cry but I took good care not to look at the worst moment when the hero kills his father to save his country — I am always very excited when I come home — still much more than when I have read an interesting book. It will interest you to know that I wear little things in my hair now also for small occasions — generally my emerald butterfly or my too little flys in brillants! Saterday we had the old gentlemen of the "Voogdij Raad [Council of Guardians]"[289] for dinner — as usual their manners were none — M<sup>r</sup> Six did not ask about you to my great consternation!!!!!!

I received this week my two dames du Palais — a thing I half found amusing & half "benauwd [stressful]"!!!!!!

I wonder if you are painting very much? I always still have a lot of ambition — I am now beginning to paint in my free time a joke with two copper pots which I bought at Venice.[290] Yesterday I went to Pulchri Studio & saw some very good oilpaintings & many most remarkable. One of Israels[291] representing a woman walking on the heather at moonlight — the whole thing looked as black as ink & he asks only 12500 glds. for it — only a very mall sum !!!!! There were some pictures where you could see that the artist had painted with his knife & thumb & some which could not have been distinguished from a Japaneeze screen!

I am working hard at our India both with Prof. Kan & from a book which I read & make notes about in my free time — it is hard work — but very interesting. Prof. Blok is now coming to a very exciting time in history: the revolution of 1795. I am asking him every moment all sorts of questions & discussing heaps of things. I have been wondering how the poor old hearty has been keeping lately & if it still feels so for- lorn! You poor old Darling! I think here things are going well — ofcourse I am sometimes impatient but on the whole I try to make things easy.

Now I think I must finish! With hugs & heaps of love, Darling, I will always remain your most affectionnately devoted

Wilhelmina

---

288  François Coppée (1842–1908) was a French playwright and poet. In 1884 he was elected a member of the Académie Française.

289  The Council of Guardians consisted of the following men: Baron W. van Goldstein van Oldenaller, envoy in London, chair (Oldenaller Nijkerk); Mr J. Röell, Minister of Foreign Affairs; Baron A.N.J.M. van Brienen van de Groote Lindt (Huize Clingendaal Wassenaar), chamberlain to the late King Willem III; Mr J.AE.A. van Panhuys, vice-president of the Council of State; A.J. Swart, former member of the Coucil of State; Baron E.W.J. Six van Oterleek, chair of the Audit Office; J.G. Kist, president of the Supreme Court of the Netherlands; and C. Polis, procurator-general to the Supreme Court of the Netherlands.

290  This work has not been recovered.

291  Jozef Israëls (1824–1911), a student of Jan Adam Kruseman (1804–62) and Jan Willem Pieneman (1779–1853), was one of the best-known painters from the School of The Hague. He also wrote and made etchings and lithographs.

I have just received your dear long letter — you don't know how happy I am to have heard from you, Darling — I was horrified at your description of your knee & bruises.

I will answer in my next letter all you tell & ask me. Thank you heaps of times for your dear telegram. With my dearest love I always remain your most devoted

Wilhelmina

PALAIS LA HAYE
February 7 1897

155  Dearest of Darlings,

You really can not realise how happy you make me with your dear long letters, I get quite enthousiastic in reading them! What a sweet old Darling you are to have read through books which you think would do for me. I am immensely looking forward to my lessons about the administration of our colonies; they are to begin about March but it must depend a little how Professor Kan gets on with our [underlined twice] India. My repitition of Asia went off quite well & your notes proved a great help, you sweet old Darling! My conscience has smitten me very hard for having written you such a long letter about your bycicle — but I am sorry to say — you deserved it fully! How is your knee now — has it got better? How about the teeth; are they better? You poor Darling, what a blow you must have had! It must be a wonderful thing, that expanding machine — is it strech you out? I would [underlined three times] be estonnished to see you quite thin. Your poor dear mother, how dreadful that she has such atacks — I suppose it comes partly from the weather — I wonder if you will still send your sister away if your mother does not like it when she is so ill! My head aches are gone for ever — I don't know any more what it feels like to have a head. You can't imagine in what a state the roads are here! First there was a great layer of snow & ice, then it thawed, then it froze again & then it snowed, then it hailed & rained & then it has been thawing for good. There are sorts of brown icy crusts every where!!!!!!!!

But I walk bravely through it all. I have not been up to anything very interesting just lately: Tuesday we went to the theatre to see "In politiek [In politics]", a comedy translated from the German. The whole thing consists of a young officer who comes to see the daughter of his colonel in private clothes when it has been forbidden for military men to go out in anything but in their uniform[292] — the colonel comes home & the young officer is hidden in a cupboard — afterwards he is found out & punished. The whole thing is very stupid but you can't help laughing. Thursday I rode with 5 of the gentlemen & 2 ladies a caroussel in the ridingschool — it went splendidly & was most amusing. We have had several dinners with the "suite" but that is all. When I think that I look a special beauty

---

292  Wilhelmina has made a mistake here: she meant to write that the officers are only permitted to wear their uniforms when they go out.

on such occasions I have Marie[293] called to come & admire me. She seems to be very happy in her new position & is delighted when I have her called. To morrow we are going to the opera for the first time this winter. The "Nederland-sche Tooneel [Dutch theatre company]"[294] is working up some of the pieces of Shakespear.[295]

I am very glad for then I will be able to see them acted.

Hoping you are getting better, Darling, I always remain your most affection-nately devoted

Wilhelmina

PALAIS LA HAYE
February 14 1897

156 My very dearest of Darlings

Mother & I we both thank you heaps of times for your two sweet letters & we are both very glad to hear that your sister is a little better.

Poor old Darling — it must be hard work for you to take care of your mother & sister now that just your mother is so ill. What a fright for you at Liverpool to hear that your sister had broken down!

You must only not trouble to write long letters for of course I quite well under-stand that you have no time & the moments you have <u>must</u> be used for rest. I am very pleased you have given me a long account of your sister for you know she has grown quite a dear friend to me by your always talking about her! I am so <u>very very</u> [underlined four times] glad that your mother allows you to wait upon her — how happy you must be to do so much for her! How awfully busy you must be with all the household to take care of. What a happy thing for you, Darling that the bruises are better. What a comfort to eat again substantional food! Of course Darling there is <u>not</u> a word true about the betrothal of cousin Pauline.[296] You must have been going about a lot at Liverpool! What a pity for you not to have heard Nansen,[297] it must be very interesting to hear him talk.

293 'Mary' refers to Marie Benner (see letter 33, note 50), who had left shortly beforehand and was succeeded by Miss M.A. van Overzee (see letters 25, note 35 and 141, note 240).
294 The Dutch theatre company known as 'Het Nederlandsche Tooneel' was founded in 1876. It was the company's aim to put its ideas regarding the ennoblement and development of drama into practice. The company was based at the royal theatre (Koninklijke Haagsche Schouwburg) in The Hague, but it also performed in Amsterdam.
295 William Shakespeare (c. 1564-1616), England's greatest playwright and poet, wrote c. 38 tragedies, historical plays and comedies, sonnets and longer poems. He had a great influence on the development of the English language.
296 The engagement between Pauline of Württemberg (1877-1965) and Friedrich of Wied (1872-1945), son of Prince Wilhelm of Wied (1845-1907) and Marie, Princess of the Nether-lands (1841-1910). Pauline was the daughter of Emma's sister Marie of Waldeck-Pyrmont (1857-1882), who had married in 1877 Wilhelm II, in 1891 King of Württemberg and was thus Wilhelmina's first cousin. Pauline and Friedrich married on 29 October 1898; see letter 230, dated 13 November 1898.
297 Fridtjof Nansen (1861-1930) was a Norwegian Arctic explorer, scientist and diplomat. He was awarded the Nobel Peace Prize in 1922. Between June 1893 and June 1896, he made a

I have waited hitherto to give you an account of the notes which my ladies make at the lessons of the Professor for I thougt it unjust to judge then from the first times they did it, but now you ask about how their assisting at the lectures is managed, I will tell you all about it. Ofcourse they are very interested in the lessons & they form the chief topics of conversation between us. We have arranged that the one who is on duty assists at the lessons so that one assists 2 of the same lessons consecutively & then the other also at 2 so that every four lectures they come again. They both make very good notes although their language can not be compared in conciseness to yours, you old Dear.

They have had difficult notes to make for with prof. Krämer. I have been learning about John Law[298] & his financial theories & with India the names are not easy & I am very severe about their spelling. Miss van Ittersum has gone home for some time as one of her sisters is ill. Last Monday I went to the French opera, I saw "le Source" a most amusing "opera comique" we remained for the beginning of "il Pagliacci"[299] I don't quite like the opera as much as the theatre − I find one loses the plot rather by the singing & music! Tuesday we went to the theatre & saw "Abt Constantijn" a piece half serious, half comical.

And just fancy yesterday we saw the opera of Hamlet!![300] I was delighted to hear it for though the play loses very much by being changed into an opera, it gives me a better idea than reading it. Although the ghost looked <u>most humanly substancial</u>, I passed a fairly restless & sleapless night − always being afraid it might come walking in my room. Hamlet had got himself up so ghastly that he looked much more weird than the ghost. Ophelia looked so ghostly that when she apeared for the first I thought it was the ghost. To morrow there is going to be a "thée dansant" − I will find it a great joke to see the potillon[301] − it is the only time I can get a glimpse of it.

I hope so much your mother & sister will soon get better, you Darling. With heaps of love I remain your most devoted

Wilhelmina

particularly interesting and adventurous journey to the North Pole that proved to be of inesti-mable scientific value.

**298** John Law (1671-1729), a Scottish economist and mathematician. One of the first academic economists, he based his theories on the issue of bank notes backed by gold, silver or land.

**299** Here Wilhelmina may be referring to the comic opera 'I Pagliacci' ('Clowns') by Ruggiero Leoncavallo (1858-1919), which was premiered in Milan on 21 May 1892, conducted by Arturo Toscanini.

**300** 'Hamlet', an opera in five acts based on the play by William Shakespeare (1564-1616), by the French composer Ambroise Thomas (1811-1896).

**301** Here Wilhelmina means the 'cotillon', a dance for introduction into society or the finale to a ball; also known as a quadrille.

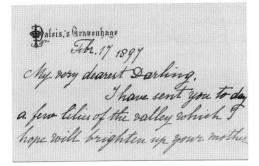

Card featuring the blue monogram of 'Paleis 's Gravenhage', which accompanied the bouquet of liles of the valley that Wilhelmina sent to Miss Winter's mother, Febr. 17 1897.

Paleis, 's Gravenhage

Febr. 17 1897

**157** My very dearest Darling,

I have sent you to day a few lilies of the valley which I hope will brighten up your mother & sister & knowing that you are very fond of their scent I thought you would like to have them.

I found the ball most amusing.

With my dearest love I will ever & always remain your most affectionnately devoted

Wilhelmina

PALAIS LA HAYE

February 21 1897

**158** My very dearest Darling,

Thank you so much for your two dear letters; how dreadful for you Darling, that your mother has been so bad again — I suppose you must be very busy with all the things you have to do — I wish I could have a good long look at you in your dear little home looking after your patients & giving your orders right & left & am sure you must look such an old Darling amidst all your surroundings! How do you feel, old Darling, are you very tired? I wonder if you are now sleeping with your mother or if you let the night-work be done by one of the trained nurses!

What a pity that your sister must still remain in bed — is she a good patient — I wonder if you will manage to get her away! I am sending you to morrow some

State portrait of Queen Wilhelmina, taken to mark her forthcoming investiture.
Photograph: H.R.F. Kameke, The Hague, 18 February 1897.

grapes — I think you told me your sister might eat fruit & I am sure that if neither your mother or sister can eat them you will be quite willing to help demolish them!!! Don't only trouble to write when you get parcels from me for that is quite unnecessary!

My ball was most amusing. I danced after the cercle & presentations the quadrille with the "Comte de Grelle"[302] the Belgiam minister — I luckily made no mistake & both this dance & the lancers[303] went very well — specially the latter I enjoyed very much; M^r Grovestins[304] was my cavalier. I found it quite a pity when it was finished. I talked the whole evening like a machine which is wound up for a few hours & can not stop untill the machinery has runn off. I found the cotillon very amusing to watch. I wore for the occasion the first gown I ordered myself at Paris. It was made in pale green satin & trimmed with white ribbons all down the skirt with yellow lace between & the body was covered with lace & here & there white ribbands. Ofcourse I wore my emeralds & my new emerald diadem.[305] Last Thursday I was photographed in the gown I had on for the ball gala & in the crown jewels — some of the photographs were done with the royal mantle for they are to be soled at my majority & are to be coppied for medals & used for making pictures also all for my majority.

By the by, I have now made up my mind about what I am going to give mother for her birthday — she knows all about it for it was a matter she had to be consulted in. I am going to have myself painted for her -- she is to say by whom, in what low gown, in what jewelry & in what position, then I am sure she will have it quite as she likes.

We intend to go very much to the theatre this week. Mother has now made up her mind to take a girl to sew to take Geeske's[306] place, she is very handy & is making my summer gowns. She is a daughter of the groom Halstein,[307] it is a pretty girl. I thought this would interest you.

With my dearest love & hoping the patients are getting better, I remain your most affectionnately devoted

Wilhelmina

302 The 'Comte de Grelle' is the Count of Grelle-Rogier, who had been envoy extraordinary and minister plenipotentiary of Belgium since 3 December 1894.

303 Les lanciers or 'the lancers' is an old dance and an abbreviation of quadrille des lanciers, a square dance for lance-cavalrymen.

304 Baron J.E.N. Sirtema van Grovestins (1842–1919) was adjutant to Prince Alexander (1851–1884) between 1874 and 1880, and then to King Willem III; and from 17 April 1891 to Queen Wilhelmina. He helped to carry the latter's royal robes during her investiture in 1898. In December 1899, he was appointed Grand Master of the House of H.M. the Queen. The court made grateful use of his advice and experience.

305 The emerald diadem (see letter 146, note 250).

306 Geeske (see letter 103, note 132, and letter 141, note 241).

307 A47a-III-2. In Emma's petty cash book entitled Weihnachten etc, which covered presents, there is a reference to Anna Halstein for the year 1897, on p.122.

February 28 1897

**159**   My own Dearest Darling,

Thank you so much for your dear long letter. I quite forgot last time I wrote to ask you if it was your friend "Anny" the one who was n't quite write in her head who has died — you poor old Darling it must have been difficult to tell your mother & sister about it!

I think you are the nicest, dearest, sweetest of Darlings I ever knew (except mother ofcourse) to have remembered about my mesuring — I have had it done on the 27<sup>th</sup> to be able to tell you about it in writing today — <u>I have grown 1 cent. Meter.</u> How dreadful for your poor sister to have to keep in bed still & just for her who is accustomed to such an active life. Poor old Sweety you must be occupied with your mother so ill! Is she now a little better? How amusing to think you are cooking, what a help your former experience must be! What an immense price the seats must be of Nansen's lecture[308], how delightful it would be for you to go & hear him for he is your greatest hero I think!!!! Just think! I have now got my little dog & he has not yet killed any chickens — he is an awful mischief & I have constantly to be on the look out for him — he is n't yet trained only so far that he behaves properly in the house — I have to teach him to run with the carriage, to obey me & to follow me when I ride. I find it mad fun looking after him, but he often has to get such a thrashing. We have been very much to the theatre lately Monday we went to see Zampa,[309] Thursday Mignon[310] & Friday "the Merchant of Venice"[311] in Dutch ofcourse. I am always so interested in the people & characters of the opera's that I don't listen at all to the music & I find it in fact very annoying that there always is music in an opera! There is one very fine voice this year in the French opera which is quite worth while hearing. The moment when the statue moves in Zampa makes you go creepy-crawly. Ofcourse I found Mignon charming after all you told me about it. The "Merchant of Venice" was given very well & had a great success. The part of Shilock was played by one of our best actors who nearly overdid his part. He looked a regular old Jew & during the trial he made himself angry that he was panting for breath — he imitated so well the Jews skratch their necks, heads & cheeks. It was quite disgusting. Ofcourse there was no getting me away untill the whole thing was finished. Mother is a good old Darling to sit there so patiently the whole evening!

Oh dear me!!! I have quite forgotten to tell you that mother has received the books for the notes & thanks you very much for ordering them. Mother is

308  Nansen (see letter 156, note 297).

309  That was on 22 February. The comic opera 'Zampa' was written by Ferdinand Hérold (1791–1833). The premiere took place in Paris on 3 May 1831.

310  The comic opera 'Mignon' was written by Ambroise Thomas (1811–1896). The premiere was held in Paris on 17 November 1866.

311  The comedy 'The Merchant of Venice' was written by William Shakespeare (1564–1616), the English playwright and poet, in 1596/97.

keeping very well — ofcourse she has to put up with a lot of nice teezing from me, a thing I find very necessary & good for her. I went all my mischief on her, I think she likes it however.

With all my dearest hugs & love I will always remain your most devoted

Wilhelmina

**160**  My dearest Darling,

Thank you very much for your sweet, long letter. As usual all you tell me about your mother & sister interests me very much — what a comfort that your mother is a little better but what a time it seems to take till your sister is quite well again. I am sending you some grapes to morrow! You old Darling, you are not mistaken in thinking that I dislike high heels, in fact I <u>hate</u> them just as much as ever. You are very unjust to think I am forgetting old Swell, this is not at all the case I hear from time to time how he is & he is in a good state of health & don't intend to forget him — "Foppie" will only take Swell's place where the old doggy cant any more like during the riding & driving in the carriage — in the house supposing, Swell will not lose his place & for the walks both dogs will come. I ride very regularly but I find it such a matter of course that I don't often mention it like also going to the theatre I will no more tell you each time for then it gets monotonous, don't you find I am right?

I have ordered a new habit from Guterbock[312] — it is to be "demi saison." The tailor came over lately — it was quite a new man — just fancy he spoke such wonderful English that miss v. Overzee & I agreed it could not be an Englishman, she asked him & he said he was a Dutchman but had lived a long time in France! You can understand I was not very sorry about M^r Swart. Poor Mss van Naghel[313] has died, I am very sorry for her family but it is a blessing for her for just lately she not only couldn't speak but also couldn't recognise her own people. The storms we have had here have also been awful.

Of course I have very strong ideas about Cretan affairs, for I hate the Turcs & admire the Greeks. To tell you the truth I am not following the question at present for I find it very uninteresting & lasting very long. I am following with much attention the trial of Rhodes.[314] Lately I have read very regularly the paper

---

**312** Güterbock (see letter 80, note 101).

**313** Baroness S. van Nagell van Ampsen and Schimmelpenninck van der Oije (1828–1897) was made Dame du Palais to Queen Emma on 22 August 1881. She succumbed to a stroke on 3 March 1897.

**314** This is a reference to Cecil John Rhodes (1853–1902), the British imperialist and mine magnate in South Africa, colonizer and statesman. His aim was to unite the various South African colonies and republics into one large state under British rule. This brought him into conflict with Paul Krüger, who was fighting for South African independence. In 1899 this resulted in a war between the Boer Republics and Great Britain, known as the 'Boer War'. Rhodesia was named after Cecil Rhodes.

Prof. J. de Louter (1847-1932), Professor of Dutch constitutional law and administrative law and international law at Utrecht, tutored Wilhelmina between the spring of 1897 and August 1898 in the constitutional law and governance of the Dutch East Indies and the Netherlands. This was followed by lectures in political economy in 1899 and international law in 1900.

Dr C. Hofstede de Groot (1863-1930), director of the Rijksprentenkabinet (the national collection of prints, designs and photographs) in Amsterdam, gave lessons in art history between March 1897 and February 1898. He also arranged the use of historical prints from the Prentenkabinet and coins and medals from the Koninklijk Penningenkabinet (the royal coins and medals collection) in The Hague for the lessons given by Professor Blok, and also for his own lessons. Emma took personal care of the artworks and artefacts for as long as they were at the palace.

during my hairdressing in the morning. In the evening when I go to the theatre or have a dinner & my head has to look its very best & my hair has to be done, I generally learn my lessons for the following day. By the by, yesterday I had my last lesson of professor Crämer[315] about the history of art & tomorrow I am beginning a new timetable with two new masters: professor de Lauter & M^r Hofstede de Groot.

The first is beginning his lectures to morrow & is to teach me about the constitution & laws of our India -- the latter is commencing his lessons next Tuesday & is to give me lectures upon the history of art of the middle ages & modern times.

Of course I am very much looking forward to both new lessons. I am sorry to say that I can't admire a ladies'club like you describe it — I certainly aprove very much having rooms for ladies which come up for the day but I would only be able to admire it if were managed in a less masculine fashion, but you will say I am meddling in other peoples affairs & would better do to mind my own, right you are, old Darling, & I beg your pardon for such enterference.

Do you give painting lessons to Ethel or only help her, I am sure you really could give good lessons, without any joking!

To day I went to church alone with Mrs. van Hardenbroek — this is also a thing I have quite got use to! I have lately been very busy in ordering all my summer things I am very good & always ask mothers advice — you see I know still very well how to sing my own praise!! The time of trying on is still to come. Yesterday we received the prince Albert of Prussia[316] who has come to his country seat here for a few days. I made brave efforts at my German!

315 See p. 30, note 62.
316 Albert of Prussia (1837–1906), the son of Princess Marianne of the Netherlands (1810–1888) and Albert of Prussia (1809–1872), paid a short visit at the end of the afternoon of 6

We are intending to go out very much this week: we have a party in town, the dutch opera, & a feast given by Pulchri Studio in honour of its jubilee of 50 years existence. Last Wednesday I heard such a beautiful concert of Diligentia: there were splendid voices & just fancy the renowned Grieg[317] came over to direct the orchestra which played the whole evening his music.

He was decorated & got a reath & general Cool made him a fine German speech (of which I didn't understand a word) & named him member of Diligentia. It was a grand affair.

I really think I must now end, with all my dearest love & hugs, I always remain your most affectionnately devoted

Wilhelmina

P.S. I must just tell you still about my grand plans for mothers birthday, I am thinking of acting some little comedy on our stage at the Loo. Don't you find it a good Idea?

Ofcourse it is a dead secret — only some of the ladies & gentlemen know about it — I only thought you would like to know about it!!

PALAIS LA HAYE<br>March 14 1897

**161**  My dearest Darling,

As usual I devoured you dear long letter, thank you so much for it. How dreadful that your two patients are only recovering so sowly! Before I forget it I must tell you — I am sending you some grapes. Poor old Darling, I am sorry I hurt your feelings about the club, but you see I <u>had</u> as friend to give my opinion in a graphic manner for we had arranged that we would be quite open with each other!

I am sure you must like very much having Ethel over for Sunday for you always like occupying yourself with children. And what a good thing for her to come to such a dear auntie in such a sweet house on her holidays! By the bey, how is your head at present? Is it keeping pretty well? Have you read about the death of Visscher[318] in the paper? I thought Lelienvelds[319] death would not have very

March 1897. He had inherited the house 'Rusthof' on the River Vliet in Voorburg. He re-sold it in 1904. Information provided by Mrs M.E. Spliethoff.

317 On 4 March 1897, in the GK&W concert hall, the Norwegian composer, pianist and conductor Edward Grieg (1843-1907) conducted the Amsterdamsch Orkest during the so-called 'Grieg concert' organized by the committee of the Diligentia concerts chaired by General Kool (1841-1914), chief of the Military House and Wilhelmina's tutor on military affairs. The songs were sung by Miss Anna Blauw and Corver, and Raoul Pugno played Grieg's piano concerto opus 16. The General informed Grieg that he had been made an honorary member of the society. Subsequently, after the concert, Grieg was informed that the Queen-Regent, who had attended the concert with Wilhelmina, had made him an officer in the Order of Orange-Nassau (De Tijd, 5 March 1897).

318 This may refer to Martinus Visser (born 1842), who was employed in 15 September 1891 as valet to Queen Wilhelmina, and dismissed honourably as of 1 November 1896.

319 This refers to David Pieter Lelienveld (1848-1897), who entered royal service on 1 May

much interested you as he did no longer go out with us these last years. My new professors are very interesting. Prof. de Lauter[320] gives lessons which are very difficult to follow if one is not attentive, but if I listen well I can follow quite easily; of course the subject itself is very dry, but as I am so very interested in our India I like the lectures immensely. Mother makes the notes & the ladies are not present. Prof. Can[321] now only gives me one lesson a week. I am learning about the climate of india — it is very dry uphill work but now I think that part is done. Doctor Hofstede de Groot gives splendid lessons although he has never done it before, ofcourse they are most interesting & the ladies make the notes. Just think auntie Lily has at last come — I am delighted — she has got very thin & has to be fed very often & strengthened. She came last Wednesday. We have been out a few times in the evening together, it is most amusing. Thursday we went to the Dutch opera[322] & saw Hans & Grietje [Hansel and Gretel][323] translated from the German. Friday we assisted at a party at Mrss van Lyndens. I found it very amusing: she had a man come over who sang al sorts of comical things. One could not help laughing: a song imitating the different ways of dancing, a would be Italian & Spanish song where you could hear that it was French with some letters stuck on. Yesterday we assisted at the feast of Pulchri Studio which was given in the building in the "dierentuin."[324] You can't think how lovely it was the whole thing was so refined & artistic. The hall in which the feast was held was crowded with people of whom a great number were in a costume the national or costumes of the last century the men as well as the women. It made the assembly look most picturesque! The stage was ornamented with a large Dutch seen with a windmill a large windmill stood next to the stage & all along that side of the room there were old Dutch houses drawn up where one could get refreshments or see some amusing thing. The other side was done in the same way whilst at the end of the room opposite the stage there was an old portcullis & a baby town groped round it.

1876 as a coachman and died on 24 February 1897.

320  Wilhelmina is often careless when writing names, writing 'Lauter' rather than 'Louter', and further on, 'Can' rather than 'Kan'. Professor de Louter taught Wilhelmina constitutional law.

321  Prof. Kan (see letter 133).

322  The Hollandsche Opera opened in Amsterdam in 1888, directed by J.G. van der Goot, with a performance of the opera *Catharina en Lambert* (1888) by Cornelis van der Linden (1839–1918). A split occurred in 1894, leading to the founding of the Nederlandsche Opera directed by conductor G. van der Linden and based in the Stadsschouwburg in Amsterdam.

323  The libretto for the musical fairy-tale 'Hänsel and Gretel', to music by Engelbert Humperdinck (1854–1921), was written by his sister, Adelheid Wette. It was premiered on 23 December 1893 in the Hoftheater in Vienna, conducted by the German Richard Strauss (1864–1949).

324  Between 1863 and 1968, the zoo of The Hague, the Koninklijk Zoölogisch en Botanisch Genootschap (Royal Zoological and Botanical Society), was located on the corner of the Benoordenhoutseweg (now the Zuid-Hollandlaan) in The Hague. This is now the site of the provincial government building.

**March 15** Passing through the portcullis one came in a large refreshmentroom. We were received by Mesdag[325] & others. The thing began by Mesdag making a speech & giving mother a book with the history of Pulchri in it. Then we saw the first tableau vivant an allegory upon Pulchri — it was splendid. It was planned out by Josselin de Jong.[326] The next represented de Ruyter[327] by Solebay from a picture of Rochussen. No 3 represented the harvest of the vines by Alma Tadema.[328] No 4 was Washington[329] crossing the Delaware. The time between the tableaux we passed in walking about & looking at the different establishments & in seeing a country dance executed in national costumes, a very pretty fairy dance, singing etc. Every thing was lovely & can't say which I found the best executed. Just fancy, last Thursday I went with Mrss van Hardenbroek[330] to the hospital & saw the children — don't you find that plucky? Yesterday I went for the first time to the german church! I have now decided that Bles[331] is to paint me. [Colour plate v-8]

**325** Hendrik Willem Mesdag (1831–915), an artist, watercolourist, etcher and lithographer from the School of The Hague and an art collector with his own museum, was chairman of Pulchri Studio between 1889 and 1907. Together with his brother, Taco, in 1896 he obtained the house on Lange Voorhout that had belonged to the former minister Gijsbert van Tienhoven. The Pulchri exhibitions were shown there from 1901.

**326** Pieter de Josselin de Jong (1861–1906) undertook a number of commissions for Queen Emma, including a drawing of King Willem III on his deathbed, 23 November 1890; Royal Archives, inv.no. AT/0211. A second example can be found the Paleis Het Loo National Museum, on loan from the Geschiedkundige Vereniging Oranje-Nassau (Historical Association of Orange-Nassau), inv.no. A1472; a portrait of the regent Queen Emma at her writing table, c. 1893, in black watercolour, which was used for the cover of the catalogue of the exhibition 'We are still here', inv.no. SC/0535. He also did a three-quarter-length portrait of Queen Emma in 1893, inv.no. SC/0581, which used for a lithograph that she presented to individuals who had supported her during the regency. Lastly, a half-length portrait of Queen Wilhelmina, for which the queen posed shortly before her investiture in August 1898, on the back terrace of Soestdijk Palace, inv.no. SC/0508. Royal Collections, The Hague (Spliethoff 1898, image opposite title page).

**327** Michiel de Ruyter (1607–1676), a Dutch admiral. In the disastrous year of 1672, during the Third Anglo-Dutch War in the Battle of Solebay, he prevented the combined French and English fleets from landing on the coasts of Zeeland and Holland, despite their superior numbers. This scene was captured by the Rotterdam-based painter Charles Rochussen (1814–1894).

**328** After completing his studies, the Dutchman Sir Laurens Alma Tadema (1836–1912), born in Dronrijp, worked in Antwerp and then in England from 1870, where Queen Victoria knighted him in 1899. He was celebrated for his scenes of Ancient Greece, Egypt and Rome.

**329** George Washington (1732–1799) was a general and the supreme commander of the colonies in the American War of Independence, and the first President of the United States (1789). In 1776, during the American Revolution, Washington crossed the Delaware River, which runs along the Atlantic Coast of the United States.

**330** Mrs Van Hardenbroek (see p. 77, note 91).

**331** Queen Wilhelmina, signed *David Bles f.*, Paleis Het Loo National Museum, on loan from the Royal Collections, The Hague, Inv.no. SC/0431. The portrait was commissioned by Queen Wilhelmina for the Queen Emma's birthday on 2 August 1897. Rem, p. 170, erroneously reports that it was commissioned by Queen Emma. David Josef Bles (1821–1899), who studied with

As I am to be photographed for his picture to day I will tell you another time about the acting. With all my dearest love & hugs I remain, Darling your most affectionnately devoted

Wilhelmina

PALAIS LA HAYE

March 21 1897

162    My own dear old Darling,

Thank you so much for your sweet long letter. I <u>am</u> [underlined three times] happy to hear that your two patients are getting better; it is quite grand of your mother to be able to get up — it has n't happened for a long time, has it? I am very much afraid that it does not occur to me that I can often through a ray of sunlight upon the path of so many a sufferer — if it did I think I would always smile, but I find it very difficult to always think of that & you must say, one day one feels more disposed for smiling or shewing sympathy than the other, ofcourse I always try. You don't know Darling, what a happiness it is to have a dear sweet old friend to whom I can write about all these things, you are as it were cut out for it: we understand eachother so well & can write all we like & know we are understood, you precious One! I wish I could hug you up to pieces!

"Bless" is a very old gentleman who paints generally interiors with oldfashioned people, he also painted a charming picture of his daughter — if he paints me like that it will be perfect.

You must be very occupied with your patients, Ethel & the lecture, are you still thinking of lecturing yourself in the TownHall? Ofcourse we are not coming over for the feasts in May & June & July.

Last Friday I presided at a meeting of my fellow-actors & actresses for mothers birthday; we read the two pieces[332] we mean to play; M[r] de Ranitz[333] is the director, I am busy trying to learn my part as I am a great duffer at learning by heart I must begin early; you know it would never have done to have tried acting during schoolroomlife for as it is I still find difficulty to find time for it & what would it have been formerly! The ball of Tuesday was delightful, I wore my chiffon Paris gown with roses & my pearl "poires" sewn on in the front. My partners were M[r] du Tour[334] & M[r] Okolichani[335] (the Ostrian). I am having mad

Cornelis Kruseman (1797–1857), among others, produced historical, satirical and humorous oil paintings; he also did watercolours and etchings.

332  The two plays that were performed were: *Een lief Vers [A sweet verse]*, a comedy in two acts by Lodewijk Mulder, and *Uit Liefde voor de Kunst [For the love of art]*, a comedy in one act, freely translated and rewritten from the French version of the play written by Eugène Labiche (1818–1890).

333  Mr S.M.S. de Ranitz (see letter 51, note 70).

334  'Mr du Tour' is the chamberlain Baron M.W. du Tour van Bellinchave (1835–1908), who entered royal service on 19 February 1869.

335  This refers to Mr A. Okolicsányi von Okolicsna, the Austrian envoy extraordinary and minister plenipotentiary from 12 December 1894. His daughter May was invited one of Wilhelmina's children's parties on 6 April 1895 (A50-V-16).

fun with auntie Lily; next Saturday Elisabeth & Victoria Bentheim[336] are coming here.

Wednesday there is to be another ball. Just fancy how sad — last Sunday there was a M^r Beelaerts van Bloklandt[337] who got a fit in the Willemskerk & died that same evening, it was a healthy man of 55 with a wife & children & a lot of affairs & occupations. They have celebrated grandly the 100^th birthday of William I of Germany[338] in the german church.

My little Foppie is still a dreadfull mischief & I have my hands full with him. He now runs after the carriage. I now don't anymore let mother read my letters so all faults come down upon me.

Do say if you think my handwriting & spelling has improved. With all my dearest love & hugs, I always remain your most affectionnately devoted

Wilhelmina

PALAIS LA HAYE
March 24 1897

**163**  Dearest Darling,

I just want to come & tell you myself about the great grief we, mother & I, have just had: my dear auntie "Sophie"[339] had died. She went off yesterday evening quite quietly after having been ill for one or two days. None of her people were there except Lily the wife of her son.[340]

You will understand what a grief it is to mother & me, I can't yet quite believe it, I am trying to help mother as much as I can.

With all my dearest love your most affectionnately devoted

Wilhelmina

Between 28 March and 20 June 1897, the letters were written on mourning paper due to the death of Sophie, Grand Duchess of Saxe-Weimar. There was one month of full mourning, one month of half mourning and one month of light mourning.

---

**336**  Elisabeth (1886-1959) and Victoria (1887-1961) Bentheim are the daughters of Emma's sister Pauline, Princess of Bentheim-Steinfurt.

**337**  This is Mr Gerard Jacob Theodoor Beelaerts van Blokland (1843-1897). He died on 14 March.

**338**  Emperor Wilhelm I (1797-1888) was the King of Prussia. In 1871 he was crowned the first German Emperor in the Hall of Mirrors at Versailles. His son Friedrich III (1831-1888) ruled for just 99 days. From 1918 (when Germany became a republic) until his death, Friedrich III's son Wilhelm II (1859-1941) would remain in exile at Doorn House in the Netherlands.

**339**  Sophie, Grand Duchess of Saxe-Weimar and Princess of the Netherlands; see p. 26, note 51. Queen Emma and Queen Wilhelmina were particularly fond of Sophie, as she was able to tell them a great deal about Dutch matters and customs. She was a mine of information for both women after the death of King Willem III.

**340**  Sophie had one son, Carl August (1844-1894), who was married to Pauline of Saxe-Weimar-Eisenach (1852-1904).

the only direct representative
of my family — would that I
were a worthier one! —
You know how I miss you these
days for dear mother has so
much to do that I scarcely see
her, specially the first days, &
I can't talk to other people about
my Auntie & I can't talk about
any thing else. People in
general & I in particular don't
easily talk about things they
feel deeply to people who they
only know since a short time
it is such a blessing to have a
loving friend on the other side of
the sea to whom one can tell
every think & who one is sure not
to worry with such things for
although both my ladies have
been charming to me during
my grief I feel it can't be
very interesting for them to
always hear the same conversation & I ... somewhat
to talk to them all day about
my Auntie. I now receive con-
dolence with a serious face &
don't grin; Wednesday I
received Mrs. v. Hardenbrook, Thurs.

I suppose it must be better for
me otherwise it would not have
happened — I must learn to
stand on my own legs. But
Auntie is not dead for me; She
lives, it is not a reason that
because She has left this world
She should be dead — She inspires me & I suppose all who
knew her, to do the good &
I feel inspired to follow her
example & to try & be a blessing
for my people, I feel that the
loss has brought me closer to ...
but also to my people. What
a great thing for people to
be able to say about Her that
all what She created lives for us
& that Her thoughts & ideas &
deeds live on & inspire others
to do the good & teach them
to be a blessing for the world
on their turn! —
Mother is keeping well although
she is tired & upset by all
her sorrow.
You will find me very selfish
to have not yet asked how
your mother & sister are. Do

Pages 6 and 7, and 10 and 11, from letter 164 in which Wilhelmina unburdened her heart to Miss Winter after the death of her aunt Sophie, the Grand Duchess of Saxe-Weimar: '[…] I'm now the only direct representative of my family' and '[…] I suppose it must be better for me […].'

The Hague, March 28 1897

**164**    Dearest of Darlings,

Your dear letter did me a lot of good & I thank you very much for the dear
sympathy you showed me. Mother told me I was to thank you also in her name
for your sweet letter & kind sympathy in her great grief. I think it will interest
you to know how every thing went here as well as in Weimar.

Already during the day of the 23$^{\text{de}}$ mother had heard from my cousin of Weimar
that my dear Auntie had an attack of influenza & the Dutch lady[341] who always
was with Auntie telegraphed that She had bronchitis, that She was weak, but
there was no danger.

Just before we go to the theatre mother gets a telegram from the same lady
saying that the forces were not yet augmenting, but there was no danger. We go
to the theatre but I can't say I liked sitting there for I could not help thinking
about Auntie. In coming home "Smelting"[342] stands in the corridor with two
telegrams. Mother opens the one — I the other. They were both from my cousin
Weimar; one saying that Aunties state had become dangerous & the other
brought the fatal news. Auntie had dined that evening at 6.30 & was weak from
coughing, but still quite well & suddenly She became so weak that She had to be
helped to get up from her chair & to walk. Miss v. Rennes (the Dutch lady) & the
doctor undressed her & She was only just in bed when She went off quite quietly.

It was certainly the most quiet & peaceful death She could have had & one
only can be thankful that She suffered so little but it is dreadful to think that
nor my uncle nor my cousins of Reuss & Mecklenbourg[343] were there. I also had
hoped that when the moment of parting had come I should have been at my dear
Auntie's side & once having got the fatal telegram I hoped we would go to the
funeral which is to be to morrow, but we could n't go for there was no service
where ladies could go. This is a great grief to me for I can't say how I would have
liked to be present.

With her the last of fathers family had died & I am now the only direct
representative of my family — would that I were a worthier one! –

You don't know how I miss you these days for dear mother has so much to do
that I scarcely see her, specially the first days, & I can't talk to other people about
my Auntie & I can't talk about any thing else. People in general & I in particular
don't easily talk about things they feel deeply to people who they only know
since a short time & it is such a blessing to have a loving friend on the otherside
of the sea to whom one can tell every think & who one is sure not to worry with

341 Originally from the Netherlands, Miss van Renesse was a lady-of-the-bedchamber to
Grand Duchess Sophie.
342 Smelting (see letter 14, note 25).
343 Heinrich VII, Prince Reuss of Kösteritz (1825–1906) and Duke Johann Albrecht of
Mecklenburg-Schwerin (1857–1920) were married to Marie Alexandrine (Zitta) and Elisabeth
(Elsi), respectively, the daughters of Grand Duke Carl Alexander and Sophie, Grand Duchess
of Saxe-Weimar and Princess of the Netherlands. Johann Albrecht was a half-brother of Prince
Hendrik.

such things for although both my ladies have been charming to me during my grief I feel it can't be very interesting for them to always hear the same conversation & I scruple some what to talk to them al day about my Auntie. I now receive condolences with a serious face & don't grin; Wednesday I received Mrs. v. Hardenbroek[344] & Thursday Mrs v. Knobelsdorff.[345] You can well imagine what that cost me. I now manage to behave as I really feel. As usual I have not shed a tear but feel the loss all the deeper. I tried to be as much as possible alone & I felt I couldn't do any thing. I have the greatest difficulty to learn my lessons for my thoughts wonder of to my Auntie & I can't yet realise I will never see her again. I feel that I couldn't do anything what is not stricly necessary.

I am not riding these days & I only remain out for two hours in a landau which is shut till out of town. You must think it is the first great grief I have had since I am old enough to realise what it is to lose somebody one loved. I had so many things I wanted to ask my Auntie & she would have been such a help to me when I am grown up to tell me how things went in her time. But I must miss all that now.

I suppose it must be better for me otherwise it would not have happened — I must learn to stand on my own legs. But Auntie is not dead for me; She lives, it is not a reason that because She has left this world She should be dead — She inspires me & I suppose all who knew Her, to do the good & I feel inspired to follow her example & to try & be a blessing for my people, I feel that Her loss has brought me closer to mother but also to my people. What a great thing for people to be able to say about Her that all what She created lives for ever & that Her thoughts & ideas & deeds live on & inspire others to do the good & teaches them to be a blessing for the world on their turn! –

Mother is keeping well although she is tired & upset by all her sorrow.

You will find me very selfish to have not yet asked how your mother & sister are. Do tell when you write next!

With all my dearest love & hugs I always remain your most devoted, affectionnate & loving

Wilhelmina

The Hague , March 29 1897

165     Dearest Darling,
I quite forgot to tell you yesterday that I am sending you two of my photographs which have been made for my picture; I will send you afterwards a third one but I thought you would like to have those which I had as soon as possible; the one which is coming later is by far the best. I feel very proud that I now can give away as I like — it is the very first time I pay them myself.

With all my dearest love & hugs I always remain your most affectionnately devoted

Wilhelmina

---

344  Mrs van Hardenbroek (see p. 77, note 91).
345  Mrs van Knobelsdorff (see letter 153, note 281).

**166**  My own dear Darling,

Your two dear letters did me a great deal of good. You dear old Thing, I <u>am</u> glad
I could do that little thing for you to give you those photographs — the third will
reach you this week. I <u>am</u> sorry that your two patients are only getting better
so slowly. The proofs of the first photographs were very good, but they are not
going to be made as they were only intended for modles for painting pictures. I
had mine of course also made for the picture but I thought at the same time that
I would give some to the people I knew the best & in the first place to my old
friendy on the other side of the sea.

Therefor I also had them touched up what the first had not been, they looked
<u>too</u> awful & black, but it seems to be better for the artist who has them as model.
My auntie Lily is still staying on for a little time. I say Darling, you will make me
quite vain if you go on praising me so much, I really believe you think I am half
an angel & if you were to have a look in that wicked heart of mine you would
think otherwise you old Darling.

Mother and I we have been having many audiences this week — a thing I did
not feel in the mood for!

Elisabeth & Victoria Bentheim[346] are coming here the 7th, I would find this very
pleasant, but I am not quite in the mood to entertain just now, but their coming
could not easily be put off. I am also to have the pleasure of Stuwart[347] this week,
but this time not for long.

Mother is also very lucky with her teeth this time, a thing which pleases me the
more as she has not been well last week; she has been very tired from all the grief
& is thoroughly done up, I hope she will soon get stronger for she feels so: "slap
[weak]"!

After last Monday I began my usual life again, a thing that cost some amount
of trouble as I did not feel inclined to. But I am certain my dear Auntie would
not have approved of this I tried to begin life with new energy. I am filled with
<u>one</u> desire & that is to try & work hard & learn as much as I can to be a worthy
& good queen for my own dear people. I feel keenly the responsibility which
rests on me as the only one on earth who now can still make my people happy in
future & I feel bound if possible still tighter to <u>my</u> Netherlands since the last of
its native princesses have died. My one great object in life is to make my people
happy & I am more resolute than ever to cling to my task till the last moment of
my life. I am trying in my free time to work up different subjects to try & learn
about many interesting questions. Never a minute of the day is waisted but on
the other hand I don't go at it so wildly that I make myself ill. Now I am working
at India in an interesting book & learning more for a joke the Arabian characters.

---

346  Elisabeth and Victoria Bentheim (see letter 162, note 336).

347  This refers to James Stewart, whose business was based on Laan Copes van Cattenburch
40, The Hague. See the invoice dated 1 January 1897, which Stewart sent for services delivered
on 3 October 1896 (A47a-III-9 Jan. 1888-April 1897 and A47-III-45).

As it is I don't learn very much, not as much as I would like, but it always helps me later to better understand Indian affairs.

I feel that all the further I get, also on the point of moral development, all the more I see how small & little I am! You see I am getting wise & thinking about what I have to do to improve & get a good queen, has made me think about myself also: I have lately been thinking very much & I feel I have grown older & realise better my responsibilities. I mean to try & work hard at myself & you know if I once use my strong will I can do a great deal, to follow the grand exemple set me by my noble Mother & Auntie putting aside all other things & thoughts which might be in my way to obtain my great object in life to be a blessing to my people to which I will give up all my thought, love & life!

You will think me very exagerated in my language but I really mean what I say & as their there was nothing very interesting to write about I thought I would tell how I felt upon this point.

With all my dearest love & hugs I will always remain your most devoted

Wilhelmina

The Hague, April 11 1897

**167**  Dearest of Darlings,

Thank you so much for your sweet letter. I am glad to hear that your sister has been able to travel; I can well understand that you have a lot to do; what a good thing that your mother is now accustomed to all your ways & lets you help her! What a happy thing also for you, for you must have now achieved the one great thing you feared you would never get done. By being allowed to help your mother you must feel you have an object to whom you can devote all your thought & all your love. My mother is still rather seedy; she has had fever & feels rather down, but both my auntie & I we preach to her that she is to keep quiet, a thing she is now trying to do. Eggs are not going to be hunted this year; it is too much trouble & I have too much to do these last days in town. What dear little things those kittens of yours must be; kittens are always so dear, if they are only very young. My cousins Bentheim are very merry & it is n't difficult to amuse them. They are such monkies.

My auntie helps entertain them. Last Thursday Mother and I received many old ladies in audience & also the deputation of the 1st chamber who came to condole. Last Saturday I had Stewart, a thing which was not of the pleasantest. To day my auntie & I we went to church together with Mrs. van Hardenbroek.

This afternoon Anna Bentinck[348] has been confirmed; you will understand how interested I was when I heard this. Yesterday I had an assembly of my fellow actresses & actors, we read over for the second time our pieces to get accustomed to act with one another. Mother has not yet decided about our travelling. It is very difficult to fit all the visits we have to make to the family, in with our other plans. Perhaps you have heard already that mother is taking a French

---

348  Anna Bentinck (see letter 123, note 171).

lady travelling with us who is to freshen up my notions of French. She will stay on at the Loo till she has been with me all together 4 months. Ofcourse there is no question of lessons or any thing of the kind; she only comes to me as lady in waiting for four months & is to talk to me. I hope she will be a nice girl, for otherwise it will be unbearable. I understand it is very necessary for me to learn more thoroughly my French, but a new lady only for four months is not agreable. She is called: "Mademoiselle de Joannisse."[349] I am sorry, Darling, that I can not tell you many interesting things, but we live so quietly that there is nothing worth telling. Excuse there for my short letter.

With all my dearest love, I always remain your most affectionnately devoted & loving

Wilhelmina

The Hague, April 16 1897

**168** My very dearest Darling,

I just want to come and write you a few words for Easter to tell how much I am thinking about you & your feelings at this time. My thoughts wonder as it were quite by themselves over the sea to come & watch your daily occupations & your going to church. I know how you will like having all the services conducted in the way you are accustomed to & going as often as you like; it must be such a time ago that you have not been home for Easter, you poor old Darling! I wish, I wish we could just meet for giving one another a great big hug next Sunday to wish each other a blessed & happy Easter.

But alas; this can not be!

How we will then doubly do it in thought!

What a lot there has all the same passed since last Easter in both our lives & what a lot has changed; but there is one thing which will never, never, change — our mutual love & affection. I know we will both think back to the past in these coming days, with a feeling of gratitude for all we have received in our lives. There have come many changes in my life since last year & it is the first Easter after I am grown up & just in these days I feel deeply all the responsibilities I have in life & what I would <u>like</u> to <u>be</u> & what <u>I am</u>. But I must not go on like this for it is not very interesting for you! It may interest you to know that I very much liked my quiet morning at home to day; I read my periodicals this morning & went to church this afternoon; next Sunday we are going to Holy Communion in

---

**349** Ada de Joannis (born after 1863, died 1951) was temporarily a French companion to Wilhelmina, to help her to practise her French. Wilhelmina wrote in *Eenzaam maar niet alleen*: 'Our relationship was not limited to a few months in 1897. As she was pleasant and cheery company, she was often asked back. She became my friend. Ada was from Alsace. Before she came to me, she had been staying with my future husband's sister and spent many months at his parental home. She was thus acquainted with my future mother-in-law's whole family. Unawares, she told me much about my future family and established, as it were, a relationship between my future husband and myself, even before we saw one another again after our first meeting as children in Weimar.'

*Gouda in vreugde [Happy Gouda]*, allegorical print to celebrate Queen Emma and Queen Wilhelmina's visit to Gouda on 24 April 1897, incorporating the stained glass by Dirk and Wouter Crabeth in Gouda's St Janskerk, candles from the 'Gouda' candle factory, and pipes from the P. Goedewagen Messrs pipe and pottery factory, all three of which were visited. Lithograph by Jan Toorop (1858-1928).

the "Kloosterkerk."[350] I have had two headaches this week which have both gone over within one day, so you see they are not very bad! By the bey, how is your dear old noddle?

We are going Saturday week for half a day to Gouda[351] & from there on to Amsterdam, so I suppose you will hear still once from me before my journey; from Amsterdam we are going to Stuttgart & from there to Vienna & from there in the mountains. Mother is a little less tired. Auntie Lily is leaving us next Tuesday but after Amsterdam we join again to go to Stuttgart & Vienna, after Vienna she goes back to Arolsen. I am madly looking forward to seing my cousin Pauline![352]

How are your patients keeping, how is your sister?

I am sending you a frame for Easter for one of my large photo's; I hope it will come in time & be large enough.

---

**350** See letter 146, note 255.

**351** To commemorate this visit, which took place on the afternoon of 24 April 1897, Jan Toorop made the lithography 'Verheugd Gouda [Happy Gouda]', see above.

**352** Pauline, Princess of Württemberg, stayed at Paleis Het Loo between 16 and 28 June 1897 (see letter 156, note 296).

Wishing you again & again a very blessed & happy Easter, I remain your most affectionnately devoted

Wilhelmina

The Hague, April 23 1897

**169**  My own very dearest Darling,

You don't <u>know</u> how happy you have made me with your pretty cards[353] & dear letter! Thank you <u>so</u> much for all of them.

What a Darling you are to have painted me a card yourself! I <u>can't</u> tell you how madly delighted I am with it & how nicely & artisticly you have done it. The colouring & shading is so soft & the background is so splendidly washed in. And what a sweet card you enclosed in your easterletter & what sweet words were written inside & then your darling letter; you have quite spoilt me, Deary!

Where is your sister staying? Is she up in Liverpool?

What ever <u>can</u> be the matter with her, that she is not getting much better! Poor old Sweety, it <u>must</u> be very tiring to feel you are in the back and call all day & then that you have not a moment to yourself; I wish I could come & comfort you a little, you seem to be rather down at present! Does your mother allow herself to be helped?

Can you talk over things with her or is she not well enough to understand?

I am sure you will not have envyed me these last days with packing. I <u>have</u> had <u>such</u> a lot to do.

We have an extra lot of little pass times at Amsterdam.[354] Just think the brother of the late grandduc of Mecklenburg is coming to Amsterdam to announce the death of the grandduc[355] & there have come over two princes[356] of our India who are bringing presents & have also to be received! I don't think I have yet told you that this time in Amsterdam & travelling miss van Stirum[357] is coming with me &

---

353  A50-VII-c5. Three daffodils, watercolour on thick cardboard, 26.7 x 18.3 cm, signed at bottom right: *E SW 97*.

354  The annual visit to Amsterdam was held between 24 and 30 April 1897.

355  Friedrich Franz III (1851–1897), Grand Duke of Mecklenburg-Schwerin, died on 14 April. He was the son of Friedrich Franz II (1823–1883) and the latter's first wife, Augusta von Reuss-Schleitz-Köstritz (1822–1862). His brother Johann Albrecht (1857–1920) married Elisabeth of Saxe-Weimar (1854–1908), daughter of Sophie, Grand Duchess of Saxe-Weimar, Princess of the Netherlands and the sister of King Willem III. After the death of his first wife, Sophie of Württemberg (1818–1877), Willem III proposed to his cousin Elisabeth, but she refused him. Friedrich Franz and Johann Albrecht were half-brothers of Hendrik, who married Wilhelmina in 1901. Hendrik was a child of the third marriage of Friedrich Franz II to Marie von Schwarzburg-Rudolstadt (1850–1922).

356  E10-IVBb-6. On the evening of Tuesday 27 April 1897, at 9:30 p.m., in the throne room of the Royal Palace on Dam Square, Amsterdam, Emma and Wilhelmina held a ceremonial reception for three (and not two, as Wilhelmina writes; EvH) 'Bornean' princes, who came to present gifts to Wilhelmina on behalf of their father, the Sultan of Kutai in Northern Borneo. Two of his sons would attend Wilhelmina's investiture in 1898: Amidi Pangeran Mangkoe Negoro and Hassanoedin Pangeran Sosro Negoro.

357  Van Stirum (see letter 141, note 239).

miss Rengers is going home. I mean to try my very best to make things easy for mother. Ofcourse all the lessons have now finished & I have said good bey to M[r] Gediking[358] for good & to prof. Can[359] till the month of September.

I quite forgot to tell you how indignant I was about your asking whether I opened your letters instantly; why Darling I always read them immediately it is only for people I don't care for that I don't open the letters.

Nansens[360] speech <u>must</u> have been very interesting after your description & what a good thing you were able to go!

You asked me in your last letter who is acting in the two pieces which are to be played at the Loo.[361] M[r] de Ranitz organises every thing & the four ladies & I & M[r] v.d. Poll, v.d. Bosch, Tets, Stirum, Suchtelen, DuMonceau the young one, Loudon, Clifford & Bentinck are going to act. The pieces are called "Een lief vers [A sweet verse]" & "Uit liefde voor de kunst [For the love of art]". I am in a flying hurry so excuse if I don't give any more details at present. I don't think I will have time to write at Amsterdam nor at Stuttgart so till Vienna, Darling! With all my fondest love & hugs I remain your most affectionnately devoted

Wilhelmina

Amsterdam, April 29 1897

170    My very own dearest Darling,

Thank you so much for your two dear long letters; I wish I could make you feel how dreadfully destressed I was to hear that you have so many worries just at present!

You poor, dear old Darling, how unhappy you must be! I would give any thing to be able to come & comfort you & it is dreadful to feel that just now when I want to fold you in my arms closer than ever, I am going further away from my own old darling! But I am sure of one thing which comforts me: that where ever we are there is always <u>One</u> who is with us & who will comfort you much better than I & in whose hands I can as it were leave you behind in safe keeping! How

---

358 Heuven 1989, p. 30. When bidding farewell on 20 April, Wilhelmina thanked Gediking warmly for everything he had done for her over the years. She made particular mention of the patience with which he had clearly explained things to her that she had not previously understood. She presented him with a large photograph of herself, signed and with the inscription: 'In grateful memory of the years 1887-1897'. Emma presented him with the officer's medal of the Order of Orange-Nassau.

359 Kan (see p. 114, letters 133 and 161).

360 Nansen (see letter 156, note 297).

361 Private secretary Mr S.M.S. de Ranitz (1846-1916); the four ladies-in-waiting Lady F.L. Henriette van de Poll (1853-1946) and Baroness Cornelia M. van Heemstra (1847-1931), who was also a governess, Miss Anny J.J. van Burmania, Baroness Rengers (1868-1944), and Lady Adolphine W.A. van Limburg Stirum (1877-1961); the adjutants Mr Willem F.H. van de Poll 1843-1918), Mr Willem J.P. van den Bosch (1848-1914), Mr Albert S.E. van Tets (1851-1936); chamberlain and master of the royal shoot Count Ernst L. van Limburg Stirum (1857-1899); the three aide-de-camps Mr C.L. 'Luc' van Suchtelen van de Haare (1860-1943), Joseph H.F. Dumonceau (1859-1952) and Frederik W.J. Loudon (1862-1935); Marshal of the Court Hendric A. Clifford (1850-1908); and Principal Equerry Baron C.A. Bentinck (1848-1925).

dreadful Darling, that your sister has broken down again & that your mother is worrying & making herself ill! Poor old Darling, you have no luck this year. How are you keeping under all this? It must be difficult to keep courage under it. I weeped hard in getting your last letter, the more because I am missing you very much these days. It is so dreadful not to have a dear friend to fall back upon & nobody to look after the time & to grumble at me when I don't do things rightly; it is all very strange! I don't think I have any more time to write. I have just told miss van Overzee to send a letter with further details; don't be horrified about what she writes for I have told her exactly what to put & I hope they are things which will interest you. Hoping that things may go better with your patients I remain with hugs & love, your most affectionnately devoted

Wilhelmina

Following their annual visit to Amsterdam, on Friday 30 April 1897, Emma and Wilhelmina Amsterdam left on a special train to travel abroad. Until around 16 May, they were accompanied by Elisabeth (Lily) of Waldeck-Pyrmont. They stayed in Stuttgart (1-2 May), Vienna (3-14 May), Alt-Aussee (Salzkammergut-Stiermarken, 14 May-8 June), Weimar (8-10 June) and finally in Arolsen (11-14 June).

Vienna, May 11 1897

**171** My very dearest Darling,

Thank you so much for your dear letter of the other day; I will answer later once your letter more in detail; for to day I just have time to give you my address at Aussee & tell you in a laconic way the most important things I have done. My address is: "Alt Aussee Hôtel Seewirth Steiermark"

I enjoyed Pauline very much, saw Saturday my uncle's stud,[362] Sunday large dinner; journey Monday very long, Tuesday made visits, Emperor came to us, were to dine at his villa Thursday, but by death of sister[363] empress idea was given up, Wednesday I had bad cold, afternoon fever in bed, next day quite well, Wednesday morning visit to museum, was repeted several times, museums are splendid, fine pictures, sketches, objects of art-industry, antiquities, natural history, Thursday went to park to see horses & carriages, Friday royal stables, palace, Schönbrunn[364] (residence out of Vienna), Saturday show of horses of Spanish school, Sunday went to church, afternoon visit to cloister of Neuburg[365]

362 The letter of 16 May refers to Pauline's studio. 'My uncle's stud': this could refer to a studio belonging to King Wilhelm II of Württemberg (1848–1921), who was married to Marie, Emma's sister. Wilhelmina may have made a mistake by writing 'my uncle's studio'.
363 Duchess Sophie Charlotte Auguste (1847–1897), the sister of Elisabeth, Empress of Austria, was the ninth child of Duke Maximilian in Bavaria (1808–1888) and Princess Ludovika of Bavaria (1808–1892). She died on 4 May 1897.
364 Schönbrunn Palace, the summer residence of the Habsburg family outside Vienna, acquired its current form under Empress Maria Theresa (1717–1780) and is an example of Austrian rococo. In 1996, the palace, gardens and Gloriette (belvedere) were added to the UNESCO List of World Cultural Heritage Sites.
365 Klosterneuberg Monastery is an Augustinian monastery to the north of Vienna, situated

near Vienna, Monday shopping, Tuesday lunch at Dutch Ambassy, to morrow lunch with crown princess,[366] Thursday trip to Buda Pest, Friday leave for Aussee, dearest love

Wilhelmina

Alt-Aussee, May 16 1897

**172**   Dearest of Darlings,

Thank you so much for your dear letters & other useful parcels which arrived here just an hour after us so that you must not think you made a mistake in sending them to Alt-Aussee, you old Darling. I am sorry to hear that your mother is again less well, how is she & your sister these last days? What darlings your kittens must be, but I thought you hated kittens? I mean to write a very long letter this time but I don't yet know if I will have time to send it off to day. I think I will begin from the time we left Amsterdam.

We met auntie Lily soon upon coming into Germany. In Stuttgart I went about a good deal with auntie Lily & Pauline;[367] I must say she was charming & I found it delightful seeing her in her own home. We saw her studio which is situated in the park. The progress she has made, is really wonderful & her establishment is grand. I talk very much German now & had often to do so in Stuttgart, the more because there were many princes & princesses come for the wedding of the prince of Schaumburg Lippe[368] which was to be shortly after we left. I found my stay delightful.

Pauline is coming over to England with her parents & on her way back she will stay with us, but ofcourse without her parents. My uncle Frits & auntie Tilly[369] were also at Stuttgart, it was most amusing. The weather was fine & warm the first day at Stuttgart but afterwards it has been very cold & I was glad to have my fur. In Vienna we had much rain & only one warm day, the rest of the time it has been as cold as in January & here in Aussee there is every where snow & it

in the hills above the River Danube. The monastery was founded in 1114; the Gothic basilica, originally Romanesque, has a baroque interior. Much of the complex was built between 1730 and 1834.

**366** 'Crown princess' probably refers to Stephanie of Belgium (1864-1945). On 10 May 1881, she married Crown Prince Rudolf (1858-1889), the only son of Emperor Frans Josef and Empress Elisabeth of Austria. Rudolf and his lover, Baroness Marie von Vetsera, committed suicide together in 1889.

**367** This refers to Pauline, Princess of Württemberg (see letter 156, note 296).

**368** This concerns the marriage of Prince Albrecht of Schaumburg-Lippe (1869-1942) and Duchess Elsa of Württemberg (1876-1936), which took place in Stuttgart on 6 May 1897. Albrecht was the elder brother of Bathildis of Waldeck-Pyrmont. There had been talk of a marriage between Elsa and Prince Alfred of Saxe-Coburg (1874-1899), the only son of Alfred I, Duke of Edinburgh and Duke of Saxe-Coburg, and Marie of Russia. For Coburg (see letter 227, note 565).

**369** Friedrich and Bathildis of Waldeck-Pyrmont, the brother and sister-in-law of Queen Emma. Charlotte of Schaumburg-Lippe (1864-1946), the older sister of Bathildis and Albrecht, became the second wife of Wilhelm II of Württemberg in 1886 and was thus Pauline's stepmother.

Emperor Franz Josef (1830-1916), pictured in the period when Wilhelmina visited him. Cover image from the book *Franc Jožef*, Gregor Antoličič (ed.), Cankarjeva založba, Ljubljana 2016.

is also very cold & wet & it rains nearly the whole day. There are really <u>very</u> fine collections of pictures at Vienna & this time I admired them very much, you see I have quite changed. I found specially interesting a private collection of sketches & etches: the "Albertina",[370] one of the finest things I ever saw. The shops were beautiful & I went twice shopping & bought a lot of fine things for mother, most things for Soestdijk. Vienna is very known for fans & leather-work.[371] A thing I found most amusing was the Prater[372] (public park) there are very fine horses in Vienna & just there in the Prater one see's very many.

The cabs drive very quickly. The private carriages have also beautiful horses just like Bavo & Beppo & they have also the same harness & go at the same speed; I don't think I ever saw horses race in the way they do in the Prater. The coachman & carriage are shockingly untidy. And they don't wear any livery so that one can't see if the gentleman is driving or the coachman it looks most extraordinary! I also went to see the horses ridden in the Spanish school.[373] It is most wonderful. The animals are quite like on the old pictures, with fat necks, long tails & a heavily built body. Their rider makes them throw all their force on their hind-legs & bend those to the ground & lift up their front-legs & hoist the whole of their body up in the air & remain in that position for several seconds.

You can understand what a good exercise that is for both rider & horse. There was one horse which jumped like a stag, he began with the exercise before discribed & then had to throw up also his hind-legs so as to jump with all fours

370 The Albertina is a museum with a collection of 65,000 drawings and 1,000,000 prints. It was named after the founder, Duke Albert Casimir of Saxe-Teschen, in 1776. The museum has occupied its current site, Archduke Albert Palace in Vienna, since 1795. In 1920 it was merged with the imperial court library.

371 The Rodeck Bros were the best manufacturers of fans in Vienna. I am grateful to Mrs F.M. Hovinga-van Eijsden for this information.

372 The Wiener Prater is a large park in Vienna. Originally an imperial hunting ground, it was opened to the public in 1766 by Emperor Joseph II. A 4.5 km-long path runs through the park, bordered by horse chestnut trees. The park is celebrated for its Ferris wheel, which dates from 1897.

373 This is the 'Spanish Riding School' in the Hofburg in Vienna. Founded in 1572, it is the world's oldest existing riding school, which displays classical equestrianism with Spanish-bred stallions.

high up in the air & come down on exactly the same place he started from. It was most wonderful & specially that the man kept on.

The Emperor came twice to pay a visit, he is such a kind old gentleman; I asked him for his photograph & had to write a fine letter to thank him.[374]

Mother & I we were very pleased to see a sweet loving auntie of mothers the Archduchess Marie Rainer;[375] we dined there & went often to see her. All the visits we had to make were very interesting & a perfect novalty for me.

We went for a day to Buda Pesth[376] which was very interesting; Buda is so prettily situated on the mountain near the river. The Hungarians are so utterly different to Austrians. We saw the Rumbolds[377] at Vienna & the Metternichs;[378] the daughter Metternich was an old playfellow of mine of the year 85 at "Königswart"[379] & it was most amusing to see her again. Auntie Lily has now left us; as usual the parting was tragical!

May 17) The weather has really got much better since yesterday & I have been able to take a walk without being quite soaked, the sun is shining brightly & the scenery is very fine. Yesterday I had a mad walk; I went all round the lake & on the otherside the snow had not yet melted & in some places we sank in till our knees, but nor I, nor miss v. Stirum, nor miss de Joannis have been any the worst for it; I don't think it can harm in this climate!

374 Between 1848 and his death, Franz Josef I of Austria (1830–1916) was Emperor of Austria and King of Hungary. In 1854 he married his cousin Elisabeth (Sisi) of Bavaria. Their only son, Rudolf, committed suicide in 1889.

375 Archduchess Marie Rainer is Maria Caroline (1825–1915), daughter of Henrietta Alexandrine of Nassau-Weilburg (1797–1830) and Archduke Charles, Duke of Teschen, the son of Leopold II of the Holy Roman Empire. Maria Carolina married Archduke Rainer of Austria (1827–1913), the grandson of Leopold II. Maria Carolina and Emma's mother Helena were the great-granddaughters of Princess Carolina of Orange-Nassau (1743–1787) and Carl Alexander of Nassau-Weilburg (1735–1788), via their son Friedrich Wilhelm (1768–1816).

376 Budapest, the capital of Hungary, was founded in 1873 through the unification of Buda and Óbuda on the right bank of the Danube, and Pest on the left bank.

377 The identity of 'the Rumbolds' is not known.

378 This must refer to Prince Paul C.L. von Metternich-Winneburg (1834–1906) and his wife Melanie, the Countess of Zichy-Ferraris and Vásonykeö (1843–1925) and their third child, Pauline (1880–1960), who was born in the same year as Wilhelmina. Paul was the son of Prince Clemens W.N.L. von Metternich-Winneburg (1773–1859), who chaired the Congress of Vienna in 1814/15. He was also Count of Königswart in Bohemia, the location of one of the Metternichs' favourite castles.

379 On 9 May 1885, Queen Emma and Princess Wilhelmina left for Arolsen, with King Willem III following them on 13 May to take the waters in Carlsbad, a spa town in Bohemia popular with the nobility in the 18th and 19th centuries. Königswart also lies in Bohemia. On 21 July, the royal family departed for Het Loo via Frankfurt. From a letter from Wilhelmina, written by Queen Emma, to Wilhelmina's nurse, Lady M.L. de Kock and sent from Königswart on 19 June 1885, we know that Queen Emma and Princess Wilhelmina had joined King Willem III, who was at that time staying in Königswart. Wilhelmina: 'Father was at the station. I have got two new dolls ... Rosa and ... Clara ... There is a donkey cart, which Father chose in Carlsbad, which I ride in. I love Königswart, it is very beautiful and pleasant. Yesterday father, mother and I paid a visit to a great-aunt ...' (G28-3).

The country round about here is lovely! The hôtel is situated on a small hill overhanging the lake & my sittingroom looks out on the water. I look into a great many vallies & looking through those I see a great many mountaintops all covered with snow. Notwithstanding the snow there are already many flowers out & the vegetation is very rich. I am out as much as possible & love my morning walks which are generally rather mad although I don't rush very madly! I get up at 7 in the morning & go to bed at 8.$^{30}$ or 8.$^{45}$; my appetite is alarming.

I am very busy here, with going out & seeing miss de Joannis who has now arrived; she seems very pleasant & easy to get on with & I think she is very merry when one gets to know her better.

I am very busy making a workbag for mother's birthday; I have begun the work quite myself & also drawn it, half imitating that pretty tablecloth I have at the Hague, you know all handwork! I am working on cream silk & wonders of wonders — on a frame; I can't do much of it at a time for as I can never feel myself if my eyes are tired & I have nobody to ask if the work is fatiguing to do, I have to be careful.

I have reserved a little time every day for learning my play & I talk with a lot of feeling & energy to the four walls! Most amusing, don't you find? The play in which I take the greatest part "uit liefde voor de kunst [For the love of art]" has the following plot: a rich countess (this I am to be) has taken in her service a new footman (young DuMonceau)[380] & this man does & says the most clever & extraordinary things & both she & her maid (miss v. Ittersum) are quite at a loss what to do with him. This footman is not really a usual servant but an artist who bought the livery of a footman to take service under this countess to be able to draw her for he has found her such a good model for a picture he is painting of Judith[381] at the moment she cuts off Holophernes's head; but the countess has one drawback: she always smiles & the artist wants an angry looking woman. He does nothing but to try & make her furious but utterly in vain. At last the maid comes in & tells the countess that her dress for the ball of that evening will not be ready; the artist draws out his sketchbook & the whole thing comes out!

The other play is as follows: Nicht [female cousin] Venkel (I) & neef [male cousin] Venkel (M$^r$ Bentinck) have a feast in honour that they have had 12 ½ years their factory & for that occasion their uncle & aunt are giving a dinner; they ask a youn man living there to make "een lief vers [A sweet verse]" for they have read in a birthdaybook somewhere a piece of poetry of his.

Ofcourse this young man is not at all a poët & can't do it a bit. He asks a friend to help him they make together such an awful, long thing that every body falls asleep while it is being read. The composer of the verse hopes by making it so awful that he will never be asked to make one again for he does not like to be

380  Count Joseph Henri Felix Dumonceau (1859-1952), (see letter 51, note 71).
381  According to the Book of Judith, Judith, a rich, pious Jewish widow, plied General Holofernes — whose army had threatened her village in the mountains, Bethulia — with wine at his camp and decapitated him. She then returned to Bethulia with his head, whereupon the soldiers fled in a panic, pursued by the Jews.

considered a professional poët. The End is that his friend who helped make it marries with a young ward of "Tante Venkel". I think I must end now!

With all my dearest love I remain your most affectionnately devoted

Wilhelmina

Alt-Aussee, May 28 1897

**173**    Dearest of Darlings,

I have just got this afternoon your sweet, long letter; thank you so much for it, Darling; it is always delightful to get your Darling letters & to converse together like in the olden times! I <u>am</u> so sorry, Darling to hear that your poor mother is so ill again; it <u>must</u> be sad for her if she gets those attacks more frequently. I am so pleased you write to me so openly about all your worries about your mother for you know you always will find in me a warm sympathiser in all your troubles & worries; poor old Darling, it must be a sad & difficult time! I am not astonished that you have no time for going out! How is your dear old head? I am getting on quite well with miss de Joannis, she is easy going; we always read my dear Corneille[382] in the morning; it is lovely to hear the Cid, Polyeucte etc. again. It is such a good thing that she is not at all pushing; one can see that she has been in the habit to do duty as lady in waiting. Here the weather is quite respectable & during my walks I suffer from the heat!

You don't know what a fool I feel at acting; I am very curious to know whether I will suffer from stagefright! I am so glad that you tell me something about Julie Liotard for to tell you the truth I have not heard from her since new year I don't quite know if I owe her a letter or not! I congratulate you with your nephew's succes. It is grand of him to come out the first; will marry now? I think bicycling must be a great joke for you, but I always maintain the old theory that walking is always the best of exercises; would it not be better for your sister to take long walks in stead of bycicling. You sent me such an amount of sulphur lozenges that I don't think I will want any for a long time, thank you Darling. Are they making a great feast of the Queen's Jubilee[383] in Walden?

We are leaving Alt-Aussee not before the 8th of June but it is not yet quite decided for the little Josias[384] at Arolsen having got hoopingcough mother does not know if we can go there. I am having a fine time here. We have made many expeditions; there are so many little lakes about here & it is delightful to row about on them. Mother is allowing me this year to make long walks of four hours with the ladies & gentlemen in the mountains, we start after breakfast & take bread & butter with us to sustain us till lunch. Every body seems to find I climb so well, but I find I puf & blow still very much.

---

**382** Pierre Corneille (1606–1684), a French playwright, wrote the tragicomedy *Le Cid* in 1637 and the tragedy *Polyeucte* in 1643.

**383** In 1897 Queen Victoria (1819–1901) celebrated her sixtieth year on the throne of the United Kingdom, to which she had acceded in 20 June 1837. From 1877, she had also been Empress of India. She was the last sovereign from the House of Hannover.

**384** Josias of Waldeck-Pyrmont (1896–1967), the eldest son of Emma's brother Fritz.

Mother is keeping very well & I hope she is resting here. To day we went to see a saltmine close to Alt-Aussee. We had to put on large new cloaks & the gentlemen slipped on linnen jackets & little caps like the English soldiers ware. We looked very funny! I miss v. Stirum miss de Joannis were driven in a little cart into the mine, sitting like a man on horseback. It was very interesting to see in the rock the different layers of salt! There was also one staircase along which one could go down like in the "montagne russe".[385] We saw a lake like there was also near Halle at Igls! I think we will come back to the dear old Loo about the 14th June. Mother told me I might tell you that we are thinking of asking you to come to us this automn at the Loo; but ofcourse Mother can't yet say for certain as you know till then there can still come many things in between. Mother also thought that just <u>that</u> time would be so good for miss de Joannis having left I would have more time to spend with you & at the end of September life is very quiet at the Loo. If however you might just not be able to come, there could ofcourse be found another time for your visit. Oh Darling, what a lovely thing that would be; it is a thing to look forward to the whole summer! What do you say about the plan? I would be positively mad of joy if you were to come over! I had to keep that good news for the last of the letter for a final treat!

With all my dearest love & hugs I remain your most affectionnately & madly delighted & looking forward to your visit

Wilhelmina

Wilhelmina enclosed a press cutting in Dutch, entitled *Rejuvenation and regeneration. Our tribute to Queen Victoria*, with the words: something very nice about Queen Victoria, I thought you might like to read it. Dearest love

Wilhelmina

Alt-Aussee, June 4 1897

**174** My own dearest Darling,
I have just got your dear letter; thank you so much for it Darling; I <u>can't</u> say how <u>glad</u> I am about your coming over to us; you will be able to represent yourself so much better my life as it is now than you can at present & we will be able to understand & represent ourselves both our surroundings much better. My Darling! are you really meaning to go to America, to that horrid unknown place? Have you already got a position over there? Or are you only going to see over there if you can get something to do? Or is it to see if change of surroundings will do the poor old hearty good? Don't please go Darling, without having looked at it from all sides!

I <u>will</u> be glad to have an opportunity of talking to you & saying many things that don't go so well by letter, I think it would be wretched for you on the other side of the Atlantic. By the bye, mother wished me to tell you that if it made the journey or any thing else to do with your going over or getting an occupation

---

**385** The term 'montagne russe' is another word for roller coaster.

over there in any way more difficult you were _really_ to say so for then there could easily be found another time for coming to us.

We are having here very fine weather & great heat. Every other day we make fine expeditions for the whole day you know. We are leaving here the 8<sup>th</sup>. Our next address is the "Belvédère"[386] at Weimar. There we remain till the 11<sup>th</sup> then we go to Arolsen, "Tientje"[387] having given his consent.

The 14<sup>th</sup> we come to the Loo. Luckily my cousins of Mecklenburg & Reuss[388] are to be at Weimar.

My various occupations are getting on very well & I think they will get ready in time.

With all my very dearest love I will always remain your most devoted,

Wilhelmina

Het Loo, June 20 1897

175   Dearest of Darlings,

Thank you _so_ much for your three dear letters; oh Darling, I _am_ sorry & ashamed about not having written before, but to tell the troth at Weimar & Arolsen I never had a moments time in my room & coming here I was awfully busy with my rooms, my lessons & my painting, embroidering & acting; in fact this is the first moment I have had to write; but all the same I feel very guilty! I was very sorry to hear that you have had to give up the idea of the work you were hoping to get in America, but on the other hand I was delighted to hear that the American plan was given up for I always still think it would have been _very_ lonely in that horrid place. Poor old Darling it must be very wearijing work looking for occupation; I can understand that you can't stay at home & I wish, I wish I could come & comfort you. You were such a Darling to send such dear letters saying how you thought about me during my stay at Weimar & my arrival here. Pauline[389] gave me all your dear loving messages; I am also madly looking forward to your coming here not only for all our comfortable talks, but also to be able to show you all my new rooms!

The days at Weimar were dreadful, but my cousin of Mecklenburg[390] was touching in all her love & sweetness; I really don't know what we would have done without her & her husband there. We started from Aussee at nine in the morning & arrived at the Belvédère at 11<sup>30</sup> at night. My uncle came to meet us

---

**386**  The Belvedere on the outskirts of Weimar is a baroque country house that was built between 1724 and 1732. After 1811, the French gardens were largely transformed into an English-style park.

**387**  'Tientje' refers to Mr G.P. van Tienhoven (1836–1901), Wilhelmina's physician. He evidently gave her his permission to travel on to Arolsen, something that had initially been questioned due to the little Josias Waldeck's whooping cough.

**388**  These are Elisabeth (Elsi), Duchess of Saxe-Weimar (1854–1908), married to Duke Johann Albrecht of Mecklenburg-Schwerin, and Marie Alexandrine (Zitta), Duchess of Saxe-Weimar (1849–1922), married to Heinrich VII, Prince of Reuss (see letter 164, note 343).

**389**  Pauline (see letter 156, note 296).

**390**  Cousin Mecklenburg is Elisabeth (Elsi) (see note 388).

at Jena in the train. He was awfully changed! The arrival at Belvédère was most painful. To come into the house where formerly my Auntie used to live; to see all the places which all call Her back into my mind & to see all the places as it were still waiting to receive Her & knowing that she was gone for ever, was to much for me & I felt perfectly miserable.

The next day mother went with my cousin to the vault where my Auntie is buried & I met them with my uncle & cousin of Mecklenburg at Weimar to see my Auntie's rooms. My cousin of Mecklenburg was very kind & a great help with my uncle. I saw my Auntie's rooms, the places where she had passed her last moments here on earth & also where I had always sat with her when I went for the golden wedding.[391] Then we saw her museum[392] that she had opened of Schiller & Goethe last year. In the afternoon I had a quiet talk with my cousine whilst her husband occupied my uncle. She gave me all the things my Auntie had destined me in Her testament.

In the evening my cousin of Weimar came with Sophie Renata & brothers & the boys Weimar.[393] I had a nice talk with Sophie R. after dinner. The next morning we saw some more museums & in the afternoon I went for tea & dinner to Ittersburg[394] (the place of my cousin of Weimar) mother only coming for dinner. It was nice to see Sophie R. again, but rather slow work.

At Arolsen it was very nice & I enjoyed seeing the dear old place very much. It was only a too great contrast with Weimar. I was delighted to be home again; only it was so sad not seeing my dear "old Bones" here. You as it were quite belong to the Loo & I thought so much about you; it was very lonely going about & seeing all the dear places without you by my side.

---

391 Emma and Wilhelmina — Miss Winter was also in the retinue — were in Weimar between 3 and 10 October 1892, to attend the festivities surrounding the golden marriage anniversary of Sophie and Carl-Alexander of Saxe-Weimar, including a service of thanksgiving and a gala dinner on 8 October. At the dinner, Wilhelmina sat between her uncle and King Albert of Saxony.

392 This is the Goethe-Schiller Archive, which Grand Duchess Sophie founded in Weimar as a worthy repository for the archives of Goethe and Schiller. The building was inspired by the Petit Trianon at Versailles; see letter 216, note 529 (Brena, p. 27).

393 Sophie Renate (1884-1968) was a daughter of Princess Marie 'Zitta' of Saxe-Weimar Eisenach, the daughter of Sophie and Carl-Alexander of Saxe-Weimar, and Heinrich VII, Prince of Reuss. On 12 December 1909 she married Heinrich XXXIV Reuss (1887-1956). Besides her stillborn brother Heinrich in 1877 and her sister Johanna (1882-1883), who died young, her brothers were Heinrich XXXII (1878-1935), Heinrich XXXIII (1879-1942) and Heinrich XXXV (1887-1936).

394 Ettersburg Castle was built in 1706 as a hunting lodge to the north of Weimar. In the 18th century, it was the meeting place of the literary-musical circle around the duke's mother, Anna Amalia, which included figures such as Goethe, Herder and Wieland. Carl-Alexander and Sophie of Saxe-Weimar used it as a summer residence, receiving, among others, the writer Hans Christian Andersen and the pianist-composer Frans Liszt. In 1918 the castle was transferred to the State of Thuringia. In 1998 it was added to the UNESCO List of World Cultural Heritage Sites, as part of 'classical Weimar'.

My rooms are <u>lovely</u>, I am delighted with then. I will begin from coming up the big stairs to describe them.[395]

Workroom[396] — Green carpet, old painted ceiling, old brown oak doors, red marble chimeny piece with old oak, large writing table & opposite me masters chair, globe, leather on the walls.

Drawingroon[397] (former music room) — soft yellow silk on walls, light carpet, ceiling painted light, doors painted, chairs pale yellow figured silk with white wood.

Sittingroom[398] (mothers former study) — carpet green, ceiling cream coloured, walls light green silk tables chairs from old sittingroom.

Bedroom[399] (formerly fathers) — blue-gray paper on walls, chairs & tables white wood blue-gray.

Dressingroom[400] (fathers former bathroom) — cream paper on walls, cream curtains, dressing table large looking glass brown polished wood.

Bathroom[401] — you know.

I am very much enjoying having Pauline here, it <u>must</u> have been plesant to see Pauline[402] again, she had written to say she would like to see you to mother at Weimar. I found back all my animals & kissed old Swell in your name, I am trying to be nice to him.

I have already been sitting for Bless[403] a few times, I have to go to him in full dress at least for the next few times.

Tuesday we are to have the first grand repetition on the stage ; last Saturday I had a private one with M^r de Ranitz & miss van Ittersum, I <u>did</u> feel a fool although I know my part very well but don't yet say it with enough feeling.

You heard that miss van de Poll's sister-in-law had just had a little boy?[404]

---

395 See Renting for the uses of all the rooms over the centuries.

396 Archives of the Intendancy of the Royal Palace and Estate of Het Loo, 1806-1971 (1975), E 9c, inv.no 1148, inventory of the furniture on the 1st Floor (9 August 1905). When Paleis Het Loo was restored in 1984 as a museum, the 'Study of H.M. the Queen no. 78' (1975) was rearranged in its original function as the bedchamber of the king-stadholder Willem III (1650-1702). Wilhelmina's study was moved to the floor below during the restoration. The wall covering is imitation gold leather and comes from the Ryozo Wall Paper Co., the wallpaper factory of Yamaji Ryozo in Tokyo (which was in business between c. 1890 and 1940).

397 Idem, 'Drawing room of H.M. the Queen no. 77' (1905), arranged as King Willem II's (1792-1849) drawing room.

398 Idem, 'Sitting-room of H.M. the Queen no. 76' (1905), arranged as the drawing room of Queen Sophie (1818-1877), the wife of King Willem III (1817-1890).

399 Idem, 'Bedroom of H.M. the Queen no. 70' (1905), arranged as King Willem III's bedroom.

400 Idem, 'Dressing room of H.M. the Queen no. 73' (1905); cabinet by Hondecoeter.

401 Idem, 'Bathroom of H.M. the Queen no. 72' (1905); still the existing bathroom.

402 This is Pauline, Princess of Württemberg (see letter 156, note 296).

403 Bles (see letter 161, note 331).

404 This refers to Mr Fredrik Harman van de Poll, who was born on 14 June 1897 (died 1922), the son of Mr Willem H.J. van de Poll (1867-1921) and Anna A.G. Gevaerts (1873-1941).

With all my dearest love & hugs I always remain your most affectionnately devoted

Wilhelmina

Het Loo<br>June 27 1897

**176** Dearest of Darlings,

Thank you so much for your dear, long letter. I must say that I can't say that my cousin Pauline has made me very beautiful on the photos she made of me. The acting went off quite well & it was most amusing. I hope very much that Alice Albany[405] may come here during this year & then I will be able to see how tall she has grown.

Don't say she is taller than I for you know I have still grown since you saw me. I swim every day in my bath & play very much tennis with all three my ladies. The heat here is very great & I ride now in my white habits, leaving off all under-clothes which are not absolutely necessary. After all the papers say the Jubilee must have been very fine, how nice it must have been for your brother to go up to London, it <u>would</u> have been nice for you also to go down to see it but I can understand you can't & you have no time.[406]

Did you read about how the ships were smashed again at Scheveningen? It must have been very bad! I wish there had come here the thunderstorm you have had at Walden for it is awfully hot for every body has got a painful noddle to day & one has a feeling that one would like to jump out of this atmosphere & come somewhere near the northpole. How is your old heady now?

And how are your sister & mother?

Excuse if this letter is rather under the impression of the heat for spelling & writing is not beautiful to day. Pauline leaves to morrow; she sends you her kindest greetings.

With all my most dearest love I always remain your most affactionnately devoted

Wilhelmina

Het Loo<br>July 10 1897

**177** My very dearest of Darlings,

I just got your dear letter yesterday, oh! Darling! how dreadful for you to have to begin the whole old worry afresh; how awful that your sister had a new relapse!

---

[405] Alice Albany was the daughter of Emma's elder sister Helena and Leopold of Albany (see letter 109, note 143). Alice married Alexander Teck, Earl of Athlone (1874-1957). Alice would always stay in touch with the Dutch royal family and would attend important events. For example, she attended the marriage of Princess Margriet of the Netherlands and Mr Pieter van Vollenhoven on 10 January 1967.

[406] The 'Jubilee' was the 60th anniversary of the reign of Queen Victoria, who had succeeded King William IV of Great Britain and Ireland (1765-1837) on 20 June 1837.

Is she now at home, or still away? And your poor dear mother, what a shock for her! I will have to begin a sermon upon not writing if you are so busy; never trouble about writing Darling, you know I quite understand you have no time! You are <u>really</u> not to send any letters until you have more time.

But I will go on writing to you all the same. I am very busy still with sitting for Bless & acting; Wednesday afternoons & Thursday mornings are quite given up to it. For the rest life is going on as usual. I am hard at work with lessons; prof Blok has arrived at the year 1830 (belgian revolution) and there are many differences of opinion.[407] Last Wednesday I drew my first plaster head with M[r] Jansen[408] & it went fairly well. I am trying on my own accord to paint scenes in the park in oils, you will imagine how <u>beautiful</u> [underlined three times] that must get for M[r] Jansen never tought it me & I only go by what I heard him say about it to you last year.[409] To morrow there is to be a gala dinner for the Persian ambassador who comes to announce the death of the late Shah.[410] — I am to wear my persian decoration[411], you may imagine how <u>beautiful</u> [underlined twice] that will be!!!! I saw back Foppie the other day since the journey & I was most astonished that he was very pleased to see me. Mother sends you her love.

Hoping, Darling, that both your mother & sister will soon get better, I remain your most affectionnately devoted

Wilhelmina

**407** The Belgian Revolution, which broke out in 1830 in the Southern Netherlands, led to the founding of the state of Belgium. The Northern and Southern Netherlands had been united during the Congress of Vienna in 1815, when King Willem I had become king.

**408** Mr Jansen (see letter 143, note 248).

**409** Wilhelmina would do many paintings and drawings and at Het Loo and Soestdijk for her calendars, which she made for her loved-ones each year.

**410** On Monday 12 July 1897, the two queens received a visit from the Persian ambassador Nasser ol-Molk, as part of an official tour of the European courts to announce the reign of Mozaffar ud-Din Sjah Qajar (1853–1907). He was taken from Apeldoorn Station to Het Loo by the state carriage and an escort of cavalry, and entertained to a gala dinner in the Gallery of Het Loo. Mademoiselle de Joannis was also permitted to attend. As Consul-General Bosschart wrote from Teheran, the ambassador was also visiting in order to 'express his good wishes for the prosperous and solemn relations between the two states, and furthermore to express the empire's satisfaction and joy regarding the demonstration of harmony and friendship made by the Netherlands to the ruler of Persia.' It was later communicated that 'the Persian Ambassador was extremely taken with the excellent reception that he received in the Netherlands and, after his return here, immediately sent a telegram on this subject to His Majesty the Shah' (see Barjesteh, pp. 78–79). The shah of Persia who had died, was Naser ud-Din Qajar (1831–1896) of the Qajar dynasty. He had ruled between 1848 and 1896. The Qajar dynasty was in power between 1786 and 1925. It was succeeded by the Pahlavi dynasty, which ended in 1979.

**411** On 26 February/27 March 1895, Wilhelmina was awarded the Grand Cross of the Order of Nichan-i-Aftab (Order of the Sun). She received the medal during the visit of the Special Ambassador of Persia. Barjesteh wrote erroneously (p. 64) that the medal was presented by Mozaffar ud-Din Sjah to Wilhelmina in 1900. My thanks to my former colleague G. Sanders for this information.

**178** My very dearest of Darlings,

Thank you so much for your dear letter. I <u>am</u> [underlined twice] glad to hear that
your mother & sister are getting better; I had remembered that your mothers
birthday was the 13<sup>th</sup> but you know I always forget if it is in June or July. You
old Dear! how strange it must have seemed to be home that day! You must not
think <u>too</u> much of my attempts at oilpainting Darling, for I have no time to give
to it at present; I say, you <u>must</u> paint a great deal when you come here! I am
trying to keep as calm as possible about the birthday because otherwise I could
n't possiby do all I have to. The galadinner went off very well but it was very
hot. The Persians spoke admirably French & had quite european manners! Prof.
Krämer has lately been giving most interesting lectures: I asked him to describe
in a few lectures the leading ideas & questions of the 17<sup>th</sup> & 18<sup>th</sup> century: he has
been talking about arts & sciences, philosophy, litteriture & he has finished up
with the economical state of Europe in the 18<sup>th</sup> century & what the enlightened
princes of that age did for the development of their states.— It was intensely
interesting.

Bless is really making the picture like me; the other day mother came for my
last sitting & stood for an hour behind him, making him change all the time little
details & in that hour my face on the picture had quite another aspect. It is not
quite decided how many people are to be invited for the performance of the 2<sup>d</sup>
but I don't think their will be very many, about 60 or 70. The acting will come
instead of all other plans of illumination.

We have not been having so many storms here; how dreadful for the poor
people who have had all their windows smashed I <u>do</u> [underlined twice] pity you
that your garden has been spoilt! It <u>must</u> has been interesting to hear the lecture
about education, poor England seems not to have been seen from a very satisfactory light; let's hope that soon it will be as far in its educational systems as it is
now in its physical development![412]

I am sorry to say I am still as bad in reading my papers as formerly & I only
read what I <u>absolutely must</u> know: the politics, for the rest I only live & hope the
kind people, like you supposing, will tell me about the other interesting things
that happen, so I did <u>not</u> read about the regattas. But ofcourse I am very proud
of my countrymen if they win a prize.[413] The weather here is not at all warm & I
can't understand how it comes that it is so hot in England.

---

**412** Important discoveries were being made in the United Kingdom at that time: in 1894, the
noble gas argon was discovered by the physicist Lord Rayleigh (John William Strutt 1842–1919)
and the chemist Sir William Ramsay (1852–1916), who also discovered the noble gas helium in
1896. In the same year, Lord Ernest Rutherford (1871–1937) studied the magnetic detection of
electrical waves, whilst the physicist Lord Kelvin, William Thomson (1824–1907) researched
cathode rays in 1897, and the physicist Sir Joseph John Thomson (1852–1940) experimentally
established the existence of the electron.
**413** From 1839, the Henley Royal Regatta was held annually in the first week of July in Henley-

The day before yesterday we had the garden party; I had a white silk dress with white toque with feathers; one found I was well dressed & I did my best to be kind. Miss de Kock is staying here for a few days & I am very much enjoying the comfortable little talks I am having with her. I am in an awful hurry to get every thing ready for the 2ᵈ. A work is still to be finished repetitions are to take place, rides & drives are to be taken, tennis is to be played, lessons are to be done, orders are to be given here-there-& every where people are to be spoken to, a perfect calm to be kept & last but not least, a good temper is to be kept!!!! I am keeping quite well & so is mother.

With my very dearest love I remain, Darling, your most affectionnately devoted

Wilhelmina

In the meantime, Queen-Regent Emma had been searching for a new appointment for Miss Winter. She found work for her with the Wied family. Diagonally across the top of the first page of the following letter, written on mourning paper, she wrote:

Don't destroy this letter at least not the part containing the conditions for the situation with the Wieds.

The Loo, July the 19ᵗʰ 1897

179    Dear Miss Winter,

Happily today I have good news for you. I have found temporary work for you. — In the course of the winter & spring I wrote to several persons to try to find some work for you. My Aunt of Wied[414] was one of the last I wrote too & from her I got what I consider good news for you. She asks me to offer you the following temporary situation.

My cousin of Wied & his wife[415] would like to have you for their girls from now until the end of January 1898.

They would wish you to teach the girls english (I suppose including litterature) & to be a pleasant companion not only for the girls but for the whole homeparty. — I asked what would be your duties & got this answer: To feel happy & at home with us and teach the girls english. —

You would not have any grave responsibilities because Miss v. Harbon[416] is still with the girls & in charge of their education.

on-Thames, with the trophy being the Grand Challenge Cup for the best men's eight. In 1897 the cup was won by New College, Oxford.

414  Marie, Princess of Nassau (1825–1902), the half-sister of Emma's mother, married to Hermann of Wied (1814–1864).

415  This is Wilhelm of Wied, who married Marie, Princess of the Netherlands (1841–1910) in 1871. They had five children: Friedriech (1872–1945), who married Wilhelmina's cousin Pauline of Württemberg (1877–1965) in 1898; Wilhelm (1876–1945), who became King of Albania in 1914; Victor (1877–1946); Louise (1880–1965); and Elisabeth (1883–1938). The last two never married.

416  Miss von Harbon was the governess of Louise and Elisabeth of Wied.

You know enough about the life of the Wieds to realise that you would form one of the home circle and enjoy family life. You also know that they spend the summer & automn at Monrepos[417] & the winter in Italy at St Margarita.[418]

The Wieds offer you 100 marks (hundred!) a month & of course would pay your travelling expences coming & leaving. I suppose you will find that little, but you must realise that you have no heavy duties & that you need make <u>no</u> expenses whatever. You do not require anything more than you would want at home at Saffron Walden & with your dresses of last year you would be ten times more elegant than all the ladies in the house of the Wieds. —

I think you will like this proposition as it has many good sides. I shall just mention them to you.

I I think you will find later on more easily some work if you have been, after leaving the <u>Queen</u> of the Neth., in a smaller establishement.

II In going to the Wieds you will get known again in another circle of people & by that be able to get more easily some work after leaving there. My Aunt would be willing to recomend you & Marietje[419] I am sure to & they both know <u>very very</u> many people. —

III I think it will be nice for you to go to Italy even if you stay only in one place & live quietly.

IV I think the life will be pleasant for you. You always got on well with Miss v. Harbon & I am sure you would find no difficulty in remaining on a good & pleasant footing with her as your duties would not clash; she remains in charge of the education & you would teach the girls english & be a bright companion for them; & although you had not the training of them you would be able to influence them & do them a great deal of good & at the same time be able to contribute to the comfort & happiness of the life of the Princess & the ladies. I also believe you would feel at home quickly, because the Princess is a Dutch woman & knows about your former life. — I naturally do not wish to exercise any influence on your decision, it is only <u>you</u> who can judge if that kind of life would suit you for a few months. I have no idea if you can leave your mother.

If you accept the situation I think you ought to write yourself to the Princess my cousin; if you wish to refuse pray write to me & I shall forward an answer.

You need not fear loosing the chance of seeing Wilhelmina if you accept the offer of the Wieds. I would let you come to us on your way to Germany. —

I feel quite sure that you will not be able to leave home before a fortnight & that would just suit me, because after the 4th of August you would be very welcome here. My girl would have had time to get over the fatigue and excitement of my birthday and would be able to give you <u>all</u> her free time, what would be quite

---

417 Monrepos Castle dates from the 18th century and was the summer residence of the Wied family in the 19th century. It had been raised and painted white, and was also known at that time as the *Weisse Schloss*. It was demolished in 1969, because it had become too expensive to maintain.

418 Santa Margherita Ligure is a municipality in the Italian province of Genoa (Liguria region).

419 By 'Marietje', Emma will have meant Marie of Wied, Princess of the Netherlands.

Family photograph of the Wieds in 1900. Standing, from left to right: Crown Prince Friedrich; Princess Louise; Prince Wilhelm; Princess Marie of Wied, Princess of the Netherlands; Prince Wilhelm, the later King of Albania. Seated: Princess Pauline, the wife of Prince Friedrich; the Queen-Widow Marie of Wied, Princess of Nassau and half-sister of Emma's mother, holding Prince Hermann, the eldest son of Friedrich and Pauline; Prince Victor; and Princess Elisabeth. Photograph: Hermann Koch, Neuwied.

impossible before the 2$^d$ of Aug. — I would ask you to spend 4 to 6 days with us, for that time Wilhelmina would be able to give up her french, if you were to stay longer Wilhelmina could all the same not spend all her time with you and that would make you both feel miserable. —

The address of my cousin of Wied is "Monrepos" pres de Neuwied sur Rhin Allemagne. —

Wilhelmina is <u>very</u> well but fearfully busy nearly too much so. I have not time to write any longer today. I am myself well, but very worried by business matters. — My letter is dreadfully untidy, but I have had to write by fits & starts. I hope you can read & that I have been clear. — Wilhelmina sends her fondest love.

I must finish. Believe me dear Miss Winter

Your affectionate                                                                    Emma

Het Loo
July 25 1897

**180**     My very dearest Darling,

Just a few words to day to tell you how madly delighted I am to hear that you have accepted the position the Wieds have offered you & that you are coming here. I am ofcourse awfully sorry you can't stay here as long as I had hoped but you see as miss de Joannis is still here I couldn't give up my french & seeing her for very long; ofcourse now that you are only coming for such a short time I will be able to give up much more time to you. Mother told me to thank you very much for your letter. I am still very busy; my work for mother is finished, but have still to mount it. I rehearse every day for an hour & next Thurday, Friday & Saturday there are to be the last grand repetitions I have got lovely costumes[420] to play in: riding & driving are all put aside & I sit stitching away at my work during my free time; I all the same keep strictly to the rule of exercise & in latter part of the day I play tennis or walk.

Auntie Helen[421] is here at present but unluckily without the children, she stays till Wednesday. The weather has got fine again here since it has been spoilt a few days ago by constant thunderstorms of which I didn't hear the worst having been at night; there must have been one very bad clap for it must have been like the end of the world & it has struck the fine copper beech near my conservatory (the lightening ofcourse).

How are both the patients going on?

With all my very dearest love I remain you most affectionnately devoted

Wilhelmina

P.S. what do they say at home about your new occupation?

Het Loo

August 4 1897

**181**    Dearest of Darlings,

Thank you so much for your dear telegram & two lovings letters. You don't know Darling, how I thought about you on the morning of mothers birthday when I got your letter. How the poor old hearty must have ached during that day & I wished I could have comforted that forlorn old darling on the other side of the sea. For me the day was a grand success. I had prepared the presents in my drawingroom the picture being amount them. We breakfasted there & the morning passed like always on those occasions in opening letters & telegrams & receiving our people. In the afternoon I drove mother myself & at $5^{45}$ there was the dinner during which I drank to mothers health; there were about sixty people all of which assisted to the evening performance. This began at $7^{30}$ & ended at 11. First was acted the "Lief vers [A sweet verse]" then the "Werkstaking [The strike]

---

**420** The violet-grey striped dress that was worn by Wilhelmina in the play 'Uit liefde voor de kunst [For the love of art]' has been kept. Wilhelmina probably bought it in Vienna during her stay in the city in May 1897, judging from the label in the dress from the couturier *Ludwig Zwiebac & Bruder*, Wien, MU/3975. The gown was exhibited for the first time at the exhibition 'Het Witte Loo, van Lodewijk Napoleon tot Wilhelmina 1806-1962 [The White Loo, from Louis Napoleon to Wilhelmina 1806-1962]' in 1992 (Heuven 1992, pp. 113-119), and also at the exhibition 'Koninklijk Gekleed Wilhelmina 1880-1962 [In Royal Array, Queen Wilhelmina 1880-1962]' in 1998, both held at Paleis Het Loo (Elzenga, pp. 112-114). The other dress was not kept.

**421** Emma's sister Helena, the Duchess of Albany, stayed at Het Loo between 23 and 28 July.

'In memory of 2 August 1897' reads Queen Wilhelmina's inscription on this photograph of the cast of the play *Een life vers [A sweet verse]*, in which she was photographed with her household one day after the performance of two plays on the occasion of Queen Emma's birthday. From left to right: the adjutants W.J.P. van den Bosch and A.S.E. van Tets, aide-de-camp C.L. van Suchtelen van de Haare?, lady-in-waiting Elise G. van Ittersum, aide-de-camp F.W.J. Loudon, lady-in-waiting Baroness Anny J. Juckema van Bermania Rengers, lady-in-waiting A. Dolly W.A. van Limburg Stirum, Queen Wilhelmina, director S.M.S. de Ranitz, crown equerry Baron C.A. Bentinck, lady-in-waiting/superintendent F.L. Henriette van de Poll, marshal of the court Baron H.A. Clifford, adjutant W.F.H. van de Poll.
Photograph: H.W. Wollrabe, 's Gravenhage, court photographer to Her Majesty the Queen.

(translated from the grève des Forgerons") & then the "Liefde voor de kunst [For the love of art]". [Colour plate VI-9] In the first we all looked very funny in our costumes of about 1855. And I felt most decidedly "benauwd [nervous]" during my first appearance on the stage, but that went of soon enough. All my fellow actors & actresses played quite splendidly. There was great enthusiasm among the audience & we were often called back by the acclamations. I knew my part well & did not feel nervous in acting.

The next day we were all photographed together & had lunch with all the actores & actresses during which I stood up & made a speech to thank all those who had helped me & drank to their health.

After that goodbeys were said to the gentlemen who had to go back home & with that ended that pleasant time of acting & rehearsing, I am very sorry it is now over for I have enjoyed it very much.

I am still going to be very busy this mounth for we are going to have many visits & we are going about a good deal. To day my cousin of Mecklenburg is coming & Saturday my uncle of Weimar.[422] They both go on the 9th. Mother can't yet quite say the exact hour or date she will ask you to come on, but she thinks the 20th so that will quite come out with your going to the Wieds.

The weather was very fine for the birthday & since the heat has set in. How are the patients? With all my very dearest love I remain your most affectionnately devoted

Wilhelmina

Het Loo

August 15 1897

**182** Dearest of Darlings,

Thank you so much for your dear letter of last week.

I <u>am</u> glad you are coming next month for I think that miss de Joannis will have gone by that time; you can't imagine how mad I am about your coming. It will be so delightful. Mother said I was to tell you that if you had no objection to starting on a sunday she would like you to come on Monday the 13th already, so that then you would stay for a week. In the beginning of September we will be very busy with the visit of the king of Siam[423] and we will have the whole house full so that we could not have you before the 13th but then I would be able to be very much with you, you old darling!

My trip to Zutphen[424] was very interesting; it had to be put off for one day, the weather being so bad on the date on which it was fixed, that it would have been madness to attempt it. The next day it was very fine. We saw in Zutphen itself the church & the hospital, from there we drove to "Nederlandsch Mettray"[425] an institution for training naughty boys. The enthousiasm was very great every where & you don't know how much trouble the poor people had given themselves; it was most touching. I tried to look sweet & I hope I succeeded.

---

422 Between 4 and 9 August 1897, Elisabeth (Elsi), Duchess of Mecklenburg-Schwerin, came to stay, while her father Carl-Alexander, Grand Duke of Saxe-Weimar, would stay between 7 and 9 August.

423 The King of Siam was Rama V (1853–1910), of the Chakri dynasty; he was also known as King Chulalongkorn the Great. He was educated by European tutors, among others. With a regent for the first four years, he ruled between 1868 and 1910. He made two journeys to Europe, in 1897 and 1907. With the two princes, Svasti Sobhana and Mahisra, he stayed in The Hague between Monday 6 September and 9 September 1897. On 7 September he travelled to Het Loo by train, and set off back to the royal capital by train at 9:20 p.m.

424 The trip to Zutphen took place in the afternoon of 10 August 1897.

425 'Nederlandsch Mettray' was a Protestant reformatory for non-criminal youth with behavioural problems, founded in 1851 by Dr Willem Hendrik Suringar. It was established as an agricultural colony on the Rijsselt estate in Eefde, near Zutphen, modelled on a similar institution in the French municipality of Mettray. In 1998 the reformatory was transformed into the Rentray judicial juvenile institution. Early 2012 saw the Regional Archive of Zutphen's completion of the digitization and conservation of the archives of the Nederlandsch Mettray for the period between 1850 and 1961.

I very much enjoyed my cousin Elsi of Mecklenburg, she came a few days before her father; the latter remained for a day.[426] Auntie Lily came last Friday & went Saturday.[427] It was a short but delightful visit. We are going to Dordrecht[428] next Wednesday, Tuesday we are going for that purpose to the Hague for from there the journey is shorter. Thursday we come back here. Plans of visiting Arnhem[429] are also being thought of. You see we have a good deal to be done during this month.

I am glad to hear that your sister is better, it does not astonish me that you are having such intense heat for here it is awful. I can vividly imagine in what a state you must be, but you must never forget that it is very good for getting slighter; I wonder if I will find you looking well; you dear old Sweety! What you tell me about Dolly Maule I find very remarkable, I wonder if she is groing after all in a normal way?

I am now beginning to think about plans for Xmas or rather New Year. I want to make an almanac for mother with twelve views of the Loo;[430] so I am setting out every day with my lady on duty & miss de Joannis to find a place in the park which is good for sketching & then we sketch away bravely all three.

I think I must now finish.

With all my dearest love I ever remain your most affectionnately devoted.

Wilhelmina

Het Loo
August 29 1897

183    Dearest of Darlings,

Thank you so much for your dear letter; I am ashamed that I have let you wait for two weeks for a letter but I couldn't find any time; both with the Hague & the lessons that had by that to be caught up & with the visit of my uncle Fritz & auntie Tilly[431] & Arnhem, I had a good deal to do.

Before I begin to tell you more in detail what I have been about, I want to ask you to write & tell me about your birthday wishes. You must choose between my giving you books or an atlas or piece of furniture. Please say which of these things you would like best & name me the titles of the books, or the title of the atlas, or which piece of furniture you would like, but you must be quite open about it. My day at Dordrecht was very interesting; the people were so nice &

---

426  See note 422.
427  Elisabeth of Waldeck-Pyrmont stayed from 13 to 14 August.
428  The trip to Dordrecht took place on 18 August 1897.
429  The trip to Arnhem took place on 28 August 1897.
430  All kinds of locations around Paleis Het Loo were sketched by Wilhelmina in pencil on prepared cardboard, gilt-edged, 36.5 × 20.5 cm., six pages, for the calendar for the year 1898 that she gave to her mother. Royal Collections, The Hague, A47-IVa-2 (see Spliethoff, p. 82).
431  Emma's brother and sister-in-law Fritz and Tilly (Bathildis) stayed at Het Loo between 23 and 28 August 1897.

Dr H. van der Stadt, a physics teacher at the secondary school in Arnhem, gave Wilhelmina weekly lessons on electricity between October 1894 and February 1896. Queen Emma also attended the lessons. Until that time, this had been the responsibility of Wilhelmina's tutor Gediking. A separate room was set up at Het Loo, known as the laboratory. It had a table for experiments and was connected to the gas and water supply.

enthousiastic. I found the town itself most quaint. The races at Clingendaal[432] were very interesting & there did not happen any accidents; but you know Darling, I don't quite so much care for races as formerly; I find that I have still so much to learn that I don't give so much thought to sports in general, as I used to, not that I don't like them but that I find the time is precious & I want to use it for working. I paid my first visit alone to my cousin of Baden[433] at Scheveningen. We were received in a most enthousiastic manner yesterday at Arnhem. Among other things we saw an exhabition of shoppeoples ware made in Arnhem[434] & in one building.

D$^r$ van de Stadt showed us round his division, among other things also the X rays.[435] He made me hold my hand behind a screen so as to let me see my bones, of course without photographing them. Just fancy I am going to assist at the manoeuvres on horseback, it will be delightful. I enjoyed very much the visit of my uncle & auntie. You don't know how glad I am about your saying that my spelling was improving; I think that by writing to you so often I will perhaps get to write without mistakes!

I will be thinking a great deal about you on the 31$^{st}$.

With all my dearest love & hugs I remain your most affectionnately devoted

Wilhelmina.

Het Loo
September 1 1897

184  Dearest of Darlings,

You <u>can n't</u> imagine <u>how</u> madly delighted I am about your dear work you made for me. You are a Darling to have given up such a lot of time & trouble

432  The races at Clingendaal were on 19 August 1897.

433  Wilhelmina's cousin in Baden is the Hereditary Grand Duchess of Baden, Hilda Ch.W. of Nassau-Weilburg (1864–1952). She was the daughter of Adolf of Nassau-Weilburg (1817–1905), a half-brother of Emma's mother Helena, who became Grand Duke of Luxembourg after the death of King Willem III. In 1885, Hilda married Friedrich II, Hereditary Grand Duke of Baden (1857–1928) (see also Fasseur 1998, p. 401).

434  For the trip to Arnhem on 28 August 1897 they left by train at 12.18 p.m. and were back at Het Loo at 7:49 p.m.

435  This concerns the discovery of X-rays by the German physicist Wilhelm C. Röntgen (1845–1923), begun on 8 November 1895. Two weeks later, he took the first photo of his wife's hand. On 28 December he published his scientific article *Über eine neue Art von Strahlen [On a New Kind of Rays]*. In 1901 he won the first Nobel Prize for Physics.

to working the lovely blotter; thank you so much for it Darling; I was just very much in want of a new one at the Hague so I think I will use it there. What an awful work it must have been making all those little stitches how beautifully you have done it Sweety!

It was so nice getting your dear letter; it came the morning when I was at breakfast. You are quite right Darling the new year I begun yesterday is a very important one for me, the one I have finished is however not <u>less</u> important -- it has separated us two and has brought great changes in both our lives. We have both lived through hard moments, but we can be certain that there is One Who we can trust & Who has let the events take place as the have done for both our bests. That for the past, but now for the present.

My dear mother has again spoilt me awfully. Just fancy she made me two handworks: a sofarug & a tablecloth. She <u>must</u> have worked awfully hard to finish them.

Then she gave me three fans a <u>very very</u> fine piece of jewelry with rubies[436] then a very lovely screen for my drawingroom, a chair, a table etc. My aunties & uncle sent also very pretty things. The day passed as usual & very pleasantly, in the morning, receiving the presents, congratulations from the dogs, breakfast, letters, telegrams (by the bye, thank you very much for yours), receiving first ladies, then gentlemen, lunch, drive with mother to see the festivities, gala dinner and then an illumination of the old Loo & little lake, it was lovely & most enjoyable. Dear mother had given herself such a lot of trouble & the day was delightful & a grand success & as I grow older I realise more & more thoroughly that Heaven has given me its <u>greatest</u> gift in giving me such a darling mother, the best woman that has ever lived on this earth, who will guide me & help me also <u>and</u> as much in the difficult task that will be layed on my shoulder next year, as she has heatherto done during the whole of my life. It is not a blessing that is granted to every body to possess somebody here on earth who not only knows all ones inward thoughts & understands one in all respects, but who lives for one & helps one like my dear mother does. And all the same what I have just said does not yet faintly express how I feel about her & how <u>much</u> a want to <u>try</u> and be for her. Now Darling I must finish, don't forget to tell me about your birthday wishes.

With all dearest love & many many loving thanks for the beautiful present I remain your most affectionnately devoted

Wilhelmina

---

436  This is probably the large brooch that belonged with the peacock-tail diadem. They both formed part of the large parure in diamonds and rubies that had belonged to Queen Sophie. In 1897/98, Queen Emma had a necklace and a diadem made for Wilhelmina at the jeweller's Schürmann in Frankfurt. The central peacock-tail design could be detached and worn as a brooch; see Brus, pp. 66–67. The members of the Royal Family still wear these jewels on a regular basis. My thanks to M. Loonstra, former curator of the Royal Archives, for this information.

1 Part of the 81-piece silver 'surtout de table', or table centrepiece, given by King Willem III to his daughter Wilhelmina in 1888. The service was manufactured by C.J. Begeer and designed by M.J. Lens, Utrecht, December 1888. In 2008 it was displayed in Paleis Het Loo at Christmas time. See letter 17, 27 December 1888.

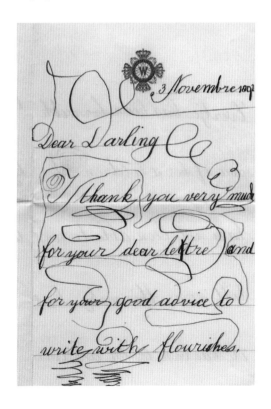

2 Letter from Wilhelmina to Miss Saxton Winter featuring a beautiful monogram and dated 3 November 1892, showing her attempt to imitate the florid handwriting style of centuries past. See letter 84, 3 November 1892.

3  Left-hand panel of a screen with views of Het Loo, depicting the dogs Dash, Daisy and Swell, and to the right, behind the bush, the gamekeeper Mekking. Painted by Jan Willem van Borselen. See letter 51, 1 January 1891.

4 Portrait of William of Orange after Anthonis Mor, presented to Queen Wilhelmina by Emperor Wilhelm II of Germany at Christmas in 1894. See letter 115, 22 December 1894.

5 *De Vaandeluitreiking [Presentation of the flag]*. Queen Wilhelmina presents new flags and standards to the infantry regiments and the cavalry, accompanied by her mother, on Malieveld in The Hague, on the afternoon of Thursday 21 September 1893. Painted by Jan Hoynck van Papendrecht. See letter 115, 22 December 1894.

6 *Wilhelmina een tweespan mennend en Emma tijdens een rit door de Kroon-domeinen op Het Loo in de Zilveren Slede [Wilhelmina, driving a pair of horses, and Emma during a drive through the crown estates of Het Loo in the Silver Sled]*, around 1895. The sled was manufactured by P. Schreuder & Co., Düsseldorf, in 1885, and was named after the silver leaf used to cover the vehicle. Watercolour, 24.5 x 31.5 cm, by Otto Eerelman (1839-1926), signed at the bottom right, from the estate of lady-in-waiting/superinten-dent Lady F.L. Henriette van de Poll. See letter 154, 31 January 1897.

7 *Chrysanthemum*. Wilhelmina also captured chrysanthemums in watercolour in 1895; signed 'W 1895'. See letter 191, 7 November 1897.

8  *Portrait of Queen Wilhelmina*, a painting that Wilhelmina commissioned from
David Bles for her mother's birthday on 2 August 1897. See letter 161, 14 March 1897.

9 Silk gown by Ludwig Zwieback & Bruder, Vienna, worn by Queen Wilhelmina in her role as the Countess of Brandensteen in the play *Uit liefde voor de kunst [For the love of art]*, on the occasion of Queen Emma's birthday, in the theatre of Paleis Het Loo, Apeldoorn, on 2 August 1897. See letter 181, 4 August 1897.

10 Baby bath on a wooden stand and jug, painted by Queen Wilhelmina as a gift for Mrs Irma van Pallandt-van Hardenbroek's baby. See letter 205, 22 January 1898.

11 *De terugkeer van de Vissersboten bij avond bij Santa Margherita [The return of the fishing boats in the evening at Santa Margherita]*, Easter 1898, painted for Wilhelmina by Miss E. Saxton Winter. See letter 215, 10 April 1898.

12  *Gezicht op het Schloss Schwarzburg [View of Schwarzburg Castle]*, painted
by Wilhelmina and signed W 15/5 1900, as seen from the Weisser Hirsch
Hotel during her holiday in Schwarzburg, Thuringia. She would meet
Prince Hendrik at Schwarzburg Castle. See letter 247, 24 May 1900.

13  On 25 November 1998,
a buckle with four decorations belonging to Miss
Saxton Winter were auctioned
by Spink & Son, London, as
lot number 1159, and acquired by
Paleis Het Loo National Museum:
1. Golden Wedding medal 1892, on
the occasion of the Golden Wedding of Grand
Duke Carl Alexander and Sophie, Grand Duchess
of Saxe-Weimar-Eisenach and Princess of the
Netherlands, in 1892. Silver gilt, by G.B. Loos / Uhlmann. 2. Marriage medal
1899, on the occasion of the silver wedding of Queen Victoria's son Alfred and
Marie of Saxe-Coburg-Gotha. Silver, by M. von Kawaczynski. 3. Marriage medal
1901, on the occasion of the marriage of Queen Wilhelmina and Prince Hendrik
of Mecklenburg-Schwerin, the Netherlands. Silver, by Koninklijke Begeer / Pier
Pander. 4. Investiture medal 1898, the Netherlands, on the occasion of the investiture of Queen Wilhelmina in 1898. Bronze, by Koninklijke Begeer / J.H.P. Wortman.
See letter 230, 13 November 1898.

185　My own very dearest Darling,

You know how I will think about you on your birthday and how many loving and good wishes I will be making for you! I hope, Darling, that the new year you are beginning may be in all respects a happy and blessed one and that where the last one brought sad moments, the new one will bring many happy moments. How sad it was also to leave me you always had the satisfaction to have helped at a great work and I always find the feeling that one has done one's duty is <u>the</u> greatest satisfaction one can have, and that certainty gives rest to the soul and helps one bear the burdens of life. I hope also so much that the new work you are soon beginning will give you a great deal of satisfaction and will open to you a new life of working and occupations.

　As you are coming over so soon I thought it would be better to give my presents when you are here myself. So, Darling, don't think I have forgotten your birthday if you only get flowers and no other presents. I am sending you some flowers of the Loo as I think they will be able the best to bring over all my good wishes as all these years. How are your mother and sister. I think I must now finish,

　With all my best wishes for a blessed year, I ever remain your most affectionnately devoted

Wilhelmina

Het Loo

October 3 1897

186　Dearest Darling,

I just want to come and tell you that we arrived here yesterday. Mother is trying to rest today; I was tired because at the Hague I did not sleep enaugh.

　Today it is awful weather. How are you? Had you a good journey? How is life at "Monrepos"? Friday evening was passed in a delightful way. With all dearest love and hugs ever your very devoted Wilhelmina

For the following letter, Wilhelmina used writing paper with a different logo: a slanting crowned 'W' in the top left-hand corner. This is different from the one used at that time with 'Het Loo' at the top of the page in the centre, with a crown printed over the 'H'. Moreover, she wrote '1896' instead of '1897'.

Het Loo

October 10 1896 [should be 1897]

187　My very dearest Darling,

Thank you many many times for your sweet letter; it <u>was</u> so dear of you to write so openly to me & to tell me all about the life you are leading. You know <u>how</u> interested I will have been. I <u>am</u> glad you are having more to do for I am sure you will feel much happier. What a joke that you are to keep my cousin of Wied also company! Then you will have plenty of time to talk to her about Louise! I can well imagine how funny you must find it not to work after a timetable! What sort of work are you making your girls do? Does Louise study very much her piano? It <u>must</u> be lovely now at Monrepos how you will like the walks through the woods! My cold has quite passed away now. I need scarcely tell you <u>how</u> [underlined twice] delightful I found it to have you at the Loo & to have a few little talks with you also still at the Hague!

I hope so much, Darling, that you will feel quite at home now, in your new surroundings.

We have had here very fine weather & three days frost; these last two days were dark, but only very little rain fell. The air is perfectly lovely & I have begun to ride again. The first times I was very stiff but now no more. I take frantic exercise lately, because besides the rides I take also long walks; it is just as if I couldn't ever get tired!

Lessons have begun again. Prof. Krämer has now got up to Napoleon[437] & gave during the last two lectures a very interesting description of his character. Prof. de Louter[438] has begun the "Nederlandsch Staatsrecht [Dutch constitutional law]"; it is very hard work, but of course most interesting. Prof. Kan[439] (I hope I have spelt his name well) has begun giving me lectures upon the climate in general & the statistics of the means of existence of the Netherlands. Prof Blok is to come back this week to give me in 10 or 8 lessons a revisal of the whole of the Dutch history. I have a great deal to do at present with lessons, riding walking, driving & with the work I am making for Xmas for mother & with drawing my almanac. This week I will be very busy: to morrow I am going with mother to Soestdijk for half a day; Thursday I am having Stuwart[440] & Saturday we are going for the afternoon & evening to Arnhem for audiences & a dinner. Mother is resting a little now I hope. We have been having my step-grandmother[441] here for a few days last week. What have you heard lately from home, Darling?

Louisa wrote my such a nice letter the other day; I hope to answer her this evening. Do you know when you are going to Italy? Do you often see my Aunt of Wied? Has the prince come back? How does conversation go at meals?

I think I must now stop chattering for the present, Darling!

---

437 Napoleon Bonaparte (1769–1821) was a French soldier and political leader during the final phases of the French Revolution. During the Napoleonic Wars, he brought much of Europe under French control in the first decade of the 19th century. He was Emperor of France between 1804 and 1815. In 1815 he suffered a decisive defeat at Waterloo, after which he spent the rest of his life imprisoned by the British on St Helena.

438 J. de Louter (see letter 160, p. 160).

439 Prof. Kan (see letter 133, p. 114).

440 'Stuwart' is the same as 'Stewart' (see letter 166, note 347).

441 This is Louise of Sleeswijk-Holstein-Sonderburg-Glücksburg (1858–1936), whom Emma's father married in 1891, after her mother died in 1888. In 1892 their only son, Wolrad, was born. He would die in the First World War in 1914. The widowed Princess of Waldeck-Pyrmont stayed at Het Loo between 4 and 8 October 1897.

With all my dearest love, I remain your most affectionnately devoted

Wilhelmina

Het Loo, October 17 1897

**188**  My very dearest Darling,

Your dear last letter was a <u>great</u> joy to me & I thank you so much, Darling, for the confiding way you have again spoken to me in. It is always such a pleasure receiving your dear letters & knowing that I have such a dear faithful friend; as I think I already told you, it is such a joy to have a friend in which one can take interest & with which one can live a part of their life & help bear their burdens!

Al you tell me about your occupations interests me very much. I envy you that you can sit & listen to Louisa's music as much as you like. I wonder what she will say about Shakespeare when you get up to him in literature & I wonder if she will admire him? I can quite well imagine you find Louisa more interesting than Elizabeth for you know <u>how</u> nice <u>I</u> find Louisa! How delightful for you to be able to develop & help her on; I am sure that <u>now</u> you don't feel any more that you have not enough to do!

How stupid of the people to have kept her back for such a time!

Is Elizabeth also listening when you read out loud? I suppose both girls don't know much about english questions of the day!

I <u>am</u> glad, Darling, that you have good news from home; but how sad for your sister that she is not getting stronger! I can imagine <u>how</u> tiresome you must find not to be able to get out alone. The woods must be lovely, here they are getting every day redder & yellower. Steward was not very bad last time, he is coming back once this week.

<u>Do</u> be careful with your teeth & have them looked at before going to Italy! The day of yesterday passed off very well.[442] The weather was <u>very</u> fine & <u>hot</u> so that I put on my gown of the opening of the Chambers for the audiences. We took tea with Mrs. Mollerus[443] & dressed for dinner; I had on my white & gold dress with pearls on the bodice & my pearl diadem. Mr. Mollerus made a beautiful speech (just to make you feel bad in the throat you know) which mother answered splendidly. She is rather tired to day but otherwise very well. I am only a little sleepy to day. The people were as always most enthusiastic. We came back here at a little before eleven. To day we had service in the chapel & I found the sermon beautiful![444] I have been working very hard last week & reading something that is interesting me very much: namely a speech that was held in honour of my Auntie of Saxe Weimar on the date of Her wedding this

---

442  On 16 October 1897, Emma and Wilhelmina, accompanied by nine courtiers, left for Arnhem by train at 12:18 p.m., to attend a dinner held in their honour by the Provincial States of Gelderland. They were back at Het Loo at 10.35 p.m.

443  In 1870, the local magistrate of Apeldoorn, Gustaaf W. Mollerus (1842–1919), a member of the Liberal Union (a progressive liberal political party), married Anna M.J.A. Bas Backer (1844–1911). The couple had seven sons and one daughter.

444  The Rev. T.F. Westrik of Zutphen conducted the service in the chapel of Het Loo.

year by a professor in front of the different literary society which she founded.[445]
The professor speaks of Her with great reverence & points out very well all the
qualities of her family. I think that in that simple, scientific historical speech one
has praised Her more & payed Her more homage than in all that one has hitherto
done in Her memory.

But I suppose you have heard all about it a long time ago as you are living in
Germany!

I think I must now finish. With all my dearest love I will always remain your
most affectionnately devoted

Wilhelmina

Het Loo, October 24 1897

**189**   Dearest of Darlings,

Thank you many, many times for your dear long letter; you are a Darling to have
answered me so quickly & to have reminded me about Louisa's birthday.

What a goody you are to beg for her to have a free Monday; what are they
going to do? Are their brothers Victor & Fritz[446] such teases as Willy? I can
understand what a relief it must have been to you to have a quiet talk with my
Auntie of Wied. She is always so affectionnate & full of kind thought to all that
come to her. What is that book: "Coriolanus" you talk about? Elizabeth must
be rather like me in her spelling I should think; I pity you if you have to give her
dictation lessons. Where n't you glad to get hold of my cousin of Wied; or have
you now opportunity of talking to her? We are having cold weather again and
also here the leaves are falling rapidly. Life has been very quiet lately & I am
sorry that my letters <u>have</u> to be uninteresting since we are back here, but I would
really not know what to write about unless I began to tell you what we had been
eating & drinking every day. The days, the weeks fly by without any thing interesting happening. Miss van Ittersum told me you had had a cruel deception the
other day, for that you had hoped to travel back with her for a little way & by her
hasty break up from Wiesbaden she could n't have you. Have you already heard
that she has been called back home two days after she arrived here as her sister
was much worse?[447] We are getting every day news how her poor sister is. Miss
van de Poll is having her holiday at present so I am going out very much with

---

445  The commemorative speech is kept in the Royal Archives, inv.no. ER.15-F29: Kuno Fischer,
*Grossherzogin Sophie van Sachsen, Königliche Prinzessin der Niederlande. Gedächtnisrede in der
Trauerversammlung am 8. October 1897 zu Weimar gehalten*, Heidelberg 1897. On 8 October 1842,
Sophie had married Carl-Alexander of Saxe-Weimar-Eisenach in the Gothic Hall of Kneuterdijk Palace. Ernst Kuno Berthold Fischer (1824-1907) was a professor of philosophy at Berlin
University.
446  Victor (1877-1946), Fritz (1872-1945) and Wilhelm (1876-1945), brothers of Louise
(1880-1965) and Elisabeth (1883-1938) of Wied.
447  This concerns her sister, her junior by one year, Maria Adriana, Baroness van Ittersum,
born in 1852, who died on 30 October 1897 in Utrecht; she was the sixth child in a family of
twelve.

Family photograph of Prince Alexis (third from right) and Princess Pauline (seated in the middle) of Bentheim-Steinfurt with seven of their eight children, from left to right: Friedrich (the youngest), Karl Georg, Victoria, Victor Adolf (standing), Eberwyn (the eldest, in uniform), Elisabeth and Emma; their eighth child, Alexis, is not present. Photograph: Georg Rothe, Burgsteinfurt.

mother now & trying to make myself useful. It is so comfy being so much with mother. To morrow my auntie & uncle of Bentheim[448] are coming for a few days.

I can't imagine it is already just a year ago today that I was confirmed; what a lot has happened in that year! I feel ever so much older than this last year. I have had such a lot more experience of life, it has taught me a good deal, it has taught me how to take people & how to look upon them. How are your people at home; you must write and tell me more often how they are, for you know it interests me very much to hear about them.

With all my dearest love I will always remain your very devoted

Wilhelmina

Het Loo
October 31 1897

190 My very dearest Darling,

Thank you so much for your dear, sweet letter. How dreadful for poor miss van Ittersum to have lost her dear sister, I am sure you will be thinking just as much about her as I am doing and feeling full of loving sympathy for her in this dreadful time she is living through. I heard that miss Rengers had written to you on a card to tell you!

448 The Prince and the Princess (Emma's sister Pauline) of Bentheim-Steinfurt stayed at Het Loo between 25 and 30 October 1897.

I am ashamed to not have remembered the name Coriolanus,[449] but as you say we did not read it and it is rather a bad name to retain. The weather has become very cold here so that I am fast taking to winterclothes. I am glad, Darling, that you have in my auntie of Wied somebody to whom you can talk openly and about things here! All you tell me about Frida Solmes[450] interests me very much, does she and her sisters get on well with my cousins? Was the prince of Wied there for Louisa's[451] birthday? Do you still read to my cousin of Wied when you are alone with her? Thank you so much for the news you give from home. I congratualte you with the success of your nephew; it is grand for him to have come out the first of the examination. Will he now be able to marry? Is it dangerous for Lilian Maule[452] to be working at a place where there is an epidemie of typhoid? I should think it was very evident what you had to do at Wiesbaden — you must also go to the dentist! My auntie and uncle of Bentheim have left yesterday; my uncle was rather well and enjoyed his stay very much I think. My auntie Lily came here yesterday and as going again to morrow. She liked very much her stay in Scotland and since she has been back in Claremont[453] she has been up to London very often. What a sad thing the Duchess of Teck[454] has died; it must be a great loss to the old Duke and to the Duchess of York!

When do you think you will be going to Italy; are you looking forward to it? Mother is very busy and a little tired also by the anxiety about miss van Ittersum. I have as usual a lot to do. My lectures upon history of art are very interesting at present for I am learning now about the Italian Renaissance and have now just reached Lionardo da Vinci and Michelangelo. I only sometimes find it difficult to drum all these Italian names into my head. Sometimes great

---

449 'Coriolanus' was the more or less legendary Roman patrician who fell into conflict with the plebeians in 491 BC and was exiled. He went to neighbouring Volsci and led the Volscian army in an assault on Rome in 489–488. According to tradition, he was persuaded by his mother and wife to return into exile.

450 The identity of Frida Solmes is unclear. See letter 192.

451 Louise of Wied was born on 24 October 1880 and was thus almost the same age as Wilhelmina. She died in 1965.

452 This probably refers to Lilian, the eldest daughter of the Maule family; see the biography of Miss Winter, p. 17.

453 The 18th-century country house of Claremont, located just outside London in Surrey, had a park designed by Lancelot 'Capability' Brown (1716–1783), who is seen as the originator of the English landscaped garden. The house was given by Queen Victoria to her son Leopold in 1881 when he became Duke of Albany, for his marriage to Emma's sister, Helena, Princess of Waldeck-Pyrmont. After Leopold's death in 1884, Helena continued to live there with her children Alice and Charles Edward.

454 Mary Adelaide, the Duchess of Teck (1833–1897), died at Windsor Castle on 27 October. Three days of light mourning were held at the Dutch court. The granddaughter of King George III of Great Britain (1738–1820), she had married Frans P.K.L.A. of Württemberg (1837–1900), Duke of Teck. Their daughter Mary (1867–1953) became the wife of King George V (1865–1936) of Great Britain.

discussions take place with M<sup>r</sup> Hofstede de Groot[455] about the old pictures and idealistic and realistic conceptions in art — I of course always more admiring idealistic pictures.

I am still drawing trees in my drawinglesson and began last Wednesday painting in watercolours some trees from one of the rooms of the palace for my auntie Lily for Xmas.[456]

It will be next Tuesday just a year ago you left; I suppose you will thinking very much about it that day. It was a sad day and yet it seems a short time ago; I think that must come somehow because we have seen eachother such a short time ago! Nothing yet reminds that November will soon be here; only the trees are becoming barer and barer and perhaps we will be able still to skate here; it would be to delightful.

I must now finish. With all my dearest love I always remain your most affectionnately devoted

Wilhelmina

Het Loo<br>November 7 1897

**191**  Dearest of Darlings,

Thank you many, many times for your dear letter; you must not think that I take it amiss when you don't write regularly for I quite well understand that you have now a lot to do & can't dispose of your time like you could at home. Poor old Darling, if your teeth will only hold till after Italy! It must all the same have been interesting to see Wiesbaden; is it a pretty town? Do the girls like shopping as much as I? So you are soon going to Italy; I wonder if it will be very cold! November has now quite set in here with its fogs & cold. I still ride very much. Miss van Ittersum is coming back here to morrow & I hope I will not find her very much changed. Tuesday there are to be a lot of gentlemen invited to come and shoot the stags and Wednesday also; it will be quite an excitement having so many people in the house. I am very busy with all the preparations for the eve of the 5<sup>th</sup> of December & Xmas.

I have taken a rage for painting chrysanthemums.[457] They are lovely flowers to paint. [Colour plate IV-7] By the by, are you painting; does Louisa paint? Are both girls still doing so much music?

Mother is well but rather tired for you know — she has always very much to do in the autumn.

---

455  Mr Hofstede de Groot (see letter 160, p. 160).

456  Wilhelmina would paint trees her whole life. She considered them most beautiful when they were bare, because then their character was revealed. See Spliethoff 2006, *Koningin Wilhelmina Schilderijen en tekeningen [The paintings and drawings of Queen Wilhelmina]*, which includes many examples of trees.

457  *Wilhelmina. Schilderijen en tekeningen*, pp. 76–77, includes a watercolour of two chrysanthemums, but it is dated 1895.

Dr E.F. Kossman (1861-1945), a German teacher at the grammar school in The Hague, taught Wilhelmina German from the beginning of 1895 until the beginning of 1898. In addition to German literature, he tutored her in the literature of Russia, Spain, Italy and Scandinavia.

Are you doing much reading for your self now? Are you getting the english newspapers? I am getting rather interested in the german literature; M$^r$ Kosman has come up to Schiller[458] with me; I don't think I have already told you that — if I have, I hope you will forgive me for it is sometimes difficult to remember from one week to another what I wrote — but the lessons are very nice. The last time I read a little part of Mary Stuart, & of Joan of Arc. I am fond of Schillers plays.

I am sending you my last photographs.[459] I think it would be nice if you would show them once to my auntie of Wied.

When you show them to the princesses you must only promis them in my name also some, but I will send those later. When you see my auntie will you please tell her that I send her my very dearest love. Do please say the same to my cousin & to Louisa and Elizabeth.

With all my very dearest love I always will remain your most affectionnately devoted

Wilhelmina

Het Loo
November 14 1897

192     My very dearest Darling,
Thank you many many times for your dear, long letter. All you tell me about my auntie & cousins interests me very much. I can imagine how dreadful the girls must find it to learn by heart their catechism, but you see Darling, as I belong myself to the old fashioned sort of people, I find it better that they should be brought up <u>too much</u> in the orthodox way than <u>too</u> little; but I should think they could do that without learning by heart. Mother has n't yet made any decided plans how we are to spend the evening of the 5$^{th}$ of December; we don't quite know if we are going to feast it in small or large society or not at all for I think it will be very sad for miss van Ittersum if we feast it!

You must now have a lot to do it seems for this last letter you must have written late in the evening though the "nonsense" you pretend you have written about I

---

458 J.Ch. Friedrich von Schiller (1759-1805) studied law and medicine. In 1780 he became an army doctor in Stuttgart, but he followed his heart and became the author of plays, poems and philosophical writings. He wrote the play *Maria Stuart* in 1800 and the play *Jeanne d'Arc* (Joan of Arc) in 1801. He lived in Weimar, where he became great friends with Goethe.
459 These photographs were taken on 23 September 1897 by Adolphe Zimmermans, The Hague (see Elzenga, p. 40).

can't discover; but you know, Darling, you must not sit up late at night writing to me, for that is bad for your eyes! And you would be tired.

I don't find it very wise of you to own up to Louisa that you gleaned your knowledge in your later life! with prof. Kan.[460]

What an interesting history that picture of Lionardo da Vinci you wrote to me about, must have had. By the bey, do you ever get to see the pictures of the girls father? I have now begun to learn about the Dutch masters like the van Eiks[461] & van der Weide[462] & Lucas van Leyden.[463] What a good idea for you to chose the "Pickwick Papers" to read out of to the Solmes[464] girls!

Miss van Ittersum came back in the beginning of last week; she is of course very sad bur she is well and is slowly commencing again her work.

The weather is still very fine & even quite hot. I can't give you any good news about poor old Swell;[465] he has lately been very lame & can't go out any more, he remains at the: "Wildmeesters [game master's]". I go & see him every day. The doctor hopes he will get better but is not certain, in every case it will last a few weeks. I have taken two long walks this last week & I enjoyed them very much. I don't think I told you that mother & I we interviewed the other day a lady which is to come in our service in the beginning of January to do the same duty for me as miss de Vries[466] does for mother; she is a very nice girl and is called miss "Kramer van Baumgarten."[467] It is n't of course pleasant to get accustomed to another new lady, but I must have two & I hope I will soon get use to her! I have been riding a great deal lately; the dear Loo is now also so lovely.

What have you heard from home; how is your mother bearing this heat?

With all my dearest love, Darling, I ever remain your most affectionnately devoted

Wilhelmina

460  Kan (see letter 133, p. 114).

461  By 'the van Eiks', Wilhelmina is referring to the brothers Jan and Hubert van Eyck. Jan van Eyck (1390–1441) was a Flemish artist and one of the most celebrated representatives of the Flemish Primitives. He played an important role in the development of the art of oil painting. Hubert (c. 1366–1426) was Jan's elder brother.

462  'Van der Weide' refers to Rogier van der Weyden (1399/1400–1464), an artist who was one of the Flemish Primitives. He is considered one of the most important painters of the 15th century.

463  Lucas van Leyden (1494–1533) was a painter, draughtsman, engraver, maker of wood-cuttings and etcher from the Northern Netherlands. He is counted among the greatest engravers in the history of art.

464  Solmes (see also letter 190).

465  Swell (see letter 21, note 34).

466  Miss de Vries is a lady-of-the-bedchamber (see letter 123, note 172).

467  This refers to Bernardina Aletta Agatha Cramer von Baumgarten. In November 1897, Emma told the Treasurer that she would come for a trial period, for an annual allowance of 700 guilders. Nothing more about her can be found in the administration (E8-VI-33).

**193**

My very dearest Darling,

Thank you so much for your dear long letter, you don't know <u>how</u> glad I am
to get your letters; it is just like talking with you! We are going to town on
December the 2$^d$. I am very glad we are remaining here so long for then there is
not such a rush for packing at the end of November. All you tell me about the
painting of the prince interests me very much, I could formerly not at all imagine
how he painted; has he got a studio?

Swell is better but not yet able to take walks of longer than a quarter of an hour.
Mother said that he would have to be shot if he did not get better but now he
is improving & I would find it dreadful if that had to happen. I go and see him
every day and bring him some liver; he now quite expects me every afternoon.

I formerly wrote my "Maleisch" in latin characters so from <u>left</u> to <u>right</u> in the
ordenary way; but this last winter I tried to write it in Arab characters from <u>right</u>
to <u>left</u> beginning at the top of the page. Wilhelmina is  ولك لك م رن ١

You see it is rather difficult but not so much so as one would think. Does Louisa
play the organ in church during the service? How do you do Darling about going
to church; do you go to the german church? And what about speaking German.
The poor girls, how dread for them to have to be operated; just think what a fuss
<u>I</u> would have made and only for removing those scars! What a lucky thing your
sister is getting stronger; was she able to take care of your mother? I have also
always heard one must be careful of one's things in Italy, but I have never <u>myself</u>
experienced the Italians stealing although I find they sometimes look thorough
thieves. The whole people look so poor!

I don't wonder your reading Hamlet made such an impression on Louisa; do
you remember how mad I got about it. After having seen it on the stage I never
can think of it in the evening without getting nervous & I need only think of the
appearance of the ghost to get quite uncomfortable in my bed. The weather her
has been rather hot! I have been riding again a good deal and yesterday I walked
back from the "Uddelermeer" Foppie goes ofcourse with me on those long walks.

Have you read in the papers about the awful fire[468] there has been in London?
There must have been many acres destroyed! I am reading now more regularly
the newspapers & I now read three: the "Nieuwe Rotterdamsche Courant", the
"Algemeen Handelsblad" and the "Haarlemsche Courant."

I now also read what there is done in the chambers![469] Have you already heard
from engagement of miss Rengers's brother[470] with a miss Rengers in Friesland?

---

468 On 19 November 1897, during a large fire on on Jewin Street in Cripplegate, London, 56
houses were completely destroyed, 15 burned out and 20 damaged.
469 The Upper and Lower House of the States General.
470 This concerns the younger brother of Baroness Rengers: Edzard Hendrik Juckema of
Burmania, Baron Rengers (1872-1951). On 28 April 1898 he married Quirina Jacoba van
Welderen, Baroness Rengers (1868-1942).

Mother has just received your letter this afternoon & thanks you very much for it. She is well but has a great deal to do.

I have just picked these flowers this afternoon during that we were inspecting the hothouses! I thought you would like to have them.

Don't trouble to write, Darling, if you have to much to do with packing & travelling, I will give you news, even if I don't hear from you.

With heaps of love, I ever will remain your most affectionnately devoted

Wilhelmina

Het Loo
November 28 1897

**194** My very dearest of Darlings,

Thank you so much for your dear last letter and the pretty photograph; it is so sweet of you to have thought of sending me the picture of Erasmus and just painted by Holbein;[471] it must be pretty and the photograph gives such a good idea of how the picture is in nature. In Vienna I just saw a lot of Holbein's sketches, but only few of his pictures. It must be very interesting for you to see Basel; you seem to be giving about a good deal with the Princess, that must be a good thing for you otherwise you wouldn't see much of the town, as the girls are kept at home!

Is miss van Suchtelen and von Harnier back and the Bylandts going to Santa Margherita. [472] By the Bey you ought to try & learn Italian. What a joke that you are reading "Crown and Sceptre"[473] to my cousins; I wonder if they don't also start when you come to the secret passage! How agreable to arrive two hours later at Basel, wasn't my cousin furious? The two poor girls! it must be a dreary way of passing their time in a strange town. Till yesterday we had here very fine weather but these two last days it has rained the whole day and there is such a "halo" blowing that one feels very content to sit comfortably in ones room. I love hearing such a strong wind in the evening! it makes you feel so snug & comfy.

**471** Hans Holbein (1497-1543), the German painter and graphic artist. After working in Basel, he travelled in 1526 via Antwerp to London. He was acquainted with the Dutch priest, humanist, writer, theologian and philosopher Desiderius Erasmus (1466/67/69-1537) and the English humanist, lawyer and statesman Thomas More (1478-1535). In 1536 he became court painter to Henry VIII (1491-1547). His artistic style developed from late Gothic and Renaissance to a free classicism.

**472** E10, IVb, no. 9 Journal of 23 October 1895. At the dinner on 24 September 1897, the following were named in the retinue of the Prince and Princess of Wied: Count C. van Bylandt, Marshal to the Court [Count Carl H. van Bylandt (1843-1916), chamberlain extraordinary to Queen Wilhelmina and Marshal of the Court to the Prince of Wied, married Hélène M.L.P. Freiin von Wintzingerode in 1874]; Miss van Suchtelen van de Haare, lady-in-waiting; and Miss [Marie] von Harnier, lady-in-waiting.

**473** The book *Crown and Sceptre* was written in 1890 by George Manville Fenn (1831-1909), who wrote many books for boys. It tells the story of two families in Devon, whose friendship turns to enmity at the time of the English Civil War in the 17th century.

After your description I don't think that the Cathedral at Basel must be very beautiful, besides I don't think I heard about it in my "Kunstgeschiedenis" [history of art] and I think I learned about all edifices built in a pure style. Are you always still so fond of Gothic architecture? I think I am fonder of the Roman style! I am very glad you hate as much as I the Electric trams with wires going overhead. That concert would have been just something for me, specially as it was a mass!!!!!!!!!!!!!!!!!

It would be pleasant for you to have a little with my auntie of Wied in coming back from Italy. I never stayed at Basel, I only came often through with the railway, only once we dined at the restaurant at the station coming back that time that your mother was so bad & you had gone home from Gersau! So you see I don't know Basel!

I have been passing my time this week in working hard for the professors, reading, trying on, working, driving, riding, seeing M^rs Hoefer,[474] (who even inquired after you & is going to Italy this winter (perhaps you will meet her)) and painting and making preparations for Santa Claus which we are only going to feast quietly between us the 6^th of December, the fifth falling on a Sunday & dirty papers strings etc. making such a mess for the servants to clear up. Are you feasting it at Santa Margherita. What a joke it would be if they asked you to dress up as Santa Claus; I think you would have a grand success!

Did I already mention we were going to the Hague on December the 2^d! So to morrow will have begin the packing!

Is the prince of Wied already at Santa Margherita or is he still always being blown about on his yacht? Are the girls having lessons at Basel? I am to have a good many lessons at the Hague in the beginning: prof. Blok[475] has not yet finished so he goes on for a time, that means two uncalculated for extra lessons; prof. Kan[476] come also still Thursday, for the last time however and prof. Krämer[477] is to come three times a week!

With all dearest love I ever remain you very affectionnately devoted

Wilhelmina

Paleis, 's Gravenhage
December 5 1897

195    My very dearest Darling,

I was very glad to hear that you had arrived safely at Santa Margherita and Mother asked me to thank you very much for your letter. I have sent of yesterday two frames which I hope will still reach you in time for Santa Claus. I thought they would do perhaps for my new photographs and as I do not think you have much room, I have chosen small frames! We are now quite established here,

---

474  Mrs Hoefer is the former governess of Wilhelmina, Baroness C.M. van Heemstra (see p. 27, note 55).

475  Prof. Blok (see letter 133, p. 114 and 151, note 273).

476  Prof. Kan (see letter 133, p. 114 and 135).

477  Prof. Krämer (see p. 30, note 62, letter 133, p. 114).

although I feel still asif it were a dream to be again beginning the winter. At one place not very far from here I saw last Thursday from the train the ground covered with snow and in arriving here it was quite cold. To day the frost was not so sharp. I began immediately in arriving here my new timetable & I had on Thursday my last lesson of Prof. Kan, after the lesson I said good bye to him; the poor old man was quite upset. I have still a great deal to do, Darling, so I think I must finish.

Mother is very tired at present and did not feel well in church to day.

With all my very dearest love, I always remain your very affectionnately devoted

Wilhelmina

Paleis, 's Gravenhage<br>December 12 1897

**196**  My very dearest Darling,

Your two dear letter were again such a pleasure to me; but before I begin to answer them I must first tell you that I got on St. Nicolaas evening a parcel coming from the post from Italy and in opening it I found it was a box of delicious fruit and violets. Now I find it very wonderful that kind Santa Clauses travel about even in Italy and I wonder if you would be so kind and thank them.

But now without joking I find it so sweet of you, Darling, to have thought about sending me such lovely goodies (I don't know how you call such fruit and violets done in sugar). They are simply lovely and they have such a nice strong taste. I only got your first letter last Monday (Dec. the 6<sup>th</sup>) so that is why you have waited such a time for the answer!

Swell was much better when we left the Loo and he could walk without limping. What a satisfactory way it must be of spending one's life for the ladies of the Princess just something for you and me to enjoy. How things must have changed since you left Scheveningen that you have so much more to do; I can well imagine how trying it must be for you to get your orders from miss de Harbon[478] but as you say it only for a short time! Here there have been also very bad storms but I don't think they have done so much harm than in England. The other day I walked through the downs to the shore or rather to the sea for the tide was so high that there was scarcely any shore left, only just enough for miss Rengers & myself to walk; the storm was awful and we had great difficulty to walk against the wind.

On the whole however the weather is mild and fine; to day it is raining hard. I don't think I would like such hot weather as you are having in Italy, in this time of the year.

I can well imagine you are getting rather frightened of the Prince's yacht. What a dangerous boat; does the Princess go yachting also? What a pity that you saw so little of the St. Gotthard; when I came back that way last year the weather

---

**478**  Miss von Harbon (see letter 179, note 416).

was dark, but one could see very well; every thing was covered with snow & big icicles were hanging from the rocks and trees. Was it foggy at Milan? When I was there last year there were fogs coming & going every 10 minutes and during the time they lasted you could see nothing and it was very cold.

Poor old Darling, it must not have been agreable travelling with your bad headaches. How pretty the scenery must be about Santa Margherita; after your description it must be just the country of which "Mignon"[479] sings. I am very glad you don't either like the dirty look of the Italians. I find the most of them look so frivolous notwithstanding their dark eyes; they look to me asif they did not think so deeply and go their way in a sort of thoughtless "don't care" way. I understand you have not had a moment to sketch. How thin you must be getting if you walk so much, I am sure that must be very good for you! If only "the fine lady" does not overdo the walking. I hope you don't remain up very late for writing to me, for then I would have a bad conscience. What have you heard about home lately is your mother quite better.

I am sorry the frames only reached you on the 9th. The evening of the 6th passed off very merrily; miss van Ittersum was not there. Every body got very amusing things and mother sent me a picture of my dear [underlined twice] William III[480] and a lovely watercolour and many other pretty things. Mother is still tired but has tryed to do the things quietly these last two days. Auntie Elisabeth is coming at the end of the week & I am looking very much forward to it. I have had and have still a heap to do before Xmas. Last week I rode out in town a few times and on Wednesday I went to the "diligentia" concert.[481] Compatriots sang & played.

My new gowns have just come from Paris, there are three lownecked: two write,[482] one made in white satin, body and skirt are embroidered with apple-blossom and here & there there are some artificial appelblossom & paillettes; the other white gown is trimmed with lace & flowers; the third is pink and also trimmed with "entredeux" of lace.[483]

The embroidered one I am going to wear for the gala ball.

Have you still Louisa alone sometimes? What a good Idea to go to to your Livorno friends on leaving the Wieds! What you read in the paper about the ceremony of my taking my oath on Sep. the 6th is quite correct! I have n't yet seen the book about Queen Victoria you write about.

Have you seen my picture in the "Almanach de Gotha"[484] and your Queen's?

479  Mignon (see letter 159, note 310).
480  This probably refers to King-Stadholder Willem III (1650–1702), who had Het Loo built in Apeldoorn as a hunting lodge in 1686.
481  This took place on 8 December 1897.
482  Wilhelmina means 'white'.
483  The 'entredeux' of lace is a lace insert.
484  The *Almanach de Gotha* is an almanac of noble families that was first published in 1763. It was published at the court of the Duke of Saxe-Coburg-Saalfeld, to which the city of Gotha also belonged. It was published for the last time in 1944. Between 1998 and 2004, six volumes were published once more in English.

To morrow we are going to Amsterdam for half a day to look at the pictures & drawings in the "Rijksmuseum" of the old masters I have been learning about; the visit is to be quite inofficial! Tuesday we are going in the same manner to Haarlem to see the sketches of the great masters in "Teylers Genootschap".[485]

I think I must now finish. With all my dearest love I remain your very devoted

Wilhelmina

Paleis, 's Gravenhage
December 19 1897

**197** My dearest Darling,

Thank you so much for your dear letter which I got to day. I <u>am</u> sorry to hear that you had such a nasty fall; your poor old heady, it has no luck! Poor queen Mary does not fly up the chimney here as in my room at the Loo. I don't think my auntie Lily will remain here the whole of the winter, I hope she will stay at least for two months. The day at Amsterdam & Haarlem were very delightful & although the weather was dark (but not rainy) we could se the pictures very well. In the morning I saw at Amsterdam the pictures of our old masters & in the afternoon I went back alone to the "Rijksmuseum" to see the drawings of the old masters, that part of the museum being under the special direction of M[r] Hofstede de Groot. We spent nearly the whole of our time at Haarlem in Teylers Genootschap, specially looking at old & modern pictures. Ofcourse I am in raptures about our old masters & I find one so fully can <u>feel</u> every stroke & every line & one feels as it were that the people & the landscapes <u>must</u> have been just as they are painted. Ofcourse Rembrandt is my great ideal & <u>the one</u> master which has never been surpassed & whose talent is greater higher and more genial than of any artist which has ever lived — at least after my idea.

It is only a good thing the Prince does not take the girls out in the dangerous boat. You must not think that the muggy weather is only in Italy, for we are having also very hot weather I can scarcely bear my winterclothes & I am generally much too hot in walking. It must be "poetic" to walk & drive in the palmavenues! How nice for you to have found some pleasant compatriots do you often go to see them? Your poor mother, how sad for her to be so seedy! I wonder if you will go to Segenhaus[486] in leaving Santa Margherita & Livorno! I have had a lot to do this week both with dinners & evening audiences. I suppose my cousin will feast Xmas & have Xmastrees; what about church, have they it in the hôtel or where & where do you go the Sundays you are free; is there an English church? Mother is still rather busy & tired. I think I must now finish,

---

**485** 'Teylers Genootschap' refers to the Teylers Foundation, an institute based in Haarlem that was founded by the merchant Pieter Teyler van der Hulst (1702–1778) and includes a courtyard, a museum and two scientific societies.
**486** Segenhaus is located nearby Neuwied, the home of Emma's Aunt Marie, Princess of Nassau (1825–1902), the half-sister of her mother Helena.

Darling! With all my very dearest love I ever remain your most affectionnately devoted

Wilhelmina

**198**  My very dearest Darling,

Just a few lines to wish you a very happy Xmas! I hope it will be blessed and happy for you in all respects and that Italian sun will not prevent you enjoying the feast as much as under the colder rays of the northern sun.

I am still very busy with the preparations so I will not write any more at present.

With all my dearest love I ever remain your very affectionnately devoted

Wilhelmina

The Hague, Dec the 22<sup>d</sup> 1897

**199**  Dear Miss Winter!

I cannot let Christmas come without sending you a few lines to assure you that I shall be thinking of you in those days, wishing you a peaceful & blessed Christmas. Happy I am afraid it will not quite be for you, so far away from your own people and country. Althoug you generally spent Xmas at home your thoughts will also be here very much I know. Wilhelmina is very well & bright. She is very much occupied by her lessons & also by her Xmas preparations. I am glad when they are all over, because she nearly is too occupied, and has too little time to herself.

We have been living quietly as yet, but after new year we will have to see more people. – I am very tired, I have been living in hurry & one rush since this automn, after Xmas I shall have a little less to do.

I am sending you a grey silk gown as a Christmas present, it will be sent to you from Milan, I hope you will like it & that it will prove usefull. I must finish. Goodbye dear Miss Winter.

May God give you peace and joy at Christmas. Believe me yours very affectionately

Emma

**200**  My very dearest Darling,

Thank you so much for your lovely picture and dear letter. It is sweet of you Darling to have found time to paint me something and I find you have done it so prettily and just for you to have copied a picture of Venice is doubly nice for me. I recognise all the known churches and one of the pretty boats with the picturesque sails. And then the pretty sky with the setting sun. You have had it framed so prettily. I do find you have done it so well.

And then you sent me such a sweet card with such pretty words written on it. You must not torment yourself with the idea that I give up too much time to writing to you for that is not the case. I <u>am</u> glad to hear you have nearly recovered from your fall.

We had a most delightful Xmas ave. The presents had all succeeded very well and mother has spoilt very much again. I got amoung other things two fans (one from mother & one from auntie Lily[487] painted by her), a lot of pretty things for the Loo, lovely lace to trim an umbrella, two chandeliers for my dressing table, you know all mounted in gold, teatables, a lovely umbrella mounted in tortishel silver and diamants ect.[488]

My workbag for mother got done in time. We played madly yesterdayevening quite like formerly. Mother is very tired but is taking rest during the xmas days. It is lovely having auntie Lily here. The other day I went alone with her & M^rss van Hardenbroek to the Diligentiaconcert. Thursday there was a concert of the Nederlandsche Zangschool [lit. the Netherlands Singing School][489] in honour of its fortyyears existence. Mother, Auntie & I went to hear the "Cantate" which was sung very well. The words were beautiful. It recalled the history of forty years. Just something for me: for they sang about the beauty of our own dear language, then about our independence: about William the Silent about our dear country being the place of refuge for all who were persecuted for their ideas, about poets being born and living on our soil and our light and landscape inspiring our Rembrandt; then coming to more modern times they sang about us & father under whose protection the N.Z.S. was founded, then a solo sang a prayer for us, during that time the people stood up & then the solo sang a prayer for our country and then we gave the impulse to get up. It was very impressive! Dec. 26. To day we were all to skate. the ici does not yet bear many people but it is very fine; this evening however it is thawing a little. It is quite ideal xmas weather with hoarfrost lying on the fields and trees. All you tell me about the house you are living in interests me very much; I suppose all those italian palaces make you the same impression as they did me: that of miserable forlornness!

Poor old Darling, it is all the same not very nice for you to let xmas go by without going to church. What a pity that you will not stay at Livorno! How you will enjoy having the girls in their free time during their holydays. Do you go on the small boat or on the dangerous one? I can understand <u>how you</u> love being on

---

487 Wilhelmina's Aunt Lily, Princess Elisabeth of Waldeck-Pyrmont, came for a long stay from 20 December until 18 February 1898. She was accompanied by her lady-in-waiting, Miss von Mauve. The fans were not found!

488 Judging from the costly design featuring tortoiseshell, silver and diamonds, this was probably a parasol.

489 On Thursday 22 December, the celebratory concert of the Koninklijke Nationale Zangschool voor Handwerkslieden (the Royal National Singing School for Artisans), of which King Willem III had been a patron, took place in the GK&W building in The Hague, on the occasion of its fortieth anniversary.

the water; that has always been the element that has had the greatest attraction for you and has always given you rest.

With all dearest love I ever remain your most devoted         Wilhelmina

PALAIS LA HAYE<br>December 28 1897

**201**   My very dearest Darling,

I hope you will get these lines in time to wish you a very happy New Year. I hope it may be blessed & happy for you in all ways & that sunshine & light may be on your path. The New Year brings a great many new things in everybody's life: disagreable & agreable things, sorrow & joy & the New Year will also bring many new things in your life, but I am sure it will bring many sunrays. I know that not every thing in life is easy nor light to bear, but I also know that all difficulties can be overcome with God's help if we look at life in the way He wishes us to namely: in receiving gratefully & profitably the blessings in life & appreciating them & when difficult times come looking up to Him for help. But what am I writing to you about! You will think I am growing into a clergyman; but you see Darling at the end of the year one thinks of those things more; and I am sure you think specially much about the New Year as it will bring many changes in my life. I know I am beginning a difficult year; but I am not dreading it, for I know the One who put me in my position will help me to do the right & in the second place I know I can make myself usefull to my dear people & I can try & be a blessing for them, besides it is always beautifull to be able to do something for those that one loves! And you know my proverb is :"let us hope the best". Well Darling, let us then both hope for the best; we would have no faith if we could not "hope"; and faith we both have, strong and firm so let us then begin the New Year in a happy satisfied way, hoping that the future may be happy for both of us.

I have sent you a little parcel in which you will find a book with poëms & a card which I painted for you.

With all best wishes for the New Year and dearest love, I ever remain your very devoted

        Wilhelmina

# 1898

Paleis, 's Gravenhage<br>January 2 1898

**202**   My very dearest Darling,

Thank you many, many times for your sweet lettre & lovely calendar which has just arrived this morning. It was so dear of you to think of having it sent from home & it is so kind of your sister to have looked after it. Both drawings &

'Major General Kool tutoring H.M. the Queen in military science. A member of the Military House (to a fellow-soldier): "This is a stroke of luck, now we'll also get the hang of what's going on."' Political cartoon by Johan C. Braakensiek (1858-1940); supplement of the *Amsterdammer, Weekblad voor Nederland*, 26 December 1897.

Lieutenant-general A. Kool (1841-1914), Chief of the General Staff, tutored Wilhelmina in military affairs in the first four months of 1898. The lectures were difficult and involved a lot of work; Emma made notes.

words are simply lovely! Never think, Darling, that I would ever take anything you wrote to me amiss; all you point out to me about mother are things I often think about deeply; my thoughts often wander on to the future both in respect to mother & my work; to both I mean to devote all my heart & love. And I hope to succeed with Gods help to ever remain a good, obedient, thankful & loving daughter to my mother and ever encourage that inflexible intimacy that has ever so happily existed between mother and myself and that has always been greater than with any body else.

I know all your efforts have been concentrated upon obtaining that and I am sure you would rejoice now as you always did also formerly in seeing <u>how</u> intimate mother & I we always are together.

But as I said in the beginning I like getting a sermon, for it is always a good thing to be reminded of ones sacred duties.

I <u>am</u> glad you liked the Xmas tree & that you had nice presents. We went to church on New Years eve & on New Yearsday; I suppose you will have come to one or the other service to! Reception[490] etc. passed of all right; I wore a blue silk gown trimmed with cream lace & blue velvet. To morrow will be the galaball![491] I don't think I told you that Prof. Blok has left off his lectures; it was very sad

490  On Saturday 1 January 1898, there was a reception in the Red Drawing Room in Noordeinde Palace for the chairmen of the Upper and Lower Houses of the States-General, the ministers, the members of the Council of Guardians, the Governor of the Residency, the Director of the Cabinet and later, in the small dance-hall, for the Military and Civil House.
491  There were 936 invitees to the gala ball.

saying good bye to him & he himself was very sorry; he finished up in a splendid manner: wishing me a happy life and a good and glorious reign!

We are awfully merry my auntie and I and we do a good deal of laughing. There is now no question of skating any more; the weather is as mild as before Xmas. General Kool is beginning his lectures next Friday.

I think I must finish now, with all my very dearest love I ever remain your most affectionnately devoted

Wilhelmina

PALAIS LA HAYE

January 9 1898

**203** My very dearest Darling,

Thank you so much for your dear long letter. I can understand how you enjoy rowing & being on the water! I can well imagine <u>how</u> sorry you will be to give up Louisa it will be quite a loss for you.

What a pity that you don't get on so very well with miss von Harbon,[492] formerly you used to find her rather a nice woman; I think it often happens that people seem agreable upon the first acquaintance, but upon knowing them better they don't seem so nice as one had thought.

I <u>am</u> glad to hear that you find one of the ladies nice for then you can't feel so very homesick. Does the Mediterranean look something like the Northsea when it is stormy? Please think of telling me when it is quite certain you are going to Segenhaus? Miss Cramer[493] came last Tuesday & I am growing used to her now. She seems to be a very nice girl. The gala ball went off all right & I enjoyed seing auntie Lily dance: of course I had a great many people to talk to & I only saw my auntie during the quadrille which I danced too. Tuesday we are all three going to the Cassino. We have been last Friday to the theatre where we saw "de Bruiloft van Cloris en Roosje [The marriage of Cloris and Roosje]"[494] a piece they always play at new year and inwhich the actors & actresses wish every one a happy new year & make their remarks upon the leading questions of the day. It was very amusing; ofcourse their were many jokes made about the smell of the "grachten [canals]". The people are dressed in dutch costumes. I have had my first lecture of general Kool, it was most interesting.

With all my very dearest love I ever remain, Darling, your very devoted

Wilhelmina

---

**492** Miss von Harbon (see letter 179, note 416).

**493** Miss Kramer von Baumgarten (see letter 192, note 467).

**494** The comic opera *De bruiloft van Kloris en Roosje [The marriage of Kloris and Roosje]* was written by Dick Buysero in 1644. The actor Thomas van Malsem, who probably played the role of Gijsbreght in the first years of the 18th century, made an adaptation of the opera, with Thomasvaer and Pieternel as the parents of the bridal couple.

**204**  My very dearest Darling,

Thank you many, many times for both you dear letters. I <u>am</u> sorry to hear your mother has been so bad again and how dreadful that she has been in such pain. So your poor sister can not yet take care of her, has your mother to have a nurse? And just you being such a way away; do you talk about home worries to the princess or to the girls or miss von Harnier?

All you tell me about your rowing interests me very much, I can well imagine how you must enjoy it!

The lessons of general Kool are very interesting, but they give both mother and me a good deal to do. Mother makes notes for those lectures and she has always a lot to write. I learned my last lesson in 1¼ hour working hard. What a awful thing that procession must have been you saw the other day. I does not astonish me you found it repulsive. It is just the "show" that the Italians make of their religion that is so antipathetic to me; specially because I often feel asif it <u>only</u> were a show and nothing more! It always made me feel impatient and sad when I was in Italy to see the light, thoughtless way they seemed to treat religious matters. It would be a good thing for you to get some other work to do; not only that you think you are "<u>not</u> wanted" as you say at home, but also I am sure you would feel much happier if you had something to do! I can well imagine how down you are by the bad news from home; but let us hope for the best; I think it must be a very good sign that your mothers sickness has been less, for then she will only have to pick up forces.

You asked me how the Cassino went off; I found it very amusing and I danced quadrilles.

To morrow we are giving a small dance; there have been a few people invited and I am looking very much forward to seeing my auntie dance the cotillon. I always find it so nice to watch all the merry faces turning round in front of me (if I need not turn with them).

I think I must finish. Hoping Darling that the news from home will soon become better, I ever remain with heapes of love your very devoted

Wilhelmina

**205**  My very dearest Darling,

I want to just come and tell you what I have been about lately. Last Monday was the ball[495] & I enjoyed very much seing my auntie dance. I danced two lanciers[496] and a quadrille and I wore a blue gown; the bodice consisting of tulle and trimmed with velvet of different shades of blue; specially the bodice suited me

---

**495**  This was a <u>small ball</u> with 495 guests.
**496**  A *lancier* is a dance.

very well. Luckily the dancing began early and finished at 12.³⁰ of the night. The weather has been very bad this week: mild & muggy, and there has been a very high wind. I am very busy at present; I don't know if I told you, I am making a bath and two cans for M^rs van Pallandts[497] baby: they are painted white and I am painting flowers with festoons of babyribbon on them, I hope it may get nice. [Colour plate VII-10] Did I tell you about the dreadful earthquake there has been at Amboina[498] in our India? There have been about 50 people killed and eversomany wounded!

January 23) I have just had your letter; thank you very much for it; I am so glad to hear that your mother is getting better. I can well imagine how nice you would find it to go home by boat but would it be very practical if the princess of Wied wanted you to go to her to first arrive at Amsterdam and then go down to Segenhaus?[499] In every case, Darling, mother has told me I might write and ask you if you pass the Hague by rail to just stay here for 24 hours for us just to be able to have a look at you before you went over home. I would be delightful if I could just see you? I do hope you will find soon something to do for it must be sad not having any permanent occupation!

I can understand you don't wish to stay any longer at Sante Margherita for if you are to give up your lessons you will practically not have any time with Louisa!

To morrow we are having the large "thé dansant". Mother has been very tired again; she is much to busy; I think however she is picking up again.

Hoping to hear from you if you are passing the Hague and if so when that will be, I ever remain your very devoted

Wilhelmina

PALAIS LA HAYE

January 30 1898

206  My very dearest Darling,

Thank you so much for your dear letter I just got to day. We would be very pleased to have you here if it did not make the journey complicated for you or if the trains fit in well. So then as you say in your letter you will let mother or me

---

**497** 'Mrs van Pallandt' is Baroness Irmgard Thecla van Hardenbroek (1871–1958), who married Hans Willem, Baron of Pallandt and Lord of Waardenburg and Neerijnen (1866–1929) on 1 October 1896. In 1898 they had a daughter, Julie Eliza (1898–1971), (see letter 122, note 167).

**498** Ambon is an island of the Indonesian archipelago known as the Moluccas. In 1600 the first Dutch trading post was established on Ambon, which had been taken by the Portuguese in c. 1512. The island played an important role in the spice trade. In 1605, the Portuguese colonies were taken by the East India Company. Between 1796 and 1802 and between 1810 and 1814, the island was occupied by the British. In 1945, the Republic of Indonesia declared its independence. This was followed by the transfer of sovereignty by the Netherlands in 1949. On 25 April 1950, the Republic of the South Moluccas was declared on Ambon. In the same year, however, the Indonesian army brought an end to the republic and Ambon was brought definitively under Indonesian control.

**499** Segenhaus (see letter 197, note 486).

know when it is decided when you leave exactly Santa Margherita and when you will arrive here. It will [underlined twice] be delightful having a look at you Darling; we will be able to talk so much better than be letter; I am looking so much forward to having you here and it will be so nice to be together and I will be able to find time to see you for a good long time during the day you are here for you see Darling I can put aside things during one day that I could not leave if you were to stay longer and I would find it such a pity if you were to pass at such a short distance of me and that I should not have a look at you. I can understand you will not like the idea of staying with the Wieds after your lessons have finished. What a good thing your mother is getting so much better; how ever can your sister miss your Godchild for so long when she herself is always so week; or is she now better; your Godchild is always so wanted at her home! I am happy to say I don't think the news you heard from Atjeh[500] was altogether correct, for the troops have been having skirmishes but we have always been the gaining party with scarcely any loss. From time to time there are sent out a few hundred men to clear the neighbourhood of enimies and at those occasions there occur little skirmishes but the enimy always flys, unluckily we have not yet caught Toekoe Oemar[501] their chief. I am painting the little bath with forgetmenots, roses and buttercups, artificial flowers bound up in a wreath; so you see I am painting it from nature. I am sorry I forgot Elizabeths birthday poor girl it must have been sad for her to be ill about that time. I am very glad you see Italy with fine weather for that is necessary to get a good impression of it otherwise it is an awfal place. We are having here very mild weather but just these last days have been colder and to day there is a perfect deluge. With all my very dearest love I ever remain your most devoted

Wilhelmina.

Paleis, 's Gravenhage
February 6 1898

**207**  My very dearest Darling,

Thank you many, many times for your dear letter that I got this morning. I just want to say still, about your coming here, that although you are ofcourse welcome every day of the week, I would have the most time to see you on

---

**500**  With the 1871 Treaty of Sumatra between the Netherlands and the United Kingdom, the Netherlands gave up its African colonies on the Gold Coast in exchange for the whole of Sumatra, including Aceh in the north. Aceh had been an autonomous sultanate since 1500. In 1873 the Netherlands declared war on Aceh. This was followed by a long and bloody conflict. Only in 1904 was General J.B. van Heutsz (1851–1924) able to take Aceh, but the revolts continued. In 1949 the whole of the Dutch East Indies, including Aceh, was transferred to the Republic of Indonesia.

**501**  Teukoe Oemar (Aceh ?–Aceh 1899), from a powerful family and a well-known figure in the Aceh War. He submitted to the Dutch government in 1892 and led a legion that drove out the 'rebels'. In March 1896, he took his legion over to the enemy side. In June 1898, during the Pedir expedition by Colonel J.B. van Heutsz, he was forced to retreat. He was badly wounded in 1899, and died of an infection.

Rear Admiral F.J. Stokhuyzen (1842-1930) succeeded Lieutenant-General A. Kool; he was chief of the naval staff and taught for only one month, as he subsequently left for the Dutch East Indies as vice-admiral. Wilhelmina also found these lessons extremely interesting and Emma once again made notes.

Tuesdays, Thursdays and Sundays, so that if you could manage to be here during one of those three days of a week I would have the most of you.

What a dreadful place Nervi[502] must be; I always dislike places which are populated with people which have a certain disease.

Do you remenber <u>how</u> I hated Davos? What a charming person that princess Salm you talk about, must be, after your description I should think it would be just somebody I would like so much!!!!!!

I <u>am</u> glad to hear your mother is getting better. What books have you been reading lately to the girls and my cousin? It has been dreadful weather here lately; in the beginning of last week we had awful storms with downpours of rain hail and snow just asif it were March.

I have been learning in my lessons of history of arts about the English artists like Gainsborough[503] (excuse the spelling) and Reynolds[504] etc. I was struck by the pretty portrets they made! Before I had the English school I had the Flemish and the French school which I both disliked and found far inferior to our school. Prof. Krämer has come up to the revolution of July and is giving me slowly on the constitutions of the most of the countries of Europe. During my lessons of M$^r$ Jansen[505] I am drawings heads; I find it very interesting but hopelessly difficult! My lessons of General Kool have had to be encreased so that I have now two lessons of an hour & a half a week of him. I will soon also begin my lectures about navymatters; the admiral Stokhuyzen[506] is to give me those lessons.

Prof. de Louter is going on at a good rate with his lectures. I am still working hard at my German and sometimes M$^r$ Kosman makes me make very difficult essays.

502 Nervi, a former fishing village, lies 7 km to the east of Genoa on the Ligurian Coast of North-western Italy.
503 Thomas Gainsborough (1727-1788) was one of the best-known English portrait and landscape artists of the 18th century.
504 Along with Gainsborough, Sir Joshua Reynolds (1723-1792) was one of the best-known 18th-century portrait painters in England; his portraits are more idealized than those of his rival.
505 From 1890 until the end of her school years, F.J. (Frits) Jansen (1856-1928), a water-colourist and from 1887 assistant director of the Royal Academy of Art The Hague, gave Wilhelmina lessons in pencil drawing and in watercolour painting, perspective, theory of colour — first inside, later outside — anatomy, horses, dogs, flowers, and some instruction in pastel and oil-painting techniques (Spliethoff, pp. 9–35).
506 Rear Admiral F.J. Stokhuyzen (see also letter 202).

I have been very sad lately about my dear Duty,[507] just think I have had to have her shot. I am very miserable about it. I think I must finish. With all my very dearest love I ever remain your most affectionnately devoted

Wilhelmina

PALAIS LA HAYE<br>February 27 1898

**208**  My very dearest Darling,

I <u>was</u> so glad to hear that you had arrived quite safe and sound on the side of the sea.[508] It <u>was</u> so delightful having you here and being able to talk over all your plans for the future and all you did in Italy and Monrepos. How have you found your home and your mother?

I have still been very busy this week with general Kool and his last lesson was most exiting. Poor mother has still had a lot to write. My bath for M^rs van Pallandt came at last and she got it yesterday evening. It really looked very nice now that it was quite ready. Have you had letters from Louisa Wied? It may interest you to hear that I am going to read that part of the book of M^r de Bas[509] that describes the battle of Waterloo. The other day I sat next to M^r Snoukaert[510] to whom I spoke about the book and he has sent it me. What do you say about the affair Zola,[511] It is now in a critical condition.

---

507  Duty (see letter 98, note 126).

508  On the evening of Monday 21 February, Miss Saxton Winter arrived for a short stay in The Hague. That evening, Wilhelmina and Emma were then attending the Mengelberg concert at the Royal Zoological Botanical Society. Miss Winter left again on the evening of Wednesday 23 February.

509  Colonel of the Cavalry F. de Bas (1840-1931) became the director of the military historical archive of the General Staff in 1897, and wrote military history.

510  Baron Albert C. Snouckaert van Schauburg (1841-1902), who became director of the Royal Archives on 28 August 1891, was commissioned by Queen Emma to develop plans for a building to house the archive. On 30 October 1896, Queen Wilhelmina placed a commemorative stone in the front of the building under construction, which would be completed in the summer of 1898 (see N. Dekking and M. Loonstra, 'De Koningin-Regentes en de geschiedenis van het Huis van Oranje', in *Wij zijn er nog*, pp. 63-73).

511  The 'affair Zola', as Wilhelmina calls it, commonly known as the 'Dreyfus affair'. On 22 December 1894, in an age that had seen a significant rise in anti-Semitism, the Jewish captain Alfred Dreyfus (1859-1935) was unjustly found guilty of high treason without any evidence, by the court-martial in Paris. Dreyfus came from Alsace, which had been conquered by Germany in 1871, and he was suspected of spying for the Germans. He was sentenced to deportation to the penal colony of Cayenne, commonly known as Devil's Island, where he had been for four-and-a-half years when the Dreyfus case was re-opened. This happened thanks to his brother, Mathieu, but in particular thanks to Émile Zola (1840-1902), who had published an 'Open letter to the President of the Republic' with the title *J'accuse* on 13 January 1898 in the radical paper *L'Aurore*, published by Georges E. Clemenceau (1841-1929). Although at the second trial on 9 September 1899, Dreyfus was found guilty by five votes to two and sentenced to ten years, the French president pardoned him ten days later. On 11 July 1906, Dreyfus was vindicated and awarded the *Légion d'honneur* (see H.L. Wesseling, 'Dreyfus na de affaire' in, *NRC Handelsblad*, 6 June 1992).

Did you stop at the Maules[512] on your way through.

The weather seems to be getting a little better to day there have been many showers but we have seen the sun whereas on the other Sundays it have rained the whole day. Mother sends you here love.

With all my dearest love I ever remain your most devoted

Wilhelmina.

**209**  My very dearest Darling,

Thank you so much for your dear, long letters. I <u>was</u> a fool to have made such stupid mistakes. When I wrote the letter I thought about our conversation and I wonder if there would be any mistakes.

I <u>am</u> so glad to hear that your mother is again a little better; has your sister left by now?

The lessons of General Kool <u>are</u> finished and I am very sorry about it I keep on thinking about them and wishing I had the General again before me to ask him lots of questions that rise in my mind now that I am disgesting what I have learned. I always have had such a military heart and I feel myself half like a soldier at his post and duty! I think mother will perhaps have a little less to write for the navy-lectures, but I don't think it will make much difference! I got a most enthousiastic letter from M^rs van Pallandt to thank me for the bath. What satis- factory news you have had of Louisa; what an excitement that concert must have been for her; <u>I</u> know who will have had the most success. If you remind me a few times I will tell you about M^r de Bas book when I have read about Waterloo. How interesting the lectures you speak about must be. I am not of your opinion about the affair Zola; formerly I was quite on his side but now no more: for 1^st when one takes his part one makes out the officers of the army for men that break their oaths for they have sworn Dreyfus guilty; 2^d when one takes Zola's part one does so because one <u>thinks</u> that the <u>evidence</u> is <u>not</u> against him, but then one condenms his judges without proofs and one does the same thing that one finds so unjust that the judges did towards Dreyfus; 3^d from a military point of view one <u>may</u> not publish the papers that proof the guilt of Dreyfus for then one publishes secrets about the fortifications of France and besides when one sits in judgement upon a spy that betrays secrets of state, one <u>may</u>, no one <u>can</u> not only keep to the forms of law, but one must condenm a spy if one is sure he is guilty, even if the forms of law have not been able to be carried out exactly. One has to chose between the forms of judgement and the good of the state. I dont say that I take part against Zola, but I only find when one hears arguments like those I mentioned, one can't condenm so much the army!

---

512  Maules; see the biography of Miss Winter, p. 17.

You know what I think about political woman and I need not tell you what I think about Lilian.[513] I am glad, darling that you have heard about something to do and I hope you will be able to go. Ofcourse I would not have talked about it to anyone but mother. I must now finish, it is time for dinner. With all my dearest love I ever remain your very devoted

Wilhelmina

PALAIS LA HAYE<br>March 13 1898

**210** My very dearest Darling,

Thank you so much for your dear last letter; what a pity that your appointment turned out to be nothing; I can well imagine how furious you must have been to have gone up to a town on a "fools errand". It strikes me that you have a good deal to do at home — more than you had thought! Aren't you glad to think that you can help your sister? Your poor mother; it must be tiresome for her that she can not come downstairs! Did n't they admire your sketches from Italy at home? We have had rather a busy week: Thursday there was a military dinner; mother has not been very well lateley and specially Thursdau she felt ill; now she is getting better but she still has fever and feels "slap [weak]". Tuesday we went to see "Antigone"[514] it has been very well translated from the Greek and I admired very much the quiet dignified language and way of acting that the actors had so well imitated. Wednesday we heard Lohengrin[515] in the Dutch opera. I found the music fine, the plot interesting, the acting good, the stage much to crowded!

I have not had much time for painting lately and my bust has not progressed much. I have been riding much lately and I mostly spend my free mornings out on horseback. It has become very cold and it is much more winter when you were here. We have had bitter north and east winds! I have just begun M^r de Bas book so I can't yet tell you much about it. I am getting very interested in the lessons of the "Schout-bijnacht [Rear Admiral]" "Stokhuizen"!

There is to be a general break up of lessons at Easter. Prof. Krämer, M^r Kosmann and the Schout-bijnacht are to finish with their lectures so that there then will remain Prof. de Louter and M^r Jansen for this summer.

I think I must now finish. With all my very dearest love I ever remain your most affectionnately devoted

Wilhelmina

---

513 See previous note.
514 *Antigone* is a tragedy written by the Greek writer Sophocles, dating from 442 BC.
515 The romantic opera *Lohengrin* was composed by Richard Wagner (1813–1883). The premiere was held in the Hoftheater in Weimar on 28 August 1850.

211   My very dearest Darling,

Thank you so much for your dear letter that I got this morning. But before I begin to answer it, I must first tell you a great news, namely mother got this morning the news that my cousin Pauline has engaged herself to the prince Fritz Wied.[516] As mother does not know if it is yet public she told me to ask you to not write any thing about it to Santa Margherita before you have heard from the Wieds in Italy about it. You will be able to imagine <u>how</u> happy mother is!

Mother has been getting better these last few days, but she is not yet strong. What a good thing your mother is getting better; it <u>will</u> be a good thing for your sister to go to the sea. All you write about your "princesses" interests me very much. You must have changed old Darling, to look at history from an "<u>un</u> [under-lined twice!!!] english point of view" I would never have thought <u>that</u> possible.

I hope my poor aunt of Sweden[517] will like having miss Mackworth for a whole month on a visit!!! I have been very busy last week but now dinners etc. are all over; I went to Diligentia last Wednesday alone; it was very "benauwd [oppres-sive]". We hope very much to still find my auntie Albany[518] at Cannes but nothing is yet fixed.

Yesterday I got the news that Mrs van Pallandt has had her baby but it is unluckily a girl.[519] Did you read in the newspaper that miss Rengers has lost an uncle. It was a M^r van Stirum who lived at Haarlem and to whom miss Rengers was much attached. I have been in one continual emotion these last days; first the death of M^r van Stirum; then the baby of M^rs van Pallandt and now the engagement of Pauline.

I think I must now finish for I have still many letters to write. With all dear love I ever remain your most devoted

Wilhelmina

212   My very dearest Darling,

Thank you so much for your dear letters. Yes, Darling, mij excitement has quite calmed down by now. I can understand <u>how</u> delighted the family at Santa Margherita will have been upon hearing the news of Stuttgart.

Mother has been better lately but just yesterday and to day she has been having a very bad toothache, just as if she was not enough tired already! We have been having nearly as bad weather here as you seem to have had at Walden.

---

516  Fritz Wied (see letter 156, note 296).

517  Queen Sophie (1836–1913), the sister of Emma's mother, was married to King Oscar ii of Sweden.

518  Albany (see letter 109, note 143).

519  Julie Eliza (1898–1971) was born on 19 March; she was the last inhabitant of Neerijnen Castle, near Waardenburg on the River Waal, in the Betuwe region of the Netherlands.

Friday we had snow and since it has been raining all the time; one can already smell the spring in the air and all the buds are growing rapidly. We have had <u>one</u> continual storm from last Wednesday till yesterday.

How extraordinary that our war against Spain should be judged in England from a Spanish (Roman-Catholic) point of view; I don't doubt that you will hold firm to your opinion and try and convince the secretary that he is wrong.

Miss Rengers is not going travelling with me this year, but it has nothing to do with the death of her uncle, but only with the marriage of her brother, which is to take place during the time I am away; she wants very badly to be present. I am very glad miss de Joannis has accepted to come with us travelling. I don't think it would be nice to arrive in the South of France just during the marriage of princess Adine,[520] I think the would be rather <u>too</u> many people.

As it is not yet decided if we are going to Cannes or to Nice it is not yet sure what road we will take to go there and if we stop on the road or not.

What a capital idea of yours to start out before breakfast on <u>such</u> a <u>run</u>; I will expect to see you back as thin as a shadow! I did n't mind about your expression of a "monkey" for I knew you did not mean it unkindly.

I think I must now finish.

With all my dearest love I ever remain your most devoted

Wilhelmina

PALAIS LA HAYE<br>April 3 1898

**213**  My very dearest Darling,

Thank you many, many times for you dear letter that reached me this morning. I am happy to say mother is rather better and has no toothache more. Do you know when Elisabeth & Louisa are to be confirmed? I suppose prince Fritz[521] will have to finish his "serious studies" before marrying! Have the history lectures finished for good or will they begin again after Easter? Are you very excited about the Cuba question?[522] I am very interested to know what will happen next!

What an undertaking to dress an English baby; but I am sure you will do it splendidly. I don't find a concert tiring any more; on the contrary I find it a great rest, for I am forced to sit still and I can not take up any thing to do like I would at home.

---

520 Alexandrine 'Adini' of Mecklenburg-Schwerin (1879-1952), the daughter of the eldest half-brother of Prince Hendrik, Friedrich Franz III, married the later King Christian X of Denmark (1870–1947). Prince Hendrik was also present at the wedding, but not Queen Wilhelmina, who was in bed with tonsillitis.

521 Fritz Wied (see letter 156, note 296).

522 The Spanish colony of Cuba, conquered in 1511, was the site of a public revolt against Spain in 1868, supported by the United States. In 1898, the unexplained explosion of the American armoured ship *Maine* in the Port of Havana led to the outbreak of war between Spain and the United States, which the latter won. Cuba was briefly under American control, before becoming a republic in 1902, with America retaining some rights in the state. This marked the beginning of a long period of unrest and turbulence.

The last Diligentia concert was very fine. There were four solo's which sang very well; the last piece was the 9th symphony of Beethoven[523] of which the "finale" is sung.

Yes, Darling, we have had a good deal to do; both with audiences, the dentist and lessons we have been very occupied. I have had a streaming cold this last week, just for the concert, audiences, dentist etc. I have had a nose as round as a plum and as red as a cherry, running eyes, a open mouth and a voice like a pig under a gate! I must have been beautiful!!!!

Mother has now secretly decided about the journey but as the "Voogdijraad [Council of guardians]"[524] has not yet given permission the affair is not yet public: Mother wishes to go to Paris for some days, then to Cannes, then to Genua perhaps, for certain to Florence and from there to Schönfels near Zug in Switserland.

This week I have still to work hard. It is beginning to look something like spring here, so perhaps we will have a green Easter. How is your mother? With all my very dearest love I ever remain your most devoted.

Wilhelmina

PALAIS LA HAYE<br>April 8 1898

214  My very dearest Darling,
Just a few words to tell you that I will be thinking very much about you on Easterday, knowing how much you like going to church and having your Easter services.

I know from olden times how much importance you attach to assist at your own services & I hope you will be able to go on Easter. I am enjoying very much my Good Friday morning as I am only going to church this afternoon and it is thus the only morning in the winter that I feel perfectly free to do what I like.

---

523  Ludwig van Beethoven (1770–1827), a German composer, pianist and conductor of his own work. He wrote symphonies, songs, piano music and chamber music. He was completely deaf when he died. The Ninth Symphony was composed between 1817 and 1824.

524  In accordance with the law of 14 September 1888 (Staatsblad No. 150) and by Royal Decree of 30 October 1888, the members of the Council of Guardians of H.R.H. the Princess of the Netherlands were appointed: Mr J. Röell; Baron A.N.J.M. van Brienen van de Groote Lindt; Mr W.A.C. de Jonge, former member of the Council of State; Baron W.A.A.J. Schimmelpenninck van der Oye; Mr G.C.J. van Reenen, vice-president of the Council of State; C. Polis, Procurator-General of the Supreme Court of the Netherlands; J.G. Kist, President of the Supreme Court of the Netherlands; and E.A.A.J. de Roy van Zuidewijn; chair of the Audit Office. Queen Emma, who was appointed Wilhelmina's guardian by the same law, would be supported by the Council of Guardians. The Council would be consulted on the choice of instructors and teachers for the underage Queen. The Council also had to give its permission for every trip abroad. In 1898 the Council consisted of the following men: Baron W. van Goldstein van Oldenaller, chairman; Mr J. Röell, secretary; Baron A.N.J.M. van Brienen van de Groote Lindt; Mr J.AE.A. van Panhuys, vice-president of the Council of State; A.J. Swart, former member of the Council of State, Baron E.W.J. Six van Oterleek, chairman of the Audit Office; J.G. Kist, president of the Supreme Court of the Netherlands; and C. Polis.

I have been again very busy with the navy lectures which are to finish this week. I have said good bye to M$^r$ Kossmann last Monday; it is always sad to finish with a lesson but I had to much to do. Mother is always tired but is keeping well. We are leaving here on Thursday evening for Paris and will remain there till the 19$^{th}$ on the 20$^{th}$. Our address is "Hôtel Continentale". In Cannes we will stay in the "Hôtel Grande Bretagne" from the 20$^{th}$ till 26$^{th}$. We will be at Genua the 27$^{th}$ "Hôtel Savoye". At Florence we will be in the "Hôtel de la Ville" from the 28$^{th}$ till May the 6$^{th}$. We arrive at Schönfels (this is the name of the Hôtel) on May the 7$^{th}$. My address there is: Hôtel Schönfels près Zug, Suisse.

How is your Mother and sister keeping.

We are having most glorious weather here: fresh and fine. All the buds are groing very fast. I don't think I will have time write again before Paris. I must end now, Darling. With all my dearest love I ever remain your most affectionately devoted

P.S of course I go by the name of Comtesse de Buren[525]

Wilhelmina

April 10 1898

215  My very dearest Darling,

You don't know how pleased I am with the sweet card [Colour plate vii-11] with the boats of Santa Margherita;[526] thank you thousand times, Darling. I find you have done it so beautifully and you have washed it so well and it is such a pretty little subject. Thank you so much for your dear letter and pretty little card enclosed in it; I find both sweet. I am sorry to hear that you have been so bad with influenza and I hope by now that you are quite better. It is troublesome having such a cold. Your poor mother, how sad for her to be ill again. I can understand you dread the coming responsibility, but can't your sister delay her journey? You poor old Darling, I am sorry you feel depressed.

You know what I always say! "Lock yourself up in your room and fight it out, not by thinking that everything is bright and easy in this world, but by owning that this world is dark and brings many afflictions, but that we must make the best of it and try and see its good sides as much as possible. Oh I know from experience that life is difficult and responsibilities way heavily upon my shoulders, but I know I must bear my burden bravely and try to go my way like a

---

525 'Comtesse de Buren' is a pseudonym. When Emma and Wilhelmina visited England in 1895, they also travelled incognito as the 'countesses of Buren'. Prince Willem-Alexander likewise took part in the Elfstedentocht skating race of 1986 under the pseudonym 'W.A. van Buren'.

526 A50-vii-c5. On the back, written in pen by Miss Winter: 'The return of the fishing boats / at evening at / Santa Margherita / Easter 1898. / E. Saxton Winter' (clearly Saxton Winter as a surname!), showing four fishing boats towards evening, with purple hills in the background against a calm sea and three low-flying birds. Watercolour on cardboard, gilt-edged, 15.5 x 20.7 cm.

hero and leave a trace behind me. I always thing it is such a responsibility but on the other hand such a comfort to think we are expected as Christians to leave a trace of light behind us on the way we have gone, and I am sure that gives us the force to go any road we are lead on. I think I will ask Julie[527] to come and see me at Paris.

I must now finish I am half affraid to send you this letter and am inclined to tear it up; but I hope you will not take amiss all I have said; if you do please throw the letter in the fire and think you have not received it.

Thank you still many times for the dear cards and letter.

With all my dearest love and best wishes for a speedy recovery I ever remain your most devoted

Wilhelmina

Cannes April 24 1898

**216**    My dearest Darling

Thank you so much for your dear letters, I am all the same writing for <u>now</u> I <u>really</u> have nothing to do; I think to spare time I will write in telegraph fashion, but first I must say that I <u>am</u> so sorry I never telegraphed sooner, but I wanted to wait till I was quite well again. I had a few days fever, but am now quite better. But I must begin to tell you what we did at Paris from the beginning.

<u>Friday</u>morning arrival, then drive through town, afternoon visit to Louvre (Grecian statues)

<u>Saterday</u>morning Louvre (pictures Italian, Dutch, Flamish school) afternoon shopping & drive.

<u>Sunday</u>morning French church & visit to monument of Coligny, afternoon visit to Madeleine (not very much to be seen) Notre Dame (fine but had thought that it would be larger, met procession (great excitement) Sainte Châpelle (fine but empty & much too much colour) then drive.[528]

<u>Monday</u>morning Luxembourg (modern pictures, sculpture & things of art-industry) lunch & reception at Dutch legation, afternoon Versailles (most interesting gardens lovely, waterworks very fine, Petit Trianon very amusing to see)[529]

---

**527** Julie Liotard (see letter 1, note 3).

**528** The statue of Admiral Gaspard de Coligny (1519-1572) is on the Rue de Rivoli. The leader of the French Protestants, he was killed by the Catholics during the St Bartholomew's Day massacre in 1572. He was the father of Louise de Coligny (1555-1620), the fourth wife of William of Orange (1533-1584). Queen Wilhelmina had a statuette of Gaspard de Coligny in her study. The Madeleine is a church that was built in 1842 and dedicated to Mary Magdalene; it resembles a Roman temple. The Cathedral of Notre Dame in the centre of Paris on the Ile de la Cité was built in early Gothic style and completed in 1345. The Sainte-Chapelle is a chapel dating from 1248 with 13th-century stained glass windows.

**529** The Luxembourg Palace dates from 1625 and was built as a Florentine palace for Maria de' Medici (1573-1642). The Palace of Versailles, commissioned as a hunting lodge by Louis xiv (1638-1715), reached its current form in 1680 under Jules H. Mansart (1646-1708). The symmetrical gardens were designed by André Lenôtre (1613-1700). In 1768, Louis xv (1710-1774) gave

'Les hôtes de la France. Les deux Reines de Hollande,' on the cover of *Le Petit Journal*, Monday 1 May 1898. During their stay in Paris between 15 and 20 April 1898, Queen Wilhelmina and Queen Emma took a number of drives through the city.

<u>Tuesday</u>morning Louvre (pictures French school, drawings of old masters) lunch in hotel given to Dutch legation, afternoon spent partly at home for visits of President & others & partly in making visits to M^rs Faure & (found it most amusing)[530]

<u>Wednesday</u>morning Museum of Clugny, Panthéon (only paintings) Sorbonne lunch at Elysée before lunch I recieved ensignes of Légion d'Honneur[531] which I wore for the occasion (lunch very amusing man people, ladies & gentlemen, very official) afternoon drive, evening we left, I felt horrid & had fever in the train, night-journey, next morning 11³⁰ arrived here. Am lunching today with the Queen,[532] looking much forward to it. With all dearest love I ever am your devoted

Wilhelmina

Schönfels, May 11 1898

**217**     My very dearest Darling,

Thank you very much that you sent the losenges. We arrived here last evening after a lot of travelling about. But before I begin to tell you about all I did these last weeks I must first answer your three last letters.

First about my impressions of Paris; I found it ofcourse a very fine place & I found it most interesting to see the French people in their own country for then

the Petit Trianon in the gardens of Versailles as a pleasure pavilion to his mistress, Madame de Pompadour (1721-1764); and in 1775 it was given by Louis XVI (1754-1793) to Marie Antoinette (1755-1793).

**530** Originally a medieval castle and changing constantly over the centuries, the Louvre was home to the French kings. On 10 August 1793 it was opened as a museum, making it one of the oldest museums in the world. Félix Faure (1841-1899) was the republican President of France between 1895 and 1899.

**531** The Musée du Cluny, housed in a Gothic mansion, contains a collection of classical and medieval artefacts, including a series of tapestries, *La Dame à la Licorne*. The Pantheon is a 19th-century building, originally built as a church, but later transformed into a civil temple to honour important Frenchmen, such as the philosopher Voltaire (1694-1778) and the writer Victor Hugo (1802-1885).

**532** The lunch took place on Sunday 24 April 1898 with Queen Victoria of Great Britain.

Queen Victoria gave the young Queen Wilhelmina this signed portrait as a souvenir of their meeting at Windsor Castle on 9 May 1895, during the educational trip to London. When Wilhelmina and Emma stayed in France and Italy between 14 April and 7 June 1898, they would see one another again in Nice. On 24 April, Queen Victoria presented Wilhelmina with the Order of Victoria and Albert. Photograph: Gustav Mullins.

one can only get an adea of their character. London & Paris are not to be compared; both are so different; I don't think I would like to live in either. I saw poor Julie for a few moments; she was ofcourse very sad & did not quite know how life would go without her mother, it was most afflicting to hear here talk. I saw the Wieds at Genua & I found both girls much improved; Elisabeth looks quite another girl with her hair up. Louisa had grown much more into an older girl; I made a great effort to talk & I really kept up a conversation with her. It may interest you to know that I had a little conversation with her mother inwhich I asked her to let the girls assist at the galadinner that is to be on my birthday; my cousin said she would be very pleased to let them come; I hope very much that Louisa having been to an official occasion once, will be allowed to go out this winter. don't you think that might be a step on the good way? I found your letter of April 15 most interesting specially the part about the Wieds.

In Cannes I did not see much being ill; I saw just still the Albanies & found Alice[533] very much grown. I went up to there little villa, which I found a sweet little nest. We went for an afternoon to Nice to see the Queen,[534] which I found

533 Helena, the Duchess of Albany, and her children Alice and Charles Edward (see letter 109, note 143).

534 Queen Victoria presented Wilhelmina with the decorations of the *Royal Order of Victoria and Albert*, although it had been the intention to do so only when she turned eighteen (see Verburg, p. 44, note 108; Verburg erroneously writes that Emma and Wilhelmina visited Queen Victoria in England in the spring of 1898.) Queen Victoria established the Order of Victoria and Albert on 10 February 1862. It was intended for female members of the British Royal Family only, but evidently also for foreign princesses. The last medal was presented to the person mentioned in the previous footnote, Princess Alice, the Countess of Athlone and Wilhelmina's cousin, who died in 1981. Wilhelmina's medal was probably sent back to England after her death, as was the case for the chain of the Order of the Garter. Information provided by G. Sanders, curator of the Museum Kanselarij van Nederlandse Orden [Chancellery of Orders of the Netherlands], Paleis Het Loo National Museum.

looking very well; ofcourse I enjoyed the visit very much; She gave me the Victoria and Albert order.

I saw also my cousin of Mecklenburg.[535] In Genoa I did not yet go sightseeing I only saw one of our boats start off to India: the "Princess Sophie"; the Schout bij Nacht Stokhuizen who gave me Navy lectures started on that boat.[536] My throatache was most disagreable; mother had "Tientje"[537] come at Genoa; he said I had got an infection in Paris & he disinfected my throat (you would be thunderstruck if you could see <u>how</u> well I behave with Tientje)

I <u>was</u> so sorry to here about poor Ethel[538] being so bad, I hope she is now quite well again!

My auntie Elisabeth has been with us till now, but she is to leave still this week. It was most delightful having her, we so used to her travelling with us that sightseeing without her would nearly be impossible. She has made herself very useful talking Italian, she being the only one who knows the language! I enjoyed very much Florence there were most beautiful things to be seen; only both beggars smells & dirt were awful.

There hade happened most unorderly things at Florence; We nearly were once in a tumult; it was not agreable: we looking at an inner court of a Paladzo when a heap of people tried to enter the Paladzo to make a manifestation at its owner to lower the price of the bread. luckily the gates were shut & they cold not get in. We could retire through another gate & get our carriages & drive on, but the tumult must have been great for the soldiers had to help keep order & all the shops closed.

We intended to pass Sunday at Milan & stop for a few hours at Ravenna to see all the beautiful churches. Ravenna was most amusing for it rained the whole time & we all looked & felt like drowned cats! We got the news there that the Italian government requested us to not go to Milan, the state of the affairs being such that we would not be safe. The insurrection had been such that 20000 soldiers had been called to restore order.

We stopped at Bologna on Sunday & enjoyed very much seeing that town. Instead of going via Milan to Schönfels as we had wished we had to go by the Brenner a great way round & had to stay for a night at Insbruck. Schönfels seems to be pretty but I have not yet seen anything of it. Have you heard that Miss van Stirum is engaged to a M^r van Lynden?[539] I can't write any more; you will understand how sorry I am to miss her.

How is your mother? Mine is well but tired. With all dearest love I remain your most devoted

Wilhelmina

---

535 This probably refers to Elisabeth of Mecklenburg-Schwerin, the daughter of Sophie and Carl Alexander of Saxe-Weimar.

536 Stokhuizen (see letter 202 and 207).

537 G.P. van Tienhoven (1836–1901) had been Wilhelmina's physician since 28 August 1891.

538 Ethel is possibly a daughter of the brother of Miss Winter (see letter 124, note 176).

539 Van Limburg Stirum (see letter 141, note 239).

**218**    My very dearest Darling,

Thank you so much for your two dear letters. One of your former letters of May 3 made a very long journey; it went first to Schönfels, then to Milan & then back here; so I only got it the other day, for it had been stopt a long time at Milan the post not working there. Before I go any further — may I condole profoundly with you for the death of Gladstone;[540] you must be sad that the "Grand old Man" is really dead!!!

I am now quite well again & painting & drawing & walking being out as much as possible. I am indeed awfully sorry that miss van Stirum is going to leave. I am so fond of her; she is such a bright, merry, sweet girl & it will be dreadfull missing her. But I must not be selfish, but be happy for her sake. I don't know if the Wied-girls know that they are to be at the galadinner. I only spoke about it to their mother. I am glad to hear that your sister has come home so much better. How nice for you to go to Oxford; I know how glad you will be to be so much on the water. I am glad to know exactly when the Wieds are to be confirmed for ofcourse I will be thinking very much about them.

I can well imagine what an awful work that doll that you dressed will have been. You asked me in one of your former letters what I thought about the war; ofcourse I am awfully sorry for the poor queen-regent of Spain[541] & all my sympathies go with her. I am sorry, Darling, that my letter is not more interesting, but we are living so quietly that there is really nothing to tell. Excuse the writing; I am just going out and did not wish to let you wait any longer for a letter.

With all my dearest love I ever remain your very devoted

Wilhelmina

**219**    Dearest Darling,

Thank you so much for your dear last letter. I heard on the day of the Wieds confirmation from my (old) cousin that the Queen of Roumania[542] had after all been present at the ceremony. All you tell me about the races interests me very much. I can see you as it were in a little boat keenly interested in all that

---

540 William E. Gladstone (1809-1898), a British statesman, who initially supported the Tories and later switched allegiance to the Liberals. Together with the Conservative Benjamin Disraeli (1804-1881), he dominated British politics in the second half of the 19th century. He was prime minister four times. He had a great sense of the value of law and liberty, and was always on the side of oppressed nations and minorities, even if this conflicted with British interests.

541 The Queen-Regent is Maria Carolina, Archduchess of Austria (1858-1929), the second wife of King Alfonso XII of Spain (1857-1885), who married her in 1879. He died in 1885. Six months later their only son, Alfonso XIII (1886-1941), was born. Marie acted as regent for him until he turned sixteen in 1902. The harsh repression of the Cuban Revolt of 1895 under the Conservative Canovas government led to the Spanish-American War of 1898, in which Spain lost its last colonial possessions (see letter 213, note 522).

542 The Queen of Romania; see Elisabeth 'Carmen Silva' (see p. 22, notes 32-33).

happens on the river & mad with excitement at the moment the racing boats go past & jumping up for the decisive moment; you dear old thing, I can well imagine <u>how</u> you are enjoying it. How agreable for lookers on to be turned over by the students! How lovely for you to be able to drive. We are leaving here the 6<sup>th</sup> & arrive at Soestdijk on the morning of the 7<sup>th</sup>. The weather is dreadful here; but we are all the same making excursions. We tried once to go to the Rigi but it was so misty that we had to give it up & went that day to Lucerne & on the lake; it was so funny to see back Gersau & Brunnen. One day we went to Zürich for shopping & yesterday we went to Göschenen & drove up the Gotthart; we came a good way further than in 1891 but the mist that had been hanging the whole day over the mountains got thicker & thicker so that we did not see much. It was colder up there than in January.

We come home from those excursions very late generally at 8 in the evening for from Zug the ascent is very steep and the poor horses have very hard work to pull us up.The road is much steeper & longer than the one going from Innsbruck to Igls!

I must end now, Darling.

With all dearest love, I ever remain your most devoted

Wilhelmina

At the top of the last page, Queen Emma has added in pencil:
Wilh. is very well indeed. Much love fr. E.

Soestdijk
June 12 1898

**220**  My very dearest Darling,

Thank you so much for your dear letter. You <u>can</u> imagine <u>how</u> madly delighted I am to be in my dear country again & how glad I am that all the unpacking is done. It went very quickly. My rooms are <u>lovely</u>;[543] my little drawingroom is the sweetest little thing I think I ever saw. Downstairs I have the same rooms as formerly, only my mothers study has become my drawingroom. Upstairs I have your little dressingroom, W.C. & bathroom & your sittingroom as bedroom. Miss v. Overzee[544] sleeps in my former dressingroom. Mother has arranged my rooms simply beautifully; she has had them got up all newly. Swell has not yet come here so I can't yet say <u>how</u> he looks! I have grown travelling as strong as a young

---

**543** E8-ixe-7e and E9d1-ivbb-11. See Paleis Soestdijk, maps 328–329. Wilhelmina used the same rooms at Paleis Soestdijk as her father, King Willem iii. They were located downstairs to the left of the vestibule (1), drawing room (2), study (3) and sitting room (4); whilst her bedroom and other rooms upstairs were also located left of the central balcony/trophy room (11). Before she was married, the drawing room (12), the bedroom (13) and the dressing room and wardrobe of the governess (14) lay in the extension of the rooms of Queen Emma, who had her apartment on the right. After Wilhelmina's marriage, the rooms upstairs on the left were arranged as follows: the sitting room of Prince Hendrik (12), the dressing room of Prince Hendrik (13) and the bedroom of H.M. (14), which would have been a shared bedroom.
**544** Miss van Overzee (see letter 141, note 240).

horse & I have so much force that I have to take a good amount of exercise to remain managable for myself! My rides & tennis & walks have begone in a most frantic fashion; but the great attraction is now at present the rowing; so you see I am now just like you! Mother gave me the permission to row alone with my ladies[545] as both can swim. We go & fish the boats out of the boathouse & start off & generally remain on the water an hour & a half. It is simply lovely. Prof. Krämer[546] is giving next Wednesday his last lessons. When those are done I will only have M$^r$ Jansen & Prof. de Louter[547] Mundays, Wednesdays & Fridays. Fridays fore twice 5/4 of an hour, the other days only for 5/4 of an hour. So I willl have very little to do, only the preparations takes a long time.

The weather is very fine & hot, for a wonder quite like one should think it must be in June. I hope so much, Darling, that you are enjoying your time at Oxford!

I must end for I must go to lunch. With all my dearest love I ever remain your most devoted

Wilhelmina

P.S. Mother has just told me to write & tell you that we are meaning to ask you to come over to Soestdijk during June or July for 8 or 10 days. Please write & tell me if that would be possible for you, or that you had arrangements for that time? You can imagine <u>how</u> delighted I would be at having you. Dearest love,

Wilhelmina

Soestdijk
June 19 1898

**221** My very dearest Darling,

Thank you so much for your last dear letter. Mother can not yet quite say when you could come over as we are expecting many visits in July but she will try and arrange to have you in the latter part of July. As we would both like to see you as much as possible we want to have you at a time when there no other guests in the house.

You need really not make such preparations, Darling, to come here as we will be leading a very quiet life out here & are wearing all our old clothes: to economise, you know, for September. I love to see you in all the dear old things of formerly, to make you look like the dear "old Bones" of olden times. I would dislike so much to see you in all new things. I was very glad to hear the doll-exhibition was a great success! The weather here was fine but cold these last days. I am going on taking most frantic exercise every day. I have been trying a new horse last week which if it is quite to my taste mother will give me. It is a sweet animal & goes like a dream.

---

**545** These ladies-in-waiting are the Countess of Limburg Stirum (see letter 141, note 239) and Baronesss Juckema van Burmania (see letter 135, note 205).
**546** Prof. Krämer (see p. 30, note 62).
**547** Mr Jansen (see letter 143, note 248), and Prof. de Louter (see letter 160, p. 160).

Queen Wilhelmina on horseback in front of Soestdijk Palace, c. 1896, part of the collection of letters belonging to Miss Elizabeth Saxton Winter. Photographer unknown.

I have taken leave of prof. Krämer this week; it was very sad saying good bey to him. Prof. de Louter, however, still gives me plenty to do & poor mother often has very much to write. She is very tired lately & always still has fever; she has dreadfully much to do.

How is your mother? I hope so much that you will be having fine weather & will still be able to be much on the water.

I must end now. With all my dearest love I ever remain your most devoted

Wilhelmina

Soestdijk
July 1 1898

**222**  My very dearest Darling,

Thank you so much for your dear letter. I can well imagine how busy you must be with the parties etc. you have been going to. I <u>am</u> happy to hear you found your mother and sister so well. You can think <u>how</u> [underlined three times] delighted I shall be to see you again, you sweet old Darling! Mother told me to write that she would ask you to come over & be here the morning of 9<sup>th</sup> of July or the 12<sup>th</sup>.[548] She can't quite say which of these two days. How prettty that play of Shakespeare must have been, acted all in the open! We are now to have many visits. First miss de Constant (Piksy)[549] is to stay here for a few days; I am looking very much forward to seing her for she was in Italy the whole of last winter and I am very fond of her & have not seen her for long. Then my cousin Pauline[550] is coming 4<sup>th</sup> of July; ofcourse I am madly happy to see her. Saturday we are to have the Gardenparty. I have also had a few audiences lately. We received the other day one of the Indian princes: the Sultan of Siak.[551] It was very interesting. Ana Bentinck has also been presented as quite grown up. It was most

**548**  Miss Winter stayed at Soestdijk between 9 and 20 July. It is unclear whether she was there the whole time.

**549**  She arrived on 2 July and left again on 7 July.

**550**  Pauline of Württemberg stayed at Soestdijk Palace with her lady-in-waiting, Miss Ulrike von Riedel, between 4 and 11 July 1898.

**551**  H.H. the Sultan of Siak ruled between 1889 and 1908. On Saturday 25 June he was met at the station and taken to Soestdijk Palace in a carriage driven by four horses, where he was received by Emma and Wilhelmina in the Stucco Hall at 3 p.m. The visit lasted 50 minutes.

amusing receiving her mother and her in a "deftig [distinguished]" audience. I am now working hard at preparations for mothers birthday; I am painting in oils a "dessus de porte"[552] for her. It is an enormous piece of canvas & I was quite alarmed when I saw this thing the first time. However, I have now got accustomed to its size & I ask sometimes M^r Jansen to look at it; he said that there was nothing yet spoilt. Don't you find it an undertaking? I think I must now finish. With all my dearest love, I ever remain your most devoted

Wilhelmina

Soestdijk July 31 1898,

**223**　My dearest Darling,

Just a few words to thank you many, many times for your dear long letter which I expected with impatience. It was lovely having you here again, you old Darling, it was only a pity the time went by so very fast. I was ofcourse very wild in getting your letter; mother read me all about the proposal my auntie of Wied has done for you.[553] You ask me what I think about it. I think it would be a very suitable position for you & I am sure that you will be able to do a great deal of good. I think the work will not be too monotonous as you are to occupie yourself both with mother & child; only it will be difficult to influence the mother as she is allready over 20 years old! How can you think that I should be horrified at your undertaking to look after the religious training of a child of another religion! You need therefor not change your views! You will understand that I am very busy at present so I will not write a long letter to day; all you tell me about the Wieds interested me very much.

With heaps of love I ever remain your most devoted　　　Wilhelmina

Soestdijk August 7 1898

**224**　My very dearest Darling,

Thank you so much for your two dear letters and good wishes. But before I begin to answer them, I must first give you a message of mother.

You wrote the other day to her to explain about the position that has been offered you! You asked mother to give her opinion upon the subject; she is so dreadfully occupied that she can't write herself, but she told me to write you her opinion. She finds you, namely, "very well qualified for the position and thinks you will be able to do a great deal of good."

I _am_ sorry, Darling, that you have had so many worries at home; it _is_ sad that your sister is ill again after having come home so well and bright; you will have been very occupied now with all the patients!

Every thing went off well on mothers birthday; the weather was splendid & the illumination was sweet. The little boats were illuminated & made a very nice

---

**552** A 'dessus de porte' is a work to be hung above a door. The location of the painting is not known.

**553** This concerns the position of governess to Prince Carol of Romania (1892–1953) (see the next letter, note 557).

effect on the water. Every now & then the lake was light by bengalfire; there was a boat with music; to complete the scenery the moon shone brightly over the whole lake. We have just had my uncle of Saxe Weimar and my cousin of Mecklenburg.[554] My poor uncle has grown very old; I enjoyed extremely my cousin.

Before mothers birthday I still had miss de Kock;[555] you can imagine <u>how</u> happy I was to have her here again. My lessons with Prof. de Louter & M<sup>r</sup> Jansen[556] have finished now. It was very sad saying good bye to both; especially to Prof de Louter; the poor man was quite upset. So now I will set hard at work to let mother give me the finishing touches before the 31<sup>st</sup> of August. I am sorry to here you found Louisa in such an unsatisfactory condition.

In Genua I found her so bright & lively! You will be leaving home comparatively soon now; for with your visit to the crownprincess[557] and my Inauguration you will have to start early for the continent. I think, but I am not sure, that I told you that I enjoyed very much the visit of the Bentheims;[558] they were not so tiring afterward than in the beginning. I grew specially fond of the eldest of the girls. The little boy was most amusing.

I think I must end now. With all my dearest love I ever remain your most devoted

Wilhelmina

Soestdijk August 14 1898

**225**  Very dearest Darling,

Thank you many times for your dear letter. I <u>am</u> glad to hear that your mother & sister are better again. Yes, sweety, it is true we did make a tour through the Betuwe[559] yesterday (do you know what is the Betuwe or have you forgotten?).

The people were most enthousiastic. The weather was so hot and the roads were so dusty and shadeless that we were cooked in an awful manner; this is

---

554 Carl Alexander, Grand Duke of Saxe-Weimar, and his daughter Elisabeth of Mecklenburg-Schwerin arrived on 4 August and left on 6 August 1898.

555 Miss de Kock (see letter 2, note 7).

556 Jansen (see letter 143, note 248 and letter 207, note 505).

557 The 'crown princess' refers to Marie, the wife of Ferdinand, Crown Prince of Romania, whose two children Carol (born 15 October 1893), the later King Carol II or Romania, and Elisabeth (born 12 October 1894), would be cared for by Miss Winter.

558 This concerned the visit from 19–27 July 1898 by the Prince and Princess of Bentheim-Steinfurt, with their son (the little boy, probably Friedrich, who was born in 1894) and three daughters, Elisabeth, Victoria and Emma (see photo p. 201).

559 The journey through the Betuwe on 13 August entailed taking the train from Soestdijk Palace to Elst, then to Doodewaard, where the queens took the ship 'De Harmonie' to Tiel. From a pavilion, the two queens listened to the music and singing of the Tielsch Stedelijk Muziekcorps and the Tiels men's choir, school children and orphans. They then did a tour of Tiel and continued their journey to Drumpt, Kerk-Avezaath, Erichem, Buren and Geldermalsen. At the end, the Queen donated 300 guilders to the 'general poor'.

On 13 August 1898 the two queens arrived in Tiel by boat, having crossed the River Waal, and were subsequently welcomed by the residents in a marquee on Nieuwe Kade. This was followed by a drive through the town. The flags flown depicted King Willem III crossing the River Waal to Leeuwen and Druten at the time of the disastrous flood of 1861.

a good beginning of the Septemberfeasts if it is going tobe so hot there will be nothing left of any of us; I will get less fat, that is one good thing.

Poor mother is quite overcome by the heat and her work; the day before yesterday she was in bed the whole day with a dreadful headache, luckily she could however go for the drive through the Betuwe! The Wieds <u>are</u> setting up in a grand way at Scheveningen.

I am quite sure you don't want my advise for painting and you are doing the sides of the portfolio very prettily. You sweet old Darling, I was most amused at the lovely arrangement in the corner of one of the sheets and was very happy to see that such things can also happen to much older people than myself. Thursday I went to Utrecht to see the Childrenshospital![560] To day it is hotter than ever. I am all of a slm-----stick (you know what that means). I am sorry to say that I think my letter has suffered very much from my temperature which I am sure, has gone up far above melting point. Please excuse it being so short. With all dearest love I remain your most affectionnately devotedly, stickily melting friend

Wilhelmina

560 That visit took place by carriage on Thursday 11 August 1898.

me. With all my dearest love I ever remain your most devoted & slim ..... stick ---

*Wilhelmina*

My very dearest Darling,

Thank you many times for your dear letter; yes Darling, as you see I have not yet quite become a grease spot, but I am not very far from that stage. I find the weather killing! I can imagine how tiresome it must be for you not to get any news from my aunt of Wied! I think the princess must soon be going to Schwalbach or however the place is called! I have still a good deal to do. Tomorrow my Paris-people are coming to try on; I hope I will like it in this temperature! Then I am to have my hair dressed a few times with my diadem & I have to rehearse with the four aides-de-camps the carrying of my mantle. All agreeable little jobs in this heat! - Don't you find?

My Mother is of course still very busy but she is better again. No wonder that your poor sister does not get much stronger in this heat. I think that all what is left of humanity will melt away. I think I must end now for my pen sticks to my hand & I am getting waves of heat all over

Queen Wilhelmina was unable to stand hot weather. This is clear from letter 226, in which she describes trying on the dress for her investiture, made in Paris, and her diadem. The writing paper features a crowned monogram that incorporates Wilhelmina's name in artful fashion.

**226** My very dearest Darling,

Thank you many times for your dear letter; yes Darling, as you see I have not yet quite become a grease spot, but I am not very far from that stage. I find the weather killing! I can imagine how tiresome it must be for you not to get any news from my aunt of Wied! I think the princess must soon be going to Schwalbach or however the place is called!

I have still a good deal to do.

Tomorrow my Paris-people are coming to try on; I hope I will like it in this temperature!

Then I am to have my hair dressed a few times with my diadems & I have to rehearse with the four aides-de-camps the carrying of my mantle. All agreable little jobs in this heat! — Don't you find?

My Mother is ofcourse still very busy but she is better again. No wonder that your poor sister does not get much stronger in this heat. I think that all what is left of humanity will melt away. I think I must end now for my pen sticks to my hand & I am getting waves of heat all over me. With all my dearest love I ever remain your most devoted & slim -----stick ----

Wilhelmina

[On a separate page, decorated with the monogram of Het Loo and written in Dutch:]
P.S.

My Mother told me that she had in the past sometimes noticed that the letters between here and Bucharest were being lost or opened. Perhaps you can find out whether that is still happening.

If so, then we must be careful!

Wilhelmina

## The investiture of Queen Wilhelmina

On 31 August 1898, her eighteenth birthday, Wilhelmina began her reign with a short proclamation entitled 'To My People'. This was followed by a service in the Grote Kerk in The Hague, a reception and a dinner, where she performed 'with an ease, a grace and a courage that bode well and are very pleasing for her and her proud mother' (Cleverens 1984, p. 47). On the day before the investiture, the *Blyde Incomste* (ceremonial entrance) was held in a splendidly decorated Amsterdam, with Wilhelmina and Emma riding in the *Crème Calèche*, a royal carriage that was a gift from her mother. The two queens were then enthusiatically cheered when they appeared for the people on the balcony of the Palace on Dam Square. At 11 a.m. on 6 September, the solemn investiture took place in the Nieuwe Kerk. Many were moved by the way in which Wilhelmina read out her speech, including Prime Minister Pierson, who wrote in his diary: 'The investiture was so deeply moving that it touched all of our souls'; and of the taking of the oath, 'When she stood there with raised hand, it was as though all were electrified' (Fasseur 1998, p. 171).

Queen Wilhelmina with her four aides-de-camp, who carried her royal robes, making her way to the investiture in the Nieuwe Kerk in Amsterdam, 6 September 1898. Photograph: Henri de Louw.

Letter from Miss Winter. Between October 1898 and 21 April 1900, Miss Winter was governess to Hereditary Crown Prince Carol, later King Carol II of Romania and his sister Elisabeth. As their mother, Crown Princess Marie, was absolutely unable to get on with Miss Winter, the latter would eventually be dismissed.

Castil Peleş, Sinaia[561]
Via Kronstadt & Siebenburgen
Oct. 1. 98

**227** My most precious Queen,

You will see by the above address that the journey has been accomplished safely. I hope that yours too, though a much shorter one, has met an equally satisfactory fate and that you are now glorying in the sweet air and beauty of the dear Loo. We[562] spent Wednesday at Munich in visiting the yearly exhibition of pictures at the Glaspalast[563] where there were some very fine ones, and in

561 A50-VIIc-S-02. This item in the Royal Archives includes a few letters from Miss Saxton Winter. Peleş Palace is located in Sinaia, c. 120 km north of the Romanian capital Bucharest. The town lies in a mountainous region in the Prahova Valley, at the foot of the Bucegi Mountains.

562 Miss Winter was travelling with King Carol I, Queen Elisabeth 'Carmen Silva' of Romania and Crown Princess Marie.

563 The Glaspalast in Munich was built following the example of the Crystal Palace in London and opened in 1854. It was destroyed by fire in 1931.

going to the studio of Fritz Kaulbach, with whom the Princess was "sitting" for her portrait.[564] <u>This</u> visit was <u>most</u> interesting, he had a lot of beautiful studies & finished canvasses, & the picture of the Princess was <u>wonderfully</u> like her & picturesque. She is certainly exceedingly pretty, & a great charm is, that there is absolutely nothing artificial about her appearance – no powder, no paint – only plenty of strong scent & jewels which could be dispensed with! We left Munich at 9 o'clock on Wednesday night & reached here at 9 o'clock yesterday (Friday) morning, more of the train than is altogether pleasant!, but I'm more thankful than I can say to have travelled with their Majesties, rather than manage the journey alone. The country all round is <u>most</u> beautiful, great solemn, rocky mountains, reminding me of Switzerland, and thick forests of fir & beech trees. The latter are just turning & their rich autumn colours are like varnished gold in the sunlight – The palace or "castle" as it is called, is also very beautiful & grand. The style is rather severe, immense quantities of heavy oak carving being employed all over the house – but it is in the most perfect taste, & proclaims itself to the work of an essentially, artistic mind. Every little detail is a complete work in itself, & I have the feeling that it reguires days or weeks to grasp the <u>whole</u>! It is very interesting to watch the entire surroundings of the court, its etiquette & all the people – Every thing is so entirely different to any former experience, but the smaller details I could only discuss if we were face to face!

The Princess left us at the railway station & drove immediately to her own house, about 10 minutes off, where she lives quite alone with her husband & children – There is an elderly widow lady who is supposed to be her lady-in-waiting, but as <u>she</u> lives here, & very seldom sees the Princess, it seems a remarkable arrangement altogether! There is a <u>very</u> choice collection of young princes coming today to stay with the young people. The young Coburg[565]

564 Friedrich August von Kaulbach (1850-1920) was a German painter who was celebrated for his portraits, particularly of women. He was painting a portrait of Princess Marie 'Missy' (1875-1938), the Duchess of Edinburgh and the daughter of Queen Victoria's son Alfred and Grand Duchess Maria of Russia (see p. 22, notes 32–33). On 10 January 1893 she married Ferdinand I, the second son of Leopold, Prince of Hohenzollern-Sigmaringen (1835-1905) and Antonia Maria of Portugal (1845-1913). Ferdinand was the king of Romania between 1914 and 1927. His predecessor was King Carol I, his father's younger brother. Theirs was not a happy marriage. They had three daughters and three sons. The paternity of Carol (1893-1953), Elisabeth (1894-1956) and Nicholas (1903-1978) was not disputed. Marie had various lovers. She had an affair with a Romanian officer Zizi Cantacuzino, known as the 'Miss Winter affair', which Miss Winter is said to have made public (see p. 22, note 34). It was said that he was the father of Marie 'Mignon' (1900-1961), the future queen of Yugoslavia. Boris of Russia was also mentioned. The paternity of Ileana (1909-1991) is uncertain. Barbu Ştirbey claimed to be the father of Mircea (1913-1916). Both had brown eyes, unlike Marie and Ferdinand.
565 This is Hereditary Prince Alfred (1874-1899), Duke of Edinburgh and Duke of Saxe-Coburg and Gotha, the eldest brother of Crown Princess Marie of Romania, who became embroiled in a scandal with a lover and tried to kill himself at the end of January 1899. He failed, but nevertheless died shortly afterwards of his wounds. After this, the dukedom of Saxe-Coburg and Gotha fell to his cousin Prince Charles Edward (1884-1954), the son of

who has just made himself a public scandal, another young Coburg[566] who
seems to wish to follow his cousins example, & the Grand Duke Boris[567] whose
reputation is not of the best, & his younger brother![568] So I don't see where
the opportunity will come in, for the Princess & myself, to become any better
acquainted than at present! The Queen has a wonderful charm about her, &
the more one sees her, the more easily can one realize the difficulties she must
meet with in life, with such an imagination & artistic temperament — There is
something appealingly sad about her, which cannot do otherwise than win the
sympathy of other women. I have no idea how long I remain here. Everyone
is specially kind. I hope darling Queen that you & the Queen-Mother are both
keeping well.

  With all my very dearest love.

  Believe me, ever, darling Queen, your most lovingly devoted friend

E. Saxton Winter

Written underneath in pencil by Wilhelmina:

do not tear up

Het Loo October 5 1898

**228**   My very dearest Darling,
At last I have found time write you these few lines. I must begin by saying that
I was so sorry not to have any time to write before the day; but I know that you
will understand that it was "force majeure" which compelled me to wait untill
to day. It is such a comfort to think that you understand so well that I have no
time! Thank you many, many times for all your loving letters and specially that
you continued writing even when you did not get any answer. I will not write
about the festivities, for I am sure you will have heard about them in the papers;
I would rather begin to tell you about my life; for I think of the two that will
interest you the most. I must all the same tell you one thing about them however:
The impression they made upon me. I felt very small and unworthy in seeing so
much enthusiasme and love all for me; it filled me if possible with more ambition
than I had to show myself worthy of so much love. Oh, if only I ever could show
my people faintly all the gratitude and love I feel towards them. In such times
I wish I had so many more means of expressing my gratitude. You mention in

---

Emma's sister Helena and Leopold, Duke of Albany, after Leopold's brother Arthur waived his
rights.

**566**  It is unclear who the other young Coburg is.

**567**  Grand Duke Boris Vladimirovich (1877–1943) of Russia was the third son of Vladimir A.
Romanov (1847–1909), the son of Tsar Alexander II and Maria of Mecklenburg-Schwerin. Boris
may have been the father of Crown Princess Marie of Romania's third child, Maria (Mignon),
who was born in Coburg on 6 January 1900. Boris was among the royal guests attending the
wedding of Wilhelmina and Hendrik on 7 February 1901 (Annals 1901, p. 284). In 1905 Boris'
older brother Kirill (1876–1938) married Victoria Melita of Saxe-Coburg-Gotha, the sister of
Marie of Romania.

**568**  This is Boris' younger brother, Andrei Vladimirovich (1879–1956).

one of your former letters the death of the Empress of Austria;[569] of course I was dreadfully sorry for the poor Empror.

I was most interest in your last letter with all the descriptions you give of different things.

During the few days at the Hague that I had no festivities I immediately set at work with the ministers; most of my mornings were filled with my work. The afternoons were spent in audiences and dessing and undressing. Some were very "benauwd [oppressive]" sup. those of the Chambers, where I was without my Mother or any lady; others were — very agreable. Here my mornings are well taken up with working & after that is done I have time to go out. After lunch I go out (mostly long works of 2½ hours) and then I have a time at home which I mostly use to get through much reading (I work up all sorts of questions of which I don't yet know all I want to) if at least I have no other duties to accomplish. After dinner I kread papers and open letters & go to bed early & sleep all night like a rose and get up the next morning as fresh as anything.

I enjoy very much the being occupied all day and I am full of courage for the future. It is also so delightful that I can now see more of my Mother than formerly. We go out very much together and chat about everything that goes across my mind or that has to do with my work. I have not had time to finish my letter the other day so I have only sent it off to day (October 7th). With all my dearest love I ever remain your very devoted

Wilhelmina

The Loo October 23 1898

229     My very dearest Darling,

Thank you so much for your two dear letters. I had so much hoped to find time to write a nice long letter before my journey, but every thing has been against; but still I have now found a little moment to write. I _am_ sorry to hear your poor mother is still so ill; it _will_ be sad for you to leave her so when you go for good to Rumania! I am for the moment in a very sad condition for I have no lady at present. Miss v. Stirum[570] left last Saturday and miss Rengers[571] is ill. She has to lye flat on her back in bed; so she can't come with me to Germany;[572] miss v.d. Poll is to take her place during the journey. Don't please do asif you knew any thing about miss Rengers, untill you here about it from someone else, for you know how she is — she dislikes that one takes any notice of her health! Untill the first of November I have no lady in waiting of mine that can do duty. That

569  On 10 September 1898, during her stay in Geneva, Empress Elisabeth 'Sissi' (1837–1898), the wife of Emperor Franz Joseph, was stabbed to death with a file by an Italian anarchist, Luigi Lucheni.

570  Van Stirum (see letter 141, note 317).

571  Rengers (see letter 135, note 283).

572  Wilhelmina and Emma went to Arolsen and Stuttgart to attend the marriage of Hereditary Prince Friedrich of Wied and Princess Pauline of Württemberg (see letter 156, note 296).

The marriage of Prince Friedrich of Wied to Princess Paulina of Württemberg was held on 29 October 1898 in Stuttgart. **1** Robert of Württemberg, son of 8; **2** Karl, Prince of Urach; **3** Victor of Wied, son of 15; **4** ?; **5** Louise of Wied, daughter of 15; **6** and **7** Ulrich and Albrecht of Württemberg, sons of 8; **8** Philip of Württemberg; **9** Maria Theresa of Austria, the wife of 8; **10** ?; **11** Katharina of Württemberg, mother of 32; **12** Marie of Wied, the wife of 15; **13** Johann Georg, Prince of Saxony; **14** Hermine of Württemberg; **15** Wilhelm, Prince of Wied; **16** Maria Isabella of Württemberg, daughter of 8 and the wife of 13; **17** and **18** Princess Pauline and Prince Alexis of Bentheim-Steinfurt; **19** Margaretha of Württemberg; **20** ?; **21** Adelheid of Anhalt-Dessau, the wife of 24; **22** Wilhelm Ernst, Hereditary Grand Duke of Saxe-Weimar?; **23** Wilhelm of Wied, 1914 Prince of Albania and son of 15; **24** Adolf of Nassau?; **25** Helena of Waldeck-Pyrmont, Duchess of Albany; **26** Hilda of Nassau, Grand Duchess of Baden; **27** bridegroom Friedrich, Crown Prince of Wied, son of 15; **28** bride Pauline of Württemberg; **29** Charlotte of Schaumburg-Lippe, the second wife of 32; **30** and **31** Queen Emma and Queen Wilhelmina of the Netherlands; **32** Wilhelm II, King of Württemberg, father of 28; **33** Elisabeth of Waldeck-Pyrmont; **34** ?; **35** Elisabeth of Wied, daughter of 15; **36** ? (My thanks to Hans-Jürgen Krüger, Fürstlich Wiedisches Archiv, Neuwied).

day the two new ones come.[573] Miss Rengers is left here with her mother, maid and nurse! So she is well taken care of! I have been very busy with ministers, my gardenparty[574] and my visit to the Rembrandt exhibition;[575] the latter was beautiful.

573 The two new ladies-in-waiting, Baroness C.E.B. 'Elisabeth' Sloet van Marxveld (1871–1941) and Baroness I.J.F. 'Pixy' de Constant Rebeque (see letter 51, note 71), were appointed as of 15 September 1898.
574 Instead of a garden party, on 19 October 1898 a matinee was held at Het Loo in the upstairs and downstairs rooms, with the exception of the Audience chamber.
575 The exhibition, entitled *Rembrandt: an exhibition of paintings assembled for the occasion of the*

I will not write any more now Darling. With all my dearest love, I ever remain your most devoted

Wilhelmina

Added by Emma:
Miss Rengers is not dangerously ill, she suffers from an irritation in the "groote darm [large intestine]"

E

Het Loo
November 13 1898

**230**  My very dearest Darling,
I am most ashamed to not have written you any letter for such a long time. I was very happy to hear from you; thank you so much for having given me news. I am glad you found the medal[576] pretty! (Colour plate VIII-13)

Miss Rengers is nearly well again and my two new ladies are very nice and I get on very well with them. I had a good deal of fun from my journey. It was very nice being at Arolsen and the baby[577] was not sick over mother during the christening but behaved very well. We travelled the whole family together going to Arolsen and then to Stuttgart.

There was a great sobbing affair at the wedding[578] and every body was very much touched. The Wieds were very merry and I had a great deal of fun with them; how merry the girls can be! The joke was that they were so astonished to see me so full of fun! I was very happy to see my Auntie of Wied; she met us at Rudesheim, came in the train till Neuwied. Have you not yet got any answer from Rumania? It is a long time coming!

It was very lonely coming home without Mother.[579] I am still very busy! We have had my auntie Albany[580] and tomorrow the Bentheims[581] are coming for my uncle to go shooting.

*investiture of Her Majesty Queen Wilhelmina,* was held in the Stedelijk Museum in Amsterdam.
**576**  The investiture medal was the first of its kind to be cast on the occasion of the investiture; Emma and Wilhelmina were inspired by German examples. The front, showing the overlapping heads of the two queens, was designed by Johan Hendrick Philip Wortman; the back, showing the regalia and a branch of orange blossom, was designed by the workshop of J.C. Begeer's royal silverworks in Utrecht (the Koninklijke Utrechtse Fabriek van Zilverwerken). The text read: 'WILHELMINA Queen of the Netherlands EMMA Queen-widow regent November 1890 August 1898 in remembrance'. The edge is inscribed 'Begeer'. Four hundred bronze medals were cast, intended for the guests, court employees and the soldiers of the royal escort.
**577**  The baby is the second child of Emma's brother Fritz and his wife Bathildis: Maximiliaan William Gustav Hermann. He was born on 13 September 1898.
**578**  The marriage of Friedrich, Prince of Wied and Pauline, Princess of Württemberg, took place on 29 October 1898 in Stuttgart.
**579**  Queen Emma stayed in Arolsen somewhat longer, returning to Het Loo on 1 November 1898.
**580**  Helena, the Duchess of Albany, accompanied Wilhelmina to Het Loo from Stuttgart on the evening of 31 October 1898. The duchess stayed until 7 November.
**581**  The Bentheims were at Het Loo between 14 and 19 November 1898.

I am in <u>one</u> excitement at present about the staircase here.[582] I have found money to have it and vestibule restaured and now I am having the paint on the walls taken off in some places to see if there is something under it. Now every hour there appears from under the paint old frescos; much to to much spoilt to be ever used again but very useful for the architect to see how it was formerly; it is most interesting.

Poor miss van Ittersum has come down a cropper from her bicycle yesterday and has hurt her foot.

She has to lie with it up; I hope for her it will not last long, for she would find it a great trial. Mother is well but always still tired.

With all my dearest love I ever remain your most devoted

Wilhelmina

Het Loo<br>December 4 1898

**231**    My very dearest Darling,

You will understand <u>how</u> happy I was to hear you <u>had at last</u> got the position! I now wonder if you could manage to come over a few days earlier that you had ment to and come and see us on your way to the other end of the world. Could you manage to stop at the Hague for two or three days? — Ofcourse I would pay you that part of the journey that you do for <u>my</u> sake if the Hague does not ly on your route! You must never think Darling, that <u>I</u> mind your using the money I give you for your birthday, for useful things like cloths on the contrary I am very glad to think that with my money you buy something to wrap yourself in during cold journeys etc. Never mind about the difficulties you will have to overcome Darling, everybody has them and you <u>are</u> [underlined twice!] plucky; so it is sure to go well! Your poor old Mother! It will be dreadful seing you go away so far!

My Mother is much better now and able to put her foot on the ground; she has driven out again. Miss v. Ittersum & Miss Rengers have still to be careful but are <u>much</u> better. M. Clifford[583] has been very bad with fever and his wife is down to take care of him; but the last two days his temperature has been much lower so that we hope he is on the good way to recovery! Miss de Vries is ill in bed with cramps in her stomach and miss Cramer[584] is laid up with cold in her side (that sounds funny! — But you see the cold has walked down from her head to her

---

582  In 1898, Wilhelmina began to restore the interior of Het Loo to its original state; that is to say, to the time of King-stadholder Willem III (1650-1702), based on the book by Daniel Marot. The task was undertaken by the Rotterdam-based ornamental painter Willem A. Fabry (1853-1925). Wilhelmina, p. 118: 'First the layer had to be removed that covered the original paintings. It was very exciting, every time a head or a figure appeared, as the designs from Marot's book came to life again' (Vliegenthart, pp. 151-171).

583  Baron H.A. Clifford (1850-1908) was appointed Marshal of the Court on 20 April 1894. In 1887 he married Claire J. van der Oudermeulen (1864-1949), the daughter of the Equerry Extraordinary to King Willem III.

584  Miss Cramer von Baumgarten (see letter 192, note 467).

Part of a fresco designed by Daniel Marot and dating from the end of the seventeenth century, in the stairwell of Paleis Het Loo. Photographer unknown, c. 1898.

side). You see the house is full of sick people so we are not going to feast Santa Clause! Under such conditions it would be difficult.

The staircase is getting on splendidly the paint is now nearly off all the walls and they have begun at taking it off the ceiling. The stench and mess and noise is something awful. But as it is all to embellish my dear Loo I grin and bear it. Please excuse my scandalous handwriting; but I have quite forgotten how to write anything but my name.

Only writing that makes you feel foolish at the end. With my very best love to you Darling, I ever remain your most devoted

Wilhelmina

the Hague December 11 1898

232    My very dearest Darling,

Thank you still many, many times for your two sweet boxes and dear letter. You don't know <u>how</u> pretty I find that way of burning, but what a dreadful work; how could you find the time? I am very exited to know when you will be coming over. All the sick people are getting on very well! My Mother has begun to walk again. Today we were out of the carriage for about twelve minutes!

I am quite settled here again. The goodbyes to my dear Loo were very heart-rending and I still miss very much its bracing air. I have a heap to do just lately; both with Xmas, business, dinners etc. But I like that very much for it makes me feel important and useful. My work with the ministers is beginning this week. I am to have 4 a week. I have just had a mad climbing party on the roof to see a dreadful fire in a breadfactory. That corner of the town was quite light up by the flames. I only hope there are no people burnt. My mother sends her love. With all my dearest love I ever remain your most devoted

Wilhelmina

December 23 1898

**233**    My very dearest Darling, Just these few words to wish you a very happy end blessed Christmas. I hope so much Darling that you will enjoy it at home!

I am sending you a little broche which I hope may be useful to you. Everything is going on all right; all the sick people are getting better herr. With all my dearest love and many thanks for your dear letter, I ever remain your very devoted

Wilhelmina

Paleis, 's Gravenhage<br>December 26 1898

**234**    My very dearest Darling,

Thank you so much foor your last loving letter and sweet cards. They are pretty little animals on both. I hope you past an as happy Christmaseve as we did. We made the whole thing much smaller than the other years.

We had it in the "kleine danszaal [small dancehall]", but all the same the whole aspect was very nice. Mother gave me as usual lovely presents;[585] one of them was a sealskin! We had seven little children[586] and I found playing with them very nice.

We have had frosty weather here also but there is not yet any question of skating. Yesterday it was very nasty weather; very cold and dark and windy; not a bit Christmas weather!

You need really not think, Darling that you were in the way here if you were to come in a time, that there festivities going on. I will be ready to have you when ever you come! Thank you Darling, I have no messages for you in Londen, only if you would perhaps be so kind to bring a box of losinges or how do you call those white things! My supply has lasted long, but now I have used it up nearly.

I don't think I told you that I was again going to have some lectures of Prof. de Louter in January; this time in economy. Perhaps that later on I also will have lectures about Indian laws and customes. Will that not be delightful; Mother will make the notes. [587] With all me dearest love, I ever remain your most devoted old friend

Wilhelmina

---

**585** One of the gifts was a fire screen for Wilhelmina's study at Noordeinde Palace, made by the furniture manufacturer C.H. Eckhart of Rotterdam. IC-22 and A74-III-46, invoice 122 (see Rem, note 322).

**586** Between 7 p.m. and 9 p.m. on Saturday 24 December 1898, the Christmas tree was decorated by the following children: Aggie Sirtema de Grovestins, Pikky van de Poll, Ilona and Max van den Bosch, Adolf Verspyck-Mynssen, Eduard van den Broek d'Obrenan and Marietje Roessingh Udink.

**587** After the departure of Miss Winter at the beginning of November 1896, Queen Emma

235    My very dearest Darling,

I hope that this letter will reach you in time to be the first to wish you a happy New Year. I hope so much, Darling, that this new year we are beginning soon may bring you a great deal of happiness and that God will bless you were ever you go and what ever you do. I know that 1899 is sure to bring its difficult moments, but I know also that God will help us to be brave and look over the mountains that are in our way; right over their tops in the future.

You will be beginning a new task that will be very difficult, but interesting, to fulfil. I am however sure that you will find it a great satisfaction to have found work at last and that you are doing good to your fellow creatures. What a sad thing that your mother is so down, no wonder however if her grandchild has left and she knows that you are going soon!

How is your sister going at present. I can well imagine how you will like going to morrow to church in the dark and coming back at midnight.

I <u>was</u> so sorry that you only got my letter, card and present on the 26<sup>th</sup> they must have been a long time on the way! Thank you many times for your last letter. I wonder if you feel "tungyhangy" out (as we used to say) about the new year. I have done for a long time, but just now I do not! Just like me I get in a estate beforehand and when the things comes about I am calmed down. The year is so long and one does not at all know what it is going to bring; it is quite otherwise than formerly for me; then I knew that every thing was leading me up to my majority, but now life has begun in all ways for me and I don't know what it is to bring.

With all my very best wishes for a happy New Year I ever remain your most devoted.

Wilhelmina

# 1899

236    My very dearest Darling,

Thank you so much for your little note just before leaving home.

So at last you are going to take up your work — I suppose you are very glad that the time for the second start has come. But I can well imagine how "benauwd [stressful]" the first few days will be. I will be thinking very often about you —

attended most of the lessons and made notes. The lessons will also have been educational for her!

specially now you will be feeling forlorn amidst strange people. I wonder if you will like your stay at Munich! Will it be as interesting as the last one? It does not feel a bit like Easter at present — no buds are yet out and it is raining hard all the time. Only the birds are sweet they are singing beautifully. There is nothing fixed about our journey, but I know we are going to Amsterdam on April the 11th.[588] After Amsterdam we leave for the mountains.[589] I don't think I will have time to write before our journey; but don't think it unkind for you know how occupied I am before leaving town and at Amsterdam I have also no time.

How are your people at home. My mothers cold is much better; she is a little more tired than in the beginning of the winter. My auntie[590] will leave after Easter. She always leaves a large hole and it is a great pity that she is going.

Are you going to Bucharest or to Sinaia?[591]

With all my dearest love I ever remain your most devoted friend

Wilhelmina

Schloss Hausbaden[592]
by Badenweiler
April 25 1899

237  My very dearest Darling,
Thank you many times for your dear letters. I am sorry not to have written till now, but somehow I have not been able to find time.

I think you must not have received my last note in which I mentioned my adress -I suppose you had already left Gotha.[593] You must have thought me a wretch not even to tell you where I was going. So you never either got my thanks for the sweet card you sent me. Thank you still many times for it, Darling.

All you tell me about your doings interests me very much. You must be busy with both children.[594] How nice for you to read to the princess. I was also very

---

588  The annual visit to Amsterdam was held between 11 and 17 April 1899.

589  Between 18 April and 20 May 1899, Wilhelmina and Emma took a holiday at the Schlosshotel Baden near Badenweiler, with excursions to Mülhausen (4 May), Freyburg (9 May) and Karlsruhe (16 May), where they had breakfast with the Grand Duke of Baden, and then went on to Baden-Baden. Between 20 and 23 May 1899 they stayed at Königswinter, from where they could visit Schaumburg Castle, which belonged to the Prince of Waldeck.

590  'Aunt Lily', Elisabeth of Waldeck-Pyrmont, was in The Hague between 30 January and 5 April 1899.

591  Cotroceni Palace in Bucharest or Peleş Palace in Sinaia (see letter 227, note 561 and letter 238, note 597).

592  Hausbaden Castle was a spa hotel near Badenweiler, not far from Basel, in the Grand Duchy of Baden. Emma's cousin Hilda of Nassau-Weilburg was married to Friedrich, Hereditary Grand Duke of Baden (see letter 183, note 433).

593  Gotha was the seat of the Duchy of Saxe-Gotha in Thuringia. The largest early baroque castle in Germany, nowadays it is home to a substantial art collection.

594  Miss Winter was governess to the later Carol II of Hohenzollern-Sigmaringen (1893–1953) and Elisabeth (1894–1956) (see p. 22 and letter 227, note 564). He was the first Romanian king to be born in Romania and baptized in the Orthodox Church. In his youth he was educated by King Carol I, who prepared him for the throne. The young prince was an intelligent student

interested to hear about the state of affairs of the country – the poor King it must not be easy for him![595]

Poor old Darling, I can well imagine the state of melting you must be in! We have not quite been so far. For at Amsterdam we had a lot of rain and stormy weather. What did you think of our expedition to Zaandam! It was simply lovely – the people were so enthousiastic. My audiences went off very well – of course I was rather "benauwd [nervous]" the first day but physically not tired. My mother is now quite better again and walks a good deal. You know she was unwell the Sunday at Amsterdam. We are here in a lovely country that I even admire! I am trying not to think of home sickness. Not withstanding the rain we are having we are out a great deal and I have a rage for painting (watercolour) that surpasses every former rage.[596] I have sometimes gone out morning and afternoon to sketch and I think you would not believe your eyes if you could see what an effort I make to be accurate in drawing and finish the things thoroughly! Please excuse my writing but I have just been signing 90 pieces of the cabinet and that has made my hand and pen somewhat shaky. How are the home folk. Poor old Darling I so well understand how lonely you must feel. I must dress to go out; so with all dearest love ever remain your most devoted friend

Wilhelmina

Palais Cotrocini[597]
Bucharest. May 1.99

238  My most precious Queen,

Accept my very loving thanks for your dear letter received a few days ago. It was so sweet of you to spare me so much of your time &, as usual, I was greatly interested in hearing how your days were being spent – What a tremendous amount of sketches you will accumulate if you are taking them "all day long"! When next we meet I shall expect to see huge portofolio's bursting with their heavy contents! I'm so glad you really admire the scenery of your present surround-

---

with an energetic character. He was King of Romania between 8 June 1930 and 6 September 1940. Elisabeth would later marry King George II of Greece.

595  Karel E.F.Z.L. of Hohenzollern-Sigmaringen (1839–1914) was prince (as Carol I between 1866 and 1881) and then king of Romania (until his death in 1914). On 3 November 1869 he married Elisabeth of Wied (who used the pen name 'Carmen Sylva'), the daughter of Prince Hermann of Wied and his wife Marie of Nassau-Weilburg, the half-sister of Emma's mother Helena. Their only child, Maria, born on 27 September 1870, died at the age of four. Carol I was succeeded in 1914 by Ferdinand, the second son of his brother Leopold.

596  Wilhelmina learned watercolour painting from her tutor Frits Jansen, who had a particular gift for the art. Little of Wilhelmina's work has been kept from this period (Spliethoff 2006, pp. 10–11).

597  A50-VIIc-S-02. In 1888 King Carol I had the Cotroceni Palace in Bucharest, which was designed by the French architect Alfred Jules Paul Gottereau (born in Perpignan in 1843), built on the Cotroceni hill on the site where Şerban Cantacuzino had built a monastery in 1679. From 1977, under President Nicolae Ceauçescu (1918–1989), the palace was used as a guest residence. From 1991, the palace was the official residence of the President of Romania.

ings and are able to enjoy the quiet free open air life — The Dutch papers had reported the Queen-Mother to be unwell at Amsterdam, so I was happy to have the good tidings in your letter that Her Majesty was really feeling better again. I feel as though there were a great many things to be written about today, & not very much time for doing it, so it is rather difficult to know where to begin. First I must tell you that next week the gentlemen appointed to represent Roumania at the forthcoming congress[598] or "conference" are leaving, I would give <u>anything</u> I possess to be going with them to the Hague! The officer who is being sent from the war office, Colonel Coanda, is an exceedingly nice man. He was for some years aide-de-camp to the Prince, & remembers seeing you several times when we were at Potsdam,[599] and he had travelled a good bit in the Netherlands & knows most of the largest towns. He is kind enough to bring you a small offering from me, which can take the place of my <u>spoiled</u> Easter present! A little Roumanian table cloth, <u>quite</u> something special to the country, worked by hand, not by any means elegant enough for your <u>sitting</u> rooms, but perhaps you could use it in one of your <u>dressing</u> rooms, & as it will <u>work</u> it may be useful? These things here are <u>not</u> expensive, so you need not worry yourself darling Queen with the feat that I have perhaps been spending a <u>lot</u> of money! I shall also enclose one for the Queen-Mother which I hope she will accept & use somewhere at Soestdijk for my sake.

We have just been celebrating Easter here — last Friday was "Good Friday" & yesterday Easter Day. It all seems so strange! I went on Friday evening with the Princess to a service in the Greek church <u>very</u> quaint & primitive, such a curious mixture of solemn ceremony and unciviliged barbarism — We all had to carry lighted candles during the <u>whole</u> service and on arrival, deposited bunches of flowers on a large kind of altar — these at one point of the service were "blessed" by the priest, namely sprinkled with holy water & incense, and everyone then received a small bunch to take away with then after approaching the priest & kissing the Bible — a procession was formed & we all walked 3 times round the outside of the church, & if our candles kept alight it was a great sign of approaching good luck. Mine was blown out <u>twice</u> so were I superstitious I might be rather uneasy for the future! To me, the most attractive part of the evening was the walk home across the park. A footman with lantern showing the road, & the nightingales singing most delightfully all around us & a gentle, warm summer breeze stirring all the trees & awaking the delicious scents of

**598** This refers to the First Hague Peace Conference, held between 18 May and 29 July 1899. It was an initiative by the Russian tsar Nicolas II, encouraged by the Austrian aristocrat and pacifist Bertha von Suttner, born Countess Kinsky of Wchinitz and Tettau. She was the only woman to attend the conference (see Montijn, pp. 329–330). The most important result of the conference was the decision to introduce voluntary arbitration. This led to the founding of the Permanent Court of Arbitration, which was later established in the Peace Palace in The Hague. A second conference was held in 1907.

**599** This may have been during the state visit that Emma and Wilhelmina paid to Germany between 30 May and 2 June 1892.

flowers. Easter Mom is supposed to be at midnight on Saturday, and at 11 o'clock when every one was feeling very sleepy and ready for bed, we had to dress for church — it was the special wish of the Princess that I should go with the rest of the household — The King went in full state accompanied by a mounted escort & military band, gentlemen in gala uniforms, ladies in light, elegant morning gowns & bonnets. It is quite impossible to tell you all the details — perhaps someday when I see you? The service began by a procession being formed, headed by the archbishop & about 6 other priests, all in exceedingly handsome vestments, & mitres on their heads, (some being much covered with jewels of great value) followed by the King, Prince Princess & their households, then ministers, their wifes etc —

Every one passed out into the open space near the church to a table or altar, when a prayer was said, incense thrown & a chant sung — The Archbishop then said aloud "Christ is risen" and everyone answered "Yes, he is risen" — A rocket was sent up, 101 cannon shots fired, the band played, and the procession reformed & entered the church again. Here all was done with the most gorgeous pomp imaginable. There is a kind of Holy inner chamber, richly decorated & entered by a small archways, where the priests remain, & from time to time one or the other of them comes out & chants a prayer, wafts incense all around & retires again — Then the Archbishop appears & the King advances & kisses first the Bible then the 3 crosses held by the Archbishop & two other priests & retires again to his place. The Prince followed suit & then the Princess — but as all the <u>men</u> of the congregation are then supposed to advance & do the same before the <u>women</u>, & as the Princess left almost immediately after she had done her duty, I [underlined twice] escaped this ordeal! We went from the church to the Palace where the King & Queen entertained over 100 guests to supper — The Queen assisted at the supper though she was not well enough to stand the heat, smell & fatigue of the church. Everyone greeted the other with "Christ is risen" — and you all supposed to crack eggs with all your friends — These old traditions are very quaint and one wonders how they have survived the inroads of civilization — Yesterday afternoon we had a dozen children to come & look for Easter eggs with the 2 little ones here, in the garden & finished up with a romp & tea, as the day was <u>scorching</u> hot; and I had only gone to bed at 4 o'clock in the morning, I was thankful when the romping was over & I could sit down for a little rest — There are very many things that I would wish to have otherwise here — but as at present I have so little to do with the boy, I suppose I must learn to be patient & try to obtain my desires by slow degrees — but it is <u>very</u> trying — In spite of my short hours of duty for <u>him</u>, I'm never the less very much occupied, as I generally stay with the Princess for some time after lunch & all the evenings are spent together — generally helping her with whatever she is doing or playing from time to time, whist with the Prince — I foresee that my <u>own</u> painting will go to the wall & that my fancy works will face very badly! Yet, here too, as I wish to gain her confidence, I suppose I had better continue as I am doing, at least for a time. It is <u>so</u> strange to feel oneself absolutely without a friend near at hand — I

Family portrait; on the right, Hereditary Prince Ferdinand of Romania and his wife Marie, Princess of Edinburgh, with their two children, Carol (at the front, the later King Carol ii of Romania) and Elisabeth, and on the left, Marie's sister Victoria Melitta with her first husband Ernst of Hesse and their baby Elisabeth, around 1900. Photographer unknown.

don't think I shall ever be quite sure of the Eastern mind, or feel convinced that they can be absolutely trustworthy — time alone can tell! They are most [underlined twice] friendly — affectionate even — & though they mean to be discreet, I don't believe they know the way to be so, as we northern people understand the term! The boy fills me with dismay & infinite pity, he gives one so completely the impression of having been cowed and bullied by a hard authority, a natural consequence of which is, that he is half afraid to speak the truth. I must end for today. With all my dearest love sweet Queen.

Believe me ever

Your most devoted loving

E. Saxton Winter

Het Loo[600]

May 28 1899

239  My dearest Darling,

I am so very grateful to you for your dear letter and sweet present. What a pretty style of work that roumanian embroidering is. So very quaint and pretty. I made the acquainttance of Mr Coanda[601] who brought it and thanked him for his trouble. I received the first delegate of each country the afternoon at the Hague and gave the conference a gala soirée[602] the same evening; I received the Russian order by Mr de Stael[603] the afternoon. So you se I had a good deal of receiving to do at the Hague. It was most interesting to se so many people of diferent parts of the world!

---

600  The address on the envelope read: Miss Winter, Gouvernante des Enfants de Roumanie, Palais Coterouni [Cotroceni], Bucharest, Roumanie.

601  Mr Coanda was one of the Romanian delegates to the First Hague Peace Conference.

602  On 24 May 1899, a soiree took place at Ten Bosch House, followed on 6 July by another gala dinner in Amsterdam. On both occasions, the young queen made an 'excellent impression'; 'Her charming and clear voice drew universal praise' (Fasseur 1998, p. 198).

603  It is unclear to whom 'Mr de Stael' refers. Wilhelmina was awarded the Grand Cross of the Order of St Catharina of Russia on 24 May 1899.

And now I am back at my dear Loo again. By the weather being so wet and cold the summerarrangements can't we beginn so that we are leading a half and half sort of life which does not make life pleasant. But ofcourse I am very happy to be back. From Königswinter I went to Schaumburg[604] where my uncle and aunties Waldeck are. I saw the family there. I also saw my grand aunts of Wied and of Sweden, my auntie Bentheim and my cousins of Wied (not the girls).[605] It was a very merry time, only with whitsentide there were so many tourists on the Rhine that you could not at all go about. All you tell me about Roumania interest me very much. You are a Darling to write so much about what you think and feel. My Mother sends you her love and so do I and remain Darling, you most devoted friend

Wilhelmina

Het Loo<br>June 18 1899

240    My very dearest Darling,
Thank you many times for your loving letter and sweet card. I was <u>so</u> sorry to hear that you had had malaria and influenza — poor old Darling. No wonder you felt down. Who took care of you? Were they kind to you? I found your postcard most interesting as I had never seen a picture of the children. You seem took work wonders over there! I admire your energy to make such innovations!

Here the heat is getting great, till yesterday it was not a bit like summer!

Our day at Rotterdam was a grand success;[606] the people were all so enthousiastic and the trouble that even the poorest had taken to decorate their houses was most touching.

I was very unhappy in hearing what had happened at Flushing with the railway,[607] there have been so many accidents with the railway here lately — I don't know how it comes for I thing the people are generally very careful.

I am intending to receive the membres of the conference still once before they leave!

Poor old Darling, I can well imagine <u>how</u> difficult you must find your Roumanian lessons — are you going on with it Sinaia.[608]

---

604  Bathildis, the wife of Emma's brother Fritz, was from the Schaumburg-Lippe line.
605  Marie of Wied (1825–1902), the half-sister of Emma's mother Helena, married to Hermann of Wied (1814–1864) and Sophie (1836–1913), sister of Helena, married to King Oscar II of Sweden (1829–1907), Emma's sister Pauline of Bentheim-Steinfurt (1855–1925) and the children of Wilhelm of Wied and his wife Marie, Princess of the Netherlands, Frederik (1872–1945), Wilhelm (1876–1945) and Victor (1877–1946).
606  The visit to Rotterdam took place on 9 June 1899.
607  The train accident in Vlissingen took place on 1 June 1899. Due to a lack of brake pressure in the cable, 'train 87' was unable to brake and only came to a stop in the station's dining room, with three dead and one wounded as a result.
608  Peleş Palace is in Sinaia. It was the summer residence of the Romanian royal family (see letter 227).

Members of the royal household, photographed at Het Loo in 1899. Standing: senior official to the Queen's Cabinet Baron J.A. de Vos van Steenwijk, lady-in-waiting Pixy de Constant Rebecque, aide-de-camp C.L. van Suchtelen van de Haare, lady-in-waiting Henriette van de Poll and Mr W. van de Poll. Seated: the ladies-in-waiting Annie Juckema van Burmania Rengers and Elisabeth Sloet van Marxveld, chamberlain H.W.J.E. Taets van Amerongen and Mlle Ada de Joannis. Photographer unknown.

Miss Joannis[609] and miss von Riedel are here at present — it is so nice seeing then back again! I have been in a great excitement these last two mounths about my dear Geeske![610] For Overdijking,[611] seing that he could not find a position as gardener in my country that enabled him to marry Geeske, decided to start off to Amerika to try and make himself a position — he had an uncle or a cousin over there who was bootmaker. Now you can imagine how mad it is at that age to leave off the work one has done all ones life and begin to learn afresh to become a bootmaker! Besides the strange language and country are also things that would not make life easy for him. When I heard of this mad plan, I made up my mind to put a stop to it — for poor Geeske carried the burden bravely, but still I could quite well see that she was getting thinner and thinner and paler and paler

609  Miss Joannis stayed at Het Loo between 12 June and 7 July 1899 (see letter 167, note 349); Miss von Riedel is Lady Ulrike von Riedel, lady-in-waiting to the princesses of Waldeck-Pyrmont, who frequently came to visit Queen Emma. They arrived on 15 June and stayed until 29 June 1899.

610  Geeske (see letter 103, note 132, and letter 141, note 241).

611  Register of the Department of the Marshal of the Court to the King/Her Majesty the Queen, E10a, sect. 11a, No. 8. Derk Overdijking, sergeant-major gunsmith (born in Zutphen, March 1832), manservant to King Willem III from 1854, may have been the father of the Overdijking mentioned in the letter.

— she found the idea terrible. So my Mother and I tried both our hardest to work for Overdijking. There was no where a position of gardener to be had. We set all our gentlemen at work to find or even create a position for him. At last after having offered him a situation more to do with writing which he refused because he thought sittingwork was not good for him; we found a position for him at one of our gardens at the Hague.

I want to have my own plants for decorating the rooms etc. and as I had made up my mind to help Overdijking at any rate I decided to offer him to be at the head of the new hothouses that I will build. Yesterday was the most trying day of all for Geeske as Overdijking went to the Hague to talk about it to Mr. Hoeufft[612] and say if he would accept. Luckily he did and Geeske is radiant with joy. Oh Darling, if you only new <u>how</u> happy I am that we succeeded to make those two happy! It has quite been a little family tragedy — and to think that everything is now settled for the best!!

How are your home people?

I must end now — I thought you would like to know how Geeske's future was decided upon.

With my best wishes for a speedy recovery, I ever remain your most devoted friend

Wilhelmina

Miss Winter was still staying in Romania.
Miss Winter, Gouvernante des Enfants de Roumanie
Castel Peles, Sinaia, Roumanie [Palace and place crossed out and replaced by: <u>faire suivre</u> Palat Cotroceni Bucuresci]

Paleis, 's Gravenhage<br>10 December 1899

**241** My very dearest Darling,

I was <u>so</u> happy with your last dear letter and specially with the decision you have taken. To tell you quite honestly the truth you would have me "tegengevallen [disappointed]" (you know still what that means?) if you had not stayed, I only hope you will add many a six mounths to those you have promised remain. Do they feast over there where you are St. Nicolas like we do here? We had a delightful evening. The young couple[613] were here now my future uncle has left; my auntie is still staying for a little time. I am now very busy both with my work and with Xmas.

My lectures are also continuing here in town and now during the time the Chambres are discussing the budget the papers give my a good deal to read!

612 Mr J.P.E. Hoeufft van Velsen (1842–1910) was the architectural adviser to Queen-Regent Emma and House Steward of the Royal Palaces of 's-Gravenhage. Among other things, he made a design for the Royal Archives in The Hague, visiting the royal archives in Weimar and Castle Wilhelmshöhe, among others, for this purpose.
613 By 'young couple', she is referring to Princess Elisabeth 'Lily' of Waldeck-Pyrmont and her future husband Alexander, Hereditary Count of Erbach-Schönberg (1872–1944).

There were also a lot of audiences which I had to give; but I am beginning the winter with a lot of courage. My journey to Flushing[614] was very interesting; of course it gave me a good deal of work beforehand.

The weather has become suddenly very cold so if it continues in this way we will wanting our skates. I saw Miss Rengers the other day, but I did not find her looking at all well she was in little less thin than this summer, but her colour is still dreadful; she is now staying with friends or with her sister or parents. How is your mother and sister?

With all my dearest love I ever remain your true and faithful old friend

Wilhelmina

Paleis, 's Gravenhage
December 27 1899

242   My very dearest darling,

I hope these lines will reach you in time for new year to wish you a very happy new year. I know Darling, that it is not beginning in an easy and happy way for you, but I know I may all the same send my best wishes; for every one of us can be happy, even in a difficult position as yours [text missing] satisfaction of [text missing] duty. God keep and guide you, Darling, in the coming year and when the ups and downs come He will show you the way to get over them. I can well imagine how lonely you must be now, but on the otherhand you must be glad that the Hobbs[615] have left!

I am so glad the boy[616] shows love to you after all you have done for him. Do you often take him to the king? I am sure you must like the idea of going to San Remo, for it is so pretty there and must nearer your own home and the Grand-parents[617] of the Boy seem nice people as much as I know them.

614  The visit to Vlissingen took place on 29 November 1899. Wilhelmina and her mother travelled to the town to greet the German emperor and empress on their arrival from England. A steam launch brought the imperial couple from the German yacht *Hohenzollern* to shore, where they were welcomed by the two queens. Tea and refreshments were offered at the dining room in the station, and the royal parties conversed. At 5:10 p.m. the German emperor and empress left for Germany and Emma and Wilhelmina returned to Het Loo.

615  It is unclear who is meant by 'Hobbs'. It may refer to Penelope Hobbs, a cousin of Emma and Georgina Hobbs, both nannies to the children of Victoria, Crown Princess of Prussia and daughter of Queen Victoria, or another member of the Hobbs family (see Zeepvat, p. 292).

616  Carol II of Hohenzollern-Sigmaringen (1893-1953) was King of Romania between 8 June 1930 and 6 September 1940. He was the eldest son of King Ferdinand and Marie, Princess of Edinburgh, a granddaughter of Queen Victoria of Britain and Tsar Alexander II. He was the first Romanian king to have been born in Romania and baptized in the Orthodox Church. In his youth he was educated by King Carol I, who prepared him for the throne. The young prince was an intelligent student with an energetic character.

617  The paternal grandparents of the young Carol were Leopold of Hohenzollern-Sigmaringen (1835-1905) and Infanta Antonia Maria of Portugal (1845-1913). His maternal grandparents were Alfred, Duke of Edinburgh and Grand Duke of Saxe-Coburg (1844-1900) and Grand Duchess Maria Alexandrovna of Russia (1853-1920).

I received the other day Baron Gevers[618] and made him tell me about you and how you looked. I suppose you will already have heard that Mr. Gevers is going to Washington and that Baron Sweerts de Landas[619] is coming to Bucharest!

Thank you so much Deary, for your last letter. I find it dreadful to think that you attempted making something for me with all you have to in Bucharest. You are a Darling to have thought of it. I hope my calendar will reach you in time for new year; it is dreadful what a time the post takes. St. Nicholas & Christmas passed off delightfully. The young people[620] were still both their for the 5th of December; but now also my aunt Lily has gone back to Arolsen. Have you heard that my aunt has had a little girl;[621] if only the child had not come during the engagement of my aunty Lily it seems very thoughtless of the child just to come before Xmas and to put a stop to her aunt and future uncle seing each other! Mother has again spoilt me with beautiful presents: she gave me fine old furniture for my dear Loo a beautiful bracelet & her picture painted by Willy Martens.[622] He has painted her very well & I think the likeness very good — We have been skating here for more than a week but now it is all over. Today the ground is covered with snow but I don't think it will last long. I went twice on the canals and enjoyed my self madly. It is just as if you quite get an other being on the ice! Did you already hear that there have been many changes in the court? Baron Grovestins[623] has left the army and has become my "Grand Maître"; Mr van den Bosch[624] has been changed into a "Chambellan" Mr

618 Since 30 November 1896, Baron Willem A.F. Gevers (1856–1910) had been the representative of the Netherlands as minister resident in Romania and to the Court of Serbia.
619 Baron Arthur M.D. Sweerts de Landas Wyborgh (1862–1944) was minister resident in Bucharest and Belgrade between 1899 and 1901.
620 Aunt Lily and her fiancée Alexander, Hereditary Count of Erbach-Schönberg.
621 On 22 December 1899, Helena was born (died 1948), the only daughter of Prince Friedrich 'Fritz', the brother of Queen Emma, and Princess Bathildis, who also had three sons: Josias, born in 1896, Max, born in 1898, and Georg Wilhelm, born in 1902. Helena married the Hereditary Grand Duke Nikolaus van Oldenburg (1897–1970), who was the son of Elisabeth (1869–1955), the sister of Prince Hendrik.
622 The portrait of Emma by Willem 'Willy' Martens (1856–1927), oil on canvas, c. 245 × 153 cm, Paleis Het Loo National Museum, on loan from the Royal Collections, The Hague, inv.no. SC/0358 (old PL213). E 9 l c 29: letter from the House Steward of the Royal Palaces H.v.V. [Mr J.P.E. Hoefft van Velsen, also architectural adviser between 1893 and 1910], dated 29 January 1900, with advice on the placing of a new portrait in Queen Wilhelmina's drawing room at Paleis Het Loo (see Loonstra 1996, pp. 36–37). When Het Loo was extended between 1911 and 1914, the portrait was hung on the short side of the newly built ballroom, whilst the portrait of King Willem III, also by Willy Martens, 250 x 149 cm, inv.no. SC/0359 (old PL214) was hung on the other short side. Since the restoration of Paleis Het Loo in 1984, both portraits have hung in Queen Emma's drawing room. Martens was primarily a painter of portraits and genre paintings, director of the Mesdag Museum and chairman of Pulchri Studio in The Hague, where he lived from 1891.
623 Lieutenant Colonel Baron J.E.N. Sirtema van Grovestins (1842–1919) was adjutant between 17 April 1891 and 1899, after which he became Grand Master of the Royal Household until his death. He also sat on the Hofcommissie (Court committee).
624 Captain Willem J.P. van den Bosch (1848–1914) was adjutant from 17 April 1891 and

Veeckens[625] has make his promotion to Contre Admiral and has left court. In his place comes Lieutenant Zegers Rijzer.[626] Captain Schimmelpenninck[627] is coming back to me as aide de camp. And a Captain van Hoogstraten is to take the place as aide de camp in stead of Mr. Grovestins.

I have attached also to me person a few new ladies. Madame Groeninx[628] mother of the nice girl Adolphine which came to play so often, madame van Wassenaer[629] which you don't know and as Dame du Palais honoraire madame du Tour.[630] You see there have come many new faces!

Poor old Darling, it must not be nice to be called up so often in the middle of the night, but what a good thing to live near your boy and to have now for him such a large apartment. Hoping new yearsday will not be too lonely for you, I ever remain with my dearest love your most devoted old friend

Wilhelmina

# 1900

Paleis, 's Gravenhage
January 14 1900

**243** My very dearest Darling,

I was so happy to hear from you yesterday; thank you so much, Darling for your long, loving letter, your beautiful calender and your dear telegram on new yearsday. You are a darling to have written so much about your life and all things over there. How could you suggest that I might find such a long letter enoying to read. No, if you could have seen me you would written otherwise. How nice that the boy is getting on so well; you poor old Darling, I can well imagine <u>how</u> hard you have to work all day if you even washed the boy till for a short time! What a good thing that the King likes having the boy with him. I hope so much for you that the Hobbs[631] will not come back so very soon. I am so sorry for the

---

chamberlain as of 17 November 1899.

**625** Naval captain P. Zegers Veeckens was adjutant from 17 April 1891.

**626** C.C. Zegers Rijser, naval lieutenant first class, was made an adjutant on 13 December 1899.

**627** Count R.J. Schimmelpenninck (1855–1935) was appointed aide-de-camp to Queen Wilhelmina on 17 April 1891 and became her adjutant on 4 December 1899.

**628** Lady Agneta H. Groeninx van Zoelen-van de Poll (1857–1933) was appointed Dame du Palais on 6 December 1899. Her daughter was Adolphine Agneta (1885–1967), later Mistress of the Robes to Queen Wilhelmina.

**629** Baroness Cornelia van Wassenaar van Catwijck-Baroness van Boetzelaer (1868–1916) was made a Dame du Palais on 6 December 1899.

**630** Baroness Maria I.A.J.C. de Tour van Bellinchave-Huydecoper (1835–1919) was made an honorary Dame du Palais on 6 December 1899.

**631** Hobbs (see letter 242, note 615).

K. that he is having such a difficult time; what a good thing the snow has set in! What a beautiful present the King must have given you, and what a pretty composition; how thoughtful he must be to have just imagined that for you! It must be a great comfort for you that he so fully appreciates all you have done for the boy. I can well understand that you are longing for a holiday, but you can't leave your pupil alone! Poor old Darling, it <u>will</u> be a sight to see you thin! I <u>am</u> sorry that your homepeople have been ill; no wonder though, for the weather is so bad this winter. Here and specially in Amsterdam there are many people ill with influenza.

So Darling you are not a friend of Chamberlain[632] — don't you read any more the Times? It is dreadful the bloodshed in Africa![633] Ofcourse I always read with the greatest interest the warnews; only excuse me saying so, your wires bring over the telegrams in an odd fashion, if they only would wire the full truth at once!! The Boeren seem to be <u>excellent</u> shots and <u>most</u> skillful in the arts of war!

I am very occupied at present with my work, I have made up my mind to work hard this winter. I feel now much more at home than last year I feel that I know how to begin a a thing and I am getting into my business much better! You don't know how interesting my work is and how I am getting more and more to love it — I think, I hope you would find me grown much older, much more of a being with own independant thought; I am getting quite my own sphere of thoughts. Oh Darling, how you will smile in reading this bit of my letter, it must sound odd; it is only sad that one can not live up to ones ideals, at least I can't; I have melted mine into a solid shape! I hope to work away at them surely, slowly, steadily. I must add still to my last letter, about court matters that I have changed mr. v.d. Poll[634] into a chaimberlain-master of the Ceremonies & I have given that also to Mr. v. Amerongen[635] whilst Mr. v.

632 This refers to Joseph Chamberlain (1836–1914), an influential British statesman and politician and member of the Liberal Unionists, who became Secretary of State for the Colonies in 1895. He sat in the government coalition with the conservatives, led by Robert Cecil, Lord Salisbury (1830–1903). This position meant that he had the Boer War in his portfolio. In January 1900, the government was confronted with a vote of censure in the House of Commons over the conduct of the war; Chamberlain succeeded in averting it.

633 See also note 345. On 11 October 1899, the Second Boer War broke out between the Boers and the British, who were attempting to subject the South African Republic (the Republic of Transvaal), led by President Paul Krüger (1825–1904), to British rule. Krüger had already played a major role in the restoration of independence in 1883, after the annexation by Great Britain. In October 1900, Krüger left for Europe on the Dutch warship the *Hr. Ms Gelderland*, which had been sent to him by Queen Wilhelmina after secret consultations between the Netherlands and the British government, to drum up support for the Boers. This attempt was unsuccessful, however.

634 Mr Willem F.H. van de Poll (1843–1918) was aide-de-camp to King Willem III. From 1888 he was the king's adjutant and from 20 April 1891, adjutant to Queen Wilhelmina. On 12 January 1900 he became adjutant extraordinary, and in 1908 he was appointed Grand Officer in the charge of Chief Cup-bearer.

635 Baron Gerard L. M. Taets van Amerongen (1837–1901) was chamberlain from 1873. In

Pabst[636] has got the title of first Chaimberlain. I hope so much, Darling that life will be made agreable for you, so that you will stay for good notwithstanding the desire of the Hobbs for you to go; those dreadful ungrateful people!

With all my dearest love, I ever remain your most devoted friend

Wilhelmina

Paleis, 's Gravenhage
February 18 1900

**244** My very dearest Darling,

Thank you ever so many times for your pretty present which I received from Mr. Gevers as soon as he arrived here. It is very dear of you, Darling, to have found time to make something — it is such a useful thing traveling to blot letters etc on![637] How prettily you have burt it and what sweet words you have put on it. I must still thank very much for your two last letters; I was very glad to have news of you and all you tell me about yourself and your difficulties interests me ofcourse very much. I heard directly about you by Mr. Gevers and I was very glad to get by this way also some news.

What do you think of Pixy' engagement with Mr. Dumonceau?[638] Of course I am very glad the young people are happy with one an other, but oh! how could she ever consent with the difference in religion! You can imagine what I [underlined twice] think of this match!! I am very sorry I did not write sooner, but the last few sundays I have been drawing the afternoon and painting the morning so I had no time. Today as Pixy has duty and my ladies are my drawing modles and I don't wish to occupy her the whole day, but want her to have time for young Dumonceau, I have taken the afternoon for writing. There has been falling a good deal of snow here and we have had frost (not enough for skating) and storms, my riding has been stopped for a long time — I always busy having a great many people to see. My uncle and aunt Waldeck[639] are coming Wednesday

1893–94 he became Marshal of the Court and in 1900 Chief Marshal of the Court. He played an important role in organizing the investiture of Queen Wilhelmina in 1898 (Cleverens 1994, p. 197).

**636** Baron Rudolph W.J. van Pabst van Bingerden (1826–1912) was chamberlain between 1862 and 1900. In the *State directory* of 1901, he is mentioned for the first time as 'First chamberlain'.

**637** A70-VIIc-S. The present from Miss Winter was accompanied by the following short letter: 'A small token of the deepest love and dedication from a very true old friend, in the hope that the writing block will prove useful when travelling, or when taking a few days in a hotel during the spring holidays!! Bucharest 25 January 1900.'

**638** On 10 February 1900, the engagement was announced of Wilhelmina's Protestant lady-in-waiting Baroness I.J.F. 'Pixy' de Constant Rebecque (1877–1958) and the Catholic aide-de-camp eighteen years her senior, Count J.H.F. 'Felix' Dumonceau (1859–1952) (see letter 51, note 71).

**639** The Prince and Princess of Waldeck-Pyrmont stayed in The Hague between 21 and 28 February 1900. They visited the Mauritshuis, a concert given by the Bohemian string quartet at Diligentia, the 'Rozenburg' Delftware factory, a *soirée-dansante* given by the German envoy, the Count de Pourtales, an exhibition of antiquities, pottery, etc. belonging to Mr Victor de Stuers in the 'art society' of The Hague, a performance of the opera *Fidelio* in the GK&W concert hall, The Hague.

and we will have a few intertainments during their stay! Poor old Darling how dreadful that you took the influenza how do you feel now?

I will be very curiuous to see if you will soon start off for the south with the boy! I am glad you go to the Opera for I am sure that must give you some rest; how dreadfully busy you must be, Darling, not to have any time for reading! How are the home people; does your mother not feel the horrid changes in the weather? Do you read to the boy, or is he to young to like that kind of thing. Please exuse this bad writing, but I have been at my table for a good long time and then somehow to write does not improve. I never get tired of putting my name (I sometimes write it on a morning ± 150 times, this is an exception) but when I have to write other letters, than those which compose my name, my hand feel inclined to take the action of a spider over my paper.

With all dearest love and many, many thanks for the sweet present, I ever remain your most devoted old friend

Wilhelmina

Paleis, 's Gravenhage<br>March 25 1900

**245**  My very dearest,

Thank you very much for your dear letters. I have been thinking very much about you all this time in full sympathy with all you have been passing through — you poor old Darling, you must be having a difficult time. I can well imaging how hard it will be for you and the boy to part — I am <u>very</u> [underlined twice] sorry for you both.[640] What a shame that he is to be sacrifised! One must hope that some thing will turn up that will save him — you, poor Darling, have done your best and it is a great pity that you are giving up your task.

I am very sorry about the ilness of my auntie of Wied, I hope very much that she will quite recover! What do you hear of your mother and sister? If you were to leave Rumania I am will very much look forward to seeing you, you old Darling, it is such a time since I have not seen your round old face — or has it grown quite thin. I so well understand that it would be horrid for you to go back home directly as if you had been sent away! Ofcourse you are more than welcome to stay with us! Our plans are not yet settled as the day of the wedding at Arolsen has not been fixed![641]

The General Dumonceau[642] is now making his spring explorations to find an hotel in the mountains.

---

640  As mentioned in the introduction on p. 22, Crown Princess Marie of Romania was absolutely unable to get on with Miss Winter, and forced King Carol I to look for another governess for his nephew Hereditary Prince Carol, with whose education he was deeply involved.

641  The marriage between Emma's youngest sister Elisabeth, 'Aunt Lily', and Alexander, Hereditary Count of Erbach-Schönberg.

642  Count C.H.F. Dumonceau, Adjutant General and Chief of the Military House of Queen

Even if you were to leave Rumania during the time we were in the mountains I am sure we could manage to have you!

I am most busy with my work — the Chambers are always giving very much occupation! How is the pilitical state of the country in which you are living?

Are you now having summer weather — or still snow? Here I seldom saw a month of March which gave so much benefit of rain, storms and cold. The poor little buds look so cold and astonished to find nature so cold and winter-like. Dolly van Lynden[643] has had a little girl a few days ago; what a pity for her that the first child should be a girl! With all my best love I remain your most devoted

Wilhelmina

## The meeting between Wilhelmina and Hendrik

On 8 May 1900, Emma and Wilhelmina arrived in Schwarzburg, Thuringia, where they would stay at the *Weisser Hirsch* hotel until 5 June. It was there that Wilhelmina would meet her future husband Hendrik, Duke of Mecklenburg-Schwerin (1876-1934), at the family castle belonging to Hendrik's mother, Marie von Schwarzburg-Rudolstadt (1850-1922), which could be seen from the hotel. They had already met in 1892, at the golden wedding celebrations of the Grand Duke and Grand Duchess of Saxe-Weimar (Fasseur 1998, p. 213).

Schwarzburg, May 8 1900

**246** My very dearest Darling,

Please excuse my dreadful handwriting and my having taken my mothers paper pen & paper but I am writing to you before truncks etc. have come. We have arrived here safely after a hot journey; I am madly glad to be out of Dresden for I was more than sick & tired of towns. But before I begin to relate to you what I have done lately, I must first thank you very much for sending so often news of yourself! You poor old Darling, I can well imagine <u>how</u> tired & sick at heart you must be. First knowing "your boy" so unhappy and then feeling worn out yourself. I felt quite bad for your sake in reading your last letter! But, Darling, you must chear up a bit, the boy must somehow be saved and who knows if you have not been the means of saving him afterall. He will not forget so soon your lessons and amidst bad people he will think of you & your example and try to follow it!

---

Wilhelmina, always organized the travel to and from abroad. Queen Wilhelmina was very fond of him.

**643** Dolly van Lynden, Wilhelmina's former lady-in-waiting Countess Adolphine W.A. van Limburg Stirum (1877-1961), who entered her service in 1896. On 24 November 1898 she married Baron Carel van Lynden and had her only child, Carola Elisabeth Aurelia, on 21 March 1900.

How nice for you to be going to the Wieds! The little one[644] at Potsdam has been very bad & we were very worried about him, but the last tidings were better! Amsterdam was in all respects a pleasant stay;[645] only very cold and tiring; just fancy I stood one day 9 hours. I found it very nice seing the people of the whole country. We saw many interesting things during our drives.

I enjoyed our visit to Arolsen[646] very much; it was so nice the whole family had come, only I missed very much Pauline Wied,[647] who was not there through the illness of her child. It is so amusing to see how my cousin Alice and Everwijn[648] had grown. They are quite like grown up young people! The little ones at Arolsen are all three dears![649]

My auntie Lily looked sweet as bride, only she had grown very thin. The festivities were managed beautifully; there was a procession with torchtlight the first evening, the next day a ball, the day after tableaux vivants, which were lovely and then the wedding and a large luncheon afterwhich bride and bridegroom left. That evening there was a small concert to prevent tears flowing, you know. The morning after that we left. My Mother & I gave auntie Lily a brilliant diadem and my Mother worked her a beautiful scrcan. I did not go much sightseing at Dresden; ofcourse I saw at Kassel (where we stopt) and Dresden the pictures and a few other things but I was sick & tired of going about so I took it easily. The heat had got intense. Schwarzburg seems a nice quiet place amongst pinewoods; It is such a comfort to be out of the townbustle!

The weather was fine in arriving but now the rain falls asif it could never stop, nevermind, perhaps it will stop some day! My windows look out upon the river Schwarza and beyond that on the castle of the prince of Schwarzburg.[650] It is a picturesc old building on a hight; our hotel is most comfy.[651] There is a drive up

644 The 'little one' at Potsdam may refer to Hermann (1899–1941), the first child of Pauline and Friedrich of Wied.

645 The annual visit to Amsterdam took place between 24 and 30 April 1900, and included activities of a social, cultural, technical and historical nature.

646 Before their trip to Schwarzburg in Thuringia, where Emma and Wilhelmina would stay between 8 May and 5 June 1900 and where she would meet her future husband, Hendrik of Mecklenburg-Schwerin, mother and daughter first attended the wedding of Emma's youngest sister Elisabeth, 'Aunt Lily', and Alexander, Hereditary Count of Erbach-Schönberg (1872–1944), in Arolsen on 3 May.

647 Paulien Wied is Pauline of Württemberg, who was married to Friedrich of Wied (see letter 230). Their first child, Hermann, was born in 1899. Another son, Dietrich (1901–1976), would follow in 1901.

648 Alice is the daughter of Emma's sister Helena, who married Leopold, Duke of Albany, in 1882. Everwijn is Eberwijn, Prince of Bentheim-Steinfurt (1882–1949), the son of Emma's sister Pauline.

649 These are the three children of Emma's brother Fritz and Bathildis of Schaumburg-Lippe: Josias (1896–1967), Maximiliaan (1898–1981) and Helena (1899–1948). Georg would follow in 1902 and die in 1971.

650 Schwarzburg in Thuringia was the family castle of Princess Marie of Schwarzburg-Rudolstadt (1850–1922), the mother of Prince Hendrik.

651 This is the 'Weisser Hirsch' hotel, where Wilhelmina and her mother stayed between 8

The marriage of Emma's youngest sister Elisabeth of Waldeck-Pyrmont to Alexander, Hereditary Count of Erbach-Schönberg, at the family's castle in Arolsen, 3 May 1900.
**1** Captain von Pfeil; **2** Chamberlain Mr van Weede; **3** Captain Mooss; **4** Mr D.A.W. van Tets van Goudriaan, ambassador in Germany; **5** Captain Fischer; **6** Chamberlain von Alten; **7** Chamberlain Baron von Rassler von Gamerschwang; **8** Baroness von Bissing; **9** Lieutenant-Colonel von Wäldniss; **10** Baroness von Reck; **11** Miss Marwell; **12** Baroness von Süsskind; **13** Queen Wilhelmina; **14** Miss von Mauve; **15** Lieutenant-Colonel von Apell; **16** Mrs von Schmidt-Hirschfelde; **17** Countess Eda of Erbach-Schönberg; **18** Princess-Mother of Schaumburg-Lippe; **19** Hereditary Grand Duchess Hilda of Baden; **20** Princess Alice of Albany; **21** Count Gustav of Erbach-Schönberg; **22** Mrs von Rota, born von Gersdorff; **23** Queen Charlotte of Württemberg; **24** Prince Friedrich of Waldeck-Pyrmont; **25** Duchess Helene of Albany; **26** Princess Elisabeth of Waldeck-Pyrmont, the bride; **27** Princess Pauline of Bentheim-Steinfurt; **28** Hereditary Count Alexander of Erbach-Schönberg, the bridegroom; **29** Countess of Erbach-Schönberg, born Princess of Battenberg; **30** King Wilhelm of Württemberg; **31** Queen-Mother Emma; **32** Princess Heinrich of Waldeck-Pyrmont; **33** Princess-Widow Louise of Waldeck; **34** Princess Bathildis of Waldeck-Pyrmont; **35** Prince Heinrich of Waldeck-Pyrmont; **36** Count Adalbert of Waldeck-Pyrmont; **37** Prince Wolrad of Waldeck-Pyrmont; **38** Count Friedrich of Waldeck-Pyrmont; **39** Princess Albrecht of Waldeck-Pyrmont; **40** Prince Alexis of Bentheim-Steinfurt; **41** Hereditary Prince Eberwyn of Bentheim-Steinfurt; **42** Count Victor of Erbach-Schönberg; **43** Baroness van Hardenbroek; **44** Hereditary Duke Friedrich of Baden; **45** Governor of the castle Baur; **46** Countess Bernstorff; **47** Baroness Sloet; **48** Fräulein von Kregh; **49** Major Baron of Stein zu Nord and Ostheim; **50** Mrs van Tets van Goudriaan; **51** Baroness van Ittersum; **52** Major Baron von Gemmingen; **53** Lieutenant General Count Dumonceau; **54** Count van Bylandt; **55** Baron von Hadeln; **56** Colonel Sir Robert Collins; **57** Councillor Muller.
Photograph: Th. Molsberger, Arolsen.

to here of an hour so that we don't hear the railway. Paper has come to an end & darkness is falling in; so good night Darling. Ever your most devoted old friend

Wilhelmina

May and 5 June. It still exists, but it has lost its former glory and is poorly maintained. From the hotel, one has a lovely view of Schwarzburg Castle.

**247**  My very dearest Darling,

Thank you so much for your dear letter. Let me first tell you about your coming to us at Soestdijk: we leave here on June 5 so my mother told me to write you were most welcome on June the 6.

Perhaps you could manage to spin out your stay at Monrepos till that date. It is delightful to see you, you old [text missing] Darling; I expect you to be most [text missing] ic and interesting; you will be sure to talk as interestingly as a book! How dreadful that my aunt of Wied[652] has been so bad — luckily the baby is nearly quite better! I am horrified at you description of poor Elisabeth,[653] she must be quite like an old cripple! I can well imagine how happy Louisa is at getting you back again for a time; how do you find her, has she grown into an older and morally more developed girl? I am looking madly forward to coming home but all the same the stay here is most pleasant. We have had here my cousin of Mecklenburg[654], she made the whole long journey from her home to come and see us. Unluckily my mother has had a bad throat and cold and had to stay for a few days (she has quite recovered now) so she cold not see so much of my cousin than I did. It was delightful having her without my uncle Weimar. We are going to the Wartburg[655] next week for a day to see him and his old castle. I have been taking long mad walks; the country is lovely for that sort of thing. We have had all varieties of weather we could wish for: our roof has been covered with snow and it has been burnt from the heat. All these extremities are most favorable to my artistic feelings: I drew [Colour plate VIII-12] Son May the 15th the castle of Schwarzburg[656] and the green tree covered with snow and the day before yesterday I made an expedition to an old ruïne of a church[657] skorching in the sun.

I painted an old woman in Schwarzburg — the old women are most picturesc! The old castle of Schwarzburg is most interesting it is built in a most odd

---

652  This refers to the Princess-widow Marie of Wied (1825-1902).

653  Elisabeth of Wied (1883-1938) was the youngest child of the Prince and Princess of Wied. Like her older sister Louise, she would never marry.

654  Elisabeth, daughter of Carl Alexander, Grand Duke of Saxe-Weimar ('Uncle Weimar') and Sophie, Princess of the Netherlands.

655  The Wartburg, founded according to legend in 1067, lies above the town of Eisenach (Thuringia). For centuries the castle was in the hands of the ruling house of Saxe-Weimar-Eisenach. When Martin Luther was banished from the empire on 26 May 1521, he found sanctuary in the Wartburg for almost a year. The castle is on the UNESECO World Cultural Heritage List.

656  Wilhelmina also did a painting of the castle from her hotel: *Gezicht op het Schloss Schwarzburg in Thüringen [View of Schwarzburg Castle in Thuringia]*, oil on canvas 24 x 27.5 cm, signed at the bottom right: W 15/5 1900. SHVON, inv.no. 0858 (see Spliethoff et al., pp. 84–85). When the painting was described, there was no realization that it had snowed then, as revealed by the remark: 'If she [Wilhelmina] had not dated the painting precisely, 15 May 1900, one might easily think that it had been painted in winter.'

657  This ruined church is located in Paulinzella. My thanks to Bearn Bilker, Oudwoude, for this information (email of 31 January 2013).

manner! There are whole collections of pictures and mugs and glaswerk and stags etc. Do you get regularly news of Rumania?

I must end now; with all my best love, I ever remain your most devoted old friend

Wilhelmina

P.S. have you heard that I have named miss Snoek[658] my new lady in waiting. She is the daughter to mr. Snoek "Kamerheer in buitengewone dienst in Noord-brabandt [chamberlain extraordinary in Noord Brabant]", you saw him in 's Hertogenbosch. She seems to be very nice, I saw her this winter at the Hague. Miss Rengers looks much better and is coming back to me at Soestdijk, I saw her at Dresden, she was staying in the mountains near there.

W

July 15 1900<br>the hottest day I have ever felt!

**248**   My very dearest old Friend,

You were a very wise old lady not to write during the time I was getting through the "program" but you see all the same I <u>would</u> have found time to read a letter coming from you! Thank you very much for sending me such a nice loving letter. I am delighted for your sake that the heat has at last set in as you were so much in want of warmth, but for my own sake I puf and blow quite like a "halow" or how do you can such a thing? Tomorrow we are going to the Hague (journey morning early and evening after dinner. I am to see the ministers and open the exhibition of the history of the Dutch navy[659] which is to take place in my palace of the Kneuterdijk. Prof. Blok is to make a speech of 15 min.[660] I hope he likes it!! After that I will visit some gardens in the "Westland", I will not at all come home baked by the sun! It was so nice having you here[661] and being able to hear of your late experiences of humanity! You were such a Dear to tell me so nicely all about them. It was really not the war[662] that made me feel different towards you; how horrid of you to think such a thing of me — I am far too enlightened to

---

658  Marie Snoeck is Lady Adriana Maria Snoeck (1873–1948), who entered royal service on 10 July 1900 as the successor to Pixy de Constant Rebecque (see letter 51, note 71). Emma and Wilhelmina were very fond of Marie. On 30 May 1905 she married Mr Frans Beelaerts van Blokland (1872–1956). The latter, among other things, was envoy extraordinary and minister plenipotentiary in Peking, Minister of Foreign Affairs and Vice-President of the Council of State.

659  The two queens opened the historical exhibition on the history of the Dutch Marine in the Gothic Hall of Kneuterdijk Palace in The Hague on Monday 16 July. Afterwards, the queen also visited the vegetable gardens in Loosduinen and the glasshouses in Poeldijk.

660  *Speech given to H.M. the Queen on the occasion of the opening of the historical exhibition on the Dutch Marine on the 16th of July 1900* ['s Gravenhage, 1900]. The speech is not kept in the Royal Archives.

661  Miss Winter came to stay at Soestdijk Palace between 18 June and 2 July 1900.

662  This refers to the Boer War in South Africa (see letter 243, notes 633).

let that make a difference between me and any other person who felt differently than I! Besides I was not aware that I behaved any otherwise than hithertoo or that there was any question which "could ever have any distinct influence upon the love, confidence & sympathy" which have existed between us. So knowing me so well I am astonished that you could think such a thing of me! It is quite another question wheather you noticed that I was preoccupied during the time you were here, but you will remember from old that I am always exited about things which are to come & you yourself name in your letter exitements enough for me to be busy with in my mind. Both the leaving of Geesken[663] and Pixy I was dreading very much. Now about the finished program: everything went off very well. Utrecht was a grand success[664] and so was Pixy's lunch and the visit of the Bentheims.[665] Victoria & Emma were the two children which came. They have both grown much older and wiser and are quite little companions for me! The new lady[666] has arrived full of good intentions and seems a very nice young girl.

How sad for your poor mother to have grown so helpless! I can understand how peaceful life must be at home; how can you say it nearly seems too peaceful, you ought to be happy for the rest! There may come times in your life you want all your forces again! How do you feel? Your poor boy,[667] what a life one must be leading him. I must go 12³⁰ has struck and I am very hot. With all the best love ever your faithful friend,

Wilhelmina

## The engagement of Wilhelmina and Hendrik

Wilhelmina saw Hendrik again several times when she and her mother stayed with her Aunt Lily and the latter's husband, Hereditary Count Alexander Erbach-Schönberg, in König in the Odenwald, 25 km to the south of Darmstadt, between 8 and 15 October 1900. The happy event took place on 12 October. Wilhelmina in *Eenzaam maar niet alleen*, p. 98: 'We met each other for luncheon. When it was over, the others withdrew and left us alone. We were very soon in agreement and within ten minutes we appeared to the others as an engaged couple. The die is cast. What a relief that is, with every engagement!' The engagement was announced on her return to Het Loo on 16 October.

---

663 'Geesken' (see letter 103, note 132 and letter 141, note 241).
664 This visit took place on 3 July 1900. Among other things, the Provincial States of the Province of Utrecht hosted a dinner in Paushuize for Queen Wilhelmina and the Queen-Mother Emma.
665 Pauline, Princess of Bentheim-Steinfurt came with her two daughters Victoria (1887–1961) and Emma (1889–1905) on 4 July 1900 (see photo on p. 201).
666 Marie Snoeck, the new lady-in-waiting (see note 658).
667 This must refer to the young Hereditary Crown Prince Carol of Romania.

On 17 October 1900, Miss Winter, then in Saffron Walden, received a telegram from Emma at Het Loo, with the following message:

**249**    I communicate to you the engagement of Wilhelmina to the Duke Henry of Mecklenburg Schwerin who has just arrived

Emma

A day later, a telegram arrived for Miss Winter from Wilhelmina:

**250**    Many thanks for your loving telegram and letter, I cannot tell you how intensely happy I am, tender love Wilhelmina

Oct. 29 1900

**251**    My very dearest Darling,

I must begin by begging your pardon for not having written to you before now. But Darling, when one is engaged — letterwriting becomes difficult; now the Duke has left and now I must thank you thousand times for your loving telegram [text missing] ...letters and for all the wishes they contain. Oh Darling, you cannot even faintly imagine how franticly happy I am and how much joy, and sunshine has come upon my path. I hope to write later a longer letter; but let me

The young betrothed couple visit Prince Hendrik's family in Lensahn, Holstein, Germany, 4 November 1900. At the back, from left to right: Duke-Regent Johann Albrecht of Mecklenburg, Queen Wilhelmina, Prince Hendrik, Grand Duke Friedrich August of Oldenburg, Duke Paul Friedrich of Mecklenburg, Duchess Sophie Charlotte of Oldenburg, Duke Adolf Friedrich of Mecklenburg; at the front, from left to right: Queen Emma, Grand Duchess Marie of Mecklenburg, Hereditary Grand Duke Nicolaus of Oldenburg, Grand Duchess Elisabeth of Oldenburg, Grand Duke Friedrich Franz IV of Mecklenburg.
Photograph: Alb. Giesler, Eutin, Germany.

tell you still now that we passed delightful days at König[668] and here in our dear Loo, for you know how it has become the Duke's and my dear Loo. To day it has been a sad day for me for he left this morning. Luckily the parting is not for long as we meet Thursday in Hamburg on the way to Lensahn[669] where he is to present me to my new relations.

Let me add still that I have changed completely since my visit to König and you would no more know me if you were to see me, so much have I grown into the tastes and ideas of my future husband; Sunday I even dared enter into the old Loo in rooms and corners where I formerly never dared come near; now don't you find he has worked wonders?

I can't attempt to describe him to you; for I could not, even if I tried, say as much good of him as he deserves. It will always be my highest aim in life to try to be for him a wife worthy of him!

It will interest you perhaps to hear that I met at König & Darmstadt "Ducky" Missy's sister[670] & that for those present it was most amusing to see Ducky & me together! You will able to imagine the rest!

With all dearest love ever your very devoted

Wilhelmina

Paleis, 's Gravenhage
December 10 1900

252  My dear old Friend,

Thank you so much for your loving letter and dear present. How nice that it is such a useful one; now ofcourse I appreciate double all those useful in my household!

For you know I mean to be an energetic wife and do a lot myself in my own dear nest! I hope to send you soon the photographs!

We did not feast St. Nicolas this year, the Duke not being here I fear I would not have been in a frame of mind for jokes!! My Duke is coming the 17th, so you must think of me very much on that date. Oh, you don't know how [underlined twice] I am longing for my wedding to come to no more be separated from him and be able to live for him, what a happiness! Ofcourse I think very, very much of my future life and try to picture it to myself but I always discover again and again new depths of happiness. I think we are the happiest future couple that ever existed! This time has been very [underlined twice] hard for me without the

---

668 König is a health resort in the Odenwald in the German federal state of Hessen.
669 Between 2 and 5 November 1900, Queen Wilhelmina and her mother stayed in Lensahn in Oldenburg. This was the home of Hendrik's sister Elisabeth (1869-1955), who was married to Friedrich August van Oldenburg (1852-1931).
670 'Ducky' is Victoria Melita (1876-1936), who was married first to Ernst Lodewijk, the Grand Duke of Hesse (1894), and then to Grand Duke Kirill of Russia (1905). 'Missy' is Ducky's elder sister Marie (1875-1938), married to Crown Prince Ferdinand I of Romania. The parents of Marie and Victoria were Queen Victoria's son Alfred of Edinburgh and Maria Alexandrovna of Russia (see p. 22, note 33).

Duke first because ofcourse I am so frantically fond of him and secondly because hitherto I have never been separated from those I loved. So this is a new experience for me and a <u>most</u> [underlined twice] painful one.

You poor old Friendy, I can so well understand what a hard time you are going through and what a dreadful feeling it must be not having any work. God help and comfort you through this sad time!

With all my fondest love I ever remain your very devoted old friend

Wilhelmina

Paleis, 's Gravenhage
December 26 1900

253 My dear old Friend,

Thank you many times for your loving letter, good Christmas wishes and pretty card. You were quite right in thinking that Xmas would be a happy one for me! It was so delightful that words fail to describe it! My Duke spoilt my dreadfully and ofcourse my mother to! Amongst other presents I got from the Duke a sweet four in hand, black Russian horses. January will be a bad look out for me as he is leaving the 2<sup>d</sup>.

Now at present it is sweeter here than the sweetest of dreams! We are both writing at my writingtable each onone side and in the highest of spirits, as you may imagine!

You poor old friend will have passed a very sad Christmas, what a contrast with mine! I can so well imagine how often you will have thought back at years gone by. Poor old Friendy, could I only confort you a little bit. The Duke tells me to send you his greetings. With fondest love I ever remain your very devoted and faithful old Friend

Wilhelmina

Paleis, 's Gravenhage
30 December 1900

254 My dear old Friend,

Just a few lines to tell you that I wish you by the beginning of this coming year a lot of blessing and comfort and God grant also happiness. I know what a sad one this year has been for you and how very many difficulties and troubles you have had; may 1901 be in all ways a good one for you.

I know how much you will be thinking of me just now when I am beginning a new year which will bring me so much happiness. You can not imagine faintly <u>how</u> happy I am. Only if that dreadful January would pass off fast, for that will still be a bad time for me! 28 long dreary days without my Duke is hard lines; but no good grumbling about it, it <u>has</u> to be got through. We have been driving a good deal lately and have been to our dear Loo for a day to look after the Dukes rooms which are being done up all fresh. Ofcourse we are both very busy! I hope the calender I am sending you, will arrive at time.

With all my most loving wishes for the coming year, I remain your devoted old friend

Wilhelmina

Queen Emma sent a New Year's card with the text:

**255** with my most affectionate wishes for 1901 & the assurance of my loving sympathy

Emma

# 1901

On 1 January 1901, Miss Winter received a telegram from Wilhelmina:

**256** Many thanks dear letter, I hope you will be able to assist our wedding, invitation will reach you soon, much love, Wilhelmina

On 7 February 1901, Miss Winter attended the marriage of Wilhelmina and Hendrik at the Grote Kerk in The Hague. Thereafter, Queen Emma lived at Lange Voorhout Palace in the winter and Soestdijk Palace in the summer. Miss Winter stayed with Queen Emma until 12 February.

Paleis Voorhout La Haye[671]

18<sup>th</sup> of April 1901

**257** Dearest Miss Winter!
I have no time to write. I can only send a few lines & promise a letter later on. But I do not forget you. My thoughts often wonder to Saffron Walden & I would like to know more about you. Than it is such a nice feeling that I <u>know</u> that your thoughts are with me & that you really fully feel <u>for</u> & <u>with</u> me. I am well, I am quite astonished how I bore every [text missing] Amsterdam [text missing], child so awkward [text missing] felt it was so difficult for me 2<sup>d</sup> day everything better.
   Loo was easier than I thought. W. in excellent health, but still <u>quite</u> gone. Later I'll write more — I am going again tomorrow for H.s birthday for 24 hours.[672]
   I am leaving April 22<sup>d</sup> for Villa Ingenheim Potsdam where I'll spend 10 days with Duchess of Alb.[673] 3<sup>d</sup> May I go to see my sister Elisabeth Erbach at <u>König im Odenwald</u>.[674]

671 Part of the text is missing because a piece has been torn off the top of the letter, which was written on mourning paper and in a black-edged envelope.
672 Prince Hendrik celebrated his birthday on 19 April.
673 The Duchess of Albany is Emma's sister Helena. Potsdam was home to her sister-in-law Victoria 'Vicky' (1840–1901), the eldest daughter of Queen Victoria of England. Vicky was married to Frederik III (1831–1888), the German Emperor and King of Prussia, and was the mother of Emperor Wilhelm II (1859–1941).
674 The Odenwald is a woody region between Heidelberg, Mannheim and Frankfurt.

After that I'll be somewhere in the blackforest.

I must stop. Goodbye Dear.

I always am

Your very affect.

Emma

Het Loo
August 21 1901[675]

**258**  My dear old Friendy,

I must begin by thanking you many, many times for your dear letter; I was indeed <u>very</u> glad to get some news of you and I am very happy to think that you are feeling better. Often this summer have I wished to write to but somehow there always came something in between and so I think I must explain my long silence. Notwithstanding all that <u>I</u> am always happy to get a letter from you, you see I have also the theory that it is delightful to <u>receive</u> news and be lazy in giving news! You do not know how the time goes and so many duties having come upon me now the days fly by before I am aware of it! Now I must come to the point! I am happy that you are going to Segenhaus;[676] I fear only you will find my poor aunt grown very old, my mother told me she had so much trouble to find her words and one had to help her say what she wished and had to guess a great deal! Now my husband and I would be very glad if you would come to visit us on the passage going or coming back. Now my dear Friend has not been as practible as usual and did not write when she was going to travel. Please let me know that and then we can see when we can fit in your visit?[677] What a good thing for your sister to have a change of air.

We are going the 23<sup>d</sup> to Oldenburg for the christening of my godchild and we are staying till monday.[678] I am wild at the idea of this yourney.

Soestdijk[679] was pleasant but ofcourse our own dear home is much better still. Sweet home, sweet home, I have forgotten the rest of the song, but sweet home is the best of all places. O you do not know <u>how</u> happy I am!

With all the best love ever your faithful old friend

Wilhelmina

---

**675**  The letter was written on mourning paper due to the death of the above-mentioned (letter 257) Empress Victoria on 5 August 1901.

**676**  Segenhaus (see letter 197, note 486) was home to the Princess-widow Marie of Wied, a half-sister of Emma's mother Helena. In her study at Het Loo, Queen Wilhelmina had a portrait of Marie of Wied by Lou Meyboom (1873–1964), after Kate Bisschop (1834–1928), 1901, inv.no. PL287.

**677**  Miss Winter was in the Netherlands between 28 October and 6 November 1901.

**678**  Prince Hendrik was in Oldenburg between 23 and 26 August to attend the baptism of Princess Ingeborg Alix (1901–1996), the third child of Hendrik's sister Elisabeth and Friedrich August II of Oldenburg, Grand Duke of Oldenburg, whom she had married on 24 October 1896. Queen Wilhelmina was not permitted to go because her doctor, Van Tienhoven, suspected that she might be pregnant, although this proved not to be the case several days later (Fasseur 1998, p. 261).

**679**  Wilhelmina and Hendrik were at Soestdijk between 15 July and 5 August 1901.

259    My dear old Friendy,
I send you my very best wishes for your birthday and hope that the new year of
your life may be as happy for you as your old Friend on this side of the Northsea
wishes for you! Tomorrow many a warm and heartfelt wish will travel over
from the Loo to Walden! I know how tomorrow will be a day for you full of sad
thoughts of the gone-by year. Life must be very hard and sorrowful for some
people, I often think, and when hard and serious times come, one does not think
of and look up to future with much hope or assurance!

We are all in Gods hand and may He have still much happiness in store for you!

Now I must thank still once for your loving birthdayletter and all the good
wishes it contains! My birthday was most delightful; ofcourse I was very much
spoilt both by my husband and mother. The latter came over for a few days; she
has left now! The first birthday in ones own home and house spent with ones
husband is a day never to be forgotten as old as one becomes, I am sure all future
birthdays will be as happy as this one!

I was sad that the gone-by year had taken an end; it was a year so full of
sunshine & happiness and the beginning of such a happy life! With all the more
confidence have I begun the new year!

How can you think I would wish you at the bottom of the RedSea when you
come to us, now how must I spiflicate you for such an idea! No, old Friend, so
unfaithful I have not yet become and I would be very happy to have you here![680]
I hope only you will write when more about your journey is decided! I can understand that you will not have an easy job at Segenhaus and would not like to be
in all respects in your shoes! My birthdaypresent I will give you when you come,
must first hear of you what wishes you have!

I must end now! With best wishes ever your faithful old friend

Wilhelmina

Letters 260, 263, 264, and 267 were all written by Queen Emma. Letter 264 reveals, in
striking fashion, how the queen poured her heart out to Miss Winter.

260    Dear Miss Winter!
For your aproaching birthday I wish to send you from the bottom of my heart my
most affectionate wishes! May the new year have many a pleasant & even happy
hour in store for you but above all I wish for work for you. The by gone year
brought sorrow & much struggle & worry to you poor Dear, you cannot be sorry
to close it. —

680  See note 677.

Once more I must thank you for your dear letters & the nice little book with dear photo's. I am looking forward to seeing you immensely. In leaving Segenhaus you must <u>first</u> come to me as you got my invitation before Wilhelmina's, & if you first went to W. you perhaps could no more come to me in my own house, because I am to keep W. company during Henry's absence from the last of Sept. to the middle of Oct.[681] If you only leave Segenhaus in the beginning of Oct, you must first go to W. & then come to me. —

I am <u>very</u> sorry you did not get the doctors child. It would have been <u>so</u> nice for you.

I hope you are quite well again by this time.

I am sure you will have a nice time at Segenhaus[682] & an interesting one. — Do make my Aunt tell the King that <u>she</u> invented your visit & not you.[683] As the K. is so distrusting.

The birthday went of better than I thought. I was allowed to help with telegramms & letters just as of old. —

I have much to tell you about W. — She has not yet settled down. She is still quite gone & one must handle her very carefully. It is not easy, one does often not know, where one had better interfere & where hold one's tong. To me she is quite open like formerly thank God and all constraint has gone.

Only I must be most careful not to give cause to the idea that I mean to interfere.

I must say goodby.

With many fond wishes I remain your affectionate                    Emma


Christmas and New Year's card from Wilhelmina:

Printed: Old friends out valuing all the rest Tennyson[684]

261  Wilhelmina wrote underneath: 'I hope I am one of those for you and send you'

Printed: Merry Christmas and a happy New Year

Signed: 'Wilhelmina 1901'

PALAIS LA HAYE

Dec. 30 1901

262  My dear old Friend,

These few lines must just tell you that my loving thought are with you on this coming new yearsday with every good wish for the year that is beginning now so soon. May it bring you many a happy time and many a blissful moment. Life is hard and none of us in this world go through it without their portion of sadness; God grant you a great deal of happiness, you dear, treu old Friendy!

---

681  Prince Hendrik went hunting in Germany between 26 September and 15 October.
682  See letter 197, note 486.
683  'Aunt' refers to the Princess-widow Marie of Wied (1825–1902), and 'King' refers to King Carol I of Romania, to whom her daughter Elisabeth (Carmen Silva) was married.
684  Alfred Tennyson (1809–1892), from 1884 Lord Tennyson, an English poet, whose poems expressed the notion that art should strive to achieve moral objectives.

I must thank you very much for your dear letter and Xmas wishes. How sweet of you to have worked me a bag for my needle work; it must be delayed by the extra work of the post at Xmastime, for it has not yet arrived. As soon as I got your letter I told all my people to be on the lookout, but nothing has come! After newyear I hope the lines will be clear and it will come! My calender will reach you in time I hope.

How dreadful for you that your brother was so ill; is he now convalescent?

You must have been in fearful state of anxiety !

Now I must end. With fondest, fondest love, I ever remain your very devoted old friend

Wilhelmina

Paleis Voorhout
30<sup>th</sup> of Dec 1901

**263** Dear Miss Winter!

I had hoped to write a long letter but there is no possibililty to manage that ! But I have time for a few words! Many many thanks for your kind letter. I hope you got mine in good time. I am so sorry you have had such dreadful anxiety about your brother. God grant the worst is over & that he may recover quickly.

Your poor sister! How tired & exhausted she will be!

Your Xmas must have been <u>very</u> lonely indeed. — I am afraid you will still be without your sister for New Years eve & N. Years day. Poor Dear! — I send you my most loving wishes for the coming year & pray God that He may give you his choisest blessings & make your path smoother than the last years. You know how intensly I wish that new interests & duties should come into your life.

I thank you very much indeed for having got the aircushion for me. I find it beautiful. I think my child in the bottom of her heart too. But she did not say much but she accepted it with graciousness!

That is all I can expect because she must have found me meddling to have given it. — I spent Xmas better than I had feared.

I had a very comfy evening on the 23<sup>d</sup> when W & H dined alone with me & got their presents I had nicely arranged. The eve of the 24<sup>th</sup> went off quite well. It is always a little awkward to be in the same place with the same people under other circumstances. But W was quite sweet & natural. But I must keep back very much & guard my tong oh so carefully. When I came home the 24<sup>th</sup> mrs Kreusler[685] had arranged all my presents of my own family & lighted a tiny tree my brother[686] had sent. That was very nice. I met my children the 25<sup>th</sup> in church. W. was so awkward & only said goodmorning in leaving church after H. had done so. And we were only with our suite in a private staircase. I was stiff from carrying heavy things & from Rheumatism the 25<sup>th</sup> & 26<sup>th</sup>. W. & H. just came to see how I was after church the 26<sup>th</sup>. W. got uncomfortable in seeing the little

685 Kreusler (see telegram 60, note 81).
686 Emma's brother Fritz; see letter 124, note 174.

Arolsen tree. I dined in the Noordeinde the 26ᵗʰ and yesterday. W. is much more natural, telling me things, but must be handled oh so carefully. She looks better & is gaining forces rapidly. She is more "opgewekt [cheerful]" as she thinks of other things than her dissapointment.[687] I must stop. God bless you dear Miss Winter

Always your
very affectioned

Emma

# 1902

Reading the following letter, one is struck by how Queen Emma, as a concerned mother, dwelled upon the marriage of her newly-wed daughter and how she expressed herself on this topic to Miss Winter.

Paleis Voorhout
The Hague
Jan. the 2ᵈ [1902][688]

264 Dear Miss Winter!

Many thanks for your dear letter & loving wishes for the new year. Yes I am thankful that that year is closed & that I need not go through a second time what I went through. And all the same I still had a feeling of thankfulness. God really helped me wonderfully. I am astonished how I struggled through & bore every thing.

I am sorry your brother still is very weak & your sister overtired. No wonder! Your girl must be a trial, how much more difficult it must be to have to do with a woman of 25 than with a child.[689] How difficult to be tolerant now I am going to write about W. I do not think you need think one moment that another training would have preventet the present phase, or that all your work, your devotion is lost. I have the conviction that the dear own self is still there & that really she is not changed in the bottom of her soul & heart. But every thing is like flooded by the great passion that has taken possession of her. If a country is flooded under the water the land remains the same & if the water sinks gradually or can run away quietly no great harm is done on the long run. How account for the passion? That I cannot. But one see's women & men (very clever & intellectual ones) having the most curious passion for a woman or a man. I think she was attracted by his great simplicity & his open & natural manner & her instinct that he was pure. I think you saw him "op zijn all024 alleronvoordeeligst [to his least advantage]".[690] Her passion does not allow her to reason in a wholesome manner, she

---

687 Queen Wilhelmina had her first miscarriage on 9 November 1901.
688 Fasseur erroneously dated the letter as 1903: see Fasseur 1898, pp. 269–70. One indication that it is from 1902, among others, is the condition of Miss Winter's brother.
689 It is unclear who is meant here.
690 Miss Saxton Winter was in the Netherlands between 28 October and 6 November 1901.

is overexcited, lives in a continual strain & has quite perverted ideas as soon as H is connected with the thing in <u>any</u> way. Only when she attends to her state affairs she is her own self, the gifted, intellectuel woman with very much tact. In all other matters she is just now a stupid little goose without any own judgment, without caracter, without tact. — Could education have prevented a passion to take hold of her? I say no. With another man the passion would have another kind of effect, but would have flooded every thing for the moment just as well. Her behaviour to me hurt me awfully but does not worry me. What worry's me is that she has <u>quite</u> the wrong tone with him & by that gets on the wrong footing with him & secondly that she looses (that passionatiness going on for such a time & in <u>that</u> way) the respect of her surroundings. And for the future I am anxious, because this passion cannot last (she could not bear it physically) & <u>how</u> will it cease?

Will it ebb away gradually & settle down in wholesome love? Will it cease suddenly because she has been awakend to reality? But how awful than! I am sure she is quite happy not with a calm quite satisfied happiness, but one moment she is wildly happy, another disappointed, but she does not realize this as yet. Another thing that hurts me as mother & women that is, she does not maintain her dignity as woman towards the man. She licks the dust of his shoes. I cannot do anything. I spoke most seriousely to her about it before the wedding and once this summer. But mother knows nothing about those things, is to old to understand what goes on in young people. Besides she is against the son in law because he took away the child!!

I have been told when I pointed out the mistake I try to make mischief between wife & husband!!

I do not say anything if I am not asked, give no advice, even not an opinion. Then everything goes well.

She is quite natural with me again telling me everything. She really just now believes that married she can only love her husband, that nobody else neither you nor I can be anything to her. She believes that she would seem not enough in love of H. if she cared for anyone else. When H. asks me to come to her when he leaves, she told me people were not to believe that I could take his place. She also is afraid that people should think she was still just as devoted to me as formely because than they would imagine she did not love H. enough!! Poor dear if she only new that people only would approve & believe that the 2 affections could existe together. With all that she is in the phase all young people go through, that she wishes to be independant or appear so & she is very ticklish still about her dignity of married women, and just her independance & dignity she misses where she wants it most! — She does not quite realize how she hurt me to the bottom of the heart at the Loo, she only thinks of herself cannot realize other peoples feelings, but all the same she is ashamed & sorry. New years eve I said to the children, I was ashamed because I had not written to one person, she looked at me & said: "I am ashamed of quite other things." — Now I am going to answer a few points I put down out of your letter that is turned. — He does not understand how to take care of her. I own you are quite right, but that is want of education. He seems to have been brought up not to have any "egard" for his mother. She never demands a single one, even now. What regards her health he has no idea. His mother cannot teach him, she thinks one need not take any notice of the condition of a women, when in the family way. She told me so!! She did not require it. She rode for months, drove over the moors with a cart without springs! — He ought not to leave her for so many hours you are quite right but she really encouraged him most strongly possessed with the idea he could get homesick. I think you would feel more happy if you could seen them together when they are quite at their ease. H. is so tender to her than & so soft. They often are childish together especially she like a kitten but there is no lack of tenderness on his part. I wish you could have seen him sit on the floor next to her bed with his head on the bed, refusing a chair as that was hist best place! He is very shy any one should see him like that even giving her a kiss, he does not easily do that before his mother. With me they generally sit both together on one chair! I know his dreadful look when he does not dare look you in the face, but that is shyness, I own he has not the chivalrous manner he ought to have for his wife, he never had it 'enough', but what there was, <u>she</u> did away with. —

I know all the little stupid things & arrangements made since the wedding are the consequence of <u>his</u> influence. But she exagerates his wishes. I know it must be he who disaproves of the olden times & former arrangements, but because he disaproves <u>she</u> puts him more & more against them. "Elle le monte" against what <u>she</u> thinks <u>he</u> dislikes. He is at the bottom of ervery & in that way it is his fault, but she pushes him still more on the wrong way, because she exagerates his wishes & puts him still more against what he dislikes. I have heard her behave in so silly a manner to him when a question was discussed, telling him only to consult his wish, the people had to aprove of everything ect. that I only find it sensible (but <u>very</u> sad) that he attaches little value to her opinion. He comes for advice to me pretty often, she hates that I think she need not care if it is a question where age & experience are a help, in other cases I always refer him to her. She really treats him in every way as she ought <u>not</u> to do. She is childish with him, interrupts him if once is reading or occupied, treats him as if he were of a higher order than she herself & she not his equal, but far beneath him! Oh it makes me so unhappy! — Two good things I saw last week for the first time. She teased & scolded him because he picked his finger (not his nails) & was just a little vexed & showed it <u>him,</u> that he asked <u>me</u> to arrange his drawingroom in a more comfortable manner. He ought to ask her, but she has <u>her</u> rooms in such a muddle! She lacks the energy to unpack & tidy up, will not allow others to do it for her. I have often heard him beg of her not to get up in the night for him but she is so proud of that! In <u>those</u> things she finds her duty as married woman! Here in town she sees <u>much</u> more of him. They go out daily together in the afternoon. He does not smoke so long in the evening. He treats me quite as if I were his mother. If he has done a thing he thinks I wished him to do he tells & asks if he is not good. If I have made a remark telling him he did wrong, he will tell me later on 'mother I have changed that'! But I see little of him & never nearly alone. Yesterday he came to me <u>alone</u> for the first time for advice. But in that way I cannot influence him really. And she does not wish me to do so, she tries to counteract my influence, and he wants to be guided, solded, developed. He is of course not equal to her in intellect but I believe him to be a man who could make her very happy & who could fill his position plus ou moins. But he must be influenced, guided, adviced & she will not do this nor allow me or his gentlemen to do it. That makes things so bad. I think she lives in a continual agitation, because she has a vague notion every thing they do is not right, because she always is afraid that he will be homesick or unhappy & because she always wonders how people will find him, what impression he makes. I think she is very much releaved to see that town life is quite nice. He is quite happy here, she sees more of him, can run in & out very easily in his rooms. An exemple of her insane way of reasoning. She tells me she loves her mother in law just as much as she does me & is <u>quite</u> as intimate with her as with me. I except this as quite natural. Than the subjects drops. But when she has to write to the mother in l. & she asks me to help her with her german I can see by everything that she is on a friendly footing but not at all intimate.

I will terminate this letter this evening. (The 7<sup>th</sup>). I feel I cannot give you a clear view in writing. We ought to be able to talk & talk. But perhaps you can all the same now follow her developpment.

I think miss van Overzee who I am sure was often vexed with somebody for his behaviour, has considerably changed of opinion. He was very upset this autumn. I find him calmer now.

I am all right, but often very much worried. Always wondering "what next." She does not talk over things quietly, she only discusses the things with him & puts me & suite before a "fait accompli". She told me she could not make a mistake or misjudge a thing if she talked the question over quietly with him. That was all that was wanted!! He often wishes for other advice & comes to me for great things & to his gentlemen for small ones! But how much better would it be if <u>she</u> talked the things over.

But now really goodbye.

I adress to Saffron Walden.

Wit much love yours
very affectionately

Emma

Please burn this immediately

PALAIS LA HAYE
23 March 1902

**265**   [No salutation]

I am afraid I have neglected my old friendy lately, but I have had so much to do that I could not write! I hope you are quite better from your vaccination and feel bright & happy! At last spring has begun and we are leaving this dreadful town on April 3<sup>d</sup> for our dear old Loo!

We will have to go without our most enjoyable visit to Amsterdam this year as I am expecting a great event if everything goes as I have reason to hope! I am beginning the 4$^{th}$ month just now; I write this to show you that positive certainty is not yet possible to give, but that I have all reason to hope. Tuesday evening it will be put in vague termes in the paper at the same time with our not going to Amsterdam! You see, dear Friend, this time I have <u>not</u> followed your wise advise so that not my husband but I am getting the baby!! You can imagine <u>how</u> happy I am, and how much more happy I will be still when <u>all</u> doubt has gone. The winter has been rather trying for us but now that the Loo is in view all is forgotten![691]

How sad about the illness of my aunt Wied;[692] the poor Queen of Roumania[693] will not be a good nurse for my aunt! How are all your people doing: your brother and your sister?

We have first had my brother & sister in law Johann Albrecht[694] for a visit; then the Erbachs[695] came to my mother and afterwards to us; their child is a darling; Alice Albany[696] visited mother and during that time there were a great many balls given in town. Now I must end! With fondest love ever your faithful old friend

Wilhelmina

Shortly after her arrival at Het Loo, Wilhelmina contracted typhus. She was extremely ill. As a result, she miscarried a son on 4 May 1902. To convalesce, she stayed in Schaumburg between 10 june and 19 July. She wrote in pencil:

Schaumburg 1 July 1902

**266**   My dear old Friendy,

At last I have found time to answer you. At the Loo the physicians did not give much permission for writing and here I am kept pretty well occupied with sleeping, eating and being in the air. So you must not be so astonished at my long silence!

It is very dear of you to take such part in all my sorrow; I knew all the time I was ill that my mother and others kept sending you news and I knew that your thoughts were with me. My sorrow and grief is greater than words can say, I trust

---

691 Queen Wilhelmina had a miscarriage on 9 November 1901.

692 This is the Princess-widow Marie of Wied (1825-1902), the Princess of Nassau and the half-sister of Emma's mother Helena (1831-1888); Marie would die in the same year.

693 The Queen of Romania is her daughter Elisabeth 'Carmen Silva' (1843-1916).

694 Grand Duke Johan Albrecht and Grand Duchess Elisabeth of Mecklenburg-Schwerin stayed in the Residency between 4 and 17 February 1902.

695 Immediately after the Meckelenburg family, Emma's youngest sister Elisabeth, who married Alexander, the Hereditary Count of Erbach-Schönberg in 1900, came with their first child Imma (1901-1947) to stay in The Hague for about a month. The couple would have three more children: Georg-Ludwig (1903-1971), Wilhelm (1904-1946) and Helena (1907-1979).

696 Slightly overlapping with the Erbachs' visit, Princess Alice also came over from England. Princess Alice, the Erbachs and Queen Emma visited the lighthouse at Scheveningen on 12 March 1902.

to God that He may help me to be brave; you see I have a <u>very dear</u> husband[697] to live for and the idea of being spared for him and thus still able to go through this world with him and be useful to him, will be the greatest help to face life with courage!

It felt very strange to be in your old room, I thought of the gone by times, the sitting round the fire between lessons ect. My poor mother has been very tired from all the nursing, but is recovering her forces now. I am feeling much stronger and take long drives; the country here is lovery; quite like a gigantic park. The heat is great and this night there was a dreadful thunderstorm which, however has not much cooled the atmosfhere. I am sitting in the garden at present, how hot you must get with your gardening, you poor old friend

What an anxiety and disappointment there must have been over all England; how dreadful for the poor King[698] to fall ill just now! Did you carry out your plan of asking an audience from the princess of Roumania?[699] Bee Coburg[700] seems to be with her in England! I hope you will write soon and tell me what you have been up to lately and how you and your sister are doing and how your niece is getting on, my mother told me she sufferd of her longs! With fondest love ever your loving old friend

Wilhelmina

Soestdijk<br>7<sup>th</sup> of Aug. 1902

**267**   Dear Miss Winter!

This mornings post brought me your little book with the photo's, many many thanks. I am delighted to have these last photo's of my dear aunt.[701] Some of them are really very good & also the Queen[702] is very like herself. But oh the costume!! I am very sorry you had the trouble of reprinting etc. Many thanks for

---

697 Queen Wilhelmina stayed with Queen Emma at Schaumburg Castle. Prince Hendrik arrived on 10 July, after a family visit.

698 King Edward VII (1841–1910) succeeded his mother Queen Victoria (1819–1901) after her death on 22 January 1901. He was from the House of Saxe-Coburg and Gotha, whereas his mother had been from the House of Hanover. The coronation, which had been planned for 1 July 1902, could not go ahead when the king had appendicitis. Thanks to Dr Fredrick Treves, who performed what was then still an uncommon operation to allow the infected appendix to drain via a small incision, the king's life was saved and he could be crowned after all on 9 August 1902.

699 See letter 227.

700 'Bee Coburg' is Beatrice Leopoldine Victoria (1884–1966). She was the daughter of Prince Alfred, the second son of Queen Victoria and Prince Albert of Saxe-Coburg. In 1826 the dynasty acquired the double Dukedom of Saxe-Coburg and Gotha, and Ernst I and II became grand dukes. Ernst II died childless, whereupon Prince Alfred, the Duke of Edinburgh, became Duke of Saxe-Coburg-Gotha in 1893.

701 Here Emma is referring to Princess-widow Marie of Wied (1825–1902), the half-sister of Emma's mother Helene.

702 This is Marie's daughter Queen Elisabeth 'Carmen Silva' of Romania.

your dear letter. I cannot write at length, I am very occupied having to do many things myself which mrs Kreusler[703] used to do for me. —

I am awfully sorry the school will not do for you either. I only hope the lady will perhaps be forced to give up more of her work & than perhaps come back to you with a better proposition. Poor Miss Winter! I feel for you from the bottom of my heart & my heart aches for you.

I am getting on very well. I still feel awfully tired & cannot stand much, but I do no more feel ill. I simply was overstrained & overfatigued & no wonder after that I went through since Nov. last.

Wilh. & Henry were with me from 1 o cl. on the 1st till the afternoon of the 4th. It was a very nice visit. Wilh. very sweet & dear & Henry happy & jolly. Wilh. is getting on very nicely & gaining strength more & more, slowly but regularly. She is very sensible as to her health, sleeps long, rests in the daytime & feeds well. She was very tired after the dinner of 30 persons & bowing & seeing many people about her in the street & the shouting fatigued her very much, but otherwise one could not see she has been <u>so</u> ill. — Miss de Kock[704] is here for 3 days. The Bentheims are coming the 9th. I hope the Albany's the 18th. —

I must finish. Goodbye dear Miss Winter. With much love & many many thanks yours very affectionately

Emma

Etching[705] with image of the front of *Soestdijk* and on the reverse, the text:

**268**  For dear Miss Winter with every heartfelt wish for a blessed Christmas 1902 & with very very much love from Emma

PALAIS LA HAYE<br>Dec. 30 1902

**269**  My dear old Friend,

Thank you so much for your dear lettre for Christmas and the nice photograph of my Aunt Wied you sent me. How melancholy it looks to see her being pushed in her chair in the garden!

You will find me a very bad correspondent indeed that I did not write before now, but you only knew how very busy I always am and somehow time flies very fast and before you realize it, there is a year gone by! Now I send you for the coming year every good wish, may it bring you happiness, health, occupation and all the good things I wish for you!

My birthdaypresent that, bad creature that I was, I never sent you, having in Sept. no time to write, so busy was I, will I send after new year, the post having now so many letters and these getting sooner lost! I hear from mother that you have at last succeeded in finding work; I will send you my present in money this

---

703  Kreusler, Emma's lectrice (see telegram 60, note 81).
704  See p. 21, note 30. Lady M.L. de Kock stayed at Soestdijk between 6 and 9 August 1902.
705  From the Secretary to H.M. the Queen [Juliana], letter C867/79/tvW-17-12-1979, Acquisition 80/-83.

time, as you perhaps will derive more pleasure from such a present just now, when you have to begin a new life than from an object that I would choose for you! I hope you have quite recovered now and feel quite strong and well again!

How is your sister? How is your niece? We had a very comfy-cosy Christmas and enjoyed exceedingly our journey.[706] We had a little skating on our return to the Loo. When are you taking up your new work? I am sending you a calendar that I hope will arrive in time. I feel dreafully stupid at this english letter, having forgot a great deal of the langage that I aught to know; but I hope you will think more about the heart that wrote this letter, than about the authograph! I scarcely ever speak English now!

Believe me ever your old true friend

Wilhelmina

Judging from Wilhelmina's signature, she sent the short book, *A child my choice*, to Miss Winter around 1902 as a Christmas gift, with the text:

270  I found this a very pretty poetry; therfor I send it you! Wilhelmina


# 1903

PALAIS LA HAYE
3 January 1903

271  My dear old Friend,

Thank you very much for you dear letter and calendar. I am sending you hereby 1000 gulden [guilders] and hope you will be able to buy a good part of the library you write about with this sum. I find your calendar charming, very very nice indeed! So you are beginning very soon your life. I hope so much you will derive very much satisfaction from it. What a large undertaking it must be, but how interesting! You will indeed have much to do in the beginning!

I was very glad you wrote me about your future plans and life, for, as I often wrote you, they interest me very much and I am very sorry when I don't hear in a long time of you and what you are doing! As you may well imagine I read with regret the part of your letter where you wrote about "failure" etc. and that you "realize that new interests have to crowd out old ones". I don't remember having used the word "failure" in the sence you mean last autumn, neither do I think that my nature belongs to those that forget my old friends like results out of the expression: new interests have to crowd out old ones! Not having written for so long a time need not mean forgetting an old friend. I can not do more than expressing my regret that my pen kept silent for so long a time. Just as well

---

706  Between 31 October and 5 December 1902, Wilhelmina and Hendrik paid an extended visit to Mecklenburg, whereby they also stayed with Hendrik's mother, the Grand Duchess Marie, in Rabensteinfeld on Lake Schwerin.

as your friendship keeps constant and true, mine does also and therefor I take the greatest interest in your new work and life; may you be successful and feel thoroughly happy in your new undertaking.

With my fondest love ever believe me your true friend

Wilhelmina

272    My dear old friend,

I must answer just in a few words your dear letter of the other day; I am very glad that my present will be useful to you; have you still many books left from your time here like Shakespear[707] and the Tauchnitz editions[708] or are those also to be bought?

Now about the explanation you give me about new interests crowding out "old ones"; I can honestly say I did not understand those words as you now write you meant them; ofcourse that changes my whole opinion and I now fully understand what you meant and mean.

Yes I always noticed how you try not to judge my actions and words and never want it to look asif you did so and I always found that very wise dudicious and kind of you! I was not at all tired from the ball and reception; we take every day a nice brisk walk and drive. We are reading now at present a book about Juliana van Stolberg the mother of William the Silent.[709] And this makes me often think of your school, for she also had with her husband a school which was renowned in those days for the broad, good and enlightened education, tinted with the ideas of the reformation onwhich the sons and daughters of a great many raigning German princes were sent to finish their education! Now I hope very much that your school may get as renowned as that of Juliana van Stolberg. I have just now in the winter months a lot of work and affairs of state and I am very occupied the whole day. My husband sends you his very kind greetings and I ever remain your tru old friend

Wilhelmina

---

**707**  William Shakespeare (c. 1564-1616), England's greatest poet and playwright.

**708**  Bernhard Tauchnitz (1816-1895) would become known for the publication in 1841 of the 'Tauchnitz editions': affordable English-language editions of books by English and American authors, and later also of German authors, intended for school pupils and students. They would be the forerunners of the paperback.

**709**  Here, Wilhelmina probably means the book: A. van Hogendorp, *Juliana van Stolberg, gravin van Nassau-Dillenburg, 1506-1580 [Juliana van Stolberg, Countess of Nassau-Dillenburg, 1506-1580]*, Nijkerk 1902. A copy in the library of the Royal Archives bears Queen Emma's bookplate. It is unclear whether Wilhelmina had her own copy. Another book about Juliana van Stolberg that was in Queen Emma's possession was: Ed. Jacobs, *Juliana von Stolberg, Ahnfrau des Hauses Nassau-Oranien: nach ihrem Leben und ihrer geschichtlichen Bedeutung quellenmässig dargestellt*, Wernigerode 1889. William of Orange was the son of Juliana van Stolberg's second marriage, to Willem de Rijke. Juliana had a total of seventeen children from her marriages. In

Queen Wilhelmina with, on the left, her two ladies-in-waiting Baroness A.J. Anny Juckema van Burmania Rengers (seated) and, standing behind her, Miss A.M. Annie van Haersma de With, who was honourably dismissed on 1 October 1908 due to her marriage to Mr A.C. Schimmelpenninck, and in the centre, her former governess Miss Elizabeth Saxton Winter, who stayed at Het Loo between 5 and 10 September 1908 (Heuven 2011, pp. 91-94). Photograph: J.M. Guy de Coral (1867-1930).

[around 2] March 1903

**273**   My dear old Friend,

I am very sorry indeed to hear from you that you have been so ill and I can so well understand what a sour trial it must be to now, where you have got work, not to be able to begin it at once! Poor old Friendy, how bad and seedy you must still be feeling, for I know all about it how it feels to be bad, weak after an illness![710] But being plucky and having a firm will and desire to recover ones former strength helpes very much to precipitate the reconvalescance!

   Please write soon again how you are getting on. How is your sister? From here I can give you the best tidings, only the times are serious as you can see from the papers and being captain on the ship of state when the sea is rough and storm

Dillenburg she founded a court school, attended by her own children, family members and children from other aristocratic families. Queen Wilhelmina would name her only daughter after her because she considered Juliana to be 'an example of great wisdom and inner strength', someone who followed only the dictates of her conscience and allowed God alone to lead her (Wilhelmina, p. 13).

**710** Here the queen is referring to the serious illness from which she had suffered in 1902.

near at hand is not an easy task;[711] but I am calm amongst the "Halo" and do not tremble for the first gusts of wind that I get!

Winter is passing for the rest in the usual way with all the habitual entertainments (annoyenses of town life).

I would have written sooner and had every day the intention of beginning a letter but could find no time, both worries of state and paperreading taking so much of my time!

With fondest love and every good wish for rapid recovery I ever remain your true old friend

Wilhelmina

# 1914

No letters were kept from the period between 1903 and 1921, aside from a letter from the Dutch envoy in London, R. de Marees van Swinderen[712] of 1914, and one from Wilhelmina, written in 1917.

The following letter was sent to Miss Winter by the envoy Mr de Marees van Swinderen at the beginning of the First World War, which broke out after the assassination of the Archduke and heir to the throne of the Austrian empire, Franz Ferdinand, on 28 June 1914 in Sarajevo:

Netherland Legation, 32, Green Street, W.<br>Octobre 14<sup>th</sup> 1914

**274** Dear Miss Saxton Winter:

I will be always pleased to place the bag of the legation at your disposal for any letters you would like to send to Their Majesties. The bag goes by hand nearly every day, so you can send the letters at your own convenience, and you can feel quite sure that they will reach Their Majesties safely.

It is a fearful time we are going through, but I have all hope that we will succeed in keeping out of the real fighting. But bar that, the Netherlands too suffer most seriously from the situation. It gives us another opportunity to admire the great qualities of the Queen, who is watching and controling every little detail with more unselfish devotion then any of Her subjects and whose

711 This was the time of the railroad strikes. The immediate cause of the strikes was a strike in the port of Amsterdam, with which the railroad workers declared their solidarity. The strike was about working conditions and trade unions, as the employers refused to recognize the workers' organizations. The directors eventually recognized the trade unions, whereupon an end was called to the strike.

712 Mr R. de Marees van Swinderen (1860–1955) was Minister of Foreign Affairs between 1908 and 1913 and envoy to London between 1913 and 1937.

exceedingly clever and cool-headed appreciations of men and circumstances are always an invaluable help to Her Government.

If you find time some day to bring me of your letters yourself, I will be most happy to get an opportunity of making your aquaintance, and so will be my wife.

Sincerely yours

R de Mareees van Swinderen

[Underneath, Miss Winter had written:] 'de Marees van Swinderen His Excellency Minister Plenipotentiary'


# 1917

PALAIS LA HAYE
Dec. 30 1917

275   My dear old Friend,

These few lines must just tell you that my loving thoughts are with you on this coming new yearsday with every good wish for the year that is beginning now so soon. May it bring you many a happy time and many blissful moment. Life is hard and none of us in this world go through it without their portion of sadness; God grant you a great deal of happiness, you dear, true old Friendy!

I must thank you very much for your dear letter and Xmas wishes. How sweet of you to have worked me a bag for my needlework; it must be delayed by the extra work of the post at Xmastime, for it has not yet arrived. As soon as I got your letter I told all my people to be on the lookout, but nothing has come! After newyear I hope the lines will be clear and it will come! My calender will reach you in time I hope. How dreadful for you that your brother was so ill; is he now convalescent?

You must have been in a fearful state of anxiety!

Now I must end. With fondest, fondest love, I ever remain your very devoted old friend

Wilhelmina.


# 1921

Between 3 and 24 August 1921, Queen Wilhelmina and Princess Juliana took a trip to Norway on ss *Merope* of the Koninklijke Nederlandse Stoomvaart Maatschappij (the Royal Netherlands Steamship Company). They visited Haugesund, Bergen, Molde, Hellesylt, Geirangerfjord, Ålesund, Christiansund, Gudvangen, Stalheim, Trondheim, Åndelsnes, Marok, Lerik and Korsø.

Queen Wilhelmina sent the following picture postcard of the 'Hermellins fall, Stora Sjöfallet' to Miss Winter:

276   My warmest thanks for letter and dear wishes on mothers birthday. We are enjoying our trip very much, notwithstanding cold and rain. This is aspect of mountains near Sogn Fjord where we made a trip. Your loving old friend

W

277   Christmas card: windmill by a river, with the following text from Queen Emma: 'My Best Wishes' and signed: 'Emma Christmas 1921';
On the reverse: 'For dear Miss Winter with my most affectionate wishes for a blessed & peaceful Christmas.'

# 1922

Between 26 May and 1 July 1922, Queen Wilhelmina and Princess Juliana were again in Norway.

Picture postcard,[713] postmarked 'Svolvaer 10 VI 22',[714] with a bird's-eye view on Bodö, northern Norway, north of the polar circle:

278   Mij dearest love coming from the Arctic. We are just on the way to the Lofoten, and enjoy our trip immensely, the weather is keeping good, we saw the midnightsun for first time yesterday. Did you enjoy your stay at the Hague,[715] what are you up to now. Much love from your loving old pupil W

Picture postcard: 'Romsdalshorn':

279   Another loving greeting from our journey. We had such rain and cold, but are enjoying it still. Hope you are having nice holiday.

The Fjords are simply beautiful, the coast is also very pretty, ravines high mountains have <u>never</u> been my friends much love W

713 This picture postcard was bought by the author for less than the reserve price after it (catalogue number 2446B) had failed to sell at the *De Zwaan* auction house in Amsterdam on 2 July 2014. See Heuven 2015.
714 The town of Svolvaer on Lofoten, a group of islands to the west of Norway.
715 Research in the Royal Archives, The Hague, revealed that Miss Winter stayed with Queen Emma between 24 May and 6 June 1922.

# 1923

Picture postcard showing a small photo of the Ruigenhoek:

Ruigen Hoek April 24 1923[716]

280   My dear old friend, accept my warmest thanks for your dear letter and Easter-writing. It was very dear of you to write. We are now staying in our cottage near Scheveningen which is a delightful rest for me, having always the bracing air. Only it is still very cold. After my child's birthday we are starting for the Loo. She has learned English now from her "Dresser" which was formerly in mij Aunts service and nursed her very well. In May J. is to lessons from a teacher.[717] My mother is doing very well, she has quite got over her broken arm now. My husband is not here at present, he is in Mecklenburg,[718] so I can't send a message from him. With best love from J. and myself I ever remain your loving old friend Wilhelmina

# 1924

Picture postcard from Apeldoorn, Paleis Het Loo:

28/2 1924

281   A loving greeting from the dear Loo to mij old enthusiastic friend who is so thankful for a little token of thought and friendship, I am happy it did you pleasure. May "the nest egg" be used for something very pleasant! I was so delighted with your dear letter and thank you very much also for your wishes for new year and for all the love it contains. It is out here beautiful winterweather. I have been hard worked and we are resting here for a few days. Best news of Mother, my child and we both. This autumn I had a bad crisistime which was very trying, politics are horrid things.[719]

   Much love from your true old friend

Wilhelmina

716  The *Ruigenhoek* was built in 1917, during the First World War, by the architect L.J. Falkenburg of The Hague. Commissioned by Queen Wilhelmina, it lay in the Oostduinen (eastern dunes) to the north of The Hague. The name of the house was derived from a stretch of dunes near Noordwijk. The house served as a country retreat for rest and fresh air, close to The Hague. The queen did many paintings in the area, and there was a painter's studio in the attic. Wilhelmina often stayed there after her abdication. The house was gutted by fire in 1982.
717  In this and the following years, Juliana was given private tuition, among others, by Prof. F.J.L. Krämer (p. 30, note 62), who had also tutored Wilhelmina in Dutch and general history, and Prof. W.J. Muller (1858–1945), who taught Dutch language and literature.
718  Prince Hendrik was in Schwerin, Germany, between 20 and 28 April 1923.
719  Shortly after the celebrations of her twenty-fifth jubilee, Wilhelmina showed signs of over-tiredness and suffered all kinds of symptoms. In early 1925 she was prescribed rest, and stayed for some time in Switzerland (Fasseur 2001, p. 49).

Queen Wilhelmina and Princess Juliana holidayed in Norway between 26 June and 1 August 1924. Picture postcard showing a fjord, sent from Andalsnes on 17 July 1924:

**282**  Many loving messages from this beautiful country. We are enjoying our trip very much and are going much on foot. Saltaluokta is a charming station quite in the wildernis, most delightful. Much love in true friendship

W

# 1925

In the period between 1923 and 1925, Queen Wilhelmina struggled with her health. She was over-tired, and her doctor recommended that she go to Switzerland to rest. Between 4 and 20 March 1925 Wilhelmina stayed in Glarus (Walensee, Eastern Central Switzerland), Geneva and Sierre (Rhônedal).

Picture postcard: 'Abend am Wallensee':

**283**  Warmest thanks for last letter. And much love from this beautiful country where we are enjoying a short holiday all in the snow just now, are taking long walks

W

# 1926

From 1926, Miss Winter received alternating letters from Wilhelmina, Emma and Juliana, who had just turned seventeen.

Het Loo, May 15<sup>th</sup> 1926

**284**  Dear Miss Winter,

Many, many thanks for your very kind wishes and lettre. I must begin with making excuses for my being so late in answering, it is rather a shame to let you wait a fortnight! The strike cannot be an excuse.

At first as I was in my "sweet seventeen" I felt rather sedate and under the impression, but it is allready getting off, which is very pleasant. I had ever such a nice birthday, an excellent beginning for such a sweet year! Mother says, that it is sweet indeed.

I thank you very much for your useful little sermon! I also like to make sermons to younger people, it gives you such a grown-up feeling! But I am sure you did not do it for that reason.

With still many thanks

Yours sincerely

Juliana

Christmas card showing a scene of Amsterdam from Emma, 'Christmas 1926' and inside:

285 'With my most affectionate wishes for my dear Miss Winter for a peaceful and blessed Christmas'

Emma

Christmas and New Year's card for 1927 with the inscription: 'For dear Miss Winter'

286 Dear Miss Winter!

Many thanks for your dear letter & Xcard. I am <u>so</u> sorry that your dear sister is still a severe invalid & <u>I</u> understand how sad it must make you.

But you must not give way to sadness & I am sure too you don't, otherwise you cannot comfort your sister. I want to send you once more my most affectionate wishes for 1927 for you & your sister. God keep you!

Emma

# 1927

PALEIS HET LOO

May 9<sup>th</sup> 1927

287 Dear Miss Winter,

For your great kindness of writing to me for my birthday I now come to thank you very much and for all your good wishes too! Everybody spoiled me <u>so</u> much, that it would have too much for a eightiest birthday, just fancy what it must have been for an eighteenth!

Mother sends you very much love –

Have you got as splendid a weather as we have already since April 28th or 29th, and it will absolutely not stop anymore. It is such a marvel.

In September I will become a student at the Leyden university and I am going to live in the neighbourhood of Leyden together with some other students.[720] It must be too lovely for words to be a student, and you will understand I am very much longing for the coming of September, when you begin by being a novice, that means that you must make the acquaintance of all the other girls, and they try your gifts in the regions of poetry, theatre, rowing, etc.

But when I am a student Mother and Father will have me back for very fat weekends, and I will be able then to tell them de most beautiful stories.

---

720 In September 1927, Juliana went to study law and general history at Leiden University. On 29 September she joined the union of women students, the Vereeniging van Vrouwelijke Studenten te Leiden (V.V.S.L.). She would live in Katwijk with Mies Rooseboom, Marguerite Michelin and Clara de Brauw (see Withuis, 93–125).

I thank you still once very much for your very kind letter; if all your good wished would be fulfilled — then — I do not know what I would feel like — but really I do think my nearest future looks rather like your wishes really! —

Will you allow me to finish

Yours affectionately                                                                          Juliana

Between 3 and 30 August 1927, Wilhelmina and Juliana stayed in Norway.

Picture postcard: 'Fefor Höifjeldshotel':

**288**   We arrived here last Friday, terrible heat in the train, but here nice and kool, are having most enjoyable time and good rest, a beautiful country, hope to make many excursions. J. & I send you our best love & I thank you very much for your last and dear letter W

Het Loo

27 Oct. 1927

**289**   My dear old friend,

Since I received your last letter; my thoughts have been very much with you with every good wish for as speedy as possible recovery & from the very beginning I made up my mind to send you these 300 gld. [guilders] but could until now never find time for writing. My life has been one rush and most fatiguing lately.[721] Today I just came back from a trip to town with as finish an official visit to Nymegen.

I hope so much you are feeling more comfortable now; you must use my present for the doctorsbill. I wonder if your sister is well enough again to nurse you; because you must be wanting much looking after. From other people I heared your complaint must be very trying & painful; so I have great sympathy with you and wish I could do something for you; something to cheer you!

I am having good news from my mother who is out for her mountain trip and will stay a few days with us on her return.[722] The house is very quiet without my

---

721   In the previous period, Queen Wilhelmina had been busy with various activities: on 22 October she had received Prince and Princess Stephan of Schaumburg-Lippe (Oldenburg), with their mother/mother-in-law Princess Elisabeth, at Paleis Het Loo, Apeldoorn. In 1921, Stephan of Schaumburg-Lippe (1891-1965) married Princess Ingeborg Alix van Oldenburg (1901-1996), the daughter of Hendrik's sister Elisabeth (1869-1955) and Friedrich August van Oldenburg (1852-1931). On 24 October, Wilhelmina and Juliana left Apeldoorn for The Hague. Joined by Hendrik, on 26 October they received Prince Ri (the eldest son of the dethroned King of Korea) and Princess Ri (the imperial Japanese Princess Masho, of the House of Nashinoto) at Noordeinde Palace, The Hague. On 27 October the royal pair travelled by train to Nijmegen via Rotterdam, to attend the opening of the Maas and Waal Canal, then on to visit Nijmegen, and then returned to Paleis Het Loo. Prince Hendrik travelled on to The Hague, and then to Germany, where he stayed between 30 October and 16 November. Princess Juliana, who began her lectures in Leiden on 4 October, would always spend the weekends (lasting four or five days) with her parents or mother.

722   After the trip to Germany, from 2 to 10 November 1927, Queen Emma stayed at Paleis Het Loo.

child for half the week but from Fryday till Monday I have made sure of her and so then we enjoy being together most franticly!!

   With fondest love and once more every good wish for you recovery ever your true old friend

Wilhelmina

Christmas greetings from Queen Emma:
Printed: To the Past — Sweet Remembrance!
For the Present — Fair Greetings!
For the Future — Life's Best!
With Christmas Greetings
**290** Written: 'for dear Miss Winter 1927'

# 1928

Between 16 July and 1 August 1928, Queen Wilhelmina and Princess Juliana spent their holidays in Sweden and Norway, from which they would also visit Lapland and the Lofoten Islands. Wilhelmina sent a picture postcard from the Fefor Höifjeldshotel to Miss Winter.

Picture postcard: 'Fefor Höifjeldshotel':
**291** My fondest love from Norway, we are much enjoying our holiday; had beautiful weather up in the north, & fine midnightsun; it was simply beautiful.[723] Fefor is the place we stayed at ariving from the north, hope you are well W

PALAIS VOORHOUT LA HAYE

Dec. the [22<sup>d]</sup> 1928

**292** Dear Miss Winter!
I am sending you separately my Christmas card in the form of one of my new photo's & the book which a committee kindly published about me this summer.[724] As you were with me & worked with in the most serious & responsable years of my life I think you will be interested in some parts of it & quite able to understand as you do not seem to forget your dutch. — Some people to whose judgement I attach great importance & who are real friends have said very kind things much too kind, making me feel very humble & ashamed.

**723** Wilhelmina, p. 218: 'I shall not attempt to describe this massive country, with its infinite variety, the beauty of the sun and clouds, and the midnight sun, which is unforgettable for anyone who sees it ...'
**724** Dr J.Th. de Visser et al. (ed.), *De Koningin-Moeder 1879–1929. Gedenkboek ter herinnering aan den zeventigsten verjaardag en het vijftigjarig Nederlanderschap van Hare Majesteit [The Queen-Mother 1879–1929. A commemoration of the seventieth birthday of Her Majesty and her fifty years in the Netherlands]*, Leiden 1928.

Queen Emma and Queen Wilhelmina (at the front) and Princess Juliana and Prince Hendrik in 1929, to celebrate Queen Emma's fifty-year residence in the Netherlands.
Photograph: Franz Ziegler (1893-1939).

One never was able to live up to what one wished.

Enclosed I send my useful present 15 £. I do hope you & your sister are feeling fairly well & that you have good news from those you love.

My thoughts will be going to you at Xmas & old-new year with many very affectionate wishes. —

Many thanks for your last dear letter. I am all right, but my holiday was a little too short this year & I have been very busy & will be still more so in January as from all sides, all parts of the country one is overwhelming me with kindness in commemoration that I have been a dutch woman for 50 years.

How the time passes! I don't feel dreadfully old as I still can do a lot. My child & Juliana are well, just now for a week at the Loo. —

With very much love & the most affectionate wishes for Xmas I always remain your very affectionate

Emma

# 1930

293  Dear Miss Winter!

I want you to have a few lines from me on the morning of your birthday! They are to tell you that my thoughts travel out to you that day with many affectionate wishes for your welfare. I pray God that He may help you to bear the troubles & worries life brings & the trials of old age! I do so hope you will be spared illness & accidents! Poor Dear how sorely you have been tried this last year! Your stay with L. Maule[725] must have done you both a lot of good, the affectionate care alone is so comforting & recuperative!

Many thanks for your 2 dear last letters. I spent 2 days at the Loo. On the 30<sup>st</sup> we all heard the concert given in the Queen's honour at Batavia[726] the evening before the birthday, military music, singing chorus of man, women & young girls & children. We could hear the difference very well. And after Wilhelmina had thanked them herself in the telefoon we heard their enthousiastic shout & the clapping of the hands. Birthday being on Sunday the day itself was pretty quiet but Monday Wilh. went to the Hague as the people had made great festivity. — Her birthday has been celebrated throughout the country with great enthusiasme. She really has made herself such a position that one can say that she is universaly respected also by social & bolsh.[727] & loved & admired by all other parties.

One also has great confidance in her judgement & wisdom & in her character & that is more lasting than popularity. I must finish. The letter must go.

Please remember me kindly to your sister. With many very affectionate wishes for you dear Miss Winter & my very best love I always am your affectionate

Emma

294  My dear old Friend,

My very best wishes for Xmas and the coming new year. May it bring you nothing but joy and happiness and florishing health. I am forwarding in this envelop my Xmas present 120 gulden. Please buy some usefull present; something you are wanting. I hope you have got over all your illfortunes of this year that is closing and feel nothing more of your accident. At present Juliana

---

725  Maule (see the biography of Miss Winter, p. 17, and letter 123, note 173).

726  Batavia, the capital of the former Dutch colony of the East Indies; since gaining independence in 1949, it has been called Jakarta and is the capital of Indonesia.

727  'Bolsh.' refers to the Bolsheviks, derived from the Russian word *bolsjinstvó*, or 'majority', and is a reference to Lenin's Communist Party. From the 1920s, the Bolsheviks called themselves the 'Communist Party of the Soviet Union.' Before 1950, their political movement was also generally known as Bolshevism.

and I are staying here at the Loo for the Xmastrees here; but next week we return to town; it is cold weather, but not nice sunny weather. As we are much occupied I must be brief and only write a few words.

With much love of myself and Juliana I ever remain your faithful and loving old friend

Wilhelmina

Paleis Voorhout<br>Dec. the 22<sup>d</sup> 1930

**295**  My dear Miss Winter!

I want you to have a word from me on Christmas eve!

My thoughts go out to all my friends than of course the most to the old ones, who shared my life & gave me help and affection & devotion in difficult <u>and</u> happy moments in responsible years. And how you shared my responsibility & my difficulties of my task, but also my happiness.

With all my heart I wish you & your sister a peaceful & blessed Christmas in fairly good health. I wonder how you are both getting on, in this damp weather. We had many foggy days, really intense fog but not yellow.

I am all right & got over a cold in my head quickly.

Wilhelmina has been at the Loo for 6 days to give Xmas trees ect to her people there at Elspeet at Uddel at Hoog Soeren. She just returned & dined with me this evening. She is in town since the end of Novem. I since Nov. the 8<sup>th</sup>. — My dear old Ladies are keeping well.[728]

I am all right, but of course growing older & than things go slower & I want more rest in the afternoon. I walk every day. —

I am growing more shortsighted & that ought not to be the case. I follow a treatment because it is handicapping not to see at any distance. I can read without any fatigue.

Alice Athlone[729] is travelling through Africa on her return.

We have many unemployed also and there is a great malaise. — I must stop. I do so in sending you heaps of love & every good wish for Christmas. Ever your affectionate

Emma

I like this photo & drawing of my child & send it therefore as Xmascard

---

**728**  Baroness E.G. 'Elise' van Ittersum and Lady F.L.H. 'Henriette' van de Poll were ladies-in-waiting to Queen Emma from 18 October 1879 until Emma's death in 1934; see introduction above telegram 53, note 72 and p. 31, note 66.

**729**  At the end of December 1930, Wilhelmina's cousin, Alice Athlone, Duchess of Albany (1883-1981), her husband Alexander (1874-1957), Earl of Athlone, who was Governor General of South Africa between 1927 and 1930, and their daughter May (1906-1994) completed a long farewell tour of Africa and the Middle East. They returned to England on 5 May 1931. After their return, on 24 October, May married Henry Abel Smith (1900-1993). See Alice, *Overland to England through Africa and the Middle East*, pp. 188-211.

Folding card with Emma on the front, with the year written in pencil: '1931':

296 Dear Miss Winter! Many thanks for your dear letter & pretty card with loving wishes. I am so sorry your eyes are troublesome. Do be careful in going out, the motors are getting more & more impertinent.

I am all right, only my thumb is troublesome through gout & that at this moment! It is not bad but makes writing difficult & bad.

For the New Year I send you my most affectionate wishes. God grant you & your Sister good health & many happy hour.

God bless you Dear Miss Winter & keep you in His holy ? is the wish of your very affectionate Emma

# 1931

Het Loo

May 15 1931

297 My dear old Friend,

You cannot imagine <u>how</u> beautiful the surroundings are in the place I am writing from. It is All spring-glorie! Many thanks for your last letter and dear Easter-wishes. We were then still in the House of the Woods where I enjoyed immensely the quite early spring in March.

I hope you are doing quite well now and are enjoying yourself as much as we are.

We had a tiring winter with a lot of social duties; which are not as nice as at door work! My girl has started out here some social work and has taken up the responsabilities of my lady which now looks after my people and the poor; whilst she is having a long holyday; Juliana likes these functions very much and is very obsorbed in them. We have some times such nice talks about all this work, in which I of course take much interest.

We hope to start for my holyday in the middle of June;[730] we are not going to Norway this year, but to France and Germany; I hope it will not be too hot there.

Mother has just left town, and has established herself quite near to here, during that they are moving her household to Soestdijk — she always does lately and get a glimpse each time of another part of the Country — what is quite a good idea. It is so nice to know she will soon be settled in the country.[731] I wonder whether you also can enjoy sitting out and taking walks now and then. What about reading and literature now. My child is so fond of that and knows quite a

---

730 Between 15 June and 30 July 1931, Queen Wilhelmina, Prince Hendrik and Princess Juliana visited France (Paris from 16–21 June, with a visit to the International Colonial Exhibition, Troyes, Les Trois Epis, Riquewihr, Ammerschwir and Kaysersberg); Switzerland (Basel); Austria (Nikolsdorf — Lengberg Castle, and trips to, among others, Weissensee, Heiligenblut and Gross Glockner); Italy (Cortina d'Ampezzo); and Germany (Munich).
731 With this, Wilhelmina means Soestdijk Palace.

lot about it. But now I must cease chattering; otherwise this letter will never be finished. With very much love and best wishes for a happy summer I ever remain your faithful old friend

Wilhelmina

Soestdijk
Sept. the 4<sup>th</sup> 1931

**298**   Dear Miss Winter!

I hope this letter shall reach you on the eve of the 5$^{th}$. It is to convey to you my most affectionate wishes for the new year of your life! I pray & hope that your health will not trouble you as much as it has done lately & that you may be spared grief and anxiety on behalf of those you love! Enclosed I send a cheque of 25 £ so that you should be at ease if your eyes want attended to. I was horrified last year, when I ordered a specialy mounted (imitation) pair of spectacles in London, about the price! I was told that that kind of thing always 3 time the price here in the country!

Many thanks for your dear letter. I spent 3 very happy days at the Loo with my sister Erbach.[732] My child was well & in the sweetest of moods. I am very well, but feel my age & want a rest after a fatiguing day & must keep quiet before a fatigue. —

I was to a family gathering at Burgsteinfurt, for the home coming of the 2$^d$ wife of Adolf Bentheim, my brother & wife, my sister, all the Bentheims were there.[733]

The post is going. So goodbye with very much love ever your very affectionately

Emma

Christmas card with the text:

**299**   Most affectionate wishes also for your sister for a peaceful blessed Christmas & for 1932

from
Emma

---

**732**  Between 21 and 24 August 1931, Emma was in Burgsteinfurt to attend the marriage of the Prince of Bentheim-Steinfurt (see following note). Her sister Elisabeth, the Princess of Erbach-Schönberg, went back to Soestdijk Palace with her and stayed there until 9 September. Between 29 August and 1 September, they were together at Het Loo for Wilhelmina's birthday. On 3 September, the Princess of Erbach visited the former emperor of Germany in Doorn.
**733**  Victor Adolf (1883–1961), the second son of Emma's sister Pauline and Alexis, Prince of Bentheim-Steinfurt, married for the second time in 1931. His second wife was Rosa Helena, Princess of Solms-Hohensolms-Lich (1901–1963). They had three daughters and four sons together. His first marriage in 1921 to Stephanie, Princess of Schaumburg-Lippe (1899–1925), had resulted in three sons.

Badly written by Emma, who was convalescing from illness:

[Voorhout Palace]734

300    Am recovering well but slowly must avoid every exertion also writing. Miss
R.[eichardt] shall do so after N. Year. Enclosed £ 25. £ 10 are Wilhelmina Xmas
present. The other £ 15 come from me. Am sure you have extra expense illness &
perhaps crisis. W. asked me to enclose her Xmas gift as I can ensure it much love

E.

Undated Xmas and New Year's card from: 'Wilhelmina'

301    with warmest thanks for your dear xmas & new years wishes and kind sympathy
with my mothers illness. She is recovering slowly, she has to obey strictly the
doctors orders; she is very bright and happy and we go and see her every day.
Much love from us all.


# 1932

Soestdijk
Sept. the 4<sup>th</sup> 1932

302    My dear Miss Winter!
I want you to have a letter of myself on your birthday, my thoughts will be much
with you.
  I pray that God may bestow His richest blessing on you & make the new year of
your life a good one. I have so many wishes for you! For your poor eyes, for your
general health, for the welbeing of your dear sister, for all the patience you want
& (I am sure you display) & for a great amount of courage to face the difficulties
of life.
  I am enclosing a cheque for £ 25 as birthday present, as I am afraid you will be
getting doctor bills.
  Miss Reichardt<sup>735</sup> gave you news lately, many thanks for your dear letters.
  I had two very happy days at the Loo.
  With a little governess cart I went to see all the beloved spots in the park. —
  I had not been anywhere last year.
  I hope to start for a change of air on Sept. the 15<sup>th</sup>.
  With my very best love also to your sister & heaps of good wishes I ever am
your very affectionate

Emma


734  At the beginning of November 1931, Queen Emma cut short her stay in Baden-Baden with
a cold, which proved to be persistent and lasted some time. Only in the course of January did
she start going out again.
735  Queen Emma's lectrice Miss Jenny Reichardt (see letter 313, note 742).

303  Dear Miss Winter!

Today I want to send you my most affectionate wishes for a blessed & peaceful Christmas! Enclosed my present a cheque of £ 25. I am afraid this money must go to practical things. The cards enclosed are a reproduction of 2 pictures (oilpaintings) of my child.[736]

For the new year I send you as well as your sister my most affectionate wishes, may you both remain well, your eyes be less troublesome, much love and affection granted you

Ever your most affectionate old friend                                    Emma


Emma wrote on the first card: *Sidefront of the Old Loo*: With many wishes for a blessed Christmas 1932 from Emma; on the second one, she wrote: *Pond at Het Loo in autumn mist*: Most affectionate wishes for 1933.


# 1933

PALEIS HET LOO

Mei [1933]

304  Dear Miss Winter

May I bring you my heartiest thanks for your kind letter with good wishes for the coming year at my birthday?

I am making still half secret plans of going in more western directions this summer, so I hope very really to see you soon again, if another time you would be so kind as to let me tell all the news I know to you![737]

With much love and many thanks

Yours afectionately

Juliana


736 In 1932, Queen Wilhelmina held the first exhibition of her work at the Kleykamp Gallery in The Hague, in aid of the victims of the crisis. The work would then be exhibited in various places in the Netherlands, followed by exhibitions in the Dutch East Indies in 1933 and the Netherlands Antilles and Suriname in 1934. In addition to a catalogue, folders of picture postcards of the queen's work were produced (see Emerentia van Heuven-van Nes, 'Een aandachtige bezichtiging ten volle waard. De tentoonstellingen van het werk van koningin Wilhelmina [An attentive display of great value. The exhibitions of the work of Queen Wilhelmina]' in: Spliethoff, pp. 37-55).

737 Princess Juliana visited London between 1 and 12 July 1933. In addition to going to see Miss Saxton Winter, she also visited the National Gallery and the Wimbledon tennis championships, among others.

305   My dear old friend,

Many loving thanks for your letter which touched me deeply; I am so very happy and thankful my child brought you some sunshine by her visit and could bring me direct news of you and tell you all about us. I fear your poor eyes must be a great trouble for you. But I am happy she could tell me that you feel content and are well looked after.

She came home perfectly enthousiastic about all she did and saw. She had a very crowded programm. It was such a great pleasure reading all your impressions of her and what you write about the result of her education. We have indeed tried to give her much freedom and contact with the people of all classes and never check her independance where this was not absolutely necessary and so now she feels perfectly happy in going about alone and being quite herself. She is a great sunshine to us and is always a true and gay companion to her many friends.

I am at last getting rested and hope by staying here still a time to get back the strength of a young lion.

With very much love from my child and myself and best wishes for you and sister I ever remain your loving old friend

Wilhelmina

Telegram from Wilhelmina:

306   's Gravenhage, 5 september 1933:

Miss Saxton Winter, S Walden

My very best loving wishes for your birthday much love

Wilhemina [written without the 'l']

Soestdijk
Sept. the 4<sup>th</sup> 1933

307   Dear Miss Winter!

Today I want to send you my most affectionate wishes for the new year of your life & to tell you that my thoughts & prayers shall be with you on that day. I do so hope you are feeling well & that your dear Sister has recovered or is making good progress.

I am afraid you will be wanting much courage & patience as your poor eyes are giving so much trouble. I pray that God may give you strength & comfort.

Enclosed my birthday presen 25 £. I am afraid they must go to practical and necessary things.

Many thanks for 2 dear letters & wishes for my childs birthday.

I was so glad to hear about you by Juliana. When she said goodbye before leaving for England I said to her, how happy Miss Winter would be if you could go & see her, but you want have time. To my joy she anwered: A visit to Miss

Winter 'staat vast op mijn program, ik zal en moet tijd voor hebben [is on my programme, I will and must make time for that]'.[738]

Juliana enjoyed her visit to Alice[739] immensely.

The letter must go.

With heaps of love and good wishes your very affectionate

Emma

Paleis Voorhout<br>Dec. the 22<sup>d</sup> 1933[740]

**308**  Dear Miss Winter

Enclosed I send you my Xmas present £15 with much love. I hope you and your dear Sister are pretty well & have not suffered by sudden changes of weather.

Since 1890 <u>we</u> have not had such a cold in December! Miss Reichardt told you that I am keeping well.

But circumstances are very depressing just now & that tells also on my child. One hears of so much misery & poverty.

With much love & most affectionate wishes also for your Sister ever your very affectionate

Emma

New Year's card with a view on the entrance gate of 'Buren':[741]

**309**  Thanking you for your dear wishes I send you my heartiest wishes for 1934

Wilhelmina

Christmas and New Year's card:

Printed: Greetings. With all good wishes for Christmas and the New Year

**310**  'In remembrance of a too nice afternoon in Saffron Walden in 1933 Juliana'

---

738  Emma wrote the part between inverted commas in Dutch.

739  Princess Alice, Countess of Athlone, the daughter of Emma's sister Helena.

740  Queen Emma did not date the letter, but her reference to the cold weather in December suggests that it was written in 1933. In that year, it froze between 2 and 17 December, with the temperature hitting a low-point of minus 13.1 on 14 December. This would be her last letter to the English governess.

741  Wilhelmina is the Countess of Buren. Buren, which lies in the Province of Gelderland and was granted a charter in 1395, is where William of Orange married Anna van Buren. Members of the House of Orange sometimes use 'Van Buren' as a pseudonym.

# 1934

12–1–34 Picture postcard from Unterwasser:

**311** Warmest thanks dear letter, we are so enjoying this delightful stay, our young friends do all much skiing. I enjoy healthy air and rest. What you received was my present which I told you I was sending in my last telegram. Hope you are doing well and having a sunny winter. Much love from W

On 20 March 1934, Queen Emma died at Lange Voorhout Palace, aged 75.
Telegram: 20–3–1934:

**312** This morning my dear mother passed away peacefully

Wilhelmina

Emma's lectrice, Mrs Jenny Reichardt,[742] wrote to Miss Winter about Emma's last hours:

Palais Voorhout in the Hague, March 30th, 1934

**313** Dear Miss Winter,

I long to write you some lines as I know how much your thoughts will be with us, sharing our deep, deep grief. —

How is it possible, that after an illness of a few days our dear, dear Queen Mother has been taken away quite softly & peacefully!

You will remember mij last letter!

Her Majesty then was perfectly well enjoying more than the last years everything, only the morning walk tired Her, & the medical man always warned not to tire Herself by walking.

The Queen Mother had neither cold or chill until 12 March. Then the phyciciain was awfully careful, & soon afterwards Her Majesty felt quite well.

During the night from Tuesday 13th to Wednesday the 14th of March the Queen Mother got fever, was laid up, but nobody supposed any danger though the medical man desired the Royal family back from the Loo, where they had spent some days.

The state of health of the Queen-Mother did not at all seem hopeless. —
Monday March 19th even seemed to be a favorable day. Her Majesty gave orders & took interest in many things, but there was not question of bronchitis, it was an inflammation of the lungs, & when we had supposed that any danger was

---

742 In 1902 Jenny Reichardt became lectrice to Queen Emma, succeeding Mrs Mathilda Kreusler, who had come from Arolsen with Emma upon the latter's marriage, and died in 1902. Reichardt served Emma until the latter's death in 1934. Among other things, she kept the cash books of Emma's expenditure (A47a -III, Petty cash). In 1929 she made an overview of the 'State of the jewels belonging to Her Majesty the Queen Mother' (A47-V-07) and she was responsible for certain correspondence. Another lectrice to Queen Emma was Mrs J.W. Jurriaanse-Steenkamp (1901–1990), who was made assistant-lectrice on 1 April 1925 and fulfilled this role until Emma's death in 1934.

over, in the morning of the 20$^{st}$ of March, our dear, dear Queen Mother quietly sleeping passed away, when the Royal Family was with Her. It was an hour of such a great peace, that one must thank God for having blessed our beloved mistress on her deathbed, sparing Her any grief.

The Prince Frederic of Waldeck was present, but the Princess of Erbach arrived to late. [743]

I shall send you some papers. Perhaps somebodij of your friends knows Dutch & will be able to read them to you.

The Palais Voorhout is awfully desert.

I must be very busy, but the poor old Ladies in waiting?[744] Her Majesty the Queen is very kind to them, to all of us.

The Queen bears wonderfully that deep, deep grief.—

What an immense loss for all those who have known the Queen Mother & who had some relations with Her Majesty.

For me the sun for ever has gone, you will understand.

I know your grief is ours, & ours is yours, so I beg you to accept my most sincerest sympathy, dear Miss Winter.

Your devoted & obedient

Jenny Reichardt

While Princess Juliana took a vacation in England from 14 June, on 23 June, Queen Wilhelmina set out alone for Brig (Switzerland). On 29 June, she had to cut her holiday short because Prince Hendrik had had a heart attack. His second heart attack would prove to be fatal.

Kensington Palace W.8<br>July 3rd 1934

**314**  Dear Miss Winter,

Three days Father had a heart attack and to-day he has had a repetition, and now, I am leaving England.

There is one thing my heart grieves about and that you understand is, that I did not come to you. I counted coming the 10$^{th}$: I hope but also sort of expect that it will happen all the same some day.

Funny, one never can be sure about one's plans. I had such a delightful time here in England, a time of my life, it could not become more delicious than it has been now, so that is scarcely a reason to be sad.

Mother very prudently told me to-day that Father had passed away — I am longing to go to her. Though after Grandmothers death, death really does not mean anything but lovely things to me anymore and I know Mother feels so only all the stronger. Father was quite gay this morning, she said, and then it happened afterwards in a second, not in her presence.

---

743 Prince Frederik is Emma's brother Friedrich 'Fritz', and the Princess of Erbach is Emma's sister Elisabeth 'Lily'.

744 Baroness E.G. van Ittersum and Lady F.L.H. van de Poll.

Is it not lovely, so suddenly. I am so glad to know since Grandmother went, that every life is going to end happily, bij "death".

I am getting philosophic — please don't mind. If you knew how sorry I am, that I can't come that is too awful.

Much love dear Miss Winter

from your affectionate

Juliana

Letter from Jenny Reichardt:

Palais Voorhout

August 5<sup>th.</sup> 1934.

**315**   Dear Miss Winter,

just back from Soestdijk, where I had to arrange things in that big lonely palace, I got your kind letter & I haste to answer all your questions.

I was verij sorry to hear that you had a bad fall, but hope you soon will be better by the care of your dear sister.

Concerning the things, the Queen charged me to forward, I am sure, you can always use the scarp & the little knitted jacket, even the cloak, every lady of your condition can wear it, — of you can have arranged it in something you like more.

I can't give you now the Queen's address, as I ignore it, but I schall ask the Queen's Lectrice, & keep these lines until I know it. Her Majesty is making trips & changes address very often, but then letters will follow.

I was told that the Queen has the intention to return to the Hague between September 7<sup>th</sup> & 12 <sup>th.</sup>

In less than a fortnight I shall be in Germany at Niedermarsberg, where I have no relations & no acquaintances, but a dear poor <u>niece</u>, who is not quite normal. I shall be able to bring some joy in her poor life & to make the mother happy, who lives in Berlin, as her other daughters must have the occasion to finish her studies.

1. The two ladies in waiting, Baroness v. Ittersum & Miss van der Poll left the Palace Voorhout last week. They have been here the whole time, receiving many visitors & undertaking many drives by motor. The Baroness, even with her bad eyes is able to walk much. She is accompanied by her maid, & now lives with her in a comfortable flat, where one cleans her rooms & prepares the meals. —

Freule van der Poll, most deeply grieved by the loss of our beloved Mistress, has returned to Zeist in the house[745] of her parents, where she will live with her brother & with two sisters, but the youngest sister that very nice creature, gave her room to Freule Henriette and took a room or more in a house just opposite, meaning that in this way she would be more free for her pianolessons she gives since years. — We have been so preoccupied during all these months, that when

---

745  This is 'Beek en Royen' House on Tweede Dorpstraat, Zeist.

we said "good-by" to each other, we felt quite indifferent, though perhaps we shall never see each other again in this life. I regretted very much that awful state of feeling, but Freule van de Poll comforted me, saying, that it was quite the same with her. We have had to great a soul-trouble, which causes that indifference, but later we shall feel most intensly that separation, & we will write long letters to each other, –

2. — Mijn address is: Niedermarsberg ᶦ/ Westf. c/o Hernn Jesper. — Until now I ignore the street?

3. — The Palace in the Voorhout⁷⁴⁶ will be shut, — (close). Nobody will live here, — perhaps later but not now. We find this awful, but can understand it, because the financial circumstances now are <u>very</u> difficult. Also Soestdijk⁷⁴⁷ will be shut. — Only a few of servants will take care of these two palaces. —

4. Everybody is wishing that Princess Juliana will soon be married, but <u>nobody</u> knows something about this question???⁷⁴⁸

We had hoped that in England there was some change? Papers always bring all kind of news, which never are true.

I am most pleased bij your proposal, that I may give you news from time to time, and as I hope to remain in connection with the Royal families & with the Netherlands, I shall be able to give you the news — you desire to have. —

You will forgive me that untidy letter, badly written, but you understand, that my forces during the last four months have diminished. — It was awful that staying in the Palace without the dear Queen-Mother, but as I had to do all kind of duties, the last, I could do for Her, — I felt happy in doing my task.

I can understand, that Hitler⁷⁴⁹ is not appriciated in other countries, but we Germans believe in him, & think him the man God has sent us in those very

---

**746**  Lange Voorhout Palace was built in 1764 by Pieter de Swart and bought in 1845 by King Willem II. Queen Emma used it as a winter residence between 1901 and her death in 1934. Queen Juliana used it as her workplace, and it functioned as the beginning- and endpoint of the ceremonial procession on Prinsjesdag (the day of the Queen's speech). Princess Juliana sold the building to the Dutch State in 1991, and it has been a museum since 1992. In 2002, the Escher Museum was established there.

**747**  Princess Juliana and Prince Bernhard would choose Soestdijk Palace as their home after their marriage in 1937, and would live there until their deaths in 2004. With the exception of the official rooms, the palace was subsequently emptied and made ready to be opened to the public, something that was possible until 2011. Now and then, special events are held at the palace or the park is used for a special performance. On 8 June 2017, it was announced that Soestdijk Palace would be operated by the Made by Holland consortium. The palace and estate will be transformed into a platform for innovation and enterprise in the fields of water management, sustainable energy, health, agriculture and nutrition. This will provide networking opportunities for institutes, businesses and start-ups. The palace, orangery and stables will have catering and hotel facilities, and housing will be built on the edge of the site.

**748**  At this time, there were rumours of a possible engagement with Prince Carl of Sweden (1911–2003).

**749**  The Austrian-born Adolf Hitler (1889–1945) became leader of the National Socialist German Workers' Party. He became chancellor in 1933. His attempts to reverse the humiliations of the Treaty of Versailles for Germany and his expansionist politics of creating

great difficulties. So we are willing to go with him & to support him, that he can do his task, but if the bad elements prevent every success, so that that instrument will be broken, we fear, Germany will perish, not only Germany, but Europe & the Bolschivisme will be everywhere. —

Though our dear Queen-Mother could not approve that new system, Her Majesty allowed me in November to go to Germany for the election. I was very grateful, that I could do it, & I assure you, that all of us will do our best, that the new tendency will bring peace for all the countries in the world. But very great sacrifices are asked, and Hitler himself makes every sacrifice. —

Freule v.d. Poll's address is: Zeist.

Prov. Utrecht.

Holland

Baroness E.v. Ittersum the Hague.

20 Rg. Schimmelpenninncklaan

the Hague.

With many thanks for your lovely, sweet letter, I beg you to forgive me all the mistakes in this writing & to believe me with the most kind regards your obedient

Jenny Reichardt.

Between 28 July and 10 September 1934, Wilhelmina and Juliana spent their holidays in Norway: Ulvik, Hardanger fjord, Fagernes, Lillehammer, Lillestrøm and Oslo.

AASGAARDEN TURISTHOTEL

INDEH.: JOH. SVENDSEN

TELF. NO. 10           [Aasgaardstrand den] 3 Sept. [19]34

**316**   My dear old Friend,

Thank you ever so much for thinking of August the second and writing to me such a dear letter.[750] I have been very lazy just during this holiday with writing and so it lasted so long till you got your answer. We are spending both birthdays in August up here in Norway because travelling one forgets the calendar and sad dates pass unnoticed. But the real reason I am writing to day is your dear birthday. My loving thoughts will be with you with all good wishes for the coming year. May it bring you many rays of sunshine and not bother you with illness. I hope so you are doing well at present and have had a nice summer. I took a lot of rest over here as I was badly run down after all I went through, but now I am getting on all right.

We are leaving this country on Saturday and our boat is due at Amsterdam on Monday. We will have a lot to do on coming home and will begin by going to the

---

'Lebensraum' for Germany led to the outbreak of the Second World War, which Germany would lose. He would commit suicide in Berlin on 30 April 1945.

**750** Queen Emma's birthday was on 2 August.

House in the Woods and in October we hope to go to the Loo. All is so changed for us, that where ever we go we will have to start afresh.

With ever so much love I ever remain your true and faithful old friend

Wilhelmina

With very much love from my child and myself and best wishes for you and sister I ever remain your loving old friend

Wilhelmina

On the reverse of two photographs: 'Wilhelmina in white morning dress at Het Loo' and 'Wilhelmina with her daughter Juliana', Wilhelmina wrote:

Dec. 26 1934

**317** My dear old friend, I am inclosing here with my Xmas present for you. Thank you so much for all your dear letters with so much tender thought and care about me and finally for your Xmas card and letter with dear wishes. I hope you are well and bright now and your teeth don't worry you any more. We are having of course a very quiet Xmas, and have been wonderfully helped through. The 20th, 21th and 22d we had Xmas trees for different circles of our people at the Loo. I am so happy my child could pay you a visit, it was so nice hearing her tell all about it.[751] Now she wishes, to write down a few words. So much love, keep bright and well my dear old friend.

Wilhelmina.

Juliana wrote: Dear Miss Winter,
Thank you very much for the nice Xmas card, I too hope you had a happy Xmas, and that the new year will bring you nothing but the best things of its stock! I thank you very much too for your kind dear letter of this month. It was such fun coming. We need our time well, did n't we? What a nice feeling of welcome you give one always, like your sister too.—

We did have adventures on the way home, but arrived more or less at time, and saw a magnificent Hamlet.

With much love yours affectionately,

Juliana

# 1935

In Unterwasser, Switzerland, Queen Wilhelmina and Princess Juliana enjoyed a winter sports holiday with friends between 20 February and 12 March 1935.

---

751 Between 20 November and 4 December 1934, Princess Juliana was back in England, where she was bridesmaid at the marriage of Prince George, Duke of Kent (1902–1942), and Princess Marina of Greece (1906–1968) on 29 November. She will have visited Miss Winter at that time.

Telegram from Wilhelmina, s Gravenhage, to Miss Winter, dated 24 March 1935:

**318** Warmest thanks dear letter & loving sympathy, came home from skying a week
ago, passed a few days at the Loo

Wilhelmina

Between 6 August and 11 September 1935, Wilhelmina and Juliana spent their holidays in
St. Fillans, Perthshire, Scotland. On the reverse of a picture postcard showing 'Moonlight
on Loch Earn, St. Fillans', the queen wrote from the Drummond Arms Hotel, St. Fillans:

**319** Warmest thanks for your dear sympathy and letter. I send you from this restfull
place a message of dear love. I want to tell you that I hope to visit you on my
way back the 7th of next month. I hope to visit you quite in the way Juliana did
last year. Please don't make any expenses. I am looking forward to see you and
your own dear home. Much love also from J.

Wilhelmina

Het Loo 10 Nov. 1935

**320** My dear old Friend,

You will think me — I am sure — most ungrateful as to not writing before now
how intensely I enjoyed our visit to you both and seeing your dear home. It was
such an immense joy being with you, my dear, dear old friend and talking with
as in far gone by times. I was so happy to find you morally quite unchanged
and in such good spirits, notwithstanding the worry of your poor eyes! What a

Queen Wilhelmina is seen off by her ex-governess Miss Winter and her sister, after she,
accompanied by her daughter Princess Juliana, had paid them a three-hour visit in Saffron
Walden, 7 September 1935. Eastern Press Agency.

courage you must have and what a blessing to have your dear sister to help and look after you with so much love and care. I am including my present which I send you every year and which I forgot to bring, what would have been of course the most convenient for both of us. Now I must still thank you for your dear letter after our visit. I am so sorry of this delay on my side.

As Rotteveel[752] telefoned from Balcombe I was layed up with fever on Monday after having unjudiciously taken an aspirine the day before during daytime. Luckily the fever lasted only a day, we had to postpone our return home for one day, what was very nice for seeing my cousin[753] a bit more, but disasterous for our plans, for it cancelled our visit to a very important cattleshow! After that we have no quiet moment till we came here the beginning of October and I had to take some rest at that time.

As we had many nice weekends with heeps of guests I was still rather busy. So that this is the excuse for my not writing sooner.

The colours came very late, but were simply beautiful and I much enjoyed painting them. We must now be thinking of going to town soon. And wintersport comes and some rest fits in then. J. sends her love and I join in for you and your sister.

With a hug ever your true old friend

Wilhelmina

It was the last contact. Just over two-and-a-half months later, on 29 January 1936, Miss Elizabeth Saxton Winter died, aged 78, in Saffron Walden.

**752** E10-11a-8 en 9. Hendricus Godefridus Rotteveel (born 1876) became a footman in July 1904. He was made first footman on 1 April 1911, and, as of 30 April 1926, valet to Princess Juliana.

**753** Wilhelmina's cousin Princess Alice (see letter 176, note 405).

The last letter from Queen Wilhelmina to her English governess, Het Loo, 10 November 1935.

# Conclusion

One could not get a better impression of Wilhelmina than from her own direct observations, recorded in her letters to Miss Winter from when she was a six-year-old girl to when she was a middle-aged woman; certainly a better impression than that given by her autobiography, *Eenzaam maar niet alleen [Lonely but not alone]*, which she wrote in her seventies, looking back on her life. Her biography was thus coloured by all that she had experienced in her lifetime, including two world wars, the crisis of the 1930s, and a not particularly happy marriage, which had left her a widow in 1934; but also the good fortune of having had a special mother, Queen Emma, and a child, her daughter Juliana.

It will have become clear from Wilhelmina's letters, and from the accompanying notes, that it was no easy undertaking for Miss Elizabeth Saxton Winter to assist with the upbringing of an only child, as Wilhelmina was, at the Dutch court. A child who had become a queen aged ten, and who had to be addressed as 'ma'am' by her peers; a child on whom it was impressed at an early age that she would not be allowed to turn out like her feeble half-brothers; she had to be strong and tough, and stand firm on her own two feet. This was the task that Miss Saxton Winter was given when she entered the service of King Willem III in 1886, but she took her instructions from his wife, Queen Emma. The king left the education of his 'Wimmy' to his wife. The latter took up the responsibility with zeal and sought the advice of experts as to which tutors to appoint when the princess/queen had to be educated – always alone. Miss Winter was always present at her classes, whilst Queen Emma attended occasionally at the beginning, and later regularly, when she made notes on certain lessons.

The situation changed following the death of King Willem III in 1890. For Queen Emma – a foreigner aged just 32 – it was a difficult task, as a single mother and the first lady, even as regent, to have to sit on the Dutch throne in a society that was largely run by older men, whilst at the same time having to prepare her daughter, 'the little queen' who in 1890 was still playing intensively with her dolls, to assume – in just eight years' time – the role of sovereign when she turned eighteen. In this new situation, Miss Winter's task also became more difficult, because Emma had less time to occupy herself with her child. This also explains why the regent named her lady-in-waiting, Lady van de Poll, as the 'superintendent of Wilhelmina's education'. Miss Winter must have found this difficult. The fact that mother and daughter were counselled by their sister-in-law and aunt, respectively, Sophie of Saxe-Weimar, never to become intimate with the members of the royal household and to keep their distance, meant that both felt imprisoned in a cage and had almost no one to whom they could pour out their feelings. No letter expressed this better than that written after the death of Wilhelmina's aunt Sophie in March 1897.

Thus Emma — who had spent her own youth in a large, companionable but well-disciplined family –had Wilhelmina brought up, owing to the circumstances, in a very constrained fashion. This was only magnified by Emma's punctuality. Everything was scheduled down to the last minute, and it is understandable that Emma found it hard to let her daughter go after Wilhelmina's confirmation in 1896, when the girl could spend a few hours how she pleased for the first time in her life. In addition, there was a lack of real friends. During her youth, Wilhelmina was never permitted to go and play with others. Moreover, the children who were invited to play with her were selected beforehand in turn; something that did not always please them, meaning that there could have been little spontaneity. Neither was there intimate contact with the ladies-in-waiting.

All of this made Wilhelmina into the woman that she would become, and that she had to become, in her mother's opinion: a resilient, tough, disciplined woman; a woman who found her greatest pleasure in her pastimes of horse-riding, drawing and painting; in Paleis Het Loo and the surroundings; in being alone in God's nature; in her own belief in God; and, of course, also in her only child Juliana. She was a lonely woman, but luckily one who also had her own unique sense of humour. At the beginning, as shown by her letters, she also found happiness with Hendrik, although this dwindled in the course of their marriage; but after his death, she nevertheless recalled him with affection in *Eenzaam maar niet alleen*.

Various passages in Wilhelmina's letters reveal clearly how difficult things were for Queen Emma, due to the multitude of duties that her position demanded; and how grateful Wilhelmina was to have had a mother like Queen Emma. The latter was her great example, whom she considered the loveliest gift from heaven, who guided her and lived for her, and with whom she long formed, until her marriage, a kind of duality.

Wilhelmina's letters constantly reveal how she sympathized with her governess, when the latter was on holiday, and how she always cheered her up and counselled her when things were difficult at home, owing to her mother's sickness. One matter of concern was likewise her behaviour towards her governess, which she hoped to improve in the New Year. Her fault, her 'impatience', was also something on which she wanted to work. And it is understandable that she was 'benauwd [anxious]' about meeting all the guests at her first ball in early 1897, although Wilhelmina soon noticed that those present were satisfied by her merely bowing at them or saying good-day.

She also addressed politics in her letters, although not frequently. One notable example is that of the Dreyfus Affair in 1898, when she explained in detail to Miss Winter why she supported the French Army, not Zola, who had taken Dreyfus' side. The English desire to take South Africa brought her close to a confrontation with Miss Winter. Wilhelmina was on the side of the Boers, causing Miss Winter to think that she had lost a friend in Wilhelmina. The skirmishes in Aceh in the Dutch East Indies were dismissed with a comment in 1898: 'We were always the winning side.'

Wilhelmina's English and German family members played an important role, with visits, attendance at celebrations and meetings during travels. In one of the last notable letters, written by Emma's lectrice in 1934, vague reference is already made to the approaching Second World War. The outbreak of war would lead Wilhelmina to turn her back on her German family, whilst by contrast, the contact with her English cousin, Princess Alice, Helena's daughter, was maintained. On their arrival in Canada in June 1940, Princess Juliana and her two daughters, Beatrix and Irene, would even stay for a short time with Alice and her husband, the Count of Athlone, because the latter had just been made Governor General of Canada. The bond between the House of Orange and Alice would remain strong until the latter's death in 1981.

Miss Winter dedicated herself unconditionally and devotedly to bringing her task to a satisfactory conclusion. In doing so, she effaced herself. How fortunate it must have been for Emma to have found someone who thought just like she did and who was prepared to stay, even though she was often at loggerheads with Wilhelmina and occasionally driven to extremes by her stubborn pupil's behaviour. Only after Miss Winter's departure did Wilhelmina see how important her governess had been for her over the past decade. In her letters, especially those written in the years leading up to her investiture in 1898, Wilhelmina expressed herself openly and spontaneously because she fully trusted her governess. After her marriage, the correspondence became less regular, but the contact was maintained in the form of picture postcards from the summer holidays, congratulations on Miss Winter's birthday, and greetings at Christmas and New Year, including from Queen Emma and Princess Juliana.

Miss Winter made an important contribution to building the foundations of Wilhelmina's life, in which devotion to duty, conscientiousness, dedication, and attention to and involvement with the Dutch people were essential characteristics; characteristics that were passed on to Wilhelmina's successors, her daughter Juliana and her granddaughter Beatrix, and, since 2013, the current successor, her great-grandson King Willem-Alexander.

Apeldoorn, January 2017

# Sources

## Archives

Royal Archives, The Hague:
Archive of the Treasurer, E8-vɪa-33 (decisions on salaries, allowances, etc., September 1908-August 1918)
Archive of the Journals of the Department of the Marshal to the Court of H.M. the Queen, E10-ɪvb-from July 1884 (16) until October 1902 (22)
Archive of the Register of employees, Department of the Marshal to the Court of H.M. the Queen, E10-ɪɪa-8 and 9
Archive of Queen Emma, Petty cash books, A47a-ɪɪɪ-2 t/m 4 (Registers signed by Miss Kreusler, 1880-1902)
Archive of Queen Emma, Items of Lady F.L.H. van de Poll, A47-ɪx-8 (speeches given by Queen Emma, written by Lady F.L.H. van de Poll)
Archive of Queen Wilhelmina, Notebook containing the names of playmates of Wilhelmina, A50-V-16;
Archive of Queen Wilhelmina, Cashbooks of Queen Wilhelmina, A50-V-19–19b (1888–1896)
Archive of Queen Wilhelmina, Letters of Miss Saxton Winter, A50-vɪɪc-S-02
Archive of Items originating from Miss Saxton Winter, G27 file no. 352, access no. E14b
Archive of Lady M.L. de Kock, G28

Archive of CODA (Cultuur Onder Dak Apeldoorn), Apeldoorn
*Erica Adres- en Jaarboekje 1887 voor de Gemeente Apeldoorn met plattegrond van Apeldoorn en Het Loo*, Third Volume, Apeldoorn (Felua B25)

Archive of the Dutch Evangelical Broadcasting Association (Evangelische Omroep), Hilversum

## General works

*Algemene Winkler Prins*, Encyclopaedia in fourteen volumes, Amsterdam-Brussels 1972
*Encyclopedie van het Koninklijk Huis*, Winkler Prins, Utrecht 2005
Internet
Isenburg, Wilhelm Karl Prinz von, *Europäische Stammtafeln*, Marburg 1975
*Nederlands Adelsboek*, 1903–2011
*Nederlands Patriciaat*, from 1910
*Staatsalmanak* from 1880

# Literature

**Alice**, H.R.H. Princess, *For my Grandchildren. Some Reminiscences*, London 1966.

**Barjesteh** van Waalwijk van Doorn, L.A.F., 'Contacten tussen Koninkrijk en Keizerrijk. Ontmoetingen tussen Van Oranje-Nassaus, Qajars en Pahlavis', in *Jaarboek Oranje-Nassau Museum 2000*, Rotterdam 2001, p. 61–85.

**Beaufort**, Henriette L.T. de, *Wilhelmina 1880–1962, Een levensverhaal*, 's-Gravenhage 1965.

**Beaufort, W.H. de**, *Dagboeken en aantekeningen van Willem Hendrik de Beaufort 1874–1918*, published by J.P. Valk and M. van Faassen, 2 volumes, 's-Gravenhage 1993.

**Boer,** Paul den, *Het Koninklijk Paleis Noordeinde historisch gezien*, Zutphen 1986.

**Brena**, Jörg, formerly Prince of Saxe-Weimar-Eisenach, 'Groothertogin Sophie van Saksen -Weimar-Eisenach, prinses der Nederlanden, een belangrijke sociale vorstin in de 19de eeuw' in: *Jaarboek Oranje-Nassau Museum 2000*, p. 7–33.

**Brus**, René, *De juwelen van het Huis Oranje-Nassau*, Haarlem 1996.

**Buckle**, George Earle, *The letters of Queen Victoria*, third series, London, 1931, Vol. II, 1891–1895, p. 499.

**Carvalho**, Trudie Rosa de, Paul Rem and Nicolaas Conijn, *Speel Goed op Het Loo. Koninklijk Speelgoed van Wilhelmina tot Amalia*, Zwolle 2008.

**Cleverens 1984** Cleverens, R.W.A.M., *Rose Villa. Herinnering aan Mevrouw H.A. Insinger-van Loon, Dame du Palais van H.M. Koningin Emma voor Amsterdam*, Middelburg 1984.

**Cleverens 1989** Cleverens, R.W.A.M., *Sire...... (II) Herinnering aan Z.M. Koning Willem III en H.M. Koningin Emma. "Souvenirs" van C.H.F. Graaf Dumonceau adjudant en particulier-secretaris van Z.M.*, Middelburg 1989.

**Cleverens 1991** Cleverens, R.W.A.M., *Als ik mij niet vergis... 'Souvenirs' van J.H.F. graaf Dumonceau opperceremoniemeester en grootmeester van H.M. Koningin Wilhelmina 1859–1952*, Middelburg 1991.

**Cleverens 1994** Cleverens, René, *Niet verder dan ons Huis... De Koninklijke Hofhouding. Het dagelijks leven in de paleizen Noordeinde en Het Loo 1870–1918*, Middelburg 1994.

**Cleverens 1997** Cleverens, René, *De Oranje-erfopvolging rond de eeuwwisseling. Troon-pretendenten en huwelijkskandidaten 1898–1909*, Middelburg 1997.

**Conijn,** Nicolaas, 'De stal als leerschool voor de natuur' in: Carvalho, *Speelgoed op Het Loo*, Zwolle 2008, pp. 101–121.

**Crawford**, Marion, *The little Princesses. The story of the Queen's childhood by her governess*, with a foreword by Jennie Bond, London 2002.

**Dekking/Loonstra** Dekking, N. and M. Loonstra, 'De Koningin-Regentes en de Geschiedenis van het Huis van Oranje' in: tent. cat.: *'Wij zijn er nog.' Het regentschap van koningin Emma 1890–1898*, Het Loo 1989/90.

**Elzenga** E., M. Loonstra and I. Mey (eds), *Koninklijk Gekleed Wilhelmina 1880–1962*, Zwolle 1998.

**Elzenga** E., M. Loonstra and I. Mey (eds), *In Royal Array Queen Wilhelmina 1880–1962*, Zwolle 1998

**EXTRA-NUMBER**, part of the *Nieuwe Rotterdamsche Courant* of 31 August 1898.

**Fasseur 1998** Fasseur, Cees, *Wilhelmina. De jonge koningin*, Amsterdam 1998.

**Fasseur 2001** Fasseur, Cees, *Wilhelmina. Krijgshaftig in een vormeloze jas*, Amsterdam 2001.

**Fasseur 2003** Fasseur, Cees, *Sterker door strijd*, Amsterdam 2003.

**Gediking**, F., 'Een Koninklijke leerling' in: *Oranje-Nassau. Mecklenburg-Schwerin. Gedenkboek*, Amsterdam 1901, pp. 87–95.

**Gedenkboek 1901,** *Oranje-Nassau Mecklenburg-Schwerin. Gedenkboek uitgegeven ter gelegenheid van het huwelijk van koningin Wilhelmina met hertog Hendrik van Mecklenburg-Schwerin*, Amsterdam 1901.

**Groenveld**, Philippe, *Koningin Wilhelmina 1880–1962 een geschreven portret*, Zaltbommel 1990.

**Halbertsma,** Marlite, *Charles Rochussen 1814–1894. Een veelzijdig kunstenaar*, Zwolle/ Rotterdam 1997.

**Hamann**, Brigitte, *Elisabeth, Kaiserin wider Willen*, Munich 1981, 1997.

**Hermans**, Dorine and Daniela Hooghiemstra, *'Vertel dit toch aan niemand'. Leven aan het hof*, Amsterdam 2006.

**Heuven 1989** Heuven-van Nes, E. van, 'Emma's jeugd en huwelijk' and 'De opvoeding van Wilhelmina' in tent. cat.: *'Wij zijn er nog.' Het regentschap van koningin Emma 1890–1898*, Het Loo 1989/90.

**Heuven 1990** Heuven-van Nes, E. van, *Koningin Wilhelmina en haar poppenverzameling*, unpublished manuscript, 1990.

**Heuven 1992** Heuven-van Nes, E. van, 'Vertoning op Het Loo' (Queen Wilhelmina as a comédienne) in: Elzenga, E. (ed.), *Het Witte Loo. Van Lodewijk Napoleon tot Wilhelmina 1806–1962*, Apeldoorn 1992, pp. 101–129.

**Heuven 1993** Heuven-van Nes, E. van, 'Koning Willem III en de watersnood van 1861', in *Jaarboek Oranje-Nassau Museum 1993*, Zutphen 1993, pp. 69–111.

**Heuven 2003** Heuven-van Nes, Emerentia van, 'I am now the only representative of my family' in: Els van den Bent, et al. (eds), *Een Vorstelijk Archivaris. Opstellen voor Bernard Woelderink*, Zwolle 2003, pp. 155–159.

**Heuven 2004** Heuven-van Nes, Renny van, 'Koningskinderen van 1880 tot 2003' in: E. Elzenga (ed.) *Oranje in de wieg. Over geboorte en doop van vorstenkinderen*, Paleis Het Loo National Museum, Apeldoorn 2004, pp. 36–59.

**Heuven 2004-1** Heuven-van Nes, Emerentia van, Annemarieke van Schaik and Marieke S. Spliethoff (eds), *Monumenten voor Nassau en Oranje*, Rotterdam 2004.

**Heuven 2008** Heuven-van Nes, Emerentia van, *Emma Koningin der Nederlanden, Prinses van Waldeck-Pyrmont 1858–1934*, Petersberg 2008. Publication to accompany dual exhibition held in Museum Bad Arolsen and Museum im Schloss Bad Pyrmont. The German publication has the title: *Königin der Niederlande Prinzessin zu Waldeck-Pyrmont 1858–1934*.

**Heuven 2011** Heuven-van Nes, Emerentia van, 'Joan Julien Marie Guy de Coral (1867–1930), amateurfotograaf, fotohandelaar en hoffotograaf' in *Jaarboek Oranje-Nassau 2011*, The Hague 2011.

**Heuven 2012** Heuven-van Nes, Emerentia van, *Dear old Bones, Brieven van Koningin Wilhelmina aan haar Engelse gouvernante Miss Elizabeth Saxton Winter 1886–1935*, Bussum 2012.

**Heuven 2015** Heuven-van Nes, Emerentia van, 'Een onverwachte vondst. Een prent-briefkaart uit juni 1922', *Jaarboek Oranje-Nassau 2015*, pp. 256–263.

**Heuven 2015** Heuven-van Nes, Emerentia van, *Nassau en Oranje in gebrandschilderd glas*, Hilversum 2015.

**Huisman,** Greddy, *Tussen salon en souterrain. Gouvernantes in Nederland*, Amsterdam 2000.

**Itallie**-van Embden, W. van, 'Op audiëntie bij H.M. de Koningin-Moeder', in: *Nieuwe Rotterdamsche Courant*, 9 January 1929.

**Kepper**, G.L., *Gedenkboek Koningin Wilhelmina in haar openbaar leven*, 's-Gravenhage 1989.

**Klooster**, L.J. van der and J.J. Bouman, *Oranje in beeld. Een familiealbum uit de 19de eeuw*, Zaltbommel 1966.

**Kroniek van Apeldoorn**, 1882–1889, compiled by W.J. de Muinck Keizer, Municipal Archives of Apeldoorn, 1983.

**Lammers**, Fred, *Wilhelmina Moeder des Vaderlands*, Baarn 1972.

**Liefde**-van Brakel, Tiny de, Annabella Meddens-van Borselen, et al., *Jan Willem van Borselen, 1825–1892. Schilder van het Hollandse polderlandschap. Wind en Wilgen*, Alkmaar/Woerden 2002.

**Lit,** Robert van, *De poppenhuizen van jonkvrouwe Lita de Ranitz*, Voorburg no date [2010].

**Loonstra**, M., *Uit Koninklijk Bezit. Honderd jaar Koninklijk Huisarchief: de verzamelingen van de Oranjes*, Zwolle/The Hague 1996, tent. cat. Noordbrabants Museum Den Bosch, Fries Museum Leeuwarden, Museum Lange Voorhout The Hague, 27 January -1 December 1996.

**Louda**, Jiři and Michael Maclagan, *Lines of Succession, Heraldry of the Royal Families of Europe*, London 1981.

**Mandache**, Diana, *Dearest Missy. The letters of Marie Alexandrovna Grand Duchess of Russia, Duchess of Edinburgh and of Saxe-Coburg and Gotha, and of her daughter, Marie Crown Princess of Romania 1879–1900*, Falköping, Sweden 2011.

**Manning**, A.F., 'Koningin Wilhelmina' in: C.A. Tamse (ed.), *Nassau en Oranje in de Nederlandse geschiedenis*, Alphen aan den Rijn 1979, pp. 359–397.

**Marie**, Queen of Romania, *The Story of My Life*, 2 volumes, London 1934.

**Marr**, Andrew, *The Diamond Queen. Elizabeth II and Her People*, London 2011.

**Meddens**-van Borselen, Annabella, 'Leven en werk' in: *Wind en Wilgen. Jan Willem van Borselen 1825–1892. Schilder van het Hollandse polderlandschap*, Alkmaar/Woerden 2002.

**Meij**, Ietse, 'Kledingleveranties voor een vorstelijke garderobe', in tent.cat. *Koninklijk Gekleed. Wilhelmina 1880–1962*, Zwolle 1998, pp. 13–59.

**Montijn,** Ileen, *Hoog Geboren. 250 Jaar adellijk leven in Nederland*, Amsterdam/ Antwerpen 2012.

**Nihom,** Nihom-Nijstad, Saskia, *Poppen van Oranje*, exhibition on the occasion of the 35th antiquities fair (Oude Kunst en Antiekbeurs), 14 October-2 November 1983, Stedelijk Museum Het Prinsenhof, Delft, Holland.

**Onder den Oranjeboom.** *Onder den Oranje boom. Nederlandse kunst en cultuur aan Duitse vorstenhoven in de zeventiende en achttiende eeuw*, tent.cat. Paleis Het Loo National Museum, Apeldoorn, Munich 1999.

**Osta**, A.P.J., *Drie vorstinnen. Brieven van Emma, Wilhelmina en Juliana*, Amsterdam 1995.

**Paleis Soestdijk.** *Paleis Soestdijk. Drie eeuwen huis van Oranje*, Amsterdam 2009.

**Rem**, Paul, *Hofmeubilair. Negentiende-eeuwse meubelen uit de collectie van Paleis Het Loo*, Zwolle 2003.

**Renting**, A.D. (ed.), *Paleis Het Loo. Een koninklijk museum*, Foundation Paleis Het Loo National Museum 2012.

**Rooseboom**, Hans, 'Een koningin voor iedereen', in: *Beelden in veelvoud, Leids Kunsthistorisch Jaarboek* 12, Leiden 2002, pp. 371–388.

**Schenk, dra. M.G.** and Magdaleen van Herk, *Juliana vorstin naast de rode loper*, Amsterdam/Brussels 1980.

**Schipper**-Swaneveld, Tineke, 'Wilhelmina kijken tussen de dijken': Chapter 7 'De Koninginnen in Tiel 13 augustus 1898', in *Tabula Batavorum*, Vol. xvi, No. 3 — 1998.

**Spliethoff 1998**, Spliethoff, Marieke E., *Feestelijke geschenken voor de jonge koningin 1898–1913*, Amsterdam/'s-Gravenhage 1998.

**Spliethoff 2006**, Spliethoff, Marieke E., Emerentia van Heuven-van Nes, Mieke Jansen and Paul Rem, *Koningin Wilhelmina. Schilderijen en tekeningen*, Zwolle 2006.

**Steyn,** S.A. van, 'Herinneringen aan de jeugd van Koningin Wilhelmina', Supplement to *Historia*, Vol. xiii 1948.

**Tamse 1981** Tamse, C.A. (ed.), *Koningin Wilhelmina*, Alphen aan den Rijn 1981.

**Tamse 1990** Tamse, C.A. (ed.), *Koningin Emma. Opstellen over haar regentschap en voogdij*, Baarn 1990.

**Verburg**, Marcel E., *Koningin Emma. Regentes van het koninkrijk*, Baarn 1989.

**Visser,** Dr. J.Th. de et al. (eds.), *De Koningin-Moeder 1879–1929. Gedenkboek ter herinnering aan den zeventigsten verjaardag en het vijftigjarig Nederlanderschap van Hare Majesteit*, Leiden 1928.

**Vijf eeuwen Nassau Oranje's,** tent. cat. Prinsenhof, Delft 1974.

**Vliegenthart**-van der Valk Bouman, 'J.M. W.A. Fabri, "Inrichting voor Vercieringskunst- Rotterdam"', in: Elzenga, E. (ed.), *Het Witte Loo. Van Lodewijk Napoleon tot Wilhelmina 1806–1962*, Apeldoorn 1992, pp. 151–172.

**Weekly News** Column Down Your Street: Jean Gumbrell visits South Road, 'The day royalty called on the Winter sisters', in: *Weekly News*, 25 September 1986.

**Wij zijn er nog.** *Het regentschap van Koningin Emma 1890–1898*, tent. cat. Rijksmuseum Paleis Het Loo, Apeldoorn 1989.

**Wilhelmina**, *Eenzaam maar niet alleen*, Amsterdam 1959.

**Winter,** E. Saxton, *Toen onze Koningin nog Prinsesje was. Persoonlijke Herinneringen uit de kinderjaren onzer Koningin door H M's ex-Gouvernante Miss . E Saxton Winter*, translated from the English version by H.S.S. Kuyper, with a foreword by the educationalist Jan Ligthart, 2nd edn, Amsterdam, no date.

**Withuis**, Jolande, *Juliana. Vorstin in een mannenwereld*, Amsterdam 2016.

**Zeepvat 2005,** Zeepvat, Charlotte, *Queen Victoria's Youngest Son. The untold story of Prince Leopold*, Stroud (Gl) 2005.

**Zeepvat 2006**, Zeepvat, Charlotte, *From Cradle to Crown. British Nannies and Governesses at the World's Royal Courts*, Stroud (Gl) 2006.

# Family Trees

The different family trees are marked with Roman numerals.

There are a lot of relations between the different families. A footnote symbol after a person's name indicates that the same person also appears in another family tree.

The figures 1, 2 and 3 indicate on first, second and third marriages and their descendants.

# I  Nassau, Orange-Nassau, Nassau-Weilburg, Waldeck-Pyrmont

Willem IV (1711–1751) ×
Anna of England (1709–1759)

Willem V (1748–1806) ×
Wilhelmina of Prussia (1751–1820)

Carolina (1743–1787) × ·······

Louise (1770–1819) ×
Karl of Brunswick-W. (1766–1806)

Willem I (1772–1843) ×
Wilhelmina of Prussia (1774–1837)

Frederik
(1774–1799)

Willem II (1792–1849) ×
Anna Paulowna of Russia (1795–1865)

Frederik* (1797–1881) ×
Louise of Prussia (1808–1870)

Marianne (1810–1883) ×
Albrecht of Prussia (1809–1872)

Willem III (1817–1890) ×
1 Sophie of Württemberg
(1818–1877)
2 Emma of Waldeck-Pyrmont
(1858–1934)

Alexander
(1818–1848)

Hendrik (1820–1879) ×
1 Amalia Maria of Saxe-Weimar
(1830–1872)
2 Maria of Prussia (1855–1888)

Sophie*** (1824–1897) ×
Carl Alexander of Saxe-
Weimar (1818–1901)

1 Willem (1840–1879)
1 Maurits (1843–1850)
1 Alexander (1851–1884)
2 Wilhelmina (1880–1962) ×
Hendrik of Mecklenburg-Schwerin◊◊◊ (1876–1934)

Juliana (1909–2004) ×
Bernhard of Lippe-Biesterfeld (1911–2004)

Beatrix (1938) ×
Claus of Amsberg (1927–2002)

Willem-Alexander (1967) ×
Máxima Zorreguieta (1971)

Amalia (2003)

* See II    ** See II    *** See IV    **** See II    + See VI and VIII    ++ See II    +++ See V    ◊◊◊ See V

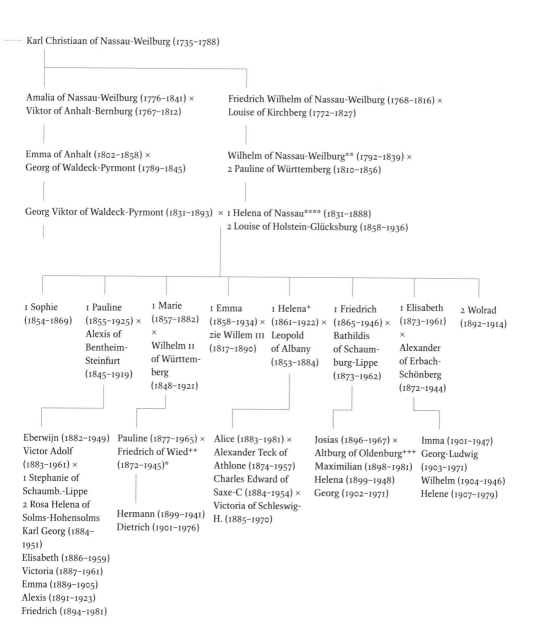

········ Karl Christiaan of Nassau-Weilburg (1735–1788)

Amalia of Nassau-Weilburg (1776–1841) ×
Viktor of Anhalt-Bernburg (1767–1812)

Friedrich Wilhelm of Nassau-Weilburg (1768–1816) ×
Louise of Kirchberg (1772–1827)

Emma of Anhalt (1802–1858) ×
Georg of Waldeck-Pyrmont (1789–1845)

Wilhelm of Nassau-Weilburg** (1792–1839) ×
2 Pauline of Württemberg (1810–1856)

Georg Viktor of Waldeck-Pyrmont (1831–1893)   × 1 Helena of Nassau**** (1831–1888)
                                                 2 Louise of Holstein-Glücksburg (1858–1936)

1 Sophie
(1854–1869)

1 Pauline
(1855–1925) ×
Alexis of
Bentheim-
Steinfurt
(1845–1919)

1 Marie
(1857–1882)
×
Wilhelm II
of Württem-
berg
(1848–1921)

1 Emma
(1858–1934) ×
zie Willem III
(1817–1890)

1 Helena+
(1861–1922) ×
Leopold
of Albany
(1853–1884)

1 Friedrich
(1865–1946) ×
Bathildis
of Schaum-
burg-Lippe
(1873–1962)

1 Elisabeth
(1873–1961)
×
Alexander
of Erbach-
Schönberg
(1872–1944)

2 Wolrad
(1892–1914)

Eberwijn (1882–1949)
Victor Adolf
(1883–1961) ×
1 Stephanie of
Schaumb.-Lippe
2 Rosa Helena of
Solms-Hohensolms
Karl Georg (1884–
1951)
Elisabeth (1886–1959)
Victoria (1887–1961)
Emma (1889–1905)
Alexis (1891–1923)
Friedrich (1894–1981)

Pauline (1877–1965) ×
Friedrich of Wied++
(1872–1945)*

Hermann (1899–1941)
Dietrich (1901–1976)

Alice (1883–1981) ×
Alexander Teck of
Athlone (1874–1957)
Charles Edward of
Saxe-C (1884–1954) ×
Victoria of Schleswig-
H. (1885–1970)

Josias (1896–1967) ×
Altburg of Oldenburg+++
Maximilian (1898–1981)
Helena (1899–1948)
Georg (1902–1971)

Imma (1901–1947)
Georg-Ludwig
(1903–1971)
Wilhelm (1904–1946)
Helene (1907–1979)

## II Nassau, Orange-Nassau, Nassau-Weilburg, Wied

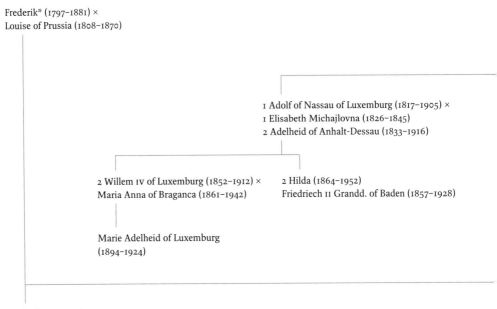

Frederik* (1797–1881) ×
Louise of Prussia (1808–1870)

1 Adolf of Nassau of Luxemburg (1817–1905) ×
1 Elisabeth Michajlovna (1826–1845)
2 Adelheid of Anhalt-Dessau (1833–1916)

2 Willem IV of Luxemburg (1852–1912) ×
Maria Anna of Braganca (1861–1942)

2 Hilda (1864–1952)
Friedriech II Grandd. of Baden (1857–1928)

Marie Adelheid of Luxemburg
(1894–1924)

Louise (1828–1871) ×
Karl XV of Sweden (1833–1916)

## III Romania

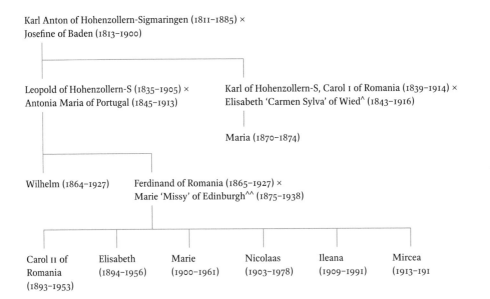

Karl Anton of Hohenzollern-Sigmaringen (1811–1885) ×
Josefine of Baden (1813–1900)

Leopold of Hohenzollern-S (1835–1905) ×
Antonia Maria of Portugal (1845–1913)

Karl of Hohenzollern-S, Carol I of Romania (1839–1914) ×
Elisabeth 'Carmen Sylva' of Wied^ (1843–1916)

Maria (1870–1874)

Wilhelm (1864–1927)

Ferdinand of Romania (1865–1927) ×
Marie 'Missy' of Edinburgh^^ (1875–1938)

| Carol II of Romania (1893–1953) | Elisabeth (1894–1956) | Marie (1900–1961) | Nicolaas (1903–1978) | Ileana (1909–1991) | Mircea (1913–191 |

Wilhelm of Nassau-Weilburg** (1792–1839) ×
1 Louise of Saxe-Altenburg (Hildburghausen) (1794–1825)
2 Pauline of Württemberg (1810–1856)

1 Marie (1825–1902) ×
Hermann of Wied (1814–1864)

2 Helena**** (1831–1888) ×
Georg Viktor of Waldeck-Pyrmont
(1831–1893)

2 Sophie (1836–1913) ×
Oscar II of Sweden (1829–1907)

Marie (1841–1910) × Wilhelm of Wied
(1845–1907)

Elisabeth 'Carmen Sylva'^ (1843–1916) ×
Carol I of Romania (1839–1914)

Marie (1870–1874)

Friedrich++ (1872–1945)
×
Pauline of Württemberg (1877–1965)

Wilhelm
of Albania
(1876–1945)

Victor
(1877–1946)

Louise
(1880–1965)

Elisabeth
(1883–1938)

Hermann
(1899–1941)

Dietrich
(1901–1976)

* See I    ** See I    **** See I    ^ See III    + See I    ++ See I    ^^ See VI and VII

## IV Saxe-Weimar-Eisenach

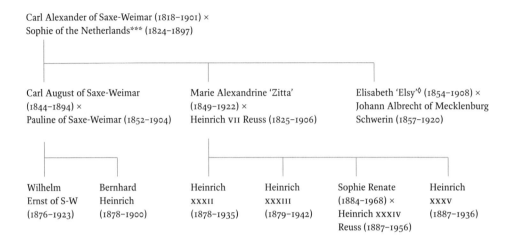

Carl Alexander of Saxe-Weimar (1818–1901) ×
Sophie of the Netherlands*** (1824–1897)

Carl August of Saxe-Weimar
(1844–1894) ×
Pauline of Saxe-Weimar (1852–1904)

Marie Alexandrine 'Zitta'
(1849–1922) ×
Heinrich VII Reuss (1825–1906)

Elisabeth 'Elsy'◊ (1854–1908) ×
Johann Albrecht of Mecklenburg
Schwerin (1857–1920)

Wilhelm
Ernst of S-W
(1876–1923)

Bernhard
Heinrich
(1878–1900)

Heinrich
XXXII
(1878–1935)

Heinrich
XXXIII
(1879–1942)

Sophie Renate
(1884–1968) ×
Heinrich XXXIV
Reuss (1887–1956)

Heinrich
XXXV
(1887–1936)

## V Mecklenburg-Schwerin

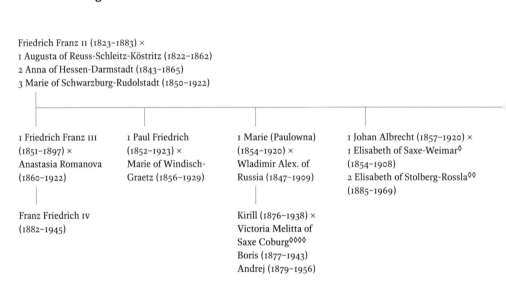

Friedrich Franz II (1823–1883) ×
1 Augusta of Reuss-Schleitz-Köstritz (1822–1862)
2 Anna of Hessen-Darmstadt (1843–1865)
3 Marie of Schwarzburg-Rudolstadt (1850–1922)

1 Friedrich Franz III
(1851–1897) ×
Anastasia Romanova
(1860–1922)

1 Paul Friedrich
(1852–1923) ×
Marie of Windisch-
Graetz (1856–1929)

1 Marie (Paulowna)
(1854–1920) ×
Wladimir Alex. of
Russia (1847–1909)

1 Johan Albrecht (1857–1920) ×
1 Elisabeth of Saxe-Weimar◊
(1854–1908)
2 Elisabeth of Stolberg-Rossla◊◊
(1885–1969)

Franz Friedrich IV
(1882–1945)

Kirill (1876–1938) ×
Victoria Melitta of
Saxe Coburg◊◊◊◊
Boris (1877–1943)
Andrej (1879–1956)

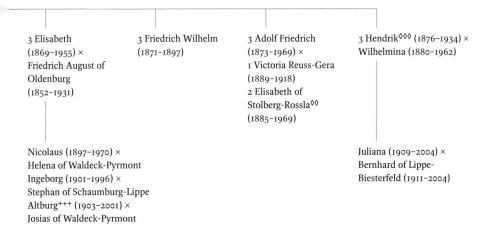

3 Elisabeth
(1869–1955) ×
Friedrich August of
Oldenburg
(1852–1931)

3 Friedrich Wilhelm
(1871–1897)

3 Adolf Friedrich
(1873–1969) ×
1 Victoria Reuss-Gera
(1889–1918)
2 Elisabeth of
Stolberg-Rossla◊◊
(1885–1969)

3 Hendrik◊◊◊ (1876–1934) ×
Wilhelmina (1880–1962)

Nicolaus (1897–1970) ×
Helena of Waldeck-Pyrmont
Ingeborg (1901–1996) ×
Stephan of Schaumburg-Lippe
Altburg+++ (1903–2001) ×
Josias of Waldeck-Pyrmont

Juliana (1909–2004) ×
Bernhard of Lippe-
Biesterfeld (1911–2004)

## vi  Hannover, Windsor

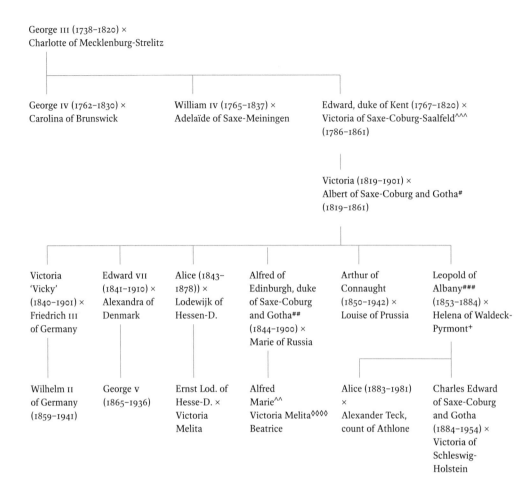

George III (1738-1820) ×
Charlotte of Mecklenburg-Strelitz

George IV (1762-1830) ×
Carolina of Brunswick

William IV (1765-1837) ×
Adelaïde of Saxe-Meiningen

Edward, duke of Kent (1767-1820) ×
Victoria of Saxe-Coburg-Saalfeld^^^
(1786-1861)

Victoria (1819-1901) ×
Albert of Saxe-Coburg and Gotha#
(1819-1861)

Victoria
'Vicky'
(1840-1901) ×
Friedrich III
of Germany

Edward VII
(1841-1910) ×
Alexandra of
Denmark

Alice (1843-
1878)) ×
Lodewijk of
Hessen-D.

Alfred of
Edinburgh, duke
of Saxe-Coburg
and Gotha##
(1844-1900) ×
Marie of Russia

Arthur of
Connaught
(1850-1942) ×
Louise of Prussia

Leopold of
Albany###
(1853-1884) ×
Helena of Waldeck-
Pyrmont+

Wilhelm II
of Germany
(1859-1941)

George V
(1865-1936)

Ernst Lod. of
Hesse-D. ×
Victoria
Melita

Alfred
Marie^^
Victoria Melita◊◊◊◊
Beatrice

Alice (1883-1981)
×
Alexander Teck,
count of Athlone

Charles Edward
of Saxe-Coburg
and Gotha
(1884-1954) ×
Victoria of
Schleswig-
Holstein

#, ## and ### See VII    ^^ See III and VII    ^^^ See VII    + See I    ◊◊◊◊ See V, VI, VII

## VII  Coburg

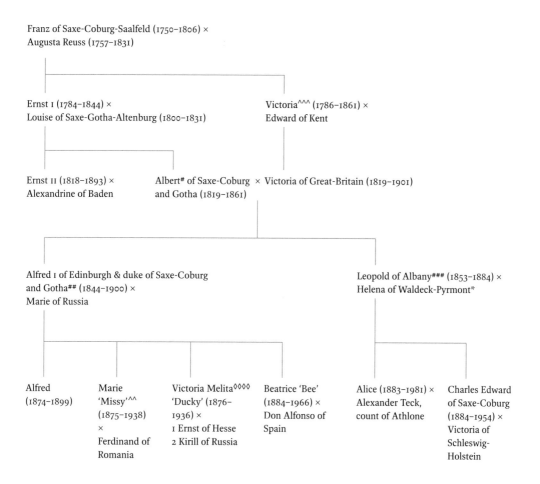

Franz of Saxe-Coburg-Saalfeld (1750–1806) ×
Augusta Reuss (1757–1831)

Ernst I (1784–1844) ×
Louise of Saxe-Gotha-Altenburg (1800–1831)

Victoria^^^ (1786–1861) ×
Edward of Kent

Ernst II (1818–1893) ×
Alexandrine of Baden

Albert# of Saxe-Coburg  × Victoria of Great-Britain (1819–1901)
and Gotha (1819–1861)

Alfred I of Edinburgh & duke of Saxe-Coburg
and Gotha## (1844–1900) ×
Marie of Russia

Leopold of Albany### (1853–1884) ×
Helena of Waldeck-Pyrmont*

Alfred
(1874–1899)

Marie
'Missy'^^
(1875–1938)
×
Ferdinand of
Romania

Victoria Melita◊◊◊◊
'Ducky' (1876–
1936) ×
1 Ernst of Hesse
2 Kirill of Russia

Beatrice 'Bee'
(1884–1966) ×
Don Alfonso of
Spain

Alice (1883–1981) ×
Alexander Teck,
count of Athlone

Charles Edward
of Saxe-Coburg
(1884–1954) ×
Victoria of
Schleswig-
Holstein

# Illustration credits

Unless stated otherwise, this concerns Dutch institutions or collections.

# Index of persons

The names of Queen Wilhelmina, Queen Emma and Elizabeth Saxton Winter are not mentioned, unless they are on photos. The pictures are shown in bold.
The names of royal and princely persons are listed with their Christian names, otherwise with their surnames.
Wilhelmina's favourite doll Susan and dog Swell are as only doll and animal in the index included.

Falkenburg, L.J. 292
Fasseur, Cees 11, 30
Faure, Félix 229
Faure, Mrs 229
Feltz, Theodoor, Baron van der 85
Ferdinand, Prince of Hohenzollern-
Sigmaringen, 1914 King of Romania
22, 237, 242, 252, **255**, 259, 272
Ffoliott, Anne 23
Fischer, Ernst Kuno Berthold 200
Fischer, Captain **267**
Flier, G.J. van der 21, 99, 111, 112, 140
Floris v, Count of Holland and
Zeeland 146
Francesco Sforza, Duke of Milaan 124
Frank, Abraham 79
Frans P.K.L.A. of Württemberg, Duke of
Teck 292
Franz Ferdinand, Arch Duke of Austria
Oostenrijk 289
Franz Josef I, Emperor of Austria, King of
Hungary 34, 176, **177**, 178, 244
Frederik, Prince of the Netherlands 11
Friedrich I, Grand Duke of Baden 251
Friedrich II, Hereditary Grand Duke of
Baden 195, 251, **267**
Friedrich III, Emperor of Germany
165, 274
Friedrich, Hereditary Prince of Wied
153, **190,** 224, 244, **245**, 246, 256, 266
Friedrich, Count of Waldeck-Pyrmont
**267**
Friedrich, Prince of Bentheim-
Steinfurt **201,** 237
Friedrich 'Fritz', Prince of Waldeck-
Pyrmont 102, **104,** 176, **194,** 200, 225,
246, 263, 266, **267**, 278, 307
Friedrich August, Grand Duke of
Oldenburg **271,** 272, 275, 295
Friedrich Franz II, Grand Duke of
Mecklenburg-Schwerin 173
Friedrich Franz III, Grand Duke of
Mecklenburg-Schwerin 173, 225
Friedrich Franz IV, Grand Duke of
Mecklenburg-Schwerin **271**

Friedrich Wilhelm, Elector of
Brandenburg 96
Friedrich Wilhelm, Prince of
Nassau-Weilburg 178
Fruin, Robert J. 114
Fuchs, H. 89

Gainsborough, Thomas 220
Gaspard de Coligny 228
Gaultier, F. 58
Gediking, Fredrik 10, 11, 14, 24, 30, 31,
42, **43,** 94, 117, 174, 195
Geeske(n), see Peters, Geeske 257, 258
Gemmingen, Major Baron von **267**
Georg Victor, Prince of Waldeck-
Pyrmont 41
Georg Wilhelm, Prince of Waldeck-
Pyrmont 260
George II, King of Greece 252
George III, King of the United
Kingdom 202
George VI, King of the United
Kingdom 9
George, Duke of Kent 36, 311
Georg-Ludwig, Prince of Erbach-
Schönberg 283
Gevaerts, Lady Anna A.G., see
Poll-Gevaerts
Gevers Deynoot, Mr P.H. 77
Gevers Willem A.F. Baron 260
Giesler, Albert, Eutin (D) 271
Gladstone, William E. 89, 232
Goedewagen, P. 172
Goedhart, Louis 56
Goethe, Johann Wolfgang von 26, 183,
204
Goldstein van Oldenaller, W. Baron
van 151, 226
Goot, J.G. van der 162
Gottereau, Alfred Jules Paul 252
Grave, J.J. Salverda de 60
Grelle Rogier, Count de 157
Grieg, Edvard 161
Groeninx van Zoelen, Lady Adolphine
Agneta 261